Studies in Church History

Subsidia

7

PROTESTANT EVANGELICALISM

W. R. WARD

PROTESTANT EVANGELICALISM: BRITAIN, IRELAND, GERMANY AND AMERICA
c.1750–c.1950

Essays in Honour of
W. R. Ward

EDITED BY

KEITH ROBBINS

PUBLISHED FOR
THE ECCLESIASTICAL HISTORY SOCIETY

BY

BASIL BLACKWELL
1990

© Ecclesiastical History Society 1990

First published 1990

Basil Blackwell Publisher Ltd
108 Cowley Road, Oxford OX4 1JF, UK

Basil Blackwell Inc.
432 Park Avenue South, Suite 1505,
New York, NY 10016, USA

British Library Cataloguing in Publication Data
A CIP catalogue record for this book is available from the British Library

Library of Congress Cataloging in Publication Data
Protestant Evangelicalism: Britain, Ireland, Germany, and America. c. 1750–c. 1950: essays in honour of W. R. Ward / edited by Keith Robbins.
    p.   cm.—(Studies in church history. Subsidia: 7)
Includes bibliographical references.
ISBN 0–631–17818–X
1. Evangelicalism—History—18th century. 2. Evangelicalism—
—History—19th century. 3. Evangelicalism—History—20th century.
I. Ward, W. Reginald (William Reginald) II. Robbins, Keith.
III. Series.
BR1840.P76 1990
270.8—dc20   90–37832

Typeset by Joshua Associates Limited, Oxford
Printed in Great Britain by Billing and Sons Ltd, Worcester

PREFACE

Professor W. R. Ward retired in 1986 from the Chair of Modern History in the University of Durham, to which he was appointed in 1965. From Devonport High School for Boys he won an open scholarship to University College Oxford in 1943. Being medically unfit for war service he was able to graduate in 1946, with first class honours in Modern History. He took up an appointment as resident tutor at Ruskin College and, a little later, began research under the supervision of Lucy Sutherland. In 1949 he took up an assistant lectureship at the University of Manchester. He received his Oxford D.Phil. in 1951 for his thesis on 'The English Land Tax in the Eighteenth Century'. At Manchester he was successively promoted lecturer and senior lecturer, and was warden of Needham Hall.

At Durham, Professor Ward fulfilled the duties of his Chair with exemplary vigour. He saw it as one of his tasks to encourage (some, less energetic than he, might say goad) members of his Department to write and publish. He supervised many theses, not only of full- and part-time higher-degree candidates in his own considerable area of expertise, but also staff candidates on subjects ranging from early eighteenth-century diplomacy to nineteenth-century American politics and twentieth-century international relations. Many of his colleagues have had good reason to be grateful for his scholarly help and advice. He has inspired many generations of students, being both tolerant and generous with his knowledge. He also undertook what must have seemed an ever-increasing administrative load. He served on innumerable university bodies, and became known for his fair and far-sighted approach to their affairs. He was Dean of the Arts Faculty from 1972 to 1974. His Department has good reason to be grateful for the way in which he defended its interests over the years and for the good-humoured way in which he guided its deliberations.

Outside the University, Professor Ward served as Secretary of the Chetham Society for nineteen years and became its President in 1984. He has been closely connected with the Ecclesiastical History Society since its foundation and served as its President in 1970–1. He has been a member of the Council of the Royal Historical Society and of the Surtees Society. In addition, he has been a member of the British Sub-commission of the Commission Internationale pour l'Histoire Ecclésiastique Comparée. He has also rendered many services to Methodism, both locally and nationally.

A perusal of the list of his published writings discloses that Professor

Ward not only writes prolifically himself, but he is also a discerning and prompt reviewer. His own scholarly interests have developed far beyond his initial researches on the land tax. For many years he has concerned himself with the world-wide ramifications of the official and unofficial ecclesiastical history and religious thought of the eighteenth, nineteenth, and twentieth centuries. It is appropriate, therefore, that this volume in his honour should focus on this particular area of scholarship. The distinctive contribution he has made has been to emphasize that the study of Protestant Evangelicalism cannot be confined within particular geographical or national boundaries. It is appropriate, therefore, that we have attempted to reflect the diversity of his own interests by assembling an international group of scholars, all of whom have been stimulated, in one way or another, by Professor Ward's writing and friendship, and who wish, in turn, to honour him. It is with a little relief that we realize that this is one book which he is unlikely to review—at least not publicly! We trust that our efforts will give him pleasure and stimulate him—not that he needs any goading—to complete the substantial projects which he still has in train. If we can be forgiven for adapting the well-known words of the Puritan John Robinson, we all hope that the Lord hath more Truth yet to break forth out of his holy Ward.

Keith Robbins

ACKNOWLEDGEMENTS

Grateful acknowledgement is made to the University of Durham for some financial assistance towards the expenses incurred in assembling this volume.

The Editor wishes to thank Dr Margaret Harvey and her colleagues at Durham, in particular Dr Anne Orde and Dr David Rollason, for their magnificent work in compiling the Bibliography of W. R. Ward's writings, and Joan Pearce for typing the Bibliography.

CONTENTS

CONTENTS

LIST OF CONTRIBUTORS

D. W. BEBBINGTON
Senior Lecturer in History, University of Stirling

CLYDE BINFIELD
Reader in History, University of Sheffield

MARTIN BRECHT
Direktor, Seminar für Mittlere und Neuere Kirchengeschichte des Fachbereichs Evangelische Theologie, Westfälische Wilhelms-Universität, Münster

SHERIDAN GILLEY
Senior Lecturer in Theology, University of Durham

DAVID HEMPTON
Lecturer in Modern History, The Queen's University of Belfast

NICHOLAS HOPE
Lecturer in Modern History, University of Glasgow

JOHN KENT
Professor Emeritus of Theology, University of Bristol

HARTMUT LEHMANN
Direktor, Deutsches Historisches Institut, Washington, D.C.

DERYCK W. LOVEGROVE
Lecturer in Ecclesiastical History, University of St Andrews

ANNE ORDE
Senior Lecturer in History, University of Durham

HENRY D. RACK
Bishop Fraser Lecturer in Ecclesiastical History, University of Manchester

RUSSELL E. RICHEY
Associate Dean for Academic Programs and Research Professor of Church History, Divinity School, Duke University, Durham, N.C.

KEITH ROBBINS
Professor of Modern History, University of Glasgow

DAVID ROLLASON
Lecturer in History, University of Durham

CONTRIBUTORS

DAVID M. THOMPSON
Fellow and Bursar, Fitzwilliam College, Cambridge

JOHN WALSH
Fellow of Jesus College, Oxford

HADDON WILLMER
Senior Lecturer in Theology and Religious Studies, University of Leeds

SURVIVAL AND REVIVAL:
JOHN BENNET, METHODISM, AND
THE OLD DISSENT

by HENRY D. RACK

OHN BENNET has always figured in biographies of John Wesley as
the man who stole his leader's 'last love'. Since he broke with Wesley
for doctrinal reasons a few years later, he failed to qualify for the biography usually accorded to Methodist itinerants. Yet Bennet deserves
something better than a footnote to Wesley's career, and not least because
his post-Methodist history (which never rates more than a bare mention
in Methodist writing) helps to illustrate other aspects of the development
of the Evangelical Revival.

In this essay an attempt will be made to see Bennet in his own right and
to show his career illustrates the complicated way in which evangelicalism
came to affect the 'old Dissent'.

I

As Professor Ward has often insisted, the eighteenth-century revival was
an international religious movement which stretched from America to
the Continent of Europe. Even within Great Britain, John Wesley's
Methodists were only part of a larger movement and by no means first in
the field. The spread and penetration of Methodism varied considerably
in different areas, and to a significant degree it grew by cannibalizing
existing local networks.[1] The initial emergence and impact of the revival
generally took place within established churches, which for England
meant the Church of England, and Wesley famously (if misleadingly)
portrayed Methodism as merely a religious society auxiliary to that
Church. The effect of the revival on Dissent has generally been seen as a late
development although, as Michael Watts has remarked, 'The Evangelical
Revival was initially an Anglican not a Dissenting movement, but it was
Dissent, not the Church of England, that reaped the ultimate benefit'.[2]

---

[1] See further in H. D. Rack, *Reasonable Enthusiast. John Wesley and the Rise of Methodism* (London, 1989), pp. 214–21.
[2] M. Watts, *The Dissenters* (Oxford, 1978), p. 440.

Yet there was some impact on Dissent from the first, if only at a scattered and individual level, and north-west England, which is the focus of this study, offers some good illustrations of how this happened.

The main arena for Bennet's activity was in his home area of the Derbyshire Peak District, in eastern Cheshire and south-eastern Lancashire, though he took extensive tours elsewhere, notably in Yorkshire. The north-west was an area of conservative and in some cases markedly High Church Anglicanism, most notably perhaps in Manchester, which had a reputation for Jacobite and Nonjuror associations. But it also contained a substantial deposit of Dissent, chiefly Presbyterian in origin. Dissent amounted to over ten per cent of the population in Lancashire with more in some towns—well above the national average.[3] In some of the under-endowed chapels of ease in large Lancashire parishes, nonconforming clergy, often with gentry support, had survived for years after the 'great ejection' of 1662. A considerable crop of Dissenting chapels followed the grant of toleration in 1689.[4] In Derbyshire, William Bagshaw, 'the Apostle of the Peak', was a member of a local gentry family who founded a string of Dissenting causes, one of which, at Chinley, was attended by John Bennet.[5] If gentry support fell off rapidly after 1689 (with the exception of the Hoghtons of Hoghton Tower and the solitary Dissenting peer, Lord Willoughby of Parham), substantial merchant families maintained a formidable presence at Cross St. in Manchester, which had at least 1,000 members for most of the eighteenth century, and there were significant congregations elsewhere, even in smaller centres.[6] In Cheshire the 'Happy Union' of Presbyterians and Independents, which had quickly broken down in London, was maintained for years in the form of the 'Cheshire Classis', which included members from neighbouring counties as well.[7]

The basis for the revival movement in this, as in other areas, was a series of scattered, more-or-less spontaneous local outbreaks, stimulated and later consolidated by travelling evangelists. Its deeper roots remain rather

---

[3] Watts, *The Dissenters* (Oxford, 1978), p. 509.

[4] P. J. W. Higson, 'Some leading promoters of . . . Lancashire chapelries', *TLCAS*, 75–6 (1961), pp. 123–63; J. Booker, *History of Ancient Chapel of Denton = Chetham Society*, 37 (1856), pp. 71–83; *History of Ancient Chapel of Birch = Chetham Society*, 47 (1859), pp. 149–50.

[5] J. Ashe, *Life and Character of William Bagshaw* (London, 1704); R. Mansfield, 'The development of Independency in Derbyshire' (Manchester, M.A. thesis, 1951), pp. 114–28.

[6] London, Dr Williams Library, MS 702.C33, Evans List, p. 58, says 1,500; F. Gastrell, *Notitia Cestriensis = Chetham Society*, 19 (1849), p. 57, says 233 families (*c.*1,150 persons) for all Dissent.

[7] *Chesire Classis Minutes*, ed. A. Gordon (London, 1917).

mysterious and cannot be explored in detail here.[8] The immediate pre-history of the Methodist societies has often been traced to the devotional religious societies which originated in the 1670s in London and later spread to the provinces. They survived into the 1730s and at least in London and Bristol supplied a framework for colonization by the Moravians, Whitefield, and the Wesleys. But this is much less evident in the north where, though a few examples are known, they do not appear to have been the source of many Methodist societies.[9] Although Bennet himself found societies in some places, they may have been the fruit of recent preaching by David Taylor, a freelance evangelist.[10]

Although many of the first converts seem to have been Anglicans (if anything), there were certainly recruits from Dissent as well. Charles Wesley at Manchester in 1756 urged the Methodists to attend sacrament at church or meeting-house and persuaded some Dissenters to attend the church.[11] Bennet at Woodley in 1745 found many Dissenters in his Methodist society.[12] At his home chapel in Chinley, the Presbyterian minister James Clegg was disgusted to find that David Taylor was attracting members of his congregation, and Bennet himself was converted by Taylor.[13]

The reasons for these defections are in some ways more obvious for Dissenters than Anglicans. If Dissenting ministers were usually hostile to the revivalists, the rank and file were sometimes more receptive. Presbyterians, like Anglicans in the 1740s, were very distrustful of teachers of justification by faith for fear that this would mean devaluing good works, and the risk of antinomian breaches of the moral law. This was Clegg's objection to Taylor.[14] Some time after 1699 Clegg had read Episcopius and Socinus and thereafter could 'never well relish the doctrines of rigid Calvinism'.[15] In the 1720s he clashed with Samuel de la Rose in Stockport over rigid Calvinism and was willing to allow a role to repentance and

---

[8] See Rack, *Reasonable Enthusiast*, pp. 171–80, for suggestions.

[9] H. D. Rack, 'Religious societies and the origins of Methodism', *JEH*, 38 (1987), pp. 582–95. But for a Cheshire example, see J. Everett, *Wesleyan Methodism in Manchester* (Manchester, 1827), pp. 139–74; *Journal of John Wesley*, ed. N. Curnock (London, 1912), 3, p. 443.

[10] Manchester, John Rylands University Library (hereafter JRUL), Methodist Church Archives (hereafter MCA), John Bennet's MS Diary, 22 Nov. 1747.

[11] Charles Wesley, *Journal*, ed. T. Jackson (London, n.d.), 2, pp. 137–8.

[12] JRUL, MCA, MS Wesley Family Letters, 2, p. 13; John Bennet to Charles Wesley, 30 July 1745.

[13] JRUL, Bagshaw MSS 25/7/5, James Clegg's Diary (also ed. V. S. Doe, Derbyshire Record Society, 2 (1978), 15 Oct. 1741; 4, 11, 24 Jan. 1742.

[14] *Ibid.*, 12, 16 Jan. 1742.

[15] Doe, *Clegg*, 1, pp. xxxviii–ix.

obedience in the process of justification.[16] It seems that, as with many other Presbyterian ministers of that generation, the softening of Calvinism was followed by a drift to Arianism.[17]

It was doctrinal development of this kind which was one factor provoking the creation of new, Calvinist, orthodox, and often 'evangelical' Independent churches, often by secession from old, Arian, Presbyterian ones.[18] Yet one should not assume that the outward behaviour of these churches necessarily altered dramatically from that of their Puritan forbears. In the conservative north-west old habits often persisted. Joseph Mottershead of Cross St. in Manchester, who died in 1771, had been present at the death of the celebrated commentator Matthew Henry in 1714. Though a reputed Arian, Mottershead continued to his death to examine applicants for admission to Communion.[19] So did Clegg, who held preparatory services for Communion, excluded sexual offenders, and attended 'double lectures' and fast days.[20] He was a physician as well as a minister, but believed his wife had been healed by prayer, and duly noted cases of divine judgement on sinners.[21] A similar pattern of discipline can be seen in the Diary of the north Lancashire Presbyterian Peter Walkden, who was to figure in Bennet's later career.[22]

Nor were the beliefs of ordinary members uniform or necessarily identical with those of ministers. Clegg records the death of an old member who was a hardened Calvinist and leader in prayer.[23] He himself had some sympathy with Whitefield and the evangelicals until antinomianism threatened.[24] Correcting the traditional picture of early eighteenth-century Dissent, which has been weighted in favour of the 'rational' type, Dr Nuttall has rightly pointed to the evidence for survival of the old ways and seekers after conversion.[25] Two further examples are relevant here. In Manchester, Richard Barlow, an early Methodist leader, was the son of an Anglican father and a Presbyterian mother. She is said to

---

[16] W. Urwick, *Nonconformity in Cheshire* (London, 1864), pp. 293–7.
[17] R. Mansfield, 'History of Congregationalism in Derbyshire' (Manchester Ph.D. thesis, 1958), p. 340.
[18] B. Nightingale, *Lancashire Nonconformity*, 6 vols (Manchester, 1893), gives many examples.
[19] Manchester, Central Library Archives, microfilm of Cross St. Register, pp. 257–69; Nightingale, *Lancs. Nonconformity*, 5, pp. 97–101.
[20] Clegg, Diary, for example, 30 Apr. 1737, 18 Dec. 1741.
[21] *Ibid.*, 27 Apr. 1721.
[22] *Diary of Peter Walkden*, ed. W. Dobson (Preston, 1866), for example, pp. 3, 14, 16, 86.
[23] Clegg, Diary, 3 Jan. 1742.
[24] *Ibid.*, 4, 5 Jan. 1742.
[25] G. F. Nuttall, 'Methodism and the Old Dissent', *JURCHS*, 2 (1981), pp. 259–74.

have recognized that the Methodists were preaching the same message as that of the orthodox founder of the Cross St. chapel. An old Presbyterian in Derbyshire said that Bennet's preaching was like that of the Puritans of his youth. It is perhaps of interest, too, that John Allen, a future Methodist preacher, was born in Chinley (Clegg's 'parish') in 1737 and had the same mixed parentage as Barlow.[26]

So far as the north-west is concerned, we know little more about the secular and religious circumstances which predisposed groups and individuals to take up the 'evangelical' way. What is clear, especially in provincial areas away from the original London–Bristol axis of the Wesleys' work, is that these leaders did not initiate the movement, but exploited earlier work. The most important of these pioneers was Benjamin Ingham, a former Oxford 'Methodist', who had accompanied Wesley to Georgia.[27] Ingham was converted by the Moravians in 1737, and in the same year began evangelistic work in Yorkshire and later in Lancashire. By 1740 he already had a round of fifty places with many organized societies.[28] He had, in fact, founded a regional 'connexion', which might have grown further had he possessed the iron will of a Wesley. In the event, he allowed much of it to be taken over, first by the Moravians, and then by the Scottish-based sect of Sandemanians or Glasites. The Moravian sources nevertheless, and with considerable justification, saw the 'awakening' in England as beginning with Ingham in the north and Whitefield in London in 1737, and not with Wesley's conversion in 1738.[29]

Ingham originally operated in Yorkshire, though he visited Manchester with Bennet in 1742.[30] The pioneer in Derbyshire, Cheshire, and Lancashire seems to have been David Taylor. Taylor was probably a native of Leicestershire who later moved to Mobberly in Cheshire, and had been in the service of Lady Huntingdon's family, where he discovered a talent for preaching encouraged by the lady herself.[31] His work in the Midlands eventually formed one source for the new sect of General Baptists of the New Connexion.[32] As so often happened, success led to his drift away

[26] JRUL, MCA, James Everett Manchester Scrap Book, pp. 412–14; J. Everett, *Methodism in Sheffield* (Sheffield, 1823), p. 27; T. Jackson, ed., *Lives of the Early Methodist Preachers*, 6 vols (London, 1872), 6, pp. 242–3.
[27] Rack, *Reasonable Enthusiast*, pp. 216–17.
[28] JRUL, MS Eng. 1062, p. 10.
[29] JRUL, MCA, M. Batty, MS Church History, p. 4.
[30] JRUL, MCA, Bennet, Diary, 1–7 May 1742.
[31] *Ibid.*, 3 July 1743; Rack, *Reasonable Enthusiast*, pp. 217–18.
[32] R. Brown, *English Baptists of the Eighteenth Century* (London, 1986), pp. 67–8.

from the Church of England into an Independent ministry, which alarmed his aristocratic patroness.[33] He was also active in the Sheffield area, where he first met John Bennet, and it is perhaps through the Bennet connection that he moved to Derbyshire and the north-west, and it was through Taylor that Bennet was converted.[34] Bennet probably absorbed some of his work later.

One of the Taylor societies absorbed by the Moravians, at the members' own request, was at Dukinfield, in Cheshire, and it is of interest to note that one of those inviting the Moravian takeover was a member of the old and probably Arianizing chapel there.[35] From the 1740s the Moravians had a congregation there, some later moving to Fairfield, near Manchester. The Moravians in the north, like Wesley, were frequently reaping where they had not sown. Individuals seem to have visited the area from 1739, but in 1742 they were formally invited by Ingham to take over his societies.[36] When Wesley took his first journeys to the Midlands and north in 1741–2 he found numerous cases of Moravian 'stillness' affecting societies which he had not founded.[37]

In Yorkshire the basis for a distinctively Methodist work was provided partly by the efforts of John Nelson, a travelling stone-mason from Birstall who had been converted partly under the influence of Wesley and Whitefield in London in 1739.[38] Back in Yorkshire his early efforts at preaching were in uneasy association with Ingham and the Moravians and Taylor. But Taylor's preaching he found a 'dry morsel', and one influenced by the Moravians he described scornfully as 'got into the poor-sinnership, who held his neck on one side and talked as if he had been bred up on the borders of Bohemia'.[39] Bennet took some journeys into this area too, perhaps because he had been commercially active there, and he maintained some contacts with Yorkshire to the end of his life.

The complexity of the sources of the revival and its relations with Dissent are well illustrated by the story of the creation of a new Independent church in Manchester. This was founded in 1756 with one Caleb

[33] Lady Huntingdon to John Wesley in *Letters of John Wesley*, ed. F. Baker (Oxford, 1982), 2, p. 75 and n.
[34] Everett, *Sheffield*, pp. 257–9.
[35] JRUL, MS Eng. 1066, Dukinfield Notes; E. E. Titterington, *Historical Sketches of the Moravian Church in Dukinfield* (London, 1910), p. 8.
[36] D. Benham, *Memoirs of James Hutton* (London, 1856), pp. 110–11.
[37] John Wesley, *Journal*, 2, p. 464; 3, pp. 215, 216.
[38] Jackson, *Lives*, 1, p. 14.
[39] *Ibid.*, p. 55.

Warhurst as its minister.[40] In 1762 the congregation acquired its own building, drew up a covenant and church order, and affirmed its doctrinal orthodoxy in the Westminster Confession.[41] The traditional accounts of the origins of this church (which can be verified to some extent from contemporary sources) seem to show that members were drawn from an existing Baptist church, a secession of rank and file members from Cross St., Scottish immigrants, and those influenced by travelling evangelists from Yorkshire.[42] There is evidence that the Methodists were highly unstable and subject to losses at this time, and at least one Methodist trustee turns up as an Independent trustee and deacon later.[43] There may have been links between the Manchester Baptists and an earlier generation of itinerant evangelists, for David Crossley, who had been active in this way as far back as the 1690s, survived to be associated with this church in the 1740s and welcomed Whitefield's preaching.[44] Caleb Warhurst had originally been an assistant to this church from 1755.[45] It is not surprising that Bennet had difficulty in establishing a society in Manchester until Charles Wesley's visit early in 1747, which may have drawn in Anglicans, perhaps in the wake of the Jacobite débâcle of 1745, but left a society very open to the inroads of Dissent.[46]

Manchester may have been exceptional in its complexity, but it is likely enough that the evangelical cause in many places was both heterogeneous and unstable. Taken as a whole, the creation of these new churches and societies marked a new phase in the region's Dissenting history, which had hitherto been dominated by Presbyterianism. For Bennet's career it is significant that the new Independent church in Manchester was one of several in the north-west with which he would be associated in his later, non-Methodist career.

[40] Manchester, Central Library Archives M185, MS Caleb Warhurst, Diary, 10 Nov. 1857. (This Diary has been disarranged and misdated, but I have corrected the dates). For Warhurst, see Nightingale, *Lancs. Nonconformity*, 5, pp. 107–16 and below, p. 18.

[41] JRUL, Congregational College Loan, Box 15, Cannon Street Church Book, pp. 1–34.

[42] R. Halley, *Lancashire Puritanism and Nonconformity*, 2 vols (London, 1872), 2, p. 447; checked by comparison with Cross St. Register and Cannon St. Church Book and Warhurst Diary.

[43] This was one Henry Hope; see C. D. Little, 'Origins of Manchester Methodism', *PWHS*, 26 (1948), p. 18; Cannon St. Church Book, pp. 15, 101.

[44] *Christian History*, 5 (2), p. 52; 6 (1), p. 35 (microfilm in JRUL).

[45] Warhurst, Diary, 18 May 1758.

[46] Charles Wesley, *Journal*, 2, p. 129.

II

John Bennet was born on 1 March 1715 (NS), the son of William Bennet, a yeoman farmer, near Chinley, where he was a member of James Clegg's Presbyterian church.[47] John was designed for one of the learned professions, and in preparation for this was sent to Ebenezer Latham's academy at Findern in Derbyshire.[48] He opted instead for a commercial career as a carrier between Sheffield and Macclesfield. At Sheffield he heard David Taylor preach and invited him (with misgivings) to Chinley.[49] Taylor's preaching induced a visionary experience of Christ in Bennet, which led to his conversion (and some execrable verse) on 1 January 1742.[50]

After accompanying Taylor and Ingham on their Gospel journeys Bennet became a preacher himself, probably in March 1743.[51] In due course he built up a 'circuit' or 'round', which at various times included some sixty places, mostly in villages, though he was successful in Bolton, where his later secession from Wesley drew off most of the society he had founded. Some of his journeys extended beyond his usual area in the Peak, west Cheshire and south-east Lancashire into Yorkshire, which he was persuaded by Wesley to visit regularly for a time.[52] He also visited London and of his own volition occasionally ventured into north Lancashire and even as far as Oxfordshire.[53] But he complained in 1749 about his circuit of 'near two hundred miles' and lack of support from Wesley.[54] He created many new societies, in addition to those probably inherited from Taylor, and organized them with monthly and quarterly meetings for oversight and in at least one place founded a 'Christian school'.[55]

Bennet originally operated as a freelance 'evangelical' though an undated record by John Nelson suggests that for a time he was 'in

---

[47] For his life see autobiography merging into diary in JRUL, MCA; supplemented for early life by summary of missing passage in Everett, *Sheffield*, pp. 257–9. for the birth date see Autobiography, p. 1, and epitaph in Mansfield, *Congregationalism*, p. 24.

[48] For this academy see H. McLachlan, *English Education under the Test Acts* (Manchester, 1931), pp. 131–4.

[49] Everett, *Sheffield*, pp. 257–9.

[50] Bennet, Autobiography, p. 15, says 1741, probably an error for OS, as Taylor's visit is dated by Clegg, Diary, 4, 5 Jan. 1742.

[51] Bennet, Diary, 20 Mar. 1743.

[52] John Wesley, *Letters*, 2, pp. 343–4.

[53] Bennet, Diary, 18 Apr. 1747; Jan. 1748.

[54] MCA, MS Bennet, Letter Book, p. 85 (Bennet to William Briggs, 3 Mar. 1749); cf. Bennet to John Wesley, 25 Apr. 1749, in MCA, MAM P6, and John Wesley, *Letters*, 2, p. 337.

[55] Bennet, Diary, 2, 3 May 1743.

connexion with the Moravian brethren' and objected to Wesley's perfectionism until Nelson changed his mind.[56] He first heard Wesley preach in
June 1742, though some accounts claim he was only introduced to Wesley
in the following year. But by May 1743 he seems to have associated himself and his 'round' with Methodism.[57] He was among the select group of
lay preachers invited to the first Methodist conference in 1744, and from
1746 was one of Wesley's 'Assistants', that is, especially trusted helpers
who soon became supervisors of the large early circuits.

In the course of his work Bennet naturally encountered opposition,
though he seems to have suffered less from mob violence than some of the
early preachers, and it has been suggested that he avoided large towns to
escape the mob.[58] Although he clearly drew in some ex-Dissenters, he
received little if any help from their ministers but rather hostility. There
were attacks by Dissenters at Woodley and Shackerley, and Clegg, his
own minister, finally cut him off from Communion.[59] After this he complained about lack of the Sacrament to the Wesleys, and at least once was
repelled by an Anglican from the Table as well.[60]

Bennet seems to have been of an anxious and rather dependent temperament, though latterly this may have been aggravated by ill- health.
Like many early Methodists he was subject to dreams, on two occasions to
visions, and once he fell into an 'ecstasy'.[61] The dreams seem to have
expressed his hopes and fears, as on the occasions when they featured an
ox and a bear, which seem to have symbolized the hostility of James
Clegg—unless they have Freudian overtones.[62] Sexual fantasies and hopes
of marriage certainly affected some of them, as in the case of a mildly
improper one in which a girl he fancied approached him in bed, and in the
conversation which followed they reflected that they could lie innocently
together.[63] The Diary does suggest a man who felt himself stretched to the

---

[56] Jackson, *Lives*, 1, p. 62.
[57] Bennet, Diary, 2 June 1742; E. A. Rose, 'Methodism in Cheshire to 1800', *TLCAS*, 78 (1975),
p. 23 (excellent account of Bennet in Cheshire).
[58] *Ibid.*, pp. 24–5.
[59] Bennet to Charles Wesley, 30 July 1745, in MCA, MS Wesley Family Letters, 2, p. 13;
Bennet, Diary, 6 Nov. 1747; 17 Mar. 1748; 2 Oct. 1748; for Clegg and Bennet, see Bennet,
Diary, 8 May 1743.
[60] Bennet to Charles Wesley, 30 July 1745 in MCA, MS Wesley Family Letters, 2, p. 13; Bennet,
Diary, Good Friday 1749.
[61] Bennet, Autobiography, pp. 15, 20; Diary, 3 May 1742; see also Rack, *Reasonable Enthusiast*,
p. 434 and 'Trinitarian visions in Methodism', *PWHS*, 46 (1987), pp. 38–9, 42.
[62] Bennet, Autobiography, p. 15; Diary, January–March 1743.
[63] *Ibid.*, 12 Sept. 1742.

limit and in need of more support than the Wesleys gave him, while the courtship of Grace Murray, which estranged him from Wesley, contains strong suggestions of his need for a wife to save his emotional and religious stability.

Despite the dreams, Bennet seems to have been less prone to supernatural and magical beliefs than some Methodists. Early in life he records an incident that looks like an attempt to raise the devil.[64] But he opposed a local 'conjuror', and his detailed account of a celebrated Cheshire healing woman is distinctly non-committal about her cures—unlike John Wesley, who promptly accepted them from Bennet's account at second hand.[65]

Bennet contributed to the early development of Methodism in at least three ways. First, it should be realized that Wesley had originally hoped to collect a body of clerical helpers, but that when they failed to appear he fell back on travelling lay preachers, who in any case were thrown up spontaneously and irresistibly by the revival—Dr Walsh's 'problem of the eloquent convert'.[66] Bennet was an early and prominent member of this band, as we have seen. From 1749 he was 'Assistant' in charge of the enormous 'Cheshire' circuit, which covered Cheshire, Lancashire, Nottingham, Derbyshire, and Sheffield.[67]

But, secondly, Bennet's work in the north-west was a prime example of the process already described by which Wesley extended his connexion from the south by cannibalizing existing networks, even though with their creators' consent. It is noticeable, for example, that although Wesley had contacts in Manchester from his Oxford days, he did not visit it between 1738 and 1747, not even on a tour in the area in April 1745. This has been explained as a precaution against the taint of that Jacobite town, but the places visited in 1745 suggest he was simply going over Bennet's societies, and Manchester did not have one until after Charles Wesley's visit in January 1747.[68] Bennet gave Wesley a ready-made network in a sizeable area.

Thirdly, although Bennet was fairly typical of the travelling preachers as a diligent visitor and supervisor of societies, in terms of Methodist

---

[64] Bennet, Autobiography, p. 5 (in shorthand).
[65] Bennet, Diary, 26 Apr. 1748; 20 Sept. 1748; 29 Mar. 1749; John Wesley, *Journal*, 8, p. 157; see my 'Doctors, demons, and early Methodist healing', *SCH*, 19 (1982), pp. 140–3.
[66] Rack, *Reasonable Enthusiasts*, pp. 210–12.
[67] Minutes of Conference (1749), in *PWHS*, 4 (5) (1904), supplement, pp. 64–5.
[68] John Wesley, *Journal*, 3, pp. 175–6; Charles Wesley, *Journal*, 1, p. 440; Bennet to Charles Wesley in *Arminian Magazine*, 1 (1778), p. 472; Everett, *Manchester*, pp. 53–5.

polity he was something of an innovator. He evidently admired the Quaker system of monthly, quarterly, and yearly meetings, and there is some evidence that he borrowed ideas and terminology from them and adapted them to Methodist purposes. As early as May 1743 he was holding monthly meetings in his own societies.[69] It is perhaps significant that at the first Methodist conference in 1744, which Bennet attended, the question of organization was discussed, and it was suggested that they might learn from 'Zinzendorf, Whitefield, the Kirk and the Quakers'.[70] In October 1748 the first two Methodist quarterly meetings were held, one in Yorkshire and the other under Bennet in Cheshire, and various officials were appointed. This was still in the experimental period of Methodist polity, and Wesley seized on the notion as valuable for all. Bennet was dispatched to spread the system elsewhere.[71] His monthly meetings, however, were not taken up, though they were used as an independent development by the Welsh Calvinistic Methodists.[72]

What caused Bennet's break with Wesley in 1751–2? The immediate, ostensible, and probably the major cause was doctrinal—a quarrel over predestinarian Calvinism and antinomianism. This was indeed the root of some of the deepest divisions in the revival, notably between Wesley, on the one hand, and Whitefield and the Calvinistic Methodists and Evangelical Anglicans on the other. It was also a factor in the numerous individual secessions of Wesley's preachers, along with a desire for independence.[73] But it has also to be said that in the Bennet case one cannot ignore the fact that they had already been estranged over a much more personal matter—the highly-charged rivalry in love between John Wesley and Bennet over Grace Murray.[74]

Only the bare outline of this tangled tale can be laid out here. Grace Murray was the widow of a Newcastle sea-captain and had been converted under Methodist influences. She became the housekeeper at Wesley's Newcastle orphan house. Wesley clearly fell in love with her, and she seems to have broken down some of his prejudices against marriage to the extent that by his own account he made agreements for marriage with her of a legally binding nature. Grace's recollections suggest

[69] Bennet, Diary, 2 May 1743.

[70] Agenda to Minutes of conference, 1744 from JRUL, MS Eng. 962, photostat of Richard Viney, Diary, 1 June 1744, and in *PWHS*, 14 (1924), pp. 203–4.

[71] Bennet, Diary, 18, 20 Oct. 1748; *PWHS*, 7 (1909), p. 78; *PWHS*, 35 (1965), pp. 1–4.

[72] M. H. Jones, *The Trevecka Letters* (Caernarvon, 1932), pp. 266–8.

[73] Rack, *Reasonable Enthusiast*, pp. 199–200, 450–61, 333–4.

[74] J. A. Léger, *Wesley's Last Love* (London, 1910); Rack, *Reasonable Enthusiast*, pp. 258–64.

that he was, as often with women, more tortuous and indecisive than this. Bennet, too, fell in love with Grace, and swayed her feelings by emotional and spiritual blackmail into promising marriage to him as well. Charles Wesley compounded the confusion by taking fright at the thought of his brother marrying someone he saw as unsuitable and socially inferior. He also believed that Bennet had the better right to her, and finally took matters into his own hands by marrying Grace to Bennet in Newcastle on 3 October 1749. Sixteen months later John Wesley made a disastrous marriage to the widow Molly Vazeille.[75]

Wesley's reaction to his disappointment shows how deeply he had been hurt and offended. By his account, very characteristically, everyone but himself had been at fault, and he bitterly resented it. Despite a formal reconciliation, it is doubtful whether he ever fully trusted Bennet again, and the feeling was probably mutual. Indeed, when Bennet finally broke with Wesley, he claimed he had not been 'in connexion' with him for the past three years, that is, even before his marriage to Grace.[76] Yet we need not doubt that doctrine and perhaps a desire for independence were major factors which were probably also at work before the marriage.

Bennet, it is to be remembered, had come from a Presbyterian background, and, as we have seen, the decay of Calvinism in that denomination had not been reflected in all its rank and file. It seems fairly clear, in fact, that Bennet began as a Calvinist, but by mid-1744 was defending perfectionism and, according to Wesley, in danger of 'running from one extreme to the other, from Calvinism to Pelagianism'.[77] In March 1747 Bennet himself said he had 'lately looked upon man as a mere machine', which inevitably leads to 'falling into the doctrine of Reprobation and Election'.[78]

It is not clear what moved him back to Calvinism, but one factor may have been an increasingly close relationship with Whitefield. By October 1749 Wesley was worried about Bennet's 'conversing much' with Whitefield, though also bitterly condemning him over the recent marriage.[79] In 1751 Charles Wesley complained that Bennet and others were moving

---

[75] Rack, *Reasonable Enthusiast*, pp. 364–7.

[76] John Wesley, *Letters*, 2, p. 491 n.; *Journal*, 4, p. 15; Bennet, Diary, 2 Apr. 1752.

[77] Jackson, *Preachers*, 1, pp. 62–3; Bennet, Diary, 25 Aug. 1744 and Letter Book, p. 41; John Wesley, *Letters*, 2, p. 107.

[78] Bennet to Wesley, 7 Mar. 1747, in *Arminian magazine*, 1 (1778), p. 472; Everett, *Manchester*, p. 55.

[79] John Wesley, *Letters*, 2, pp. 390–3.

into predestinarianism.[80] Bennet himself complained about the conduct of the preachers as the cause of his secession, but a letter of complaint to an Anglican clergyman in 1753 shows him upholding the classic pattern of Calvinist doctrine, and the issue was also made plain in a final confrontation with Wesley in 1752.[81]

Matters finally came to a hand in Bolton in 1751–2. On 31 December 1751 Bennet publicly disowned Wesley from the pulpit, saying 'Popery! Popery! I have not been in connexion with him these three years, neither will I be any more.'[82] The alienation from Wesley was aggravated, and perhaps precipitated, by a dispute over the terms of the trust deed for the Bolton preaching house, which gave Wesley control of the pulpit. Early in April there was a meeting between Wesley, Bennet, and others at Bolton, which ranged over the matters in dispute and showed that these included the Calvinist issue. The 'popery' charge reflected the Calvinist suspicion that Wesley was teaching salvation by 'works'. Bennet had also intimated that he intended to retain his societies if he could after the break. Mrs John Wesley enlivened the proceedings by storming in and saying that Bennet was 'in the gall of bitterness and bond of iniquity and that she believed me to be a very bad man etc.'.[83]

III

Methodist writers have understandably relegated Bennet's later career to a mere footnote. He is seen as having lost his societies, except at Bolton, to Wesley and then as having settled down in a small Independent church in Warburton, in Cheshire, until his death in 1759.

What actually happened was less simple and clearcut, and certainly less rapid and complete so far as Wesley's recovery of the divided societies was concerned. The story that follows can be pieced together, if rather fragmentarily, from Bennet's Diary and correspondence plus some information from the Methodist circuit accounts for the Manchester area.[84]

Bennet certainly intended to keep up an itinerant ministry in as many of his old societies as possible, and managed to do so in a substantial number, at least from his public break with Wesley in December 1751 until June 1754, when he was making preparations to take on the

---

[80] F. Baker, *Charles Wesley* (London, 1948), pp. 83–7.
[81] Bennet, Letter Book, p. 105; Diary, 1 Apr. 1752.
[82] John Wesley, *Letters*, 2, p. 491 n.; Bennet, Diary, 2 Apr. 1752.
[83] Bennet, Diary, 2 Apr. 1752.
[84] Transcript of Manchester circuit minutes from 1752 in my possession.

Warburton church. His fortunes with the societies were variable. Bolton was his greatest triumph, for there he captured 107 out of the 126 members, and it is surprising that he did not settle there.[85] The seceders built a chapel and reinforced themselves with seceders from the Arian Presbyterians at Bank St. The new congregation at Duke's Alley Chapel became an Independent church, though the original deed of the Chapel simply described them as 'Protestant Dissenters'. An early minister was John Whitford, another ex-Methodist preacher, whom we shall encounter again later.[86] As to the remaining Methodists, in October 1756 Charles Wesley said they had only forty members, and the circuit accounts suggest that they only began growing from the end of 1759, the year of Bennet's death.[87]

Stockport was another place where Bennet either retained a following or the Wesleys lost them for several years. Bennet visited them in 1752, but found them doubtful about him. The place disappeared from the circuit accounts until 1758, though a society was kept near by at Adshead. Robert Anderton, one of the Stockport leaders, was also visited for preaching by Caleb Warhurst, the Manchester Independent.[88] So perhaps the Independents absorbed some of them.

The Woodley society, already containing 'many Dissenters' in 1745, seems to have split, and in face of Methodist preachers' visits Bennet left it 'for a season'. The circuit accounts show no break, but here, too, Warhurst visited Robert Cheetham, a Methodist leader.[89] There were Dissenters in the Shackerley area, too, but here Bennet was 'coldly received', though he persisted for a few weeks, and here the accounts show a gap until July 1754.[90]

In the Peak, Bennet's home territory, matters were more promising for him. The circuit accounts show losses from the Methodists, and a letter of Wesley's shows trouble at Monyash, which was only resolved in March 1758. At Chinley the Methodist society only began in 1759—the year of Bennet's death.[91]

Elsewhere Bennet had only temporary successes, if any. He failed in

[85] Nightingale, *Lancs. Nonconformity*, 3, p. 18.
[86] W. H. Davison, *Centenary Memorials of Duke's Alley, Bolton* (Bolton, 1854), pp. 48–86; Nightingale, 3, p. 18.
[87] Charles Wesley, *Journal*, 2, p. 128.
[88] Caleb Warhurst, Diary, 6 Mar. 1759.
[89] Bennet, Diary, 1 May 1742, 22 July 1744; Warhurst, Diary, 1 July 1758.
[90] Bennet, Diary, 6 Nov. 1747, 4 Apr. 1742.
[91] John Wesley, *Letters*, 2, pp. 491–2; Jackson, *Preachers*, 6, pp. 242–3.

Manchester, though he had hopes of outlying groups in Chorlton and Stretford.[92] Many other places are mentioned up to the end of his detailed Diary in the summer of 1752, and a number never appear as Methodist places again. One clue to the fate of some of them may lie in the examples of those visited by Warhurst. One interesting one is that of Jonathan Hulme or Holmes of Stretford. This man had welcomed Ingham and Bennet in earlier years, but he was also visited by Warhurst in the late 1750s. On one occasion he received Ingham and a Baptist preacher.[93] In the Stockport area, Warhurst seems to have taken on some of Bennet's people, especially in Bredbury Green, which was his own home.[94]

As late as June 1754 Bennet could still speak of an extensive 'circuit', which he 'rambles about' with many societies to care for.[95] But this was before his ordination, and this event and the effects it had on his 'ramblings' and 'circuit' is unfortunately much less clearly documented.

If Bennet's original plan after the break was to continue at least with a reduced 'circuit', under what kind of ecclesiastical auspices and with what status did he intend to act? Here, too, it was not a simple matter of transition to the Independent ministry. The indications are that at first he thought of himself as being still a 'Methodist', though of the Calvinist sort. It seems likely that what he hoped to do was to attach himself to Whitefield's loose 'connexion', and if possible to get help from that evangelist. Whitefield did have a more-or-less organized connection, mostly in the south and west, though its stability is not very clear after 1749.[96]

But Bennet also seems to have had thoughts of ordination, perhaps even as early as 1750, and one motive may have been his recent marriage. Possibly with his wife's pregnancy in mind, he wrote to Whitefield in June 1750, apparently talking of the possibility of 'resuming his classical studies'.[97] Charles Wesley also saw merit in his 'going aside' for a time— but both Bennet and Charles were very critical of the preachers' poor qualifications at this time. Whitefield also talked of Bennet 'settling' (as a minister) and advised him to consult Doddridge about study. But he also

[92] Bennet, Diary, 13 Feb. 1752, 1–2 May 1752.
[93] JRUL, MS Eng. 1062, p. 30; Bennet, Diary, 7 Nov. 1747; Warhurst, Diary, 21 Oct. 1757, 17 Aug. 1758, 18 Feb. 1759.
[94] Bennet, Diary, 11 Apr. 1747 for Bredbury Green and frequent references in Warhurst, Diary.
[95] Bennet to Mrs Whitefield, 4 June 1754, in Letter Book, pp. 108–9.
[96] E. Welch, ed., *Two Calvinistic Methodist Chapels* = London Record Society, 11 (1975); Rack, *Reasonable Enthusiast*, pp. 282–4.
[97] For these exchanges see Whitefield to Bennet, 29 June, 9 and 15 Aug. 1750 in MCA, MS 113.1.10–12; Charles Wesley to Bennet, 10 Aug. 1750 in MCA, MS MAM P6.

offered to obtain help from Lady Huntingdon, presumably for Anglican ordination. It is probably only a curious coincidence that just at this time (when Bennet's Diary has gaps) Lady Huntingdon sponsored some students to Doddridge's academy, one of them a 'serious lad' called Bennet.[98]

Failing ministerial training, Bennet hoped to be a Calvinistic Methodist associated with Whitefield. At the point where his continuous Diary broke off, in July 1752, he had just arrived in Gloucester, evidently to attend a Whitefield 'Association' there. In October 1752 Whitefield himself was in Bennet's area.[99]

Although Bennet did not resume his Diary, the volume concludes with a kind of narrative appendix, in which he observes that because the people he frequently visited needed organization and lacked 'the ordinances' (sacraments), he was 'moved by several to take upon me the ministry' and qualify himself 'by law' (register as a Dissenting minister). What followed can only be approximately dated with the help of some other sources. He had considerable difficulty in obtaining his licence (possibly because of his wandering 'Methodism'), and in the end he succeeded through the good offices of his old minister, James Clegg, who recommended him to the Dissenting M.P. Sir Henry Hoghton.[100] This was in January 1754. In February he was still trying, unsuccessfully, to get aid from Whitefield, and in July the previous year he had already had a weaver's cottage registered by one of his adherents in Warburton.[101]

Warburton, in Cheshire, was one of Bennet's old 'Methodist' societies—it appears in his Diary as early as 1747, with a formal society there by 1749. Bennet then records in his narrative that a 'small meeting house was built for me at Warburton' and a congregation 'raised'. 'Old Mr Walkden of Stockport' (the Dissenting minister mentioned earlier) agreed to open it, and Bennet agreed to attend every other Sunday and to obtain further help. This clearly implies an intention to continue itinerating. The last event recorded in Bennet's narrative is on 12 May 1754, when he exchanged pulpits with Walkden, and Walkden administered the Sacrament to thirty people 'who could give an account touching God's deal-

---

[98] *Calendar of Philip Doddridge's Correspondence*, ed. G. F. Nuttall, *HMC* (with Northamptonshire Record Society), 26 (London, 1979), pp. 333 and n., 339–40 and n.; *Correspondence and Diary of Philip Doddridge*, ed. J. D. Humphries (London, 1839–41), 5, p. 515.

[99] Clegg, Diary, 31 Oct. 1752; G. Whitefield, *Letters* (London, 1772), 2, p. 448.

[100] Clegg, Diary, 12 Jan. 1754.

[101] Whitefield to Bennet, 11 Feb. 1754, in MCA, MS 113.1.17; Chester Record Office, Register of Dissenting Meeting Houses, Warburton, 10 July 1753.

ings with their souls'—the old Independent test of conversion for Communion. This seems to imply that Bennet was not yet ordained.

That this was the case is confirmed by an important letter to Mrs Whitefield in June 1754.[102] Here he says he is still 'rambling about as usual' and still gaining societies—more than he can handle. His Warburton church meets in classes and bands (the Methodist system). He begs for help from the Whitefieldite preachers. The letter concludes with talk of getting ordination, but a desire to continue to itinerate. He had had trouble with William James, of the Welsh Calvinistic Methodist Association (who later joined Duke's Alley at Bolton). Bennet hoped to be ordained soon at Warburton 'amongst the poor Dissenting Methodists', but to keep up his 'circuit' and preach alternate Sundays at Bolton.

In August Clegg advised him to stop Methodist-style itineracy and to obtain ordination as a Dissenter settled in one place, which Bennet promised to do. He must have been ordained by November 1754, when his baptism-register begins. What is curious is that none of the baptisms over the next four years are in Warburton, but they cover a wide area in Cheshire, Lancashire, and Yorkshire. There is a tradition that he preached in Lady Huntingdon's area around Donington, in Leicestershire, as well.[103] This evidence, coupled with the indications in the Methodist circuit accounts already noticed, may suggest that Bennet still kept up some of his rambles to the end of his life. Some of the baptisms show Bennet in the Bolton area, as one would expect, and others are near his Cheshire base. They may, of course, simply have been favours to old friends and not signs of a regular ministry in those places. The Yorkshire cases at Holme Firth, Rotherham, and in Craven, as well as some in Chowbent in Lancashire, are perhaps suggestive, since they are in places with old Presbyterian chapels or new Independent ones at the time or soon after. Was Bennet picking up dissidents for evangelicalism here?[104]

One can only guess tentatively at the reasons for Bennet's temporary success, but eventual failure to retain much of his old network, and for Wesley's recovery of most of it. Among the factors were probably the Dissenting antecedents of some of the members, views on Calvinism, personal allegiance to Bennet or Wesley. But Bennet tended to withdraw

---

[102] Bennet to Mrs Whitefield, 20 June 1752 in Letter Book, pp. 108–9.

[103] A. C. H. Seymour, *Life of Lady Huntingdon*, 2 vols (London, 1844), 1, p. 45. A document on 'Warburton Conversations 1754' formerly in MCA, but now lost, would probably throw light on Bennet's plans.

[104] For these places see under names in J. G. Miall, *Congregationalism in Yorkshire* (London, 1868).

unless he had a warm welcome, and Wesley and his preachers were more aggressive and had more resources. It is possible that ordination did lead to a contraction of Bennet's travels, but equally likely that what finally settled the matter was declining health and a premature death.

Bennet died on 24 May 1759 and was buried in the Presbyterian grave-yard at Chinley.[105] We shall see that his Dissenting friends rallied round after his death to care for the 'poor scattered flock' at Warburton and its neighbouring society at Rosthern, but the rest is silence.[106] Local history is silent about Warburton, which is not even mentioned in Urwick's *Non-conformity in Cheshire*. A Methodist pilgrim early this century could find no trace of a chapel.[107] In all probability the society as well as the remnants of the old Bennet 'circuit' faded away for lack of care, or were absorbed here and there into Independency where Wesley failed to capture them.

IV

Something more can be said, however, about Bennet's association with a local group of Independent ministers, some of whom have already figured in this story, and help to illuminate the sources of Dissenting revival in the area.

The Diary of Caleb Warhurst of Manchester throws a little light on Bennet's last months of life, and also on his associates. Warhurst was born in 1723, the son of a carpenter in Bredbury Green, near Stockport, and in all probability attended the old Independent church at Hatherlow.[108] There is no record of his conversion, which may have been through any of the new preachers in the area, although Bennet was certainly his 'beloved friend'. In May 1755 he became assistant at the Baptist church in Manchester, was drawing away Methodists in October 1756, and then, as we have seen, was ordained minister of an Independent church in November 1756. The ordainers are an interesting group.[109] James Scott of

---

[105] Mansfield, *Congregationalism*, p. 24; *PWHS*, 7 (1910), p. 116.

[106] Warburton, Diary, 28 July 1759.

[107] *PWHS*, 7 (1910), pp. 116–17.

[108] Manchester Central Library Archives, MS M162, Box 54, MS History of Cannon St. Chapel, p. 41; Nightingale, *Lancs. Nonconformity*, 5, p. 109; G. R. Axon, 'Hatherlow Chapel Baptismal Register 1732–81', *TLCAS*, 44 (1927), pp. 56–99, includes Warburton and others in the Warburton and Bennet Diaries; Urwick, *Nonconformity in Cheshire*, pp. 312–14 on the chapel. J. Cocks, *Memorials of Hatherlow* (Stockport, 1895), p. 61 confirms this.

[109] Warburton, Diary, 10 Nov. 1756. For Scott, R. Tudur Jones, *Congregationalism in England 1662–1962* (London, 1962), pp. 140–1, 152, 154; McLachlan, *English Education*, pp. 192–3. For Pye, Miall, *Congregationalism in Yorkshire*, pp. 350, 353.

Heckmondwike was head of an academy explicitly founded to counter the effects of Arianism in the north, and his students were often evangelical. John Pye was minister of an Independent church in Sheffield, whose first minister had been brother of Samuel de la Rose of Stockport. Peter Walkden, whom we have already encountered, was the last of the trio.

Warhurst's Diary shows that he was in close touch with a small group of Independent ministers, some of them ex-Methodists like Bennet.[110] On 9 May 1758 Warhurst records a visit from his 'beloved friend' Bennet and says he has 'well recovered from his illness', though with 'trials' in his church. He preached for Bennet at Warburton to a 'small auditory'. At Stockport in July 1758 John Edwards came from Leeds to preach at Walkden's church and met Bennet and Warhurst. Edwards and Warhurst stayed at Robert Cheetham's at Woodley—a Methodist from the old Bennet society there. On 14 December 1758 Warhurst says he should have preached at Warburton, but Edward Harrison, the minister of Greenacres chapel near Oldham, went instead. Bennet was by now ill again, and Harrison, John Whitford of Bolton, and Warhurst agreed to supply Warburton once a fortnight until they saw how it went with him. This was duly done, and on 2 March 1759 Warhurst visited Bennet at Chinley, finding him very weak. On 22 April he also preached at Brother Billinge's at Rosthern, where Bennet had a meeting. Finally, after Bennet's death, in May 1759, Warhurst preached for the distracted Bennet meetings. He had already been visiting some of Bennet's contacts elsewhere.

Of the little group of Independents mentioned by Warhurst, John Edwards appears to have been born in Ireland and worked there for Whitefield and Wesley. Whitefield had resisted his attempts to set up a church in Ireland, and later in Leeds, in opposition to Wesley, but he had seceded at Leeds in 1753 and founded an Independent church. He appears to have died in 1784.[111] John Whitford was a Methodist preacher from 1748 to 1754, when he left Wesley. According to Charles Wesley, the Manchester Methodists were distracted by him, Bennet, and others in 1756, as well as drawn away by Warhurst.[112] He became minister of the Duke's Alley church in Bolton at least from 1756 to 1758 or 9. He then had ministries in Yorkshire in the 1760s, but had an 'unhappy temper', and he last appears, still with problems and in fear of insanity, at Olney,

110 The following details are all from Warhurst's Diary.
111 Whitefield, *Letters*, 2, pp. 451; 3, p. 143; John Wesley, *Journal*, 4, pp. 67 n., 96 n.
112 Charles Wesley, *Journal*, 2, pp. 128–9.

where William Cowper knew in the late 1770s.[113] Edward Harrison and his Greenacres church had no Methodist connections, but close ties with Yorkshire Independency in the Craven area. He also had close ties with Scott of Heckmondwicke.[114]

But the most interesting of these rather shadowy figures (and the best documented) is Peter Walkden of Stockport, who has appeared several times in this narrative. He is interesting particularly because he provides a link between the old Dissent and the newer, evangelical type, and his role in the Bennet and Warhurst circle shows how the revival of Independency drew on survivals from an earlier period as well as from new converts and those influenced by Methodism.[115]

Walkden was born near Manchester on 16 October 1684, attended Conyngham's academy in that town, and allegedly had an M.A. from a Scottish university, though evidence for this has not been found. He was minister of Garsdale, in Yorkshire, from 1709–11 and was ordained there. It is probably significant of the tone of this church that his successor was a friend of Scott of Heckmondwike and helped ordain Scott in 1741.[116] Walkden then moved to the Chipping area, in Lancashire, and became minister of two chapels, Newton-in-Bowland and Hesketh Lane, both of which had early associations with Wymondhouses, the home of the Jollie family of Independents. Walkden's Diary in this period gives a good idea of the life of an old-style Dissenting minister in an old-fashioned, rural part of Lancashire. Here, as we have seen, he also kept up much of the old Puritan pattern of chapel life. These churches seem to have been notionally 'Presbyterian', though Walkden took part in ordinations with Independents and later attended the Cheshire Classis. In 1738 he moved to Holcomb, near Bury, and here met Scott of Heckmondwike and helped to settle him in a ministry in Craven in a church also aided by Edward Harrison, later of Greenacres.[117] In 1744 Walkden finally moved to Stockport to the Old Tabernacle Independent chapel, where he died on 5 November 1769 at the age of eighty-five.[118]

---

[113] *Letters and Prose Writings of William Cowper*, ed. C. King and C. Ryskamp (Oxford, 1979), 1, pp. 400–1 and n.

[114] Nightingale, *Lancs. Nonconformity*, 5, p. 230; G. Waddington, *History of Greenacres Chapel* (Manchester, 1854), pp. 56–8 confuses the succession; T. Whitehead, *History of the Dales Congregational Churches* (Keighley, 1930), p. 126.

[115] For Walkden, see *DNB*; *Diaries*, ed. W. Dobson (Preston, 1866); J. Bromley in *THSLC*, 32 (1880), pp. 117–42, 36 (1884), pp. 15–40, 37 (1888), pp. 117–40.

[116] Miall, *Congregationalism in Yorkshire*, p. 344.

[117] Whitehead, *Dales Churches*, pp. 123–6.

[118] Epitaph in Bromley, in *THSLC*, 32 (1880), p. 135.

The Stockport chapel was a large one, with 629 hearers in 1715.[119] Its history throws some light on Walkden's religious position, for it was here that Samuel de la Rose had offended some by his Calvinism and caused his critics to secede and found a church which later gravitated to Arian Presbyterianism—the reverse of the usual pattern of secession by the 'orthodox'.[120] The Tabernacle certainly showed signs of evangelical sympathies even before Walkden's day. His immediate predecessor was a Scotsman called James Smith (a category of minister which contributed considerably to the revival of Lancashire Independency—James Scott was another). David Taylor attended and once preached in Smith's time there, and James Clegg thought they were well suited to each other![121]

With one exception, scattered references to Walkden's time at Stockport all suggest orthodox and evangelical sympathies. The exception is a batch of letters in 1745–8, charging him with Arian views and unsoundness on original sin and salvation.[122] But this may simply have been the product of hyper-Calvinist hysteria. Certainly the associations with Taylor, Bennet, and Warhurst point the other way, and in 1742 Walkden was in friendly correspondence with Whitefield, who wished him well if he 'loved the Saviour in sincerity and preached the Gospel with the demonstration of the Spirit and with power'. He apparently also corresponded with other revival leaders.[123] It is possible that Walkden, like other orthodox Independents, had reservations about the new-style 'enthusiasts'. If so, relationships may have improved when people like Bennet and his friends broke with Methodism, turned Calvinist, and showed signs of adopting a more settled as well as ordained ministry. So one is not surprised to find this 'old Dissenter' helping Bennet at Warburton. By the late 1750s Walkden was evidently a venerable associate of the local group of evangelical Independents already described.

The friendships and contacts outlined here are a signal testimony to the mingling of old and new in the expansion of Independency in the later eighteenth century. Pye, Scott, and Walkden may all be taken to be in continuity with the old tradition, though stimulated and reinforced by the revival. Warhurst's background was probably of the same kind, though with Baptist connections as well, and he listened with some appreciation to the Wesleys, Whitefield, and the antinomian Roger

---

[119] Urwick, *Nonconformity*, p. lxi (from Evans List).
[120] H. Heginbotham, *Stockport Ancient and Modern* (London, 1892), 2, p. 50.
[121] Clegg, Diary, 11 Jan. 1742; Bennet, Diary, 22 Aug. 1743, 20 June 1743, 5 Aug. 1743.
[122] Bromley, in *THSLC*, 37 (1888), p. 140.
[123] *Ibid.*, p. 119.

Ball.[124] The effect of the revival was partly to loosen up denominational allegiances in favour of a degree of co-operation between those of evangelical persuasions until Calvinism disrupted this, as it frequently did. Bennet, Whitford, and Edwards, of course, were very much products of the revival, and specifically of Methodism, though Calvinism drove them out too, and in Bennet's case back to Dissent in another form.

The distinction between Presbyterianism and Independency in the early eighteenth century in England was difficult to draw on ecclesiological lines, and not least in Cheshire with its undenominational Classis. In Lancashire, Independency was largely a fresh creation through the revival. Walkden's case is interesting here because his early ministry was in churches usually classed as 'Presbyterian', though his later associations are clearly with renewed Independency. Indeed, by the time of his death the best way of distinguishing the two seems to be less in terms of the earlier history of the churches and people concerned than in terms of the doctrine and ethos they now upheld. Those churches and ministers by the mid-eighteenth century which were identified as 'Presbyterian' had almost always gone Arian in this area; those identified as 'Independent' were Calvinist and evangelical. They were also beginning to multiply, weakening the old staid and enclosed ways with the ecstasies and expansiveness of revival.[125]

It has to be said that the personal associations described here for Bennet's circle in the 1750s did not amount to anything like a formal association, though their tendency to work beyond a purely localized church recalled some older Dissenting habits and looked forward to the freer itineracy of some of their successors later in the century. But, compared with Methodism, this was still restricted and lacked system and support even of the kind Bennet thought insufficient for his needs in his Methodist days and still more later. The fate of his church and 'circuit' underlined these limitations and the advantages enjoyed by Wesley's connexion. Whitefield's loosely-jointed connexion, significantly, dissolved into Independency after his death. One can understand John Wesley's slighting comment on one of his preachers who deserted him for a Dissenting ministry: his 'light' had been 'laid under a bushel in a little, obscure Dissenting meeting-house'.[126] That was not Bennet's intention, but it was liable to be his fate. It was only after 1800 that

---

[124] Warhurst, Diary, 22 Oct. 1757, 23 Apr. 1758.

[125] Tudur Jones, *Congregationalism*, pp. 162–8.

[126] *Arminian Magazine*, 2 (1779), p. 95.

Independents created county associations of a new kind, dedicated to co-operation for evangelism, though even this step fell well short of the tight connexional autocracy of a Wesley.

University of Manchester

JOHN WESLEY AND THE COMMUNITY
OF GOODS

by JOHN WALSH

And all that believed were together, and had all things common.
And sold their possessions and goods, and parted them to all men, as
every man had need. And they continuing daily with one accord in
the temple, and breaking bread from house to house, did eat their
meat with gladness and singleness of heart.

Acts 2. 44–5.

AMONG the strangest of the rumours circulating about early
Methodism was the charge that it promoted the notion of
Christian communism—'the community of goods'. In the early
summer of 1739 Lord Egmont, one of the Georgia Trustees, got wind of
the story and after hearing Whitefield preach at Blackheath pressed him
whether, among other eccentricities, he held that 'all things should be in
common'.[1] The same year two anti-Methodist pamphlets raised the same
issue, and in 1740 it surfaced again in the papers when another former
Oxford Methodist, Benjamin Ingham, was accused by his local vicar of
helping to foment a violent riot of Dewsbury cloth workers by 'preaching
up ... a community of goods, as was practised by the Primitive
Christians'.[2] Ingham was said to urge a sharing of wealth so drastic that his
brother had remarked in disgust, 'if I mind our Ben, he would preach me
out of all I have'.[3]

What is one to make of these charges? They seem curiously at odds
with fashionable interpretations of Methodism as an agency of industrial
capitalism, the exemplar of a Protestant ethic dedicated to the business of
strenuous accumulation. Were accusations like these merely the product
of polemical fantasy? Early Methodism certainly attracted to itself a
cluster of apparently bizarre allegations. Once critics had identified it as a
fresh outbreak of religious 'enthusiasm' they quickly placed it in a
heresiographical tradition that stretched from the ancient Gnostics to
modern Ranters and French Prophets. Methodists were seen as clandestine

---

[1] *HMC, Egmont Diary*, 3 (London, 1923), p. 69.
[2] W. Bowman, *The Imposture of Methodism Displayed* (Wakefield, 1740), p. 61.
[3] *The Weekly Miscellany* (London), 26 July 1740.

subversives, sexual deviants, destroyers of family life, even practitioners of witchcraft. They were also regarded as potential Levellers, for the association of enthusiastic heresy with radical communitarianism was an instinctive one. A long succession of radical groups had been mesmerized by the 'love communism' described in Acts. Communitarian experiments, like those of the ill-fated Anabaptist theocracy at Munster and the Diggers, were not forgotten. It did not seem beyond the bounds of credence that the new Methodists would follow this well-trodden path.

Having laboriously forced the genie of religious radicalism back into the bottle after the Restoration, conservative churchmen were in no mood to let it out. An era which feared 'new modelling' and exalted the rights of property was hardly one propitious for a discussion of Acts 2 as a model for contemporary behaviour. To be sure, clergymen could not ignore the existence of the post-Pentecostal 'community of goods', but they treated the texts which described it with the greatest circumspection. It was a precedent to be stripped of literal application to the present day. The community of goods at Jerusalem was seen as an emergency expedient suited only to the infancy of the Church, when the Christians were still a tiny group surrounded by a hostile population.[4] No general rule was here laid down for future generations. Post-Restoration exegetes, be they Anglicans or Nonconformists, appear virtually unanimous in their opinion that this was 'an extraordinary occasion'; it was, as Bishop Thomas Sprat put it firmly, 'absolutely inimitable and never to be copied after by us'.[5] Though Richard Baxter sounded a note of wistful regret for its passing, allowing that a community of goods might be highly desirable, 'if we were here capable of it', he none the less concluded firmly that we were *not* so capable.[6] With this judgement the Evangelical clergy of the eighteenth century were generally content. The sharing of Acts 2, advised John Newton of Olney, was 'not enjoined as a precedent to be observed'.[7] Commentators stressed the brevity of its duration. They pointed to the clear implication in some of the Epistles that property was still being retained for personal use in other parts of the early Church. Surely, they argued,

[4] See J. Viner, *The Role of Providence in the Social Order* (Philadelphia, 1972), p. 88.
[5] *The Whole Duty of Man* (1748 edn.), p. 382; T. Sprat, *Sermons Preached on Several Occasions* (London, 1710), p. 93.
[6] R. Baxter, *Dying Thoughts* (London, 1683), p. 192.
[7] J. Newton, *Works*, 6 vols (London, 1816), 3, p. 83. Cf. T. Scott, *The Holy Bible with Explanatory Notes* (London, 1823), 5, p. 32; C. Simeon, *Horae Homileticae*, 16 vols (London, 1819–28), 8, pp. 268–70; J. B. Sumner, *A Practical Exposition of the Acts of the Apostles* (London, 1836), pp. 75–6.

the Apostles' injunction that the rich should give to the poor was meaningless unless propertied Christians existed to succour the needy? Even the Jerusalem Church did not practise a true community of goods: what was involved here was not the common *ownership* of property but the common *use* of property, which was a very different matter.[8]

It was conceded that there was indeed a moral to be observed in the extraordinary fraternity of the Church at Jerusalem, but it was not that of a communitarian abandonment of private property. 'The lesson to be gathered from this instance', wrote William Burkitt, the biblical commentator 'is . . . that . . . we must always relieve the saints' wants as we are able and sometimes upon an extraordinary occasion, above what we are well able.'[9] This conclusion appeared to dovetail nicely with the official teaching of the Church of England. The Thirty-Eighth Article declared that

> the riches and goods of Christians are not common, as touching the right, title and possession of the same; as certain Anabaptists do falsely boast. Notwithstanding, every man ought of such things as he possesseth, liberally to give alms to the poor.[10]

It was thus not as a precept that the primitive community of goods was to be invoked, but as an incitement to almsgiving. In eighteenth-century sermons early Christian communalism was invoked, if at all, as a generalized ideal of Christian love and benevolence, for occasional use in Charity Sermons, where it might shame the niggardliness of a congregation and fill the collecting-bag.[11]

All the same, Acts 2 and 4 could not be entirely excised from the consciousness of the Church. Though early Christian heretics and Protestant sectaries provided negative referents for the notion of a community of goods, the more positive affirmations of Christian history remained to nag at the clerical mind. It was evident to those who read the Fathers that for a considerable period the members of other early churches had contributed their weekly earnings to a common stock, which was disbursed by deacons for the relief of the suffering and

---

[8] D. Whitby, *A Paraphrase and Commentary on the New Testament*, 2 vols (London, 1703), 1, p. 609. For the similar interpretation of a modern scholar, see L. Goppelt, *Apostolic and Post-Apostolic Times*, translation (London, 1970), pp. 49–50.

[9] W. Burkitt, *Expository Notes on the New Testament*, 11th edn. (London, 1739), unpaginated, on Acts 2. 43.

[10] See Bishop Burnet's comments on this Article; G. Burnet, *An Exposition of the Thirty Nine Articles* (London, 1699), pp. 391–2.

[11] As, for instance, in Lewis Stephens, *The Great Duty of Charity* (London, 1721); R. P. Finch, *A Sermon Preached before the Sons of the Clergy* (London, 1768).

destitute. The Jerusalem precedent retained ideological force for centuries. Though private property was legitimated by the early Church, it was viewed not in terms of natural right, but as a concession to man's fallen state.[12] Though the ownership of goods was seen as lawful, Christians were reminded that they always possessed them in trusteeship from God for the relief of Christ's poor. Though the communal sharing of Acts was held up as 'counsel' rather than 'precept', and transmuted into almsgiving and charity, it had not forfeited all its force as a direct example, but still found literal expression in the communal sharing of monks and others living by rule. Here, through the centuries, the prescription of Acts 2 had continual embodiment as a 'counsel of perfection'—a way of life for those who sought to imitate Christ by the abandonment of personal possessions.

Through the channels of history and tradition a disquieting knowledge of patristic attitudes to wealth was still transmitted to later generations beyond the Reformation. Radical early Christian conceptions of riches and poverty continued to reach English Protestants, not only through the Gospels and Epistles, but through patrology, for the Reformation brought no sharp caesura in English knowledge of the Fathers. Learned Puritans like Baxter still larded their writings with patristic citations, while Laudians and post-Restoration High Churchmen set the authority of primitive tradition only a little lower than that of Scripture itself.[13] In the late seventeenth century the Church of England produced a remarkable cult of Christian primitivism which, in a quiet way, constituted a virtual religious revival, affecting many aspects of its life.[14] In the history of an idealized early Church, Anglicans found precepts and practices which could be held up to inspire, renew—and shame—an existing Church of England shaken by decades of disorder and revolution. There was a fine flowering of Anglican patristic study in writers like Fell, Wake, Bingham, Cave, Reeves, and Deacon, through whom a knowledge of early Christian thought reached not only parish priests, but also devout laymen like the

---

[12] See M. Hengel, *Property and Riches in the Early Church* (London, 1974).
[13] See G. V. Bennett, 'Patristic tradition in Anglican thought, 1660–1900', *Oecumenica*, 1971–2 (Centre d'études Oecumeniques Strasbourg, 1972); J. W. Packer, *The Transformation of Anglicanism 1613–1660* (London, 1969); H. R. McAdoo, *The Spirit of Anglicanism* (London, 1965); N. Sykes, *From Sheldon to Secker* (Cambridge, 1959), p. 113.
[14] See E. A. Duffy, 'Primitive Christianity revived: religious Renewal in Augustan England', *SCH*, 14 (1977), pp. 287–300.

Nonjuror Robert Nelson, whose aim was 'to live, as well as believe, as the Primitive Catholicks did'.[15]

It was in this atmosphere that John Wesley's spirituality was incubated. The nature of his debt to the Fathers and to primitive Christian piety has not yet been systematically studied, but it was clearly substantial.[16] Of his early life at Epworth Rectory he recalled, 'From a child I was taught to love and reverence the Scriptures . . . and next to these, to esteem the primitive Fathers, the writers of the three first centuries.'[17] At Oxford, one of the driving passions behind the formation of the Holy Club was a yearning to recapture the lost purity of the early Church—so intense that it earned him the nickname of 'Primitive Christianity' from one of his lady friends.[18] In 1733, through his friend John Clayton, Wesley came into touch with the circle of Manchester Nonjurors, notably with the learned Dr Thomas Deacon, who inspired him for a time with a zealous interest in the primitive liturgies which so preoccupied the Nonjuring 'Usagers'.[19] He sailed for Georgia in 1735 with the eighteen-pound weight of Bishop Beveridge's *Synodikon* in his baggage.[20]

Wesley's patristic studies seem to have been somewhat electic, the reading of a devout man of letters rather than of a laborious and systematic scholar. He gave pride of place to the earliest writers of all, those nearest the world of Acts. His *Christian Library* (the *Reader's Digest* of practical divinity which he later excerpted for his followers) opens with the 'small remains' of the Apostolical Fathers—Ignatius, Clemens Romanus,

---

[15] W. Reeves, *The Apologies of Justin Martyr, Tertullian and Minutius Felix*, 2 vols (London, 1709), 1, Epistle Dedicatory.

[16] See the valuable observations on this theme prefacing J. Wesley, *Sermons I*, ed. A. C. Outler (1984), pp. 59, 74–6. Professor Outler's magnificent four-volume edition of the *Sermons* comprises volumes 1–4 of *The Bicentennial Edition of the Works of John Wesley* (Nashville, 1984). This is a continuation of *The Oxford Edition of Wesley's Works*, in which several of the projected 34 volumes appeared between 1975 and 1983. This composite edition is to be distinguished from the previous standard edition, *The Works of the Rev John Wesley*, edited by Thomas Jackson, of which I have used the 3rd edn., 14 vols (London, 1872), widely available in the Zondervan photographic reproduction. All references to Wesley's *Works* are to the Jackson edition and are indicated as such. Professor Ted Campbell of Duke University is currently working on patristic influences on Wesley's thought.

[17] Wesley, *Works*, ed. Jackson, 13, p. 272.

[18] Wesley, *Letters 1 1721–1739*, ed. F. Baker (Oxford, 1980), p. 246 (vol. 25 in *The Bicentennial Edition of the Works of John Wesley*). So far two volumes of *Letters* have appeared in this fine edition, covering the period 1721–55. For those of later years I have used J. Wesley, *Letters*, ed. J. Telford, 8 vols (London, 1931).

[19] See R. Heitzenrater, *John Wesley and the Oxford Methodists, 1725–1735* (Duke Ph.D. thesis, 1972), pp. 160 ff.; F. Baker, *John Wesley and the Church of England* (London, 1970), pp. 31–3.

[20] Wesley, *Sermons I*, p. 74.

Polycarp—'contemporaries of the Apostles' whom he had studied at Oxford in William Wake's edition.[21] After these he ranked Fathers of the second and third centuries: Tertullian, Origen, Clement of Alexandria, and Cyprian. Thereafter he saw a declension, but 'even in the fourth century' he still found the pure deposit of primitive Christianity in Ephrem Syrus and 'Macarius' (from whom he quarried his doctrine of Christian Perfection), in Basil, and above all in Chrysostom, much revered by the Wesley family—'master St.Chrysostom' had been Samuel Wesley's advice to his son preparing for Orders at Oxford in 1725.[22] Wesley's vision of primitive Christianity was strongly coloured by a close knowledge of recent historical accounts. Works like William Cave's *Primitive Christianity* (1673), Anthony Horneck's *Letter . . . Concerning the Lives of the Primitive Christians* (1681), and the Abbé Claude Fleury's *Manners of the Ancient Christians* (English translation 1698), played an important role in Wesley's intellectual formation and were studied by him at Oxford. He subsequently reprinted and abridged Horneck and Fleury in the exemplary literature of his movement.[23]

Although Wesley came drastically to modify some of his Oxford views, the primitive Church continued to provide him with models for his belief and action. Not only did he justify doctrines like Christian Perfection by reference to the Fathers, but also some of the distinctive practices of early Methodism, such as the love-feast, the watch-night service, and class tickets.[24] His ironically titled *Character of a Methodist*, depicting the ideal Christian, was taken from Clement of Alexandria's *Stromateis*.[25] There is no doubt, too, that his social ethic was profoundly shaped by the vision of early Christian mutuality opened up to him by his Oxford reading. The idealized image of the primitive Church provided stark contrasts with the acquisitiveness of Walpole's England, of which, as an old-fashioned Tory, he disapproved strongly. In the Fathers he encountered a powerful consensus on the need for a drastic sharing of

---

[21] *The Christian Library*, ed. J. Wesley, 15 vols, 2nd edn. (London, 1819–21), 1, Preface, p. iii.

[22] For Chrysostom, see Wesley, *Letters I 1721–1739*, p. 171. For the influence of 'Macarius' and Ephrem Syrus on Wesley, see *John Wesley*, ed. A. C. Outler (New York, 1964), pp. 9–10, 30–1, 251–2.

[23] W. Cave, *Primitive Christianity* (London, 1673); A. Horneck, *The Happy Ascetick . . . to which is added a Letter to a Person of Quality concerning the Holy Lives of the Primitive Christians* (London, 1681); Claude Fleury, *An Historical Account of the Manners and Behaviour of the Christians in the Church* (London, 1698). For Wesley's abridgements of Horneck and Fleury, see below, nn. 26 and 29.

[24] Wesley, *Works*, 8, ed. Jackson, pp. 250–63.

[25] *Ibid.*, pp. 340–7; see the comment in *Sermons I*, p. 74.

wealth and the extreme danger of covetousness and conspicuous consumption. Behind the Fathers stood the Apostolic Church at Jerusalem, 'the pattern and mother of all churches'.[26] As Fleury or Horneck depicted it to a young Oxonian, it was an ideal community bound together by the bonds of love; an extended family, sharing its resources, prizing its poor and helpless as 'the treasure of the Church'.[27] The first Christians 'lived for the most part only from hand to mouth, upon their labour', despising luxury, giving their surplusage away immediately to the needy.[28] 'They had all their joys and sorrows common; and they might be said to be all in one, and one in all.'[29] Despite their historical remoteness, these potent images of consensual love and communal sharing possessed radical potential for those who saw them as behavioural models for the Christian world. They held just such a significance for John Wesley.

Not all Wesley's High Church mentors took a deep interest in the social teaching of primitive Christians. Their main concern was the ecclesiology and devotional practice of the early Church. When, in 1733, John Wesley consulted Dr Deacon for advice on early Christian ethics, the reply came back that 'Dr Deacon gives his humble service to you, and lets you know that the worship and discipline of the Primitive Church have taken up so much of his time that he has never read the Fathers with a particular view to their moral doctrines.'[30] For the most part, the High Churchmen who extolled the early Church were self-conscious conservatives, reaching back to the early Christian centuries not only for devotional inspiration, but also for a polemical purpose. In Christian tradition they looked for an objective deposit of dogma, fixed and static, which could be set against the enthusiastic biblicism, the destructive religious individualism—the 'private spirit'—of Puritans and sectaries. By appealing to the coordinate authority of tradition in the interpretation of the Bible, they hoped to contain the dangerous potential of *sola scriptura*. In the Fathers they sought historical evidence to defend cherished principles which had been under attack from religious radicals: Apostolicity, episcopacy, liturgy, the eucharistic Sacrifice. A similar conservatism characterized their politico-theology. In State and Church—and in the

[26] [C. Fleury], *The Manners of the Ancient Christians, extracted from a French Author* [by J. Wesley], (Bristol, 1749), p. 7.

[27] *Ibid.*, p. 21.

[28] Fleury, *Historical Account*, p. 73.

[29] A. Horneck, *Letter to a Person of Quality concerning the Lives of the Primitive Christians*, abridged in Wesley's *Christian Library*, 16, p. 425.

[30] Wesley, *Letters 1*, p. 352.

family, that 'little commonwealth', too—they extolled the religious character of magistracy; divine right, passive obedience.

In their attitude to poverty and riches, however, this inbred authoritarianism was often softened by an ethic of charity inherited from the Middle Ages and reinforced by patristic learning. Reverential views of the poor as 'Christ's poor' were still current. Strong views of the obligations of Christian stewardship, buttressed by quotations from the Fathers, are common in the High Anglican devotional literature of the early eighteenth century—as, for example, in the writings of Robert Nelson, studied by the Holy Club. In his *Address to Persons of Quality* (1715) Nelson reminded his readers that 'all the ancient Fathers who are wise instructors in matters of piety, as well as the best witnesses to necessary truth, agree in this notion; that after we have satisfy'd our necessities, and supply'd our reasonable occasions, we should employ the rest for the relief of our poor neighbours'—a point which he drove home by citation from Basil, Augustine, and Ambrose.[31] All the same, as churchmen realized uneasily, there were dangers in the transposition of primitive precedent to the contemporary world, particularly in the realm of social ethics. Prudence was necessary, as well as zeal.[32]

There were High Churchmen who did not seem to exercise that prudence, however. One of the chief mentors of Wesley's Oxford Methodists, William Law, provides a spectacular example of one in whom the ascetical ideals of the past were propagated with a literalness and intensity that struck some fellow High Churchmen as not only eccentric, but fanatical. For Law, 'self-denial, holy discipline, daily cross', were essential elements in the Christian life: Christianity was nothing if not a '*doctrine of the cross*'—a view echoed in other Nonjurors, whose privations and sense of ecclesiastical marginality may have made them susceptible to a theology of suffering.[33] His *Christian Perfection* (1726) and *Serious Call* (1729) urged that the mortification and self-denial characteristic of the primitive Christian saints were still enjoined on all those who sought to imitate Christ and follow him. The pursuit of perfection was not to be confined to the cloister, but was to be aimed at by all Christians: though God might accept lower states of piety, no true Christian could afford to do other than aim at the highest target. The right use of wealth was seen

---

[31] R. Nelson, *An Address to Persons of Quality and Estate* (London, 1715), pp. 229–30.

[32] By the 1730s the authority of the Fathers was yielding ground to the claims of 'reason'. Antiquity had suffered in the 'battle of the ancients and the moderns' which had been taking place in the previous decades; see Bennett, 'Patristic tradition', pp. 72–4.

[33] W. Law, *A Practical Treatise upon Christian Perfection* (London, 1726), p. 191.

by Law as particularly necessary for Christian discipleship. He extolled voluntary poverty; he fulminated against the retention of unnecessary property for personal use. 'The peaceful, pleasurable enjoyments of riches is a state of life every where condemned by our blessed Saviour', he insisted.[34] It was impossible to follow the dominical injunction to be 'poor in spirit' while enjoying wealth: much of Law's eloquence was devoted to the negative treatment of wealth—to riches as a hindrance to the ascetical pursuit of perfection—but he was none the less highly conscious of the positive obligations of almsgiving, which he saw as a vital element in the practice of Christian love and the *imitatio Christi*. There was no 'other lawful way of employing our wealth (beyond our bare necessities) than in the assistance of the poor'.[35]

In a later work, *The Spirit of Prayer*, part i (1750), written during his final mystical phase, he extolled the primitive community of goods at Jerusalem. This he saw as the embodiment in its fullness of the universal love which was the heart of the Gospel. Here was 'a Church made truly after the pattern of heaven, where the love that reigns in heaven reigned in it, where divine love broke down all the selfish fences, the locks and bolts of *me*, *mine*, *my own*.'[36] In a passage that alarmed some of his readers, Law declared his belief that the spirit of love which had made the primitive community of goods a natural and spontaneous reaction to human need could elicit the same response in every individual today. He emphatically rejected the notion that the primitive communalism of Acts 2 no longer had any exemplary relevance.

> Now though many years did not pass after the Age of the Apostles before *Satan* and *self* got footing in the Church, and set up merchandize in the house of God, yet this *one heart* and *spirit* which first appeared in the Jerusalem Church is that *one heart and spirit* of divine love to which *all* are called that would be true disciples of Christ. And though the practice of it is lost as to the Church in general, yet it ought not to have been lost; and therefore every Christian ought to make it his greatest care and prayer to have it restored in himself. And then, though born in the dregs of time, or living in Babylon, he will be as truly a member of the first heavenly Church at Jerusalem as if he had lived in it, in the days of the Apostles.[37]

---

[34] *Ibid.*, p. 99.
[35] *Ibid.*, p. 134.
[36] W. Law, *The Spirit of Prayer*, part i (London, 1750), p. 86.
[37] *Ibid.*

If the communal reintroduction of a community of goods still seemed far off, its spirit could be captured by every Christian who followed the path towards perfection.

Many readers were impressed by Law's all-or-nothing demands on the professed Christian, but others found his counsel of perfection alarming in its rigorism. In a best-selling tract, *The Folly, Sin and Danger of Being Righteous Overmuch* (1739), his fellow High Churchman Joseph Trapp distilled from Law's precepts the stark message that "'tis a sin to be rich', a proposition which he condemned as the abnegation of right reason.[38] Law's interpretation of Scripture, argued John Brownsword in 1739, was based on a dangerously 'levelling notion'.[39] Writing in 1760, Alexander Jephson complained that texts like Luke 12. 33 had, by Law's ruthless literalism, been 'miserably perverted to prove the absolute unlawfulness of any worldly estates and possessions and the necessity of a community of goods'.[40]

It is noticeable that each of these writers was convinced that Law's views on riches and property had infected the founders of Methodism. His strong influence on the Holy Club at Oxford was well known, having been advertised to the world through John Wesley's published *Journals*. 'I was at one time a kind of oracle with Mr. Wesley', Law remarked later.[41] His *Christian Perfection* and *Serious Call* had been closely-studied patterns for the spirituality of the Holy Club: with à Kempis and Jeremy Taylor, he was a major exemplar of the 'holy living' tradition in which the Oxford Methodists moved. Though Wesley came to break with Law, he allowed that he had learned from him how to pursue 'inward holiness, or a union of the soul with God'.[42] The extent of Wesley's debt to Law on the issue of riches is not easily determined and difficult to isolate from other parallel influences on a man who browsed and cropped unusually widely in the literary pastures of spirituality, but Wesley's frequent reference to him suggests that it was strong. Law's ethical teaching is cited incidentally at various places in the corpus of Wesley's writings, quoted at length in his eighth discourse on the Sermon on the Mount, and largely endorsed in his own abridgement of the *Serious Call* (a characteristic example of the

---

[38] J. Trapp, *The Nature, Folly, Sin and Danger of being Righteous overmuch*, 2nd edn. (London, 1739), p. 15.

[39] J. Brownsword, *The Case of the rich young Man in the Gospel all and giving it to the Poor . . . endeavoured to be set in a clear light* (London, 1739), p. 11.

[40] A. Jephson, *A Friendly and compassionate Address* (London, 1760), pp. 31–2.

[41] J. H. Overton, *William Law, Nonjuror and Mystic* (London, 1881), p. 80.

[42] Wesley, *Journal*, ed. N. Curnock, 8 vols (London, 1909–16), 1, pp. 468–9.

literary piracy which was Wesley's unwelcome tribute to those who had particularly impressed him).[43] Law's significance lay in his ability, in the context of an intensely arresting devotional treatise, to relay precepts concerning the right use of riches and poverty which were largely traditional, but expressed with a memorable rigorism and intensity.

A similar note is struck in Wesley. Many of the ethical assumptions underpinning his economic teaching were familiar enough. There was nothing new in Wesley's insistence that men were not proprietors of their possessions, but held them in stewardship from God, the Donor; that they were obligated to disburse from their own superfluities to relieve other men's necessities—these were homiletic commonplaces. Wesley's unusual reverence for the poor as 'Christ's poor', 'members of Christ', though becoming archaic, was not untypical of other High Church priests of his time. Where Wesley most resembles Law is in the uncompromising radicalism of his ethic of stewardship and in his attachment of that ethic to a perfectionist theology.

In an early sermon on *The Use of Money* he neatly encapsulated much of his economic ethic in a famous triad: 'Gain all you can; save all you can; give all you can.'[44] Methodists were to acquire wealth by all lawful means possible and regard their labour as a divine calling. They were to save every penny, by avoiding luxuries and making economies, following the example of their leader, who never wasted a sheet of paper or a cup of water if he could help it. But all this was subordinate to *giving*, for Wesley's eye was fixed firmly on distribution, not merely on production, let alone accumulation. What had been earned and saved was to be given out in charity to the poor, whom God had appointed to receive it, and by 'giving' Wesley made it clear that he meant sacrificial giving: everything beyond that needed to keep self and dependants in the plain necessaries and simple conveniences of life.[45] 'I account him a rich man', he said, 'who has food and raiment for himself and family, without running into debt, and something over.'[46] If Wesley prescribed acquisition, he sternly proscribed acquisitiveness; though he encouraged work, it was in the service of the community, not merely the individual. Like Law before him, he saw charity not as a series of episodic acts, but as a way of life, whose demands were total, continual, and embedded in the heart of the

---

[43] Wesley, *Sermons I*, pp. 268 ff.; *A Serious Call to a Holy Life. Extracted from a late Author* [W. Law] (Newcastle, 1744).

[44] Wesley, *Sermons II*, pp. 268 ff.

[45] *Ibid.*, pp. 286, 295; *Sermons III*, p. 619.

[46] Wesley, *Sermons II*, p. 560.

Christian life itself. It was an ideal to which many of his people did not aspire, but one which he firmly set himself, giving away the large fortune gained by his writing and publishing and from the legacies of well-wishers. Though recognizing the great value of money in civilized societies as stored human potential, Wesley also saw it as possessed of an almost phosphorous quality of destructiveness: it would burn him, he said, if he kept hold of it.[47] A great deal of Wesley's money was given away immediately and apparently without much forethought. On publishing a *History of England* he is said to have remarked cheerfully, 'I find that I am two hundred pounds in pocket . . . but as life is uncertain, I will take care to dispose of it before the end of the week.'[48] Remarkably for a man of his time (and again very much in the style of Law), he gave away much of his money to mendicants, often in small alms, medieval-style. Many moralists of Wesley's time saw the beggar as merely a social nuisance. Wesley saw in him the awesome image of the suffering Christ.

This is not the stuff of which the capitalist ethic is easily constructed. Wesley here hardly fulfils the role sometimes assigned to him by Weberians as a prime exemplar of the strenuous capital accumulation which is held to be a major plank of the Protestant Ethic. His concessions to the retention of capital by the tradesman or entrepreneur are grudging. When a man had provided for his family and set aside 'a sufficiency to carry on worldly business', he should 'fix [his] purpose to gain no more'.[49] Wesley viewed with evident distaste the increasing sophistication of the credit system, fearing that it would provide excuses for the selfish retention of wealth. Laying up money was no more consistent with a good conscience than throwing it into the sea, he insisted.[50] His aim was the promotion of an early Christian *koinonia*, not the sanctioning of possessive individualism.

For, like Law, Wesley regarded the primitive community of goods as retaining a prescriptive authority for Christians of all ages. Pushing his inherited High Church primitivism beyond its conventional limits, he saw the early Church as a model not only for credal orthodoxy, ecclesiological correctness, and personal spirituality, but as an important guide to

---

[47] Wesley, *Sermons II*, p. 286; J. Wesley, *The Appeals to Men of Reason and Religion*, ed. G. R. Cragg (Oxford, 1975) [vol. 11 in *Bicentennial edn of Works*], p. 87; J. Wesley, *Letters*, ed. Telford, 5, pp. 108–9.

[48] E. M. North, *Early Methodist Philanthropy* (1914), p. 122 n.

[49] Wesley, *Sermons III*, p. 276. He conceded that 'allowance' should be made for those who owed considerable sums of money to others; 'their affairs are frequently so entangled that it is not possible to determine with any exactness how much they are worth'; *Sermons IV*, p. 179.

[50] Wesley, *Sermons I*, p. 627.

contemporary social ethics. Most authors of his day drew a firm caesura between the world of the earliest Christians and the normative course of Christian history which followed it, sealing off the world of Acts, with its charismatic explosiveness and radical potential, into a separate historical compartment. Wesley, however, saw in the *koinonia* of Acts not only a vision of what Christianity had been at the moment of its miraculous conception, but of what it should and might be again.

Wesley was sustained by his vision of the primal Church at Jerusalem as a familial unity bound together by the law of love.

> Meek, simple followers of the Lamb
> They lived, and spake and thought the same. . . .
> They all were of one heart and soul
> And only love inspired the whole.[51]

He saw the sharing of Acts as spontaneous and voluntary, free and charismatic. Its participants obeyed no positive command of Christ or the Apostles; they did not need to, for 'the command was written on their hearts' by love.[52] In the warmth of mutuality, gradations of wealth and rank were melted away. There were no rich and no poor. Private property seemed irrelevant. As his brother Charles's poem on *Primitive Christianity* (printed at the end of John Wesley's *Farther Appeal* in 1744) put it wistfully:

> Propriety [property] was there unknown
> None called what he possessed his own:
> Where all the common blessings share
> No selfish happiness was there.[53]

Here at Jerusalem, wrote John Wesley approvingly, 'was the dawn of the proper gospel day. Here was a proper Christian Church'.[54]

At the same time, his historical realism, combined with his conscious- ness of the potency of original sin, led him to stress the fragility of this primal state. Even in Acts the worm was in the bud. The case of Ananias and Sapphira, who kept back part of the price of a land sale from the Apostles, showed the pertinacity of the proprietary instinct, even among

---

[51] Wesley, *Appeals*, pp. 90–1. The poem was reprinted in Charles Wesley's *Hymns and Sacred Poems*, 2 vols (Bristol, 1749), 2, p. 337, and in *The Poetical Works of John and Charles Wesley*, ed. G. Osborn, 11 vols (London, 1868–77), 5, p. 480.

[52] Wesley, *Sermons II*, p. 455.

[53] Wesley, *Appeals*, p. 91.

[54] Wesley, *Sermons II*, p. 455.

the first Christians. After the 'Mystery of Godliness', the great outpouring of the Spirit in the Apostolic era, had succeeded the 'Mystery of Iniquity', that strange intrusion of selfishness which followed like a dark shadow close behind.[55] Wesley had no doubt about 'the first plague which infected the Christian Church'; it was the love of money. With it came the second plague, 'partiality', or 'respect of persons', which sapped away at the pristine fraternity, as 'men of reputation' demanded preferential treatment.[56] Wesley noted that the richest churches were the first to be corrupted, while those which retained their original simplicity longest were poor churches like Smyrna and Philadelphia.[57] The declension was gradual; even in the late second century Tertullian's *Apologeticum* showed some Christian communities still sharing out their goods with something approaching the original generosity. But then came the crowning disaster; the conversion of Constantine and the elevation of Christianity into a religion of State. After this there 'poured in a flood of riches, honours and power upon the Christians', leaving the Apostolic Spirit as a diminishing residue among the poor and humble.[58]

Unlike most of his contemporaries, Wesley was not content to pass over the demise of Christian communalism with a mere sigh. While others pointed to the rapid demise of the primitive community of goods, Wesley remembered that it had, in fact, existed, and at the most exemplary phase of Christian history too. At an early stage he seems to have contemplated it as in some sense an attainable ideal. The easy fraternity among the Oxford Methodists, living on a bare minimum, distributing their surplusage to the poor among whom they moved, taking and giving among themselves with easy spontaneity, had perhaps already suggested to him that the primitive example was one which could be proximately implemented by a Christian community, at least in its smaller groupings. Writing later about the corporate life of the Holy Club, he noted:

> ... as to that practice of the apostolic Church (which continued till the time of Tertullian, at least in many churches), the 'having all things in common', they [the Oxford Methodists] had no rule, nor

---

[55] For the 'Mystery of Godliness' see I Timothy 3. 16; for the 'Mystery of Iniquity', II Thessalonians 2. 7. For their place in Wesley's view of early Christianity see his sermon on 'The Mystery of Iniquity' in *Sermons II*, pp. 452–70.

[56] *Ibid.*, pp. 456–7.

[57] *Ibid.*, p. 460.

[58] *Ibid.*, p. 463.

any formed design concerning it. But it was so in effect, and could not be otherwise; for none could want anything that another could spare.

From their stipends and acts of self-denial the members maintained a constant fund—in 1734 it was £80—to relieve the poor of the city.[59]

At this point in his odyssey Wesley seems to have been alert to the existence of other contemporary examples of communal sharing which might suggest the viability of the Jerusalem model. In 1735 he left Oxford for the newly-founded colony of Georgia, sailing off, he believed, to a pastorate in the wilderness, where he hoped not only to seek the spiritual peace and certitude which had so far eluded him, but perhaps to find it in the context of a Christianized communitarian life among the Indians, of whose tribal life he had romantic expectations. In the complex of motives which led Wesley to abandon the security of Oxford was the romantic hope that as a missionary among the tribes he would not only pursue a simple, ascetical life away from the distractions and temptations of Oxford, but might actually participate in a way of life close to that of the primitive Christians extolled in Cave or Fleury. Among the Indians of Georgia, he told a friend, he hoped to show his faithfulness to God 'in dispensing the rest of my Master's goods, if it please him to send me to those who, like his first followers, had all things in common'.[60]

It did not, of course, work out like that. Two years later he was back in England, in low spirits, pursued by affidavits, haunted by self-doubt and pastoral failure. His ministry had been confined to the settlers, to whom his stiff, rubrical High Churchmanship was alien. The Indians whom he encountered were plentifully endowed with original sin. Contaminated by contact with European settlers, they hardly lived up to his high hopes of them as innocent, tractable, noble savages. But the disillusionment was not total; he continued to hold the American Indian up as an exemplar of a lifestyle closer to the example of primitive Christian simplicity than that of most Europeans. The Indian, he held,

> desires and seeks nothing more than plain food to eat, and plain raiment to put on; and he seeks this only from day to day; he reserves, he lays up nothing; unless it be as much corn at one season of the year as he will need before that season returns.

[59] Wesley, *Sermons III*, p. 582; *Letters I*, p. 405.
[60] Wesley, *Letters I*, p. 441.

Though they did not know it, the Indian tribes were obeying the scriptural warning against laying up treasures on earth.[61]

In 1744 the idea of the primitive community of goods seems to have been at the forefront of Wesley's mind, though his published *Journal* gives little evidence of the fact. The early months of 1744 had produced a hard winter, and Wesley had been engaged in energetic rescue work, squeezing the last pennies out of his London societies to buy clothes and shoes for the destitute.[62] He was also brooding on longer-term expedients, such as an 'Oeconomy'; some kind of settlement-house which would be part orphanage and part workhouse, and to this end had planned to visit the Quaker workhouse at Clerkenwell, which was a model of its kind.[63] This we learn from the Diary of Richard Viney, a tailor, who had been closely associated with the Moravians, and who had long conversations with Wesley at this time. Such plans were not particularly remarkable: far more surprising was the project for a 'community of goods' which Wesley unfolded to Viney on 22 February 1744.

> 'Tis this [noted Viney] each is to bring what cash they have and put it together. If any owe small debts, they are first to be paid. Then each abiding in their own dwellings, and following their business as they do now, are to bring weekly what they earn and put it into one common box, out of which they are to receive weekly as much as is thought necessary to maintain their families, without reflecting whether they put much or little into the box.[64]

The plan, Viney told Wesley drily, would not succeed. It does not seem to have been implemented. Why not? Was it too difficult to launch? Was Wesley fearful of the outcry which might follow such an experiment in 'levelling'? The episode gives an indication of Wesley's interpretation of primitive communalism. It did not involve 'selling all' in the literal sense—in his sermons Wesley carefully rejects this interpretation of texts like Matthew 19. 21 ('If thou wouldest be perfect, go, sell all thou hast') as not relevant to ordinary life.[65] Nor was there any question of a program-

---

[61] Wesley, *Sermons I*, p. 617.

[62] Wesley, *Journal*, 2, pp. 117, 122, 125.

[63] W. Beck and T. F. Ball, *The London Friends' Meeting* (London, 1869), pp. 361–74; D. W. Bolam, *Unbroken Community* (Saffron Walden, 1952), pp. 2–17.

[64] *PWHS*, 11 (1924), p. 29.

[65] Wesley, *Sermons I*, p. 622. Jesus 'saw it needful to enjoin this in one particular case, that of the young rich ruler. But he never laid it down for a general rule, to all rich men, in all succeeding generations'. Wesley dissociated himself firmly from John of Leyden; *Works*, ed. Jackson, 8, p. 445.

matic communism of production, like that practised among religious radicals, such as the Hutterites. Viney's account suggests that Wesley envisaged an experiment similar to the scheme described by Tertullian, of which he had certainly read in Reeves's collection of early Christian *Apologiae*. Of this, Tertullian recorded:

> Every one puts a little to the publick stock, commonly once a month, or when he pleases, and only upon condition that he is willing and able, for there is no compulsion upon any; all here is a free-will offering; and all these collections are deposited into a common bank for charitable uses. . . . We Christians look upon ourselves as one body informed . . . by one soul and being . . . incorporated by love.[66]

The vision was still there in June, when the first conference of Wesley's preachers assembled at the Foundery in London. On 28 June rules were set out for the 'select societies'—the inner grouping of members who were seekers after, or had actually attained, Christian perfection, 'perfect love'; that purity of intention which Wesley saw not only as the target of spiritual growth, but also as a stage in the Christian life which could actually be *reached* as well as aspired to. Among the rules was the following:

> Every member, till we can all have all things common, will bring once a week, *bona fide*, all he can spare towards a common stock.[67]

What were the implications of this remarkable rule? Was it issued in the imperative or merely the indicative mood? Materials on the life of the 'select societies' are scanty, for they never developed as a salient feature of Methodism. Did Wesley expect the 'entirely sanctified', who had been granted a measure of love and a purity of intention comparable to that of the early Christians, to be the standard-bearers of a restored communalism?[68] Certainly the 'select societies' were intended to have an exemplary role in the Methodist movement; their members were, Wesley said, 'models whom I could propose to all their brethren as a pattern of love, of holiness and of good works'.[69] If the ideal fraternity of Acts was to be

---

[66] W. Reeves, *Apologies*, 1, pp. 333, 335.

[67] *Minutes of the Methodist Conferences*, 2 vols (London, 1862), 1, p. 23.

[68] Wesley declined to give detailed rules to the members of the select societies because they had 'the best rule of all in their hearts (the rule of love)'; *Works*, ed. Jackson, 8, p. 261. Much the same is said by Wesley of the first Christians at Jerusalem; *Explanatory Notes Upon the New Testament* (London, 1755), p. 295. This suggests that he saw a correlation between the two groups.

[69] Wesley, *Works*, ed. Jackson, 8, p. 260.

re-enacted anywhere, it should be here, among those in whom love had been raised once more to a primitive fervour.[70]

Later in the year, Wesley held up his ideal before an altogether less receptive group, the assembled dons of Oxford. On 24 August he preached his University sermon on the theme of scriptural Christianity. The text was Acts 4. 31: 'And they were all filled with the Holy Ghost'. The theme was the contrast of current English piety—especially that of the clergy and academics in front of him—with that of the first Christians:

> Where does this Christianity now exist [he enquired bitterly]? Which is the country, the inhabitants whereof are all thus filled with the Holy Ghost? are all of one heart and of one soul? cannot suffer one among them to lack anything, but continually give to every man as he hath need?[71]

Wherever this ideal place might be, it was certainly not the city or University of Oxford. He ended with a passionate demand that the assembled Masters should heed the 'young, unknown, inconsiderable men' who had launched a revival of primitive Christianity.

After 1744 there were no new initiatives, but this did not mean that Wesley had put the theme out of his mind. In his *Notes on the New Testament*, published in 1755, commenting on Acts 2. 45, he rebuffed all those who saw the community of goods as a transient expedient.

> To affirm . . . that Christ *did not design it should continue* [he declared] is neither more nor less than to affirm that Christ *did not design* [that] . . . *love should continue*. I see no proof of this.[72]

The sharing of goods, he repeated, went on far beyond the destruction of Jerusalem. Its existence was well attested long afterwards, when the Christians were no longer a tiny and beleaguered handful, but members of a fully-fledged church. It continued because it was a natural fruit of 'that love wherewith each member of the community loved every other as

---

[70] It is conceivable that Wesley read into Acts 4. 31, which described those who initiated the original sharing of goods at Jerusalem as '*filled* with the Holy Ghost', the implication that they were entirely sanctified.

[71] Wesley, *Sermons I*, pp. 19–80. The sermon was preached on 24 August 1744.

[72] Wesley, *Notes Upon the New Testament*, p. 295. Wesley's suggestion that early Christian communalism disappeared because the love sustaining it grew cold resembles his explanation for the disappearance of the miraculous gifts—the charismata—possessed by the first Christians. There is some evidence to suggest that Wesley did not rule out a restoration of some of these. Wesley cites Chrysostom in support of the idea that lack of faith was a cause of the withering of the miraculous powers of healing; *Letters*, ed. Telford, 2, p. 313.

his own soul. And if the whole Christian Church had continued in this spirit, this usage had continued thro' all ages'.[73]

If Wesley tied his hopes for a restoration of the community of goods to the progress of 'Christian Perfection' in the Evangelical Revival, he was destined to be disappointed. Although the propagation of perfect love lay close to the heart of his message—it was, he once declared, 'the grand depositum which God has lodged with the people called Methodists'—yet his hopes of extending it widely came to little.[74] In the early 1760s a perfectionist revival seemed for a time to be permeating the movement, but among some of the societies in London and elsewhere it toppled into disaster, woefully distorted by a band of bizarre enthusiasts, whose eccentricities Wesley tolerated too long for safety.[75] It never regained full momentum. The 'entirely sanctified' retained a small presence in Methodism, quietly influential as spiritual Stakhanovites, but few in numbers.

This does not seem to have affected Wesley's belief that those who seriously followed the path towards perfection must give away to the needy all their income above that required for a very modest competence. In a remarkable late sermon, *The More Excellent Way*, he posited a kind of double standard, a two-tier system which resembled the medieval and early Christian resolution of the problem of the pursuit of holiness, whereby voluntary poverty and the ascetical life are accepted as 'counsels of perfection', the rule for the spiritual élite (in medieval Christendom those self-dedicated to the rule of poverty), while less was accepted from the ordinary mass of practising believers.[76]

Following 'an ancient writer', he suggested that from the beginning there had been two orders of Christians.[77] The first was content to lead a merely innocent life, conforming to the manners and customs of the world in things that were not unlawful; doing good works and practising piety as opportunity offered, but not aiming at the highest standard of attainment. The second order aimed at Christian perfection and of them nothing less was demanded than a constant 'course of self-denial'. Wesley

---

[73] Wesley, *Notes upon the New Testament*, p. 295.
[74] Wesley, *Letters*, ed. Telford, 8, p. 238.
[75] For this episode, see S. W. Gunter, *The Limits of 'Love Divine'* (Nashville, 1989), pp. 215–6; L. Tyerman, *The Life of the Rev. J. Wesley*, 3 vols, 2nd edn. (London, 1872), 2, pp. 431–66.
[76] Wesley, *Sermons III*, pp. 265 ff.
[77] See Outler's comment in Wesley, *Sermons III*, p. 265 n. on the long history of this distinction between the 'two orders'. It is clearly visible in William Law's *Serious Call*, p. 134, where it is attributed to Eusebius. See also Law's *Christian Perfection*, pp. 12–13.

sketched the way in which the different levels of aspiration might affect the Christian life—in attitudes to devotion, recreation, food, work, money. In each of these there was a lower and a higher way. There were many, he noted, who set aside a fixed portion of their income, perhaps one-tenth or even a half, for the poor. There were thousands more who were prepared to give large sums when some particular case of suffering was brought home to their imagination. All these took the lower way. But for all those who followed 'the more excellent way' and aimed to reach 'the summit of Christian holiness', nothing less was required than a life of strenuous self-sacrifice, in which everything above the minimum needed to maintain life should be given back to the poor whom God had appointed to receive it.[78] This being done, they must make it their fixed purpose 'to gain no more'.

> I charge you in the name of God [he told them solemnly] do not increase your substance! As it comes, daily or yearly, so let it go: otherwise you 'lay up treasures upon earth'. And this our Lord as flatly forbids as murder or adultery.

Following this course, he admitted, was easier for the single than for those with family responsibilities. None the less, there was no doubt that the perfectionist track was the only safe way to heaven. The lower path was continually fraught with danger.

> How can you [he asked in his final peroration] on principles of reason spend your money in a way which God may *possibly forgive*, instead of spending it in a manner wich he will *certainly reward*? You will have no reward in heaven for what you *lay up*; you will, for what you *lay out*.[79]

Wesley thus reintroduced into Protestantism through his doctrine of Perfection something approaching the two-tier ethical system of Catholic Antiquity, but firmly laicized it, removing the perfectionist imperative from the monastic community and placing it firmly on the shoulders of the ordinary folk of his societies.

He did not slacken his pressure even on those who took the lower way. Those who belonged to the little groupings known as 'bands' were obligated to give 'to the uttermost'.[80] Constant demands were made on his

---

[78] Wesley, *Sermons III*, p. 275.
[79] *Ibid.*, p. 276.
[80] The Rules of the Band Societies contain the injunction 'to give alms of such things as you possess and that to the uttermost'; Wesley, *Works*, ed. Jackson, 8, p. 274.

people to care for the indigent of the societies—and wherever possible, for those outside them, for Wesley was always concerned lest Methodist philanthropy become sectarian and introverted. He tried various expedients to maximize the charitable commitment of his people. With mixed success he experimented with various small-scale philanthropic projects; the Newcastle Orphan House, charity schools, a poor house, a spinning-school, the first public dispensary for the poor, and—more successfully—a loan fund somewhat on the lines of those organized by the Quakers, or the medieval *mons pietatis*.[81] But the main Wesleyan remedy for poverty lay in the relief carried out by individuals or through the officers of the Methodist societies. From 1742 the class meeting, the basic unit of Methodist polity, was organized round a weekly collection which was distributed to the poor, 'as everyone had need' (a deliberate invocation of Acts 2) by the Society Stewards, who here filled a role similar to that of deacons in the early Church.[82] In periods of distress special collections were made for clothing and food. Methodists were told never to be ashamed to beg; Wesley himself had no hesitation in knocking on doors or standing at a chapel door, hat extended. In times of severe economic dislocation he acknowledged the inadequacy of such gestures, even for the relief of his own people, and banged his head against the constrictions of his situation: in the winter of 1750, when he began closely to examine the plight of his destitute London members, he concluded sadly, 'I was soon discouraged; their numbers so increasing upon me, particularly about Moorfields, that I saw no possibility of relieving them all, unless the Lord should, as it were, make windows into heaven.'[83]

Wesley did not move forward to the conclusion that the State should exert itself to re-order the economic system of the country. Though on occasion he proffered advice to the Government on economic policies which would help the plight of the poor, he kept well out of active politics.[84] To blame him for this would be to expect a great deal of a man brought up in early Hanoverian England, when the State apparatus was

---

[81] For Methodist philanthropy in Wesley's lifetime, see M. Marquardt, *Praxis und Prinzipien der Sozialethik John Wesleys* (Göttingen, 1977); W. J. Warner, *The Wesleyan Movement in the Industrial Revolution* (London, 1930), pp. 204–47; R. F. Wearmouth, *Methodism and the Common People in the Eighteenth Century* (London, 1945), pp. 205–16; L. O. Hynson, *To Reform the Nation. Theological Foundations of Wesley's Ethics* (Grand Rapids, 1984). For Quaker loan funds, see A. Lloyd, *Quaker Social History 1669–1738* (London, 1950), p. 40.

[82] Wesley, *Works*, ed. Jackson, 8, p. 262.

[83] Wesley, *Journal*, 3, p. 501.

[84] See R. M. Kingdon, 'Laissez Faire or Government Control: a Problem for John Wesley', *ChH*, 26 (1957), pp. 342–52.

small, and party politics the plaything of those whom Wesley sarcastically termed 'the great ones'.[85] His own solutions remained within the bounds of drastic but voluntary Christian philanthropy. Though he was inspired by his historical vision of the primitive *koinonia* as an agency of welfare for the poor and weak, he was also constricted by it, seeing the churches themselves as still the true agencies of poor relief. His paradigm for the caring community was the family—the small-scale, face-to-face, communal association, looking after its own in close fellowship. The first church at Jerusalem, he observed, was 'like a family'; in hard winters, as Howell Harris noted approvingly, he fed a crowd of poor at his table—'like a great family'.[86] He envisaged the local church community, revitalized by the Gospel, as the agency for the redistributive ethic of love; here, as at Jerusalem in Apostolic times, he saw the Christian answer to the problem of poverty. In a late sermon (1789) which rounded on the niggardliness of rich Methodists, he asked the rhetorical question: 'but is it possible to supply all the poor in our society with the necessaries of life?' and answered it firmly:

> It *was* possible once to do this, in a larger society than this. In the first Church at Jerusalem 'there was not any among them that lacked; but distribution was made to every one according as he had need.' And we have full proof that it may be so still. Is it not so among the people called Quakers? Yes, and among the Moravians so called. And why should it not be so with us?

The Methodists were poorer than either Quakers or Moravians, but their affluent members could still raise enough to do it.

> With two thousand pounds, and not much less, we could supply the present wants of our poor and put them in a way of supplying their own wants for the time to come.[87]

Perhaps there are echoes here of Wesley's much-admired Chrysostom, who told his congregation at Constantinople in the year 400 that if their wealth were only pooled, the poverty in it could be eliminated and the

---

[85] Wesley, *Letters*, ed. Telford, 4, p. 291.

[86] *Howell Harris's Visits to London*, ed. T Beynon (Aberystwyth, 1960), p. 89. Cf. Wesley, *Notes on the New Testament*, p. 305; 'the Church being then like a family'. See W. A. Meeks, *The First Urban Christians* (New Haven and London, 1983), pp. 86–8, for a discussion of this theme.

[87] Wesley, *Sermons IV*, p. 93.

community of Acts again realized.[88] There is certainly knowledge of the Quakers' poor relief system, which kept their own members clear of the operations of the poor law; in 1744 Wesley's project for an 'Oeconomy' was based on information about their Clerkenwell workhouse, the brainchild of the philanthropist John Bellers, whose original inspiration (whether Wesley knew it or not) had been to form 'a community something like the example of primitive Christianity that lived in common'.[89]

Looking over his movement in the last decade of his life, Wesley experienced conflicting moods of despair and confidence. On the one hand the headlong expansion of 'vital religion' in Britain and America encouraged hopes that the Gospel was at last making the final breakthrough into the self-sustained growth which presaged the millennium. Other revivals had come and gone, but the size and global extent of the evangelical awakenings seemed to suggest that at last the cycle of flow and ebb had been broken. Luther's worrying prophecy that a revival of religion was *res unius aetatis*, a matter of a single generation, would prove to be wrong.[90] Methodism was perhaps 'only the beginning of a far greater work, the dawn of the latter day glory'.[91]

But Wesley's exultation at the Mystery of Godliness was held in check by anxiety at the counterworkings of the Mystery of Iniquity. The external growth of Methodism, like that of primitive Christianity, was being vitiated by interior decay. 'It is certain that many of the Methodists are fallen', he exclaimed in a late sermon. Forty years ago they had been almost 'angels here below', living and walking as though already in eternity: now there were signs that they were getting lazy, quarrelsome, and selfish. The root cause was what it had been in the beginning of Christianity: covetousness; the love of money; the corrosive desire for more riches. With this had appeared, yet again, the 'respect of persons' which followed on from affluence and 'intimacy with worldly men'. As the Methodists became richer they lost their sense of the stewardship of wealth and pulled apart from the poor.[92] By the 1780s Wesley found himself not only up against the Old Adam, but the effects of profound economic change. What he was witnessing were the effects of industrialization, which was beginning to raise incomes in some of the trades in

---

[88] *The Homilies of St. John Chrysostom on the Acts of the Apostles*, trans., *A Library of the Fathers*, 2 vols (Oxford, 1851–2), pp. 161–3.
[89] Bolam, *Unbroken Community*, p. 2.
[90] Wesley, *Sermons II*, p. 492.
[91] *Ibid.*, pp. 493, 525.
[92] Wesley, *Sermons III*, p. 514; *Sermons II*, p. 562.

which Methodism was strongly represented. Through the mass production of cheap artefacts, new patterns of consumption were being created on a scale that constituted, in the opinion of some economic historians, a virtual 'consumer revolution'.[93] Emulation and fashion were now being praised as necessary levers of economic growth. The old mercantilist model, which had laid paramount stress on production and saving, had given way to that of the *Wealth of Nations* (1776), in which Adam Smith could state it as a 'perfectly . . . self-evident' maxim that 'consumption is the sole end and purpose of all production'.[94]

What gave tragic irony to Wesley's vision of Methodist declension was his perception that it stemmed at least as much from the virtues of the movement as from its vices: the germs of decay were not only transmitted from the external 'world', but were endemic to Methodism itself; an endogenous cancer, incubated by the very asceticism he had done so much to propagate. He mused frequently on this theme in a series of classic soliloquies which have been quoted by analysts of the Protestant Ethic from Max Weber onwards.

> Does it not seem (and yet this cannot be!) that Christianity, true scriptural Christianity, has a tendency in process of time to undermine and destroy itself? For wherever true Christianity spreads it must cause diligence and frugality, which, in the natural course of things, must beget riches. And riches naturally beget pride, love of the world, and every temper that is destructive of Christianity. Now if there be no way to prevent this, Christianity . . . cannot continue long among any people; since, wherever it generally prevails, it saps its own foundations.[95]

In the last phase of his life he unleashed a series of passionate homilies against the affluence which he saw spreading among his societies. Too many Methodists, he complained bitterly, had selectively interpreted his economic teaching: they had gained all they could, saved all they could, but only one in a hundred obeyed his third injunction—to give all they could.[96] By filtering out what they wished to take from his ethic and ignoring what they did not, they had focused greedily on those rules which encouraged personal prosperity. Many of them were not even

---

[93] N. McKendrick, J. Brewer, and J. H. Plumb, eds, *The Birth of a Consumer Society* (London, 1982), pp. 13–33.

[94] Adam Smith, *The Wealth of Nations*, ed. E. Cannan, 2 vols (London, 1961), 2, p. 179.

[95] Wesley, *Sermons IV*, pp. 95–6.

[96] Wesley, *Sermons II*, p. 561.

saving what they earned; to the aged Wesley, bred in more Spartan days, they seemed to have capitulated to the temptations of 'luxury', expressed in needless and conspicuous consumption—necklaces, expensive laces, 'spider caps', silver shoe-buckles.[97] He was dismayed to find even his clerical coadjutor, Peard Dickenson, wearing ruffles.[98] All this extravagance was at the expense of the redistributive ethic of stewardship. Those who spent their money in trifles were 'tearing from the back of the naked ... snatching from the mouth of the hungry'.[99] By the 1780s Wesley was experiencing some of the emotions of the charismatic leader who has lived so long that he feels a degree of alienation from his own movement. 'I am distressed', he exclaimed in 1789, 'I know not what to do.' Perhaps he should have exerted an altogether tighter discipline on his people from the beginning, and kept them in some kind of sectarian segregation from the world? But it was now clearly too late. 'Alas, the time is now past. And what I can do now I cannot tell.'[100]

But despite strong bouts of pessimism, Wesley seems never to have abandoned his underlying confidence that the communitarian spirit of Acts would ultimately be regained. His anxiety at the signs of *embourgeoisement* in Methodism was counterbalanced by a buoyant millennial hope. His expectations of a return to the pristine love communalism of Acts were projected on to an imminent *parousia*. He had reason to believe, he wrote happily in 1787, that the 'times of the latter day glory' were fast approaching and might already have begun, a hope which the early upheavals of the French Revolution did much to intensify.[101] In one of his last sermons, on 'The General Spread of the Gospel', he speculated on the stages by which Christianity would make its final breakthrough across the globe, jumping like a flame from one nation to another. It was his belief that in the latter days God would observe the same operational pattern which had been visible in His work from the very inception of Christianity; the Spirit would work not from the greatest down to the least, but would begin among the poor and work up to the great. In the end even the rich would enter the kingdom. There would be a second, grand Pentecost. All things would be again as at the small beginnings of Christianity, but now on a universal scale. Men, women, and children would be bonded

---

[97] Wesley, *Sermons III*, p. 260; *IV*, p. 183.
[98] Tyerman, *Life of J. Wesley*, 3, p. 621.
[99] Wesley, *Sermons III*, p. 254.
[100] Wesley, *Sermons IV*, p. 93.
[101] Wesley, *Sermons II*, p. 525. For his reactions to the French Revolution, see *Letters*, ed. Telford, 8, pp. 199, 204.

together harmoniously as they had been in the first church at Jerusalem, in a sharing community held together not by secular laws but by the unwritten law of love. As a 'natural, necessary consequence', the community of Acts would be permanently restored. This time, though, there would be no 'partiality', no differentiation of esteem, and no Ananias and Sapphira to bring back the 'cursed love of money'.[102]

Jesus College, Oxford

[102] Wesley, *Sermons II*, pp. 493–5.

METHODISM AND PROVIDENCE: A STUDY IN SECULARIZATION

by RUSSELL E. RICHEY

I DEFINING CHURCH HISTORY

IN 1884, the American Historical Association was founded. Four years later, in 1888, the American Society of Church History came into being. The two events, the founding of the ASCH as well as of the AHA, belong to the larger saga of late nineteenth century professional formation.[1] In field after field, amateur and patrician endeavours fell before what seemed a common strategy to consolidate, standardize, resource, institutionalize, and professionalize. The relation of the ASCH to the AHA is instructive. The two organizations shared much. Both drew significantly upon the idiom and structures of German historical scholarship. The guiding spirit of the AHA, Herbert Baxter Adams, plied his German training in a research seminar at Johns Hopkins whose methods and graduates swept historical efforts across the nation into the AHA orbit. His counterpart, Philip Schaff, conceived the ASCH in comparable instrumental and imperialistic terms. German-born, trained by Ferdinand Christian Baur and Johann A. W. Neander, Schaff put an indelible mark on the field of church history. The scholarship attests the leadership and legacy: a 13-volume American Church History Series (1893–7), his own

---

[1] See J. Higham, *History: Professional Scholarship in America* (Baltimore and London, 1965, 1983), P. Dobkin Hall, *The Organization of American Culture, 1700–1900: Private Institutions, Elites, and the Origins of American Nationality* (New York, 1984), and the centennial issue of *The American Historical Review* for October 1984, and in that issue particularly, D. D. Van Tassel, 'From Learned Society to Professional Organization: the American Historical Association, 1884–1900', *AHR*, 89 (1984), pp. 929–56. Van Tassel distinguishes a learned society and a professional organization in these terms: 'A learned society, therefore, may be defined as an organization, often exclusive in membership, dedicated to the preservation, advancement, and diffusion of knowledge solely through the publication of papers read at periodic meetings. While pursuing some of the same goals as a learned society, a professional organization usually distinguishes itself from other groups, sets standards of professional performance as well as guidelines for professional training programs, enhances communication among the members, serves and protects special interests of the profession by promoting legislation, among other things, and enforces a degree of conformity to professional practices and standards among its members. Indeed, a professional organization is the product of a community of people with a common sense of purpose': p. 930. In these terms the ASCH remained a learned society long after the AHA had achieved professional status.

6-volume *History of the Christian Church* (1882–92), a 3-volume *Religious Encyclopaedia* (1882–4), adapted from that of J. J. Herzog, the 3-volume *Creeds of Christendom* (1877), and the *Nicene and Post-Nicene Fathers*, the two series of which ran to 28 and 14 volumes (1886–9, 1890–1900).[2]

Some around Schaff saw the purpose of these two historical organizations—the ASCH and the AHA—as sufficiently identical to warrant merger. They formed a committee to that end. And in 1896, after Schaff's death, the ASCH, in fact, dissolved and transformed itself into a section of the AHA. While he lived, Schaff fought such efforts, preferring to see the ASCH as having its own distinct mission.[3] Programmatic aspects of that mission, for instance, pursuit of Christian unity through history, clearly lay beyond the interests of secular historians. But Schaff also believed that the conception of history itself differed. The scientific lights by which colleagues, particularly in the AHA, increasingly found their paths, Schaff viewed as only partially illuminating the historical saga. Their iconoclastic, empirical, and naturalistic tendencies,[4] Schaff denounced. He thought rationalism an inadequate beacon for church history. On the contrary, church history ought to remain a sacred rather than a natural science. Premised on belief in God's operative control of history, church history required an appropriate definition of the Church as a starting-point and a method sensitive to the activity of the Spirit in human affairs. As a working maxim, Schaff affirmed:

> The recognition of God in history is the first principle of all sound philosophy of history. . . . He who denies the hand of Providence in the affairs of the world and the church is intellectually or spiritually blind.[5]

The scientific historians were quite impatient with these views. They were especially so with their contemporaries from the older generation of American historians who indulged themselves in such speculation, tracing, for instance, the finger of Providence in American affairs. Scientific history ought rather to confine attention to the human and natural realm, to cause and effect relations, to explanations that were

---

[2] See Henry W. Bowden, *Dictionary of American Religious Biography* (Westport Conn., 1977). In this discussion I follow Bowden's *Church History in the Age of Science: Historiographical Patterns in the United States, 1876–1918* (Chapel Hill, 1971), and Higham, *History*.

[3] Bowden, *Church History*, pp. 59–61; Higham, p. 17.

[4] This formulation of history as science can be found in Bowden, *Church History*, p. 17 *et passim*.

[5] Quoted by Bowden, *Church History*, p. 52, from Schaff's *Theological Propaedeutic*, p. 236.

objective, universal, and regular.[6] Even the Church should be treated as a human institution. With such an understanding, Adams taught a course in church history at Johns Hopkins.[7]

Towards that understanding the discipline of church history gravitated in the decades after Schaff's death. The standard-bearer was Ephraim Emerton, who taught church history at Harvard from 1882 to 1918. Trained at Harvard, Berlin, and Leipzig, Emerton sought to make church history scientific. He insisted that church history be pursued with the rules that govern all history: 'Church History is nothing more or less than one chapter in that continuous record of human affairs which we give the name of history in general.'[8] He rejected out of hand the older conception of church history, repudiating, for instance, the following as an unhistorical framing of the task:

> To show when the divine force has controlled all human events, and made them subserve the steady progress of God's servants is the mission of him who treats the history of the Church.[9]

Emerton functioned with the axiom that '[T]he superhuman . . . is not a subject for the historical record.'[10] Hence church historians had no business with the controlling hand of Providence, divine interpositions, and the divine presence in the life of the Church.[11]

II HISTORY AND PROVIDENCE

This paper will trace the shift from Schaff's understanding of church history to that of Adams and Emerton. It amounts to an enquiry into the decline in belief in Providence. Or, perhaps one might say, a shift in the way in which God's activity in the world was envisioned, for the essay will monitor various claims to divine agency, not simply those that might be comprehended in a doctrine of Providence, strictly defined. The focus

---

[6] Higham, pp. 92–103.

[7] Bowden, *Church History*, p. 26.

[8] *Ibid.*, p. 106 n. From Emerton's 'A Definition of Church History', *Papers of the ASCH*, ser. 2, 7 (1923), pp. 55–6. Emerton affirmed that 'Historical evidence concerns only such things as are perceptible to human powers and can be recorded by human means. Miracles—*all* miracles— are to be excluded from the historian's function, because no human evidence can establish the fact of a miracle': Bowden, p. 109; Emerton, p. 63.

[9] *Ibid.*, p. 103: Emerton, p. 57.

[10] *Ibid.*, p. 108: Emerton, p. 62. Emerton continued: 'The *belief* in the superhuman . . . because it is a fact of human experience, has its historical record and can be studied historically'.

[11] *Ibid.*, p. 103: Emerton, p. 57.

will be on particular religious community, even a sub-variety thereof, the body known as the Methodist Episcopal Church, perhaps the leading, but certainly not the only, bearer of the Wesleyan legacy in America. The paper attempts to show that a historical presentation of the movement functioned as an essential, if not the essential, mode of self-understanding; that the Church permitted history that definitional and legitimating function because history served theological purposes; that for much of the nineteenth century those purposes placed Providence at the heart of Methodist history; that as the century wore on, those claims about Providence changed; and that by the end of the century Methodist history began to approximate the views of Emerton.[12] On one level, and most explicitly, this enquiry traces the evolution of Methodist historical scholarship. However, since such scholarship shaped and was shaped by the self-understanding of the Methodist denomination, these historiographical changes also illustrate changes in the denomination. On that level, the enquiry concerns fundamental, paradigmatic shifts in Methodist consciousness. In several respects, this study opens the question of secularization. The relation of historical consciousness to institutional, popular, and societal consciousness (here treated in terms of the relation of Methodist history to Methodism); the specific changes in historiography (here Methodist historiography); and the changing character of denominations (here only the Methodist Episcopal Church), all have been considered under the rubric of secularization.[13]

---

[12] For a related effort to show how Methodists use history for theological and definitional purposes, see my essay, 'American Methodism: A Bicentennial Review', *The Drew Gateway*, 54 (Winter, Spring, 1984), a double issue entitled *Methodism and Ministry: Historical Explorations*, special editors, J. B. Seleck and R. E. Richey, pp. 130–42; and also K. E. Rowe, 'Counting the Converts: Progress Reports as Church History', in *Rethinking Methodist History: A Bicentennial Historical Consultation*, ed. R. E. Richey and K. E. Rowe (Nashville, 1985), pp. 11–17. This effort builds on Rowe's findings.

[13] The literature on secularization is immense and the definitions various. The definition used here is one of five outlined in Larry Shiner's 'The Concept of Secularization in Empirical Research', *Journal for the Scientific Study of Religion*, 6 (1967), pp. 207–20. Shiner's third definition, 'the desacralization of the world', proves most helpful here. His other rubrics for secularization are 'the decline of religion', 'conformity with the world', 'the disengagement of society from religion', and 'the transposition of beliefs and patterns from the "religious" to the "secular" sphere'. For an alternative estimate of the literature and exhaustive survey of the same, see K. Dobbelaere, *Secularization: A Multi-Dimensional Concept*, which constitutes a full issue of *Current Sociology*, 29 (Summer, 1981). See also his 'Secularization Theories and Social Paradigms', *Social Compass*, 31 (1984), pp. 2–3, 199–219. See also 'Rethinking Secularization: Retrospect and Prospect', *Review of Religious Research*, 26 (1985), pp. 228–43. The several works of Bryan R. Wilson and David Martin have, of course, been immensely influential on this topic.

The motif of Providence is not the only window on these changes. And yet its transparency is not readily equalled. For in its infancy, as we shall observe, Methodists saw themselves in providential terms, saw through their activities, beliefs, and rituals to the workings of God. In such claims they entered to their own account a common vision. Most Americans in the eighteenth and early nineteenth century about whom we know very much believed very fervently in Providence. And they saw in both public and personal events the clear tracings of the divine hand.[14] By the end of the century, as we have noted, those who could no longer see Providence disdained those who did. That shift altered the way historians envisioned the world. It produced no less dramatic changes in denominational consciousness. In a real sense, Providence was the issue of secularization.

III HISTORY AS METHODIST SELF-DEFINITION

The Wesleyan movement understood itself in providential terms. Its revivals, preaching, structures, ethos served to renew the Church, so it thought, because they derived from the workings of the Holy Spirit. That premise made Methodists, as it made other movements who shared it, the Puritans and other Pietists, for instance, acutely sensitive to human experience. They looked within and looked without expecting to detect God at work. What they found, they shared, confident that God used even humble vessels to bear that which would save others. So men and women shared their religious experience in band and class meetings; so John Wesley broadcast those accounts in his *Arminian Magazine*; so he published journals, his own and others; and so he wrote his *A Plain Account of the People Called Methodists* and *A Short History of Methodism*. This was history as conversion narrative. Methodists turned to history, their own history pre-eminently, for redemptive purposes. History functioned not only as language about God, a theology, but more importantly as God's language, as the way God worked to achieve the renovation of the world.

Methodists generally gave history a prominent function. American

---

[14] On Providence as an American commonplace see especially J. F. Berens, *Providence and Patriotism in Early America 1640–1815* (Charlottesville, 1978); P. C. Nagel, *This Sacred Trust. American Nationality 1798–1898* (New York, 1971); H. F. May, 'The Decline of Providence?' in *Ideas, Faiths and Feelings. Essays on American Intellectual and Religious History 1952–1982* (New York, 1983), pp. 130–46; J. Bowen Gillespie, '"The clear leadings of Providence": pious memoirs and the problems of self-realization for women in the early nineteenth century', *Journal of the Early Republic*, 5 (1985), pp. 197–221; F. J. Hood, *Reformed America: The Middle and Southern States, 1783–1837* (Alabama, 1980); L. O. Saum, *The Popular Mind of Pre-Civil War America* (Westport Conn., 1980); S. Bercovitch, *The American Jeremiad* (Madison, 1978).

Methodists, in particular, gave it a peculiarly prominent place in their self-definition. When American Methodists organized themselves as an independent church in 1784, independent from Wesley (they thought) and independent from Anglicanism, they, like the nation, drew up a formal constitution. The document that resulted, commonly known as *The Discipline*, was one of three books (along with the Bible and their hymn-book) which defined and shaped the Church.[15] The initial version followed in style, substance, and order a loosely-constructed, question-and-answer document derived from John Wesley's conferences with his preachers, *The Large Minutes*.[16] Two years later, in 1787, the Church restructured *The Discipline*, announcing it to be 'Arranged under proper HEADS, and METHODIZED in a more acceptable and easy MANNER'. In this new format, the first statement the church made, before it said anything about what it believed, about Scripture, about sacraments, about authority, about polity, the first statement it made was historical. Still honouring Wesley's question-and-answer style, the Church asked, first, 'What was the Rise of Methodism so called in Europe?'; second, 'What was the Rise of Methodism, so called in America?'; and, third, 'What may we reasonably believe to be God's design in raising up the Preachers called Methodists?' The answers to these three questions provided a providential history of American Methodism. The first two answers sketched the very beginning of Methodism in Britain and America. The third answer, which Americanized Wesley's original formulation, placed a most significant construction on the first two. It was continuously cited and is still cited as the central definition of Methodist purpose. It epitomized Methodism. God's design was:

> To reform the Continent, and spread scripture Holiness over these Lands. As a Proof hereof, we have seen in the Course of fifteen Years a great and glorious Work of God, from New York through the

---

[15] The former two gave the movement its substance, the latter its form.

[16] The initial version of the American *Discipline* suggested in its title the loyalty to the Wesleyan format—*Minutes of Several Conversations between the Rev. Thomas Coke LLD. and The Rev. Francis Asbury and others, at a Conference, begun in Baltimore, in the State of Maryland, on Monday, the 27th of December, in the Year 1784. Composing a Form of Discipline for the Ministers, Preachers and other Members of the Methodist Episcopal Church in America* (Philadelphia, 1785). For comparison of the American with the Wesleyan minutes see John James Tigert, *A Constitutional History of American Episcopal Methodism*, 6th edn. rev. and enl. (Nashville, 1916), Appendix VII, which puts the two in parallel clumns. Consult this volume and N. B. Harmon, *The Organization of The Methodist Church*, 2nd edn. rev. (Nashville, 1962) on constitutional matters.

Jersies, Pennsylvania, Delaware, Maryland, Virginia, North and South Carolina, even to Georgia.[17]

Thus *The Discipline* gathered the entire Methodist movement into Providence, turned mundane into sacred history, conceived of history in redemptive terms.

Although Methodists do not seem to have drawn out its implications, they carefully preserved both the precise wording and the placement of this formulation. It continued to be their first statement about themselves. Even when they changed the very character of *The Discipline*, they retained this providential history and its prominent placement. So when, in 1790, they departed from Wesley's question-and-answer format, Bishops Thomas Coke and Francis Asbury recast this historical-providential self-understanding into a prefatory episcopal address. Two years later in further recognition of history's priority, the Church added a new section, placed it immediately after the episcopal address, entitled it 'Of the Origin of the Methodist Episcopal Church', and brought the account of Methodist beginnings up to 1784. This historical addition functioned to legitimize the Church as an institution, particularly its orders and sacraments. Thus began the definition of Methodism, or more properly, the Methodist Episcopal Church.

That body left these historical formulations intact, really for the duration of the century. However, when the movement fragmented, the new Methodist bodies honoured this principle of historical self-definition. They also began their Disciplines with history. The new groups used these initial historical statements to recognize their divergence from the Methodist Episcopal Church and to justify their separate identity. So the *Disciplines* of the AME Church, the AME Zion Church, the Evangelical Association, the United Brethren in Christ, the Methodist Protestant Church, the Wesleyan Methodist Connection, the Methodist Episcopal Church, South, the Free Methodist Church, and the Coloured Methodist Episcopal Church all begin with some sort of historical preface.[18] These later movements were less prone to discern

---

[17] *A Form of Discipline, For the Ministers, Preachers, and Members of the Methodist Episcopal Church in America* (New York, 1878), pp. 3–4. For sustained reflection on the import of the changes that the Americans made see the first seven essays in *Reflections Upon Methodism During the Bicentennial* (Dallas: Bridwell Library Center for Methodist Studies, 1985; Papers presented at the 1984 Regional Conference of the World Methodist Historical Society).

[18] See *The Doctrines and Discipline of the African Methodist Episcopal Church* (Philadelphia, 1817); *The Doctrines and Discipline of the Wesleyan Methodist Episcopal Zion Church in America, Established in the City of New-York, October 25th, 1820*, 2nd edn. (New York, 1840); *The Doctrine and*

Providence in events connected with their founding—a fact of interest in connection with the remainder of this paper—but they clearly recognized the value of history as a self-definition. By contrast, non-Methodist denominations did not seem to rely on history in this fashion.[19] At any rate, Methodists, children of Providence by their own estimation, turned to history for the frame for their church, the *Discipline*.

IV PURE HISTORY OF RELIGION IN AMERICA

The historical imperative expressed itself in various ways. The leadership clearly saw history's importance. John Wesley wrote to the American Ezekiel Cooper in 1791:

> We want some of you to give us a connected relation of what our Lord has been doing in America from the time that Richard Boardman accepted the invitation and left his country to serve you.[20]

That sort of request generated the personal accounts with which Wesley filled his *Arminian Magazine* and that found their way into the initial but short-lived American Methodist copies. It also clearly prompted *The Experience and Travels of Mr. Freeborn Garrettson*,[21] the first of many American Methodist journals to be published. Bishop Asbury, who saw his own into print, issued a Wesley-like command to the American leadership, the presiding elders, requesting more of the same:

Discipline of the Evangelical Association, Together with the Design of Their Union, translated from the German (New-Berlin, 1832); *Origin, Constitution, Doctrine and Discipline, of the United Brethren in Christ* (Circleville, Ohio, 1837); *Constitution and Discipline of the Methodist Protestant Church* (Baltimore, 1830); *The Discipline of the Wesleyan, Methodist Connection of America*, particularly in the 2nd and 3rd versions (New York, 1875 and 1849), which include a Preface by a committee appointed to prepare a short account of the Wesleyan Methodist Connection of America, to be inserted in the Discipline' (1845, iii; *The Doctrines and Discipline of the Methodist Episcopal Church, South* (Richmond, 1846); *The Doctrines and Discipline of the Free Methodist Church* (Rochester, 1870); *The Doctrines and Discipline f the Colored Methodist Episcopal Church in America* (Louisville, 1874). All were consulted in The Archives Center, Drew University.

[19] A tentative claim, based on a small sample of constitutions: *A Summary of Church Discipline . . . by The Baptist Association* (Charleston, 1774); *The Canons and Constitution of the Protestant Episcopal Church* (1829); *The Constitution of the Reformed Dutch Church* (1793); *The Constitution of the Presbyterian Church* (1821).

[20] *The Letters of the Rev. John Wesley*, ed. J. Telford, 8 vols (London, 1931), 8, p. 259. The letter was dated 1 Feb. 1791.

[21] (Philadelphia, 1791). See *American Methodist Pioneer. The Life and Journals of The Rev. Freeborn Garrettson, 1752–1827*, ed. R. Simpson (Rutland, Vt., 1984): published under sponsorship of Drew University Library.

Once in every year I wish to hear circumstantially from the presiding elders, that we may collect, as in medium, the most pleasing and interesting things of the work of God, not only for the episcopacy, but the Conferences, and the press. I think we have paid but little attention to the work of God, or pure history of religion in America.[22]

That request generated *Extracts of Letters Containing Some Account of the Work of God Since the Year 1800. Written by the Preachers and Members of the Methodist Episcopal Church, to their Bishops*.[23] Here were the raw, undigested, immediate Methodist apprehensions of the movement of God—accounts of revivals, camp meetings, revivalistic quarterly meetings.[24] Here was a 'pure history of religion' in Asbury's terms. A comparable perspective on a comparable document came from the book editors, Daniel Hitt and Thomas Ware. They gathered into one volume *The Minutes of the Methodist Conferences* from 1773 to 1813.

[T]his publication must confessedly contain the best history (as far as it goes) of the Methodists and Methodist preachers in America, now extant; from the commencement thereof to the year 1813:—shewing to the reflective mind, what the Lord hath done for us, and by us, in the space of 40 years past.[25]

The editors' claim for the *Minutes* is particularly interesting because three years earlier Jesse Lee had published *A Short History of the Methodists*.[26] Apparently, they preferred the un-interpreted legislative acts, statistical reports, listing of ministers, and charges and obituaries of the *Minutes* to Lee's account. His effort resembled theirs more perhaps than they recognized.

V THE METHODIST HISTORIANS: JESSE LEE

Abel Stevens and J. M. Buckley ranked Jesse Lee (1758–1816) next to Bishop Asbury in importance, 'the most popular . . . and one of the most

---

[22] *The Journal and Letters of Francis Asbury*, ed. E. T. Clark, 3 vols (Nashville, 1958), 3, p. 197. To Daniel Hitt, dated 30 Jan. 1801. Cf. the letter to Stith Mead ten days earlier, 3, pp. 195–6.

[23] (New York, 1805).

[24] See my 'From quarterly to camp meeting: a reconsideration of early American Methodism', *Methodist History*, 23 (1985), pp. 199–213.

[25] *Minutes of The Methodist Conferences, Annually Held in America: From 1773 to 1813 Inclusive* (New York 1813), iii. Noting the dramatic growth and prosperity of Methodism, the editors comment, 'With wonder and gratitude, we may exclaim, *what hath God wrought?*' iv.

[26] (Baltimore, 1810); facsimile edition Rutland, Vt., 1974).

effective ... of early American Methodist preachers'. A national leader, Asbury's choice to be an episcopal colleague, nearly elected to that office, and 'the founder of Methodism in New England', Lee lived the history he wrote, from his conversion in 1773 under Robert Williams, through pacificist alternative service in the Revolution, to chaplaincy to Congress.[27]

On the title page of his *A Short History of the Methodists*, Lee placed three verses from the Scriptures. They suggested the essential continuity between this first, formal history and prior Methodist efforts at historical self-understanding.

> The Lord hath done great things for us, whereof we are glad. Ps. 126, 3
> Come thou with us, and we will do thee good; for the Lord hath spoken good concerning Israel. Numb 10, 23
> We will go with you, for we have heard that God is with you. Zach 8, 29

Lee sustained the providential theme from first to last, connecting it tightly to Methodism. His preface affirmed:

> I desire to shew to all our societies and friends, that the doctrines which we held and preached in the beginning, we have continued to support and maintain uniformly to the present day. We have changed the economy and discipline of our church at times, as we judged for the benefit and happiness of our preachers and people; and the Lord has wonderfully owned and prospered us. It may be seen from the following account, how the Lord has, from very small beginnings, raised us up to be a great and prosperous people. It is very certain, that the goodness of our doctrine and discipline, our manner of receiving preachers, and of sending them into different circuits, and the frequent changes among them from one circuit to another, not allowing them in general to stay more than one year in a station or circuit, and in no case more than two years, has greatly contributed to the promotion of religion, the increase of our societies, and the happiness of our preachers.

Lee concluded on the same note, believing that his collection of facts, and ... clear, plain, and full account' would convince the reader 'that the Lord has done great things for us'.[28]

---

[27] Abel Stevens, *A Compendious History of American Methodism* (New York, 1868), pp. 517–18, 143–6; J. M. Buckley, *A History of Methodists in the United States*, 4th edn. (New York, 1890), pp. 354, 353, 181, 213–16.
[28] Lee, *Short History*, pp. v–vi; 362.

However, Lee was not content to make vague, prefatory, claims about general providential workings and leave the matter there, as would later historians. Lee found particular Providence far more important. Indeed, like John Wesley, Lee would probably have been not a little impatient with a sharp distinction between general and particular Providence. Where Lee discerned the hand of God at work, he announced it. For instance, in analysing Methodist growth in Petersburg in 1787, Lee stated forthrightly, 'That town never witnessed before or since such wonderful displays of the presence and love of God in the salvation of immortal souls.'[29] Interestingly, he was highly selective in such judgements. There seem to be two factors that govern those conclusive claims, first, Lee's proximity to the events and, second, the presence of a revival. Although he began with Wesley and British Methodism and traced the early American developments, only when his narrative reached the 1770s, his native Virginia and the labours of Robert Williams and Devereux Jarratt—after forty-three pages of earlier Methodist history—did Lee clearly discern 'a considerable out-pouring of the spirit' and conclude that 'many sinners were truly converted to God'.[30] Thereafter, Lee saw the hand of God

---

[29] *Ibid.*, p. 129. The distinction between general and particular Providence was a common one. John Wesley examined the issue in his sermon 'On Divine Providence', *The Works of John Wesley*, 14 vols (Grand Rapids, n.d.) = reprint of the standard Jackson edition in its 1872 version, 5, pp. 313–25. Wesley asked the reader, p. 322: 'You say, "You allow a *general* providence, but deny a *particular* one?" And what is a general, of whatever kind it be, that includes no particulars?' and p. 323: 'What becomes, then, of your general providence, exclusive of a particular?' However, both in this sermon and in 'Spiritual Worship', 6, pp. 424–35, Wesley did attend to both. This series of statements (each of which is elaborated) summarizes his position on general Providence:

> 'He is the true God, the only Cause, the sole Creator of all things';
> 'And as the true God, he is also the Supporter of all the things that he hath made';
> 'As the true God, he is likewise the Preserver of all things';
> '[H]e is the true Author of all the *motion* that is in the universe';
> 'The true God is also the Redeemer of all the children of men';
> 'The true God is the Governor of all things'.

Wesley distinguished God's providential government over the children of men by a three-fold circle of divine providence, p. 428: 'The *outermost circle* includes all the sons of men; Heathens, Mahometans, Jews, and Christians. He causeth his sun to rise upon all. He giveth them rain and fruitful seasons. He pours ten thousand benefits upon them, and fills their hearts with good and gladness. With an *interior circle* he encompasses the whole visible Christian Church, all that name the name of Christ. He has an additional regard to these, and a nearer attention to their welfare. But the *innermost circle* of his providence encloses only the invisible Church of Christ; all real Christians, wherever dispersed in all corners of the earth'.

[30] *Ibid.*, pp. 43–4. Lee continued, p. 44: 'The revival of religion which first began under the ministry of Mr. Jarratt, was greatly increased by the labours of the Methodist preachers, who,

primarily in the revivals, and he saw it so clearly where he saw it close up. For instance, Lee devoted some six pages to a major revival that occurred in 1775 in southern Virginia and in North Carolina. He spoke of God sending his word home upon hearts, of 'the great power of God', of 'the presence of God', of hundreds finding 'the peace of God', of the work of God increasing on every side, and of the Lord raising up preachers. He concluded, 'Such a work of God as that was, I had never seen, or heard before.' He then added,

> I have spoken largely of this revival of religion; but my pen cannot describe the one half of what I saw, heard and felt. I might write a volume on this subject, and then leave the greater part untold.[31]

We might say that Lee did indeed write a volume on this subject. His History had as its subject 'Methodism as revival'. This was providential history with a narrow, revivalistic thrust. Or perhaps we should say this was a conversion narrative expanded, a narration of a collective conversion. For it was really only in conversions and revivals that Lee saw the hand of God. He did not ignore other aspects of the Methodist economy. Indeed, he structured the book around the periodic quarterly, annual, and general conferences which functioned as the legislative, judicial and executive of the Methodist movement. He attended to the evolution of structure and authority, taking care to cite important documents in full. He wrote essentially as an apologist for the system, even though he had his own differences with Bishop Asbury and made little use of Asbury's published journals. Others before and after him—from John Wesley himself through most of the nineteenth-century Methodist historians— saw providential design in the entire Methodist system, and particular features thereof, like its itinerant principle, its provision for small groups

---

who, uniting with Mr. Jarratt in the same blessed work, were greatly owned and honoured of God and had the pleasure of seeing the work of the Lord prospering in their hands'. Lee was himself one measure of that prosperity. He had been converted by Williams, whom he regarded as his spiritual father. See Stevens, *Compendious History*, p. 49. At earlier points where religious vitalities might have warranted a comparable judgement, Lee refrained from rendering the judgement himself. For instance, of a 1760 revival in Britain, Lee said, 'Many persons, men and women, professed to be cleansed from all unrighteousness and made perfect in love in a moment'. Then he quoted Wesley, p. 21: 'Here began that glorious work of sanctification . . .'. So also Lee rendered an account of George Whitefield's 1740 revivals in New England by citing a passage from Whitefield's journal that advanced the claims about the work of God.

[31] *Ibid.*, pp. 54–9. For other revival accounts, see pp. 43, 49, 51, 74, 77, 82, 129–34, 138–40, 145, 218, 271–5, 277–80, 283–7, 289–94, 300–4, 308, 311–15, 344, 351, 356.

(classes), camp meetings, and the like. Lee would only hint at that.[32] Nor did Lee connect Methodism providentially with the American experiment. Perhaps he saw too clearly what was central in God's intentions to be concerned with what seemed peripheral. At any rate his successors put both Methodism and Providence in a larger context.

VI NATHAN BANGS

'Apologist for American Methodism' is Richard Hermann's recent description of him, and that he was. Bangs (1778–1862) wrote against Calvinists who attacked Methodist doctrine and Episcopalians who attacked its order; he also faced the critics within. But like Lee, Bangs was also a major creator of and actor in the script that he transcribed. Bangs led Methodism through the restructuring that made it a member of the nineteenth-century family of Protestant denominations, that voluntary establishment of Christianity. Most notably he had a hand in giving the denomination the rudiments of organization, by the formation of educational institutions, by creating a ministerial course of study, and by the formal adoption of the society principle through the creation of a missionary society (serving as its major officer). He also played a pivotal role in both *The Christian Advocate*, Methodism's national paper, and *The Methodist Magazine*, its first successful effort at theological journalism. Bangs was 'American Methodism's first major historian, polemicist, and theological editor'.[33]

From Bangs's pen came, in 1838–41, *A History of the Methodist Episcopal Church*, a 4-volume work, only the first of which was under 400 pages.[34] In certain respects, Bangs's providential views resembled Lee's. He also termed the 1775 growth spurt 'a remarkable revival of the work of God' and spoke of 'these manifest displays of the power and grace of God'.[35] And he would not only see in the phenomenon of camp meetings 'signal displays of the power and grace of God', but would also analyse them with some care to defend that judgement.[36] Like Lee, then, Bangs recognized

---

[32] *Ibid.*, pp. iv, v.

[33] R. E. Hermann, 'Nathan Bangs: Apologist for American Methodism' (Emory, Ph.D. thesis, 1973). L. Scott, 'The message of early American Methodism', in *The History of American Methodism*, ed. E. S. Bucke, 3 vols (New York, 1964), 1, p. 347; Stevens, *Compendious History*, pp. 367–8.

[34] I am using the 6th edn., 4 vols (New York, 1860).

[35] 1, p. 89.

[36] 2, pp. 101, 109–19.

God's handiwork in conversions and revivals. But he also wrestled with the implications of Methodism's taking its place in American society and taking its place in a Protestant establishment. That meant a conception of Providence put in a larger context and nuanced more carefully. Bangs conceded, for instance:

> We do not infer the blessing of God upon the labors of a ministry merely because proselytes are made. Mohammed made proselytes to his false religion by the power of the sword faster than Jesus Christ did by the power of his miracles and the purity of his doctrine. And any impostor, or mere formal minister, by the fascinating charms of his eloquence, or the cunning artifices to which he will resort, may succeed in proselyting others to his party without at all benefitting their souls, or reforming their lives. The mere multiplication of converts to a system is no proof, of itself, that it has the sanction of the God of truth and love.[37]

Bangs had directed much of his writings at critics who had, in various ways, implicitly or explicitly, suggested that Methodism was not of God. Bangs could not, with Lee, content himself with 'providential' results and take those results as self-evidently attesting Methodism's providential character; he had to show the providential design. He did that in a variety of ways. First, and perhaps most importantly, he elaborated criteria that allowed him to make good the claim. To the rhetorical challenge just cited, Bangs proposed the following as sustaining the providential character of Methodism:

(1) that these men preached the pure doctrine of Jesus Christ;
(2) that those who were converted by their instrumentality were really 'brought from darkness to light, and from the power of Satan to God';
(3) that those 'born of the Spirit' then 'brought forth the "fruit of the Spirit, love, joy, peace, long-suffering, gentleness, goodness, faith, meekness, temperance"'.[38]

---

[37] I, p. 360. He continued, pp. 360–1; 'We have not, therefore, enumerated the communicants of the Methodist Episcopal Church as an evidence, of itself, that its ministry were moving in obedience to God's will, and in the order of his providence. Though they had been as "numerous as the sands upon the seashore", had they been destitute of righteousness, they would be no proof that the instruments of their conversion were sent of God.'

[38] I, p. 361. The specification of three criteria and the numbering are mine.

There could be no mistaking the manœuvre. Bangs proposed as criteria of Providence, precisely what Methodists took to be their hallmarks—faithful and efficacious preaching, the new birth, and holiness. He took care, however, to locate the providential mark in the distinctiveness of Methodist commitment to orthodox belief, not in its theological novelty. Indeed, as a further criteria of Methodism's providential character, Bangs in his *An Original Church of Christ* elaborated the first point into a full-scale defence of the primitive, apostolic character of Methodism, a point that Methodists had, following Wesley, always made.[39] In his *History*, Bangs reiterated the apostolic claims on both polity—he pronounced 'the Methodist Episcopal Church Scriptural and apostolical in her orders and ordinances'[40]—and doctrine:

> The doctrine, too, which they principally insisted upon, had a direct tendency to produce the desired effect the heart and life. While they held, in common with other orthodox Christians, to the hereditary depravity of the human heart, the deity and atonement of Jesus Christ, the necessity of repentance and faith; that which they pressed upon their hearers with great earnestness was, the necessity of the new birth, and the privilege of their having a knowledge, by the internal witness of the Holy Spirit, of the *forgiveness of sins*, through faith in the blood of Christ; and as a necessary consequence of this, and as naturally flowing from it, provided they persevered, *holiness of heart and life*. On this topic they dwelt with an emphasis and an earnestness peculiar to themselves. The doctrine itself, though held by most orthodox churches . . . was allowed to sleep in their books. . . .[41]

Because Methodists recognized that they had emphasized doctrines left dormant, because they saw themselves as reviving scriptural and experimental Christianity, because they recognized Wesley's own imprint in all they were about, they could not effectively establish a historical (that is, human) connection between Methodism and the early Church. From 1784 on, they repudiated notions of uninterrupted apostolic succession.[42]

---

[39] (New York, 1837): 2nd edn. rev. (1837, 1840). I am using the 1840 edition.

[40] 1, p. 165. Chapter 3 of this volume recounted the organization of the Methodist Episcopal Church and effectively summarized the defense that Bangs had mounted in *An Original Church of Christ*. See particularly his twelve points, pp. 159–63.

[41] 1, p. 364.

[42] Thomas Coke made this point at the organization of the church and in specific reference to the church order being adopted. See his *The Substance of a Sermon Preached at Baltimore . . . Before the General Conference of the Methodist Episcopal Church . . . at the Ordination of the Rev. Francis Asbury to the Office of a Superintendent* (Baltimore, 1785).

Bangs concurred.[43] That wedded both him and Methodism generally to the doctrine of Providence. The connection between Methodism and primitive Christianity, between Methodism and Scripture, the only connection, was providential. They saw John Wesley in those terms; they saw their church economy in similar terms.

Musing retrospectively about the historian's responsibility, Bangs asserted, 'I might have conjured up a thousand fanciful theories to account for the success and influence of Methodism, without ascribing it to its true original cause, namely, the divine agency.' Both the 'entire structure' of Methodism and its introduction into this country, he thought, 'originated without any foresight of man, without any previous design in the instruments to bring about such an event, and without any of those previously devised plans which generally mark all human enterprises'.[44] This language, which echoed Wesley, pointed in Methodist minds to a Providence which was as practical and pragmatic in things structural as it was experimental in things personal. What Bangs said of camp meetings, he insisted pertained generally:

> [T]hese camp meetings were not the result of a previously digested plan, but like every other peculiarity of Methodism, were introduced by providential occurrences, and were embraced and followed up by God's servants because they found them subservient to the grand design they had in view, namely, the salvation of the world by Jesus Christ.[45]

Elsewhere Bangs spoke of the 'gospel simplicity', 'beautiful symmetry', 'providential character', and 'adaption of means to ends of the Methodist machinery'.[46] Hence, perhaps, the great Methodist fascination with their

---

[43] 1, p. 160.

[44] 4, p. 456; 1, p. 46.

[45] 2, pp. 111–12. In 'A Plain Account of The People Called Methodists', Wesley said of 'the whole economy of the people commonly called *Methodists*', 8, p. 248: '[A]s they had not the least expectation, at first, of any thing like what has since followed, so they had no previous design or plan at all; but every thing arose just as the occasion offered. They saw or felt some impending or pressing evil, or some good end necessary to be pursued. And many times they fell unawares on the very things which secured the good, or removed the evil. At other times, they consulted on the most probable means, following only common sense and Scripture: Though they generally found, in looking back, something in Christian antiquity likewise, very nearly parallel thereto'.

[46] *An Original Church of Christ*, pp. 346–7. Cf. pp. 347–8. Note the curious anomaly in Bangs and early Methodism. Providential leadings yielded a dynamic view of structure and a static view of doctrine. However, that anomaly disappeared as Bangs and others insisted that what had been dynamically given should be left alone. See *ibid.*, p. 370.

own history. It gave them God at work. Methodists knew Providence in history.

Bangs saw Providence in secular as well as sacred history. Unlike Lee, he began his history, not with Wesley, but with Columbus. Bangs set Methodism within a republican and providential schema, one that honored the relation of civil and religious liberty, that depicted the unfolding American drama as providentially ordained, and that recognized a distinctive Methodist role in the construction of a Christian civilization.[47] Bangs developed this theme most explicitly in a several-page assessment of Methodist influence, predicated upon the common assumption that 'a thoroughly reformed sinner cannot be otherwise than a good citizen, a good ruler, husband, brother, and friend'. He asserted that revivals 'had a most happy and conservative influence upon our national character'. Methodists rooted out infidelity which threatened the social order, they diverted attention from 'mere secular and political affairs', which were divisive, 'to the momentous concerns of eternity', and, most importantly, they instilled a 'vital, experimental, and practical Christianity' which exerts a conservative influence 'upon individual character, upon social and civil communities, and of course upon states and empires'. Methodists did so, thought Bangs, because the entire system functioned well in the expanding country. This applied to 'camp and other meetings'.

> Their mode of preaching, too, plain, pointed, searching, extemporaneous, and itinerating from place to place, collecting the people in log houses, in school houses, in the groves, or in barns, was most admirably adapted to the state of society, and calculated to arouse the attention of a slumbering world to the concerns of religion.[48]

Finally, Bangs argued that the cohesive, interactive, national character of Methodism had a nationalizing function, tending 'in the natural order of cause and effect, to cement the hearts of our citizens together in one great brotherhood'.[49]

---

[47] *History*, 1, pp. 20–33, 46, 280–8; 2, pp. 146–50. 'And although it formed no part of the design of its disciples to enter into the political speculations of the day, nor to intermeddle with the civil affairs of the country, yet it is thought that its extensive spread in this country, the hallowing influence it has exerted on society in uniting in one compact body so many members, through the medium of an itinerant ministry, interchanging from north to south, and from east to west, have contributed not a little to the union and prosperity of the nation' (p. 46).

[48] 2, pp. 148, 146, 147.

[49] 2, pp. 148–9. Bangs recognized the divisive spirit abroad in the land. He said, p. 149: 'It is well

Bangs, then, considered Methodism's relation to the nation a providential one and the nation itself providentially guided. And yet those were relatively minor themes, quite secondary to the far more prominently featured providences in individual lives and the far more important providential role in the Church itself. In his most important successor these priorities reversed themselves.

VII ABEL STEVENS

When American Methodism determined to make 1866 a centenary jubilee of its founding, it turned naturally to Abel Stevens (1815–97) to write a popular denominational history for the occasion.[50] Stevens had already completed standard histories under denominational sponsorship, *The History of the Religious Movement of the Eighteenth Century, Called Methodism*, a three-volume affair, and a *History of the Methodist Episcopal Church* in four volumes, then nearing completion.[51] He turned out a number of thematic and regional Methodist histories as well.[52] The spokesperson role

---

known that our civil organization, into several state sovereignties, though under the partial control of the general government, naturally tended to engender state animosities, arising out of local and peculiar usages, laws, customs, and habits of life. What more calculated to soften these asperities, and to allay petty jealousies and animosities, than a Church bound together by one system and doctrine, under the government of the same discipline, accustomed to the same usages, and a ministry possessing a homogeneousness of character, aiming at one and the same end—the salvation of their fellow-men by the same method— and these ministers continually interchanging from north to south, from east to west, everywhere striving to bring all men under the influence of the same "bond of perfectness?" Did not these things tend to bind the great American family together by producing a sameness of character, feelings and views?' Not long after Bangs wrote this, the church divided, north and south; and not to many years after the Methodist, Baptist, and Presbyterian divisions, the nation itself divided. Clarence Goen in *Broken Churches, Broken Nation* (Macon, Ga., 1985) echoing Bangs's sentiments, has carefully argued what others have intimated, that the first divisions largely determined the latter.

[50] See Abel Stevens, *The Centenary of American Methodism: A Sketch of Its History, Theology, Practical System, and Success* (New York, 1865).

[51] 3 vols (New York, 1858–61), and 4 vols (New York, 1864–7).

[52] The first of Stevens's major writings treated Providence explicitly, *Centenary Reflections on the Providential Character of Methodism* (New York, 1840). Among Stevens's other works are *Sketches and Incidents; or, A Budget from the Saddle-bags of a Superannuated Itinerant* (New York, 1843–5), *Memorials of the Introduction of Methodism into the Eastern States* (Boston and New York, 1848), *Memorials of the Early Progress of Methodism in the Eastern States*, ser. 2 (Boston, 1851), *The History of the Religious Movement of the Eighteenth Century*, 3 vols (New York, 1858–61), *An Appeal to the Methodist Episcopal Church . . . on the Question of Slavery* (New York, 1859), *Dr. Cartwright Portrayed* (New York, 1861), *Life and Times of Nathan Bangs* (New York, 1863), *The Centenary of American Methodism* (New York, 1865), *The Women of Methodism* (New York,

had been earned. Stevens guided *Zion's Herald*, Methodism's New-England-based paper for twelve years, beginning in 1848; assumed also in 1852 the editorial helm of *The National Magazine*, a Methodist venture into a more purely literary genre; accepted his election to the national weekly, *The Christian Advocate* in 1856, after having turned it down some years earlier; and moved on in 1860 to serve as corresponding editor of *The Methodists*, a post that he held until 1874. Self-consciously and forthrightly committed to Methodism's unity and national influence, Stevens strove in the controversies leading up to the Civil War to play what he took to be a moderating role. In that stance, which often meant placating the South and countering abolition, he offered what we would now think unfortunate conciliation. In that, he rather faithfully represented and led the Church.

Stevens's conception of American Methodist history cohered with and reinforced such a unitive mission. It was, in some ways, a more thoroughly and explicitly providential reading than either of his predecessors. Stevens elaborated the theory of general Providence towards which Bangs had struggled into a full-fledged historical vision. He also applied it continuously to the historical data so that the whole drama of Methodist history had an inner and consistent providential meaning. But it is a curiously attenuated Providence.

Stevens discerned Providence in the interconnecting missions of Nation and Church. Consistently, he pointed out how Methodism was providentially suited for America. Summing up Methodism's pre-Revolutionary period, he affirmed, for instance, 'In fine, the providential design and adaptation of Methodism, for the new nation, are revealed all through this period of its preparatory operations.' He saw that in the way in which Methodism seemed peculiarly adapted, like some organism to its environment, to what would be the needs of the new nation, particularly as it expanded West:

> Obviously then the ordinary means of religious instruction—a 'settled' pastorate, a 'regular' clergy, trained through years of pre-liminary education—could not possibly meet the moral exigencies of such an unparalleled condition. . . . A religious system, energetic, migratory, 'itinerant,' extempore, like the population itself, must

---

1866), *Character-sketches* (New York, 1882), *Supplementary History of American Methodism* (New York, 1899).

arise; or demoralization, if not barbarism, must overflow the continent.

Methodism entered the great arena at the emergent moment. . . . Methodism was not to supersede here other forms of faith, but to become their pioneer in the opening wilderness, and to prompt their energies for its pressing necessities. It was to be literally the founder of the Church in several of the most important new states, individually as large as some leading kingdoms of the old world. It was to become at last the dominant popular faith of the country, with its standard planted in every city, town, and almost every village of the land. Moving in the van of emigration, it was to supply, with the ministrations of religion, the frontiers from the Canadas to the Gulf of Mexico, from Puget's Sound to the Gulf of California. It was to do this indispensable work by means peculiar to itself. . . .[53]

Then followed one of the most succinct descriptions of the Methodist denominational system and its functioning. The force of his analysis, there and throughout, was to show Methodism in the details of its structure and operation to be essential to the American experiment. So Stevens believed Methodism 'to have been providentially designed more for the new world than for the old'.[54] Obviously, the argument functioned apologetically.

VIII TWO MACHINES IN THE GARDEN

Stevens also believed that America had been providentially set aside, peopled, developed, and governed with Methodism in mind, or, to be more precise, with the Protestant Evangelicalism and the Protestant Evangelical social order in mind that Methodism most fully embodied. Stevens registered both this claim about American society's religious purpose and that about Methodism's socio-political purpose with an arresting, initial metaphor. The metaphor makes the essentially providential character of Stevens's overall interpretation absolutely unmistakable.

Stevens began both his 4-volume History and the 600-page *Compendious*

---

[53] Stevens, *Compendious History*, pp. 146, 22–3. Cf. *History of the Methodist Episcopal Church*, 1, pp. 26–7. I will follow the one-volume, condensed version of Stevens's narrative. He worked these essential points into whatever scale analysis he undertook. Cf., for instance., *The Centenary of American Methodism*, pp. 147–53 with the sections just cited. There Stevens also concluded, p. 151: 'It would indeed appear that the Methodist movement was thus a providential intervention for the new nation'.

[54] *Compendious History*, p. 24; *History of the Methodist Episcopal Church*, 1, p. 28.

History with two figures whose paths he makes cross in a quadrangle at Glasgow, and whose discoveries shaped American life. The two men are James Watt and John Wesley, 'co-workers for the destinies of the new world'. Their machines—the steam-engine and 'Methodism, with its "lay ministry," and "itinerancy"'—are the forces that develop American society, two machines in the Garden, both more important for the new world than for the old.[55] Watt and the steam-engine stood in Stevens's presentation not only for the commercial and technological advances of his day, but also for all that the century then named progress. For Stevens the providential ordering concerned America as a whole—land, culture, peoples, society, economy—not just its democratic polity. So also the machine of Methodism served the entire moral order of the new nation, an order that he compared at one point to Augustine's City of God and to which he referred frequently.[56]

IX PROVIDENCE: WITHOUT TRANSCENDENCE OR IMMANENCE

American historians have long noted a subtle but important shift in Protestant relations to culture occurring around mid-century. One strand of Protestantism increasingly embraced culture, when appropriately Christianized, as the effective bearer of Divinity. A Christian civilization which in ante-bellum days had been recognized as a means to transcendent goals, symbolized in the Kingdom of God, increasingly became an end in itself.[57] Stevens invited his Methodist readers into just such an inversion of means and ends.

Stevens did so by reversing Methodist providential priorities. As we have seen, he functioned with a consistent providential motif, and he connected Methodism with the nation providentially. Indeed, when he thought of Methodism and Providence, the nation seemed almost invariably to come to mind.[58] That combination in itself would not have alarmed his predecessors. Indeed, they would have found what he said congenial. It was what he did not say that would have alarmed them, that

---

[55] *Compendious History*, p. 18 and chapter 1; *History of the Methodist Episcopal Church*, 1, p. 18 and chapter 1. Stevens does not himself call Methodism a machine, though some of his contemporaries did. See L. Marx, *The Machine in the Garden* (London, 1964), which treats the image of the machine in the garden in American literature.

[56] *Compendious History*, p. 176. See also pp. 199–200, 262, 506, 578–80 and, indeed, the entirety of this concluding chapter (XXXVI) as well as the entirety of chapter 1.

[57] This particular formulation comes from Robert T. Handy, *A Christian America* (2nd ed., New York, 1984). Compatible but differently nuanced readings prevail in the critical literature.

[58] *Compendious History*, pp. 46, 55, 107–9, 146, 199–200, 262, 266, 424–5, 506.

is, alarmed them, if they caught it. For Stevens put an incredible emphasis upon general Providence, but he slighted particular Providence. The careless reader might not have caught the shift. God language in fact abounds. For instance, the reader who expected to hear extravagant claims for Methodist camp meetings and revivals would not be disappointed to hear of a Kentucky gathering that 'the people fell under the power of the word like corn before a storm of wind', or to find said of a revival connected with the 1800 general conference that 'The Lord . . . is at work in all parts of the town', and 'Christ the Lord is come to reign.'[59] The attentive reader might have discovered that characteristically Stevens would not make such direct claims about the presence of God himself. Rather, the recognition of God at work, the particular Providences that dominated the works of Lee and Bangs, Stevens typically quoted, sometimes, as in those cited, placing the remarks in quotation marks, often implicitly attributing them.[60]

Exceptions occur. For instance, Stevens declared that God summoned Freeborn Garrettson to Methodism. He also spoke of Jesse Lee as 'endued with power from on high'.[61] On occasion, Stevens asserted that individuals were providentially led, George Whitefield for one, or events providential in character (the failure of the unpopular experiment with government by council).[62] Yet the pattern is unmistakable. Providence was, for Stevens, not so much an active agent in history as an axiom about the nature of history. Or perhaps, one should say that Providence remained an active agent for Stevens's subjects, who spoke loudly from his pages permitting him a discrete silence. In a concluding chapter, Stevens addressed himself to the reasons for Methodism's phenomenal growth and influence. He found two causes. The first, Methodism's providential adaptation to the times and circumstances, he termed primary, a fitting notation for what had been the motif of the book. The second, the proximate cause, he called 'the dispensation of the Spirit' and recognized in Wesley's Aldersgate experience and in the ethos of the movement generated therefrom.[63] An afterthought at best.

---

[59] *Compendious History*, pp. 404, 419.
[60] *Ibid.*, pp. 39, 49, 81, 84, 85, 91, 257, 442.
[61] *Ibid.*, pp. 96, 143.
[62] *Ibid.*, pp. 55, 263.
[63] *Ibid.*, pp. 578–82.

X JAMES BUCKLEY

For the Methodist volume in his American Church History Series, Philip Schaff turned naturally to its most eminent spokesperson. That was James Buckley (1836–1920), the long-term editor of *The Christian Advocate* (1880–1912) and delegate to every general conference from 1872 to 1912. His voice carried great weight in Methodist gatherings; his editorials every bit as much in Methodist thought. That intellectual gravity is well illustrated in his *Constitutional and Parliamentary History of The Methodist Episcopal Church*.[64] The extent of his influence can perhaps be gauged by the many apologetical and practical works that also came from his pen.[65] He was a formidable and conservative force in American Methodism.

Buckley's *History of the Methodists in the United States* appeared in 1896. He later issued it independently of Schaff's series in both one-volume and two-volume versions.[66] Buckley's work reflected some of the self-consciousness about historical method that Schaff and Adams espoused. He began the volume with a bibliographical preface and a bibliography of standard works. He concluded that section with a list of the official proceedings of the major Methodist denominations. In the course of his discussion, Buckley resorted to occasional footnotes to point the reader to the source or authority for a statement. In another preliminary statement, Buckley addressed himself to methodological concerns, and did so in a way that would have intrigued both Schaff and Adams. Schaff should have been pleased to find Buckley concerned with Providence, and might have seen Buckley's apparent reticence in pronouncing judgement as more than offset by his professed obligation to set forth the record so that the reader might 'estimate the relation of events to human and divine providence—the factors in the development of every form of Christianity'. For his part, Adams might well have been pleased with the following:

> Methodism is highly organized, and organization implies human centers of power. Hence the characteristics and work of individual

---

[64] (New York, 1912.)

[65] In addition to those mentioned in the text, the works of Buckley include *Christian Science and Other Superstitions* (New York, 1899); *Christians and the Theater* (New York, 1875); *Extemporaneous Oratory* (New York, 1898); *The Fundamentals and Their Contrasts* (Nashville, 1906); *Oats or Wild Oats? Common-sense for Young Men* (New York, 1885); *Theory and Practice of Foreign Missions* (New York, 1911) and *The Wrong and Peril of Woman Suffrage* (New York, 1909). For a fuller enumeration of Buckley's works see K. E. Rowe's *Methodist Union Catalog: Pre-1976 Imprints* (Metuchen, N.J., 1976), 2.

[66] (New York, 1896); *A History of Methodism in the United States*, 2 vols (New York, 1897). Reference is to *A History of Methodists in the United States*, 4th edn (New York, 1900).

men occupy a large place. The history of the body is but the history of those who have made it what it is.[67]

In actuality, Adams should have been the more satisfied. For in Buckley's hands, Providence effectively abandoned the Methodists. 'Effectively' needs to be underscored. In certain respects, Buckley was more explicit and extravagant in his theory about providential workings than his predecessors. Two significant passages, chapters 8 and 26, as we shall see, treat the doctrine of Providence. And one can certainly find scattered here and there familiar providential claims. However, Buckley made neither general nor particular Providence integral or necessary to his account. The reader might well draw his or her own inferences about providential workings; Buckley himself provided little assistance.

XI PARTICULAR PROVIDENCES

Especially remarkable is that particular Providences no longer dominated Methodist history. Buckley continued Stevens's practice of quoting or paraphrasing statements made by historical figures. However, those turn out to be infrequent and primarily concentrated in the very earliest years of the American Methodism.[68] Equally rare was Buckley's own use of providential language. By my count, at only some seven places in his narrative did Buckley unambiguously identify the hand of God at work. He called Wesley, 'The Man of Providence',[69] such a common designation that it almost could be considered Wesley's title. He spoke of Asbury refusing a call to a church and 'justly regarding himself as providentially occupied'.[70] Similarly, at a later point, Buckley confirmed another Asbury judgment, 'Well did Asbury conclude that "the hand of God has been greatly seen in all this. . . ."'.[71]

The first discussion that broke decisively with this minimalist reading came at page 201, well into the narrative. There, in chapter 8, Buckley devoted 24 pages to the relation of the human and divine in eighteenth-century American Methodism. He examined the spiritual saga of several preachers, Benjamin Abbott, Caleb Pedicord, and Jesse Lee among them, diagnosing their religious experience and practice in social scientific and

---

[67] A History of Methodists, p. xvii.
[68] Ibid., p. 49, the title of chapter 3.
[69] Ibid., pp. 170–3, 176–7, 179, 203, 205, 248.
[70] Ibid., p. 173.
[71] Ibid., p. 188. See also pp. 533, 655.

particularly psychological fashion. Buckley concluded that 'natural' explanations, though important, were not sufficient.

> There were not wanting those who constructed finely woven theories to explain the results of Methodist preaching upon natural principles, and there were others who denied that these principles had any influence. Both were in error; the former by predicating of nature effects that it never did or could produce, the latter by denying to nature the vast power which really exists to create influences which seem to many to be supernatural. Had there been no influence beyond unassisted nature neither Christianity nor Methodism as a spiritual system could have become permanent.[72]

Here, then, Buckley insisted that 'the preservation and growth of the fruits of the Spirit, and their correspondence with the plain teachings of God's Word, constitute proof of the divine origin of the movement....'.[73] So Buckley insisted upon the centrality of particular Providences to historical reality, even though he did not or could not sustain that dimension in his historical analysis.

XII GENERAL PROVIDENCE

Virtually the same statement could be made about Buckley's views of general Providence. He is the first of our historians, in fact, to abandon a providential framework for Methodist history. Neither Methodism as a providential force nor America as a providential construct shaped Buckley's narrative. In fact, the volume really lacks a unifying thread. Buckley hints at several that may have been operative in his own thinking—a germ reading of American society and religion that located its genius in the earliest arriving European cultures, peoples, and traditions,[74] a 'great man' theory of history that following Emerson saw Methodism as 'the lengthened shadow of one man',[75] an Anglo-Saxonism that deemed this particular racial stock to be the bearer of civilization, progress, and liberty, and a fierce commitment to Methodist episcopacy that made him impatient with its detractors. The latter two points are implicit in Buckley's choice of a starting-point, the English Reformation—not Wesley,

[72] *Ibid.*, p. 221.
[73] *Ibid.*, pp. 220–1.
[74] *Ibid.*, p. 97.
[75] *Ibid.*, p. 1.

nor the beginnings of American religion and society, nor the Reformation generally—but the beginnings of English religion. Of course, Wesley represents the fruition of those beginnings.

However, though the volume hints at an overriding perspective, what really provides coherence is a historicist or scientific orientation to facts. Buckley refrained not only from providential judgements, but really from interpretation altogether. He rarely permitted himself any distance from the historical process. Buckley the reporter, rather than Buckley the editorialist, charted the Methodist story. That dispassionate objectivity is particularly remarkable in the section on the slavery and sectional crisis and the division of Methodism.[76] After reporting the debates and events, Buckley did step back for what he called, 'A Calm Survey', an attempt to provide some perspective on that tragic episode in American and Methodist life. But even here he proceeded by identifying one figure in the maelstrom whom he thought afloat, Stephen Olin, and sketched Olin's views. Buckley's self-conscious commitment to historicism triumphed.

In a similar manner, Buckley stepped back from the historical process for some concluding and brief reflections about the spirit of Methodism. Here he concerned himself primarily with Methodism's future, but in so doing touched on the theme of general Providence. What he said of Methodism in his own day might well be said of his historical perspective as well:

> The founders of Methodism had no enterprises that were not distinctly subordinate to the conversion of men and their spiritual training. Now its enterprises are many and complex, often pervaded by a distinctly secular element, which contends constantly with the spiritual.[77]

He followed with an exhortation to Methodists to keep the spirit, concluding with Wesley's prophecy that the movement would die if it had 'the form of religion without the power', and lost 'the doctrine, spirit, and discipline' with which it first set out.[78] It may seem highly uncharitable to bring that prophecy down on Buckley himself. And yet, in so far as the historians gave Methodists their reality, in so far as history functioned to

---

[76] A History of Methodists, pp. 407–63, chapter 17. Buckley entitled the chapter 'Bisection of The Methodist Episcopal Church', perhaps a further indication of his effort at 'objectivity', and implicitly a recognition of Southern claims that both branches represent genuine episcopal Methodism and that neither is a schism.

[77] Ibid., p. 685.

[78] Ibid., p. 686.

define the movement, in so far as theology required a historical presentation, could one not say that here in a historicist reading was 'the form of religion without the power'? Indeed, what is striking about this theological excursus, as well as that which touched particular Providences, is that a person who wrote history as Buckley did, could still hold those views or, to invert the statement, that someone who held those views could write as he did. Or to put the matter more charitably, Providence had become for Buckley a theological rather than a historical construct.

XIII CONCLUSION

Buckley wrote for Schaff's series. He nodded also to Schaff's commitment to a providential reading of history. Providence was façade. Underneath no Spirit operated. His was a secular treatment. Adams and Emerton ruled. And since Methodism had accorded its historians great prominence, had called them to be the movement's spokespersons, had allowed them to define Methodism, Buckley's historicist interpretation is of great importance. Yet we must not make him into a scapegoat for twentieth-century Methodism's problems. For, as we have seen, the changes in Providence were a long time in the making. Lee had immediate experiences of God's Providence, saw them personally in revivals. Bangs burdened Providence with the perfection of Methodist machinery and the adaptation of church to republican order. Stevens shifted the emphasis further towards a civil theology. Buckley completed the abandonment of particular Providence and rendered general Providence a postulate. Over the century then, Providence changed radically. Burning conviction became historical theorem, experience became theory, agency became axiom.

Duke University

'COMMUNITY' AND 'WORK' AS CONCEPTS OF RELIGIOUS THOUGHT IN EIGHTEENTH-CENTURY WÜRTTEMBERG PIETISM

by HARTMUT LEHMANN

I GAPS IN THE STUDY OF PIETISM

UNLIKE English and American Puritanism, German Pietism has hardly ever been used as an example in works on religious sociology and general modern history. Max Weber, in his famous study on *The Protestant Ethic and the Spirit of Capitalism*, first published in 1904–5, pointed out that Pietism in Germany was, with regard to his thesis, in many ways similar to Puritanism in England and America. Yet those following the Weberian tradition and most of those studying religious sociology, or writing general modern history, rarely pay attention to German Pietism. This has meant that, first, most of the research on Pietism has been and is still being done by church historians. Accordingly, in works other than on church history, little can be found on Pietism. Second, until now there has been no thorough analysis or comprehensive description of the impact of Pietism on eighteenth- and nineteenth-century German society, culture, politics, or economics. Third, certain specific Pietist concepts, such as the concepts of 'community' and 'work', which possess a central position in modern sociology and were influential far beyond the ranks of the Pietists themselves, have not been investigated and thereby introduced into comparative studies.[1]

II EIGHTEENTH-CENTURY WÜRTTEMBERG PIETISM

From the early seventeenth century to the time of the French Revolution, the Duchy of Württemberg was an economically poor and divided country. In the seventeenth century this territory in south-western Germany had been badly hit by the Thirty Years War and by successive

---

[1] For a detailed bibliography of Pietism in general, as well as for its different aspects and its development in the various German territories, see *Pietismus und Neuzeit. Ein Jahrbuch zur Geschichte des neueren Protestantismus*, 1–11 (1974–85). See also the bibliography of M. Fulbrook, *Piety and Politics: Religion and the Rise of Absolutism in England, Württemberg and Prussia* (Cambridge, 1983).

wars between the Empire and France. During this time Württemberg lost approximately one-third of its population, many towns and villages were destroyed, and commerce and the trades suffered badly.

In the eighteenth century the general economic situation in Germany improved. As the population rose quickly, however, and as the dukes levied more and more taxes without developing the country's economic potential, Württemberg remained in a rather desolate state. Moreover, the country had been divided socially and culturally since the last quarter of the seventeenth century. While the dukes imitated the court of Versailles, introducing baroque architecture, baroque manners, and baroque festivities, the countryside clung to its traditional ethics and way of life, with people behaving, talking, and thinking much as their fore-fathers had done. While the court soon had an international band of musicians, dancers, architects, and courtiers, life in the villages and small towns of Württemberg was decided by the same families which had held power for centuries. Thus eighteenth-century Württemberg was torn by political, cultural, and social tensions. On the one hand, one observes the inhabitants of the countryside: devout Protestants for the most part and loyal members of their State Church, deeply rooted in their native soil and tradition, provincial and narrow-minded in their simple view of the world, considering the estates of Württemberg as the political expression and safeguard of their civil rights. On the other hand, one observes the duke and his family: Catholic since 1733, trying to rule as an absolute prince, spending enormous sums for official entertainment and a luxurious court life equal to that of larger courts in richer countries, and attempting to play a role in the sphere of European politics.

Yet not all of Württemberg submitted to the power and splendour of the dukes and their court. Some families separated themselves as far as possible from public life and from the Church. In the second half of the eighteenth century a growing number of Württembergers decided to emigrate, some to the Balkans and southern Russia, some to the New World. Still others, from the circles of the educated, compensated for the oppressions in their daily life by taking refuge in a world of spiritual free-dom. The Pietists of Württemberg were foremost among those who tried not to be corrupted by the new ways of the court.[2]

---

[2] See Fulbrook, pp. 130–52; H. Lehmann, *Pietismus und weltliche Ordnung in Württemberg vom 17. bis zum 20. Jahrhundert* (Stuttgart, 1969), 'Der Pietismus im Alten Reich', *HZ*, 214 (1972), pp. 58–95, 'Vergangenheit, Gegenwart und Zukunft im Denken des württembergischen Pietismus', in H. Löwe, ed., *Geschichte und Zukunft. Fünf Vorträge* (Berlin, 1978), pp. 51–73, and '"Absonderung" und "Gemeinschaft" im frühen Pietismus. Allgemeinhistorische und sozial-

Spener, the father of the Pietist movement, found admirers and followers in Württemberg soon after 1675. Between 1680 and 1720 Pietism in Württemberg played the role of a reform movement within the Church. Most early Pietists were to be found among the clergy, with most of their energies spent in church reform. Naturally they stayed away from the court and supported the fight of the Estates of Württemberg against all attempts to introduce absolute rule.[3] These early Pietists were frugal with their time and money and carefully used the little they possessed.

Between 1720 and 1750 Pietism in Württemberg was dominated by the towering figure of Johann Albrecht Bengel. Bengel had spent most of his life as a teacher in the school of Denkendorf, where future clergymen of the Württemberg State Church were educated. As a scholar, Bengel was well known for establishing and editing a reliable text of the New Testament. As a theologian, he commented on the past life, the present condition, and the future of true Christians. After elaborate studies he came to the conclusion that the return of Christ and the beginning of his glorious rule of a thousand years would occur in 1836. For the Pietists of Württemberg, Bengel, who died in 1752, was able to explain that their miserable condition and that of their country was part of the divine economy of salvation. He argued that in the last period before Christ's return the number of true Christians would necessarily, and according to biblical prophecy, be small. Those who were faithful to Christ's commands could also be victims of diabolical temptations and persecutions.

'Community' for these Pietists appears to have been the community of the true, reborn followers of Christ—the brotherhood of those who assembled in the Pietist conventicles, who were in brotherly correspondence on edifying matters, and who believed in salvation as predicted by Bengel. 'Work', on the other hand, seems to have been an important aspect of a truly Christian life for them. 'Work' was part of the lessons which God taught his children, who, by learning these lessons, hoped to give proof of their religious endeavours and thus qualify for heaven on Judgement Day. While, at least at first glance, the concepts of 'community'

---

psychologische Überlegungen zur Entstehung und Entwicklung des Pietismus', *Pietismus und Neuzeit*, 4 (1979), pp. 54–82.
[3] For the background, see W. Grube, *Der Stuttgarter Landtag 1457–1957* (Stuttgart, 1957), pp. 342–449; H. Lehmann, 'Die württembergischen Landstände im 17, und 18, Jahrhundert', in D. Gerhard, ed., *Ständische Vertretungen in Europa im 17. und 18. Jahrhundert* (Göttingen, 1969), pp. 183–207.

and 'work' were not directly linked with each other in the religious thought of eighteenth-century Württemberg Pietists, both concepts were closely related in the way in which they understood the history of salvation and the obligations of a reborn Christian in their time. We will explore these themes further by looking at some of the books of the generation of Württemberg Pietists after Bengel.

III FOLLOWING THE EXAMPLE OF CHRIST

Johann Christian Storr, Pietist clergyman and disciple of Bengel, explained in a series of sermons he gave from 1745 to 1751 that following the example of Christ was something blessed, something thorough and complete, yet voluntary and not impossible.[4] Only he who followed Christ would find rest for his soul. Following Christ consisted of secrets which Christians learned to believe and duties which they learned to fulfil. God had given mankind, as Storr pointed out, everything necessary for livelihood—houses, land, and other possessions—and demanded that men looked after them carefully. It would be sinful, however, if people loved their families and possessions more than they loved God. In times of persecution, in Storr's view, rather than deserting Jesus, true Christians should leave behind their homes and families, and sacrifice their lives rather than deny Christian teachings. In short, Jesus should be loved most, and following him should take precedence over everything else. In turn, according to Storr, following Christ would bring light into people's lives and bless all their professional activities. Storr stressed that it was the imitation of Christ which makes one truly committed to one's profession, truly industrious, and truly blessed. According to Storr, imitating Christ transformed ordinary houses, workshops, and offices into houses, workshops, and offices of the Holy Spirit. Nobody was happier, he concluded, than a farmer, an artisan, or a servant who followed Christ's example and tried to live in the love, patience, and hope which Christ had given.

In his sermons Storr left no doubt that following Christ was a matter of the whole person. He added that 'old Adam' was always present alongside 'man reborn'. In his eyes one consequence of this was that there was little harmony to be expected in this world. This existence offers not the fullness of life, Storr insisted, but only a foretaste of the life to come. In his view, salvation in this world was, at best, a kind of salvation through hope.

---

[4] *Die Nachfolge Christi in sieben Predigten* (Stuttgart, 1755): for the following quotations see pp. 24, 46–9, 159–60.

Another consequence was that true Christians should not lose sight of their destination. This is why life in this world is not the time of reward, Storr told his followers, nor the time of joy, but the time of trial, of struggle, of hard work, and of service. What was important for true children of God, Storr concluded, was striving to belong to the chosen few to whom God's eternal blessings were promised. Following Christ, therefore, was not a burden but glory and everlasting bliss.

IV THE PATH OF SALVATION

As another eighteenth-century Pietist clergyman and disciple of Bengel, Immanuel Gottlob Brastberger, demonstrated in his sermons, Christian perfection dealt not only with spiritual matters, but also with one's conduct in worldly affairs.[5] He who was on the path of salvation and who trusted God's economy of salvation had another orientation in his life besides worldly matters alone. Blessed are those, Brastberger exclaimed, who follow the progress of salvation and who walk on the path of godliness, as they are citizens of the Kingdom of God. According to Brastberger, members of God's Kingdom could expect royal privileges, advantages, presents, and awards, such as no earthly king would be able to give his favourites. They had more precious things to enjoy than food and drink: spiritual matters and heavenly goods which lifted up their souls and prepared them for eternal life. In Brastberger's view, all of this demonstrated the supremacy of the Kingdom of God which surpassed all earthly affairs. Members of God's Kingdom had nourishment which never perished but lasted for ever, as his Kingdom was full of justice, peace, and joy. Secular minds could not comprehend this, Brastberger explained, since they believed that true Christians could not have even one hour of joy, but must always be sad, melancholy, and gloomy. In Brastberger's view secular people were angry when they saw a lively, merry, and cheerful Christian. This made them jealous, and they called it 'licentious thoughtlessness' because they did not understand that true children of God had no reason to be anything but full of joy. According to Brastberger, this joy of the citizens of God's Kingdom was especially precious as it was the joy of the Holy Spirit. In his view, this made an enormous difference, especially comparing a simple, worldly joy to the desires of the flesh or luxury and frivolity. All of these worldly kinds of joy could never satisfy the heart of a Christian, he continued, as they were sinful,

---

[5] *Die Ordnung des Heils* (Stuttgart, 1759): new edn. (Reutlingen, 1856), pp. 644–64.

83

dangerous, and should be condemned. Voluptuous frivolity, according to Brastberger, made the human heart drunk, bewitched the soul, blinded the mind, diverted their senses, and made humanity unfit to be cultivated by the grace of God. While worldly joy led people away from God, joy in the Father, the Son, and the Holy Ghost united them with all true Christians and made them heirs of the possessions of God's realm.

Furthermore, Brastberger went on to say, as any service was more honourable the higher the lord to whom it is rendered, service in God's Kingdom was the highest form of service. There is no lord who is higher in rank than Christ, he wrote. Christ is the most powerful, the highest, the greatest, the king of kings, the lord of lords. Brastberger concluded that a true Christian served only him, and him alone; not God and Mammon, not Christ one day and Satan another, but Christ alone. In his sermons we hear in words reminiscent of Storr that serving Christ was something delightful, something voluntary and easy, and pleasing to God. Serving Christ and pleasing God was in full accordance with man's vocation, Brastberger concluded; thus servants of God become members of the community of believers and are supported, touched, admonished, consoled, and led by the prayers of their fellow Christians. It is the place where they find something better, more enjoyable, and of greater delight than in the world they left behind.

For Brastberger and the other Pietists of Württemberg, the Kingdom of God was totally contrary to the devil's reign in this world. For those who were hesitant it was important to join God's Kingdom. For those who were walking on the path of salvation it was important to be loyal and persistent. Brastberger admonished his fellow Pietists that only those who were persistent until the end of time would receive eternal salvation. According to Brastberger, therefore, remaining faithful to one's belief as a Christian was more important than anything else. Many had made a start, he explained, but had not remained firm. Quite a few had been citizens of the realm of Jesus, he wrote, but they had again joined the camp of Satan. Many had found something better than food and drink, he continued, but had again become slaves of sensual pleasures. They had worn the justice of Jesus, but had thrown it away; they had gained peace, but had given up faith and again become lost in an ocean of anxiety and fear; they had tasted the joy of the Holy Spirit, but had fallen to the enticements of frivolous, worldly sins; they had started to serve the Lord, but had again fallen and become prisoners of sin; they had been God's pleasure, but had again become rascals in his eyes; they had been kept in love and friendship by other children of God, but had left their community. According to

Brastberger, therefore, the community of true, loyal Christians was constantly endangered. As the devil would only be defeated by the returning Christ, true Christians had to be vigilant and constantly remember the progress of their souls towards salvation.

V THE SIGNIFICANCE OF 'COMMUNITY' IN THE PROCESS OF REDEMPTION

For pietists in eighteenth-century Württemberg rebirth was impossible without the intervening help of God. In their view the community of the reborn children of God had to help each member towards Christian perfection, yet each Christian had to achieve repentance and conversion alone. Redemption came from the intervening and judging God, from the helping and controlling community, and from the struggling and praying individual. Of the three sides of this triangle, the role of community was no less important than God or individual effort, even though, in the writings and sermons by Württemberg Pietists on redemption, 'community' is mentioned less often than God and the individual. For example, Philipp Friedrich Hiller, another of Bengel's disciples and a famous Pietist author of church hymns, wrote in the 1760s:

> Our time is short,
> and the world is falling.
> Everything crumbles.
> In this desert
> I shall only long to be
> where I can be forever.

> Kingdoms of this world
> come and go rapidly.
> Only where you are the king, Jesus,
> only there is an eternal empire.

> Your citizens have many privileges,
> and theirs is a blissful inheritance;
> they live in the city of God.
> Blessed the ones who have entrance.

> I am being called into your empire,
> where your son is the sovereign;
> he leads, step by step,
> into the city of God.

This is something incomprehensibly great;
this is a most charming prospect.[6]

The Pietist clergyman Gottlieb Friedrich Machtholf asked his fellow Pietists not to delay in attending to their souls. They should rush their souls to God as they would rush thirsty cattle to water, or as a bride would rush to her beloved who, in turn, would rush to her.[7] Friedrich Christoph Oetinger, next to Bengel the most learned and eminent among eighteenth-century Württemberg Pietists, wrote in an essay on the destination of man that health, strength, and skill were vital, but taken by themselves were not enough as long as there was no connection with God. God alone gave hope and perspective, Oetinger stressed; therefore, full concentration on God was necessary. He confessed that he would never forget the relation which exists between this world and eternal life. All good and all evil things of this world lose their importance if seen from this perspective. Prestige, glory, power, victories, and crowns are mere human vanities and of no value after death, and Christians should not degrade themselves by venerating them. For Oetinger, concentration on the ultimate destination was more important than anything else.[8]

Philipp Matthäus Hahn, to mention the sermons of another Pietist clergyman, stressed the continuous growth of God's Kingdom which, in his view, began in a small way and was opposed from many sides, yet advanced with irresistible force.[9] When asked about his work as a spiritual adviser, he replied that as there are beggars and housekeepers in material matters, he had become accustomed to teaching the Pietists to become good housekeepers in spiritual matters and thus acquire a spiritual treasure of their own: a fountain of life in their own hearts. According to Hahn, to obtain this spiritual treasure it was necessary to get down on one's knees and to pray to God every day, considering him as one's teacher and fountain of life. If one did not know what to ask for, Hahn explained, it was enough to utter what one felt about one's own misery.[10] As this

---

[6] *Geistliches Liederkästlein* (Stuttgart, 1762–7: new edn. (Stuttgart, 1849), part 2, pp. 38, 131, 343.
[7] *Leben und Schriften des Gottlieb Friedrich Machtholf, Pfarrers von Möttlingen*, ed. K. F. Ledderhose (Heidelberg, 1862), pp. 106–11.
[8] *Des Wirtembergischen Prälaten Friedrich Christoph Oetinger Abhandlungen von den lezten Dingen, desgleichen über Homiletik und Katechetik*, Sämmtliche Schriften, Abt. II, 6, ed. K. C. E. Ehmann (Stuttgart, 1864), p. 491.
[9] *Betrachtungen und Predigten über die sonn- und feiertäglichen Evangelien wie auch über die Leidens-geschichte Jesu für Freunde der alten Schriftwahrheit* (n.p., 1774), new edn. (Basel, 1896), *passim*.
[10] *Die Kornwestheimer Tagebücher 1772–1777*, ed. M. Brecht and R. F. Paulus = *Texte zur Geschichte des Pietismus*, Abt. VIII, 1 (Berlin and New York, 1979), p. 47.

remark shows, 'community' with God played a central part in the Württemberg Pietists' religious life.

We should not forget in this context, however, that Hahn eagerly conducted and attended Pietist conventicles in the parishes where he worked, just as Machtholf and many other Pietist clergymen did. They would never have disputed the auxiliary function of the conventicles in the process of redemption, although the community of true Christians as represented by the Pietist conventicles could neither replace nor make up for what God's grace and individual effort did not achieve. Moreover, Magnus Friedrich Roos, another disciple of Bengel, believed it was wrong to wait for the conversion of the whole people in his time. Rather, each one should look after his own soul. Everyone should be discontented with his own sin, he wrote, instead of being discontented, together with others, with the state of public affairs.[11]

All Württemberg Pietists agreed that on the day of the Last Judgement the single Christian's achievements and failures would be measured and judged. For Machtholf, this meant that one should love neither the world nor what is in it. Those who love the world are not loved by God the Father. Everything which is in the world, Machtholf continued, such as carnal pleasures, or desires of the eyes, or arrogant behaviour, is not from the Father but from the world. While the world with all its pleasures would pass away, this Pietist concluded, those who followed the will of God would remain for ever.[12] Hiller expressed the same thought in a number of hymns:

> Should I go on to love the world?
> O no, I know quite well
> that it will vanish soon
> with all its pleasures.
> There where the Father lives
> is more than in the world;
> the child whom he rewards
> receives more than goods and money.[13]

In the second half of the eighteenth century, following the example of Bengel, Friedrich Christoph Oetinger, and Philipp Matthäus Hahn, many

---

[11] *Anweisungen für wahre Christen wie sie sich in die gegenwärtige Zeit schicken und was sie bedencken und thun sollen* (Tübingen, 1790), p. 8.
[12] *Leben und Schriften des Machtholf*, p. 156.
[13] *Geistliches Liederkästlein*, part 2, p. 128.

others stressed time and again that Christ would return soon, and that time was running out for those who still hesitated to join God's Kingdom. It should be added that in theory, according to eighteenth-century Württemberg Pietists, an individual Christian could become a member of God's Kingdom without joining a Pietist conventicle. In the practical religious life of eighteenth-century Württemberg villages and towns, however, the kind of piety which Oetinger, Hahn, and their friends considered adequate for membership of God's Kingdom could only be found and expressed in close contact with the community of other true Christians as organized in Pietist conventicles. Therefore, if one attempts to form a judgement on the importance of the concept of 'community' for the Pietists of Württemberg, the opinions they expressed in their sermons and other edifying works are not sufficient by themselves but have to be supplemented by considerations and materials from social and religious history. Religious history teaches that conventicles were the greatest cause of friction between the State Church and the movement of Pietism in eighteenth-century Württemberg. Cultural history reveals that Pietist tradition and Pietist culture in Württemberg were inseparably linked with the institution of the conventicles in which Pietist patriarchs decided theological, ethical, and many other matters. The conventicles formed (and this may prove more correct for Pietism in Württemberg than for Pietism in other German territories), together with eschatology, the two constitutive and essential components of any proper definition of Pietism in Württemberg.

VI THE LIMITED VALUE OF 'WORK' IN THE STRUGGLE FOR CHRISTIAN PERFECTION

Most of eighteenth-century Pietist literature deals with edifying matters, enumerating in detail what true Christians should believe and how they should live. There are a few eighteenth-century Württemberg Pietists, however, who discuss the question of a proper Pietist lifestyle. One is the clergyman Johann Friedrich Flattich, who wrote a catalogue of twenty-seven rules of proper conduct for reborn Christians, some of which deserve our attention.[14] His first rule advised Christians not to spend much, so that they would not have to earn much. If one does not need much, Flattich explained, and if one is not pressed to earn much, one is rid

---

[14] *Leben und Schriften des Johann Friedrich Flattich, Pfarrers in Münchingen*, ed. K. F. Ledderhose (Heidelberg, 1856), part 2, pp. 3–21, 38.

of many of the problems others have. Therefore, Flattich went on to say, he had never offered much to his guests in his own house except brotherly love. His second rule states that the simpler the household, the less trouble would arise if servants destroyed something. In his third rule Flattich stated that there are different kinds of troubles. One could be troubled by fancies, by wealth, and by honour, but being troubled by fancies and by honour was considered the hardest, as these troubles could find no satisfaction with the help of God. According to Flattich's fourth rule, a true Christian had to work less hard than others since he spent less on food and drink. Some people like to go to inns on Sunday and holidays, he explained, but to be able to do this they had to work hard during the week so that they would have something to spend foolishly on these occasions. In contrast to the people of the world, Christians did not have to sweat or work as if under a curse. As they needed less, as they did not live to satisfy their desires for pleasure, and as they tried to get along and stay within the limits of orderly conduct, they could care less about making money, but still prosper better than people of the world. In subsequent rules Flattich explained that it is better to buy cheaply than to sell dearly, and better to make one's living by working than by trading. Poor people's lives were easier, Flattich stated, as they had less to care for than the rich. As he had experienced, rich people were often discontented, unhappy creatures, while the poor were satisfied with the little they had. Those who love carnal pleasures will find themselves in hell, Flattich concluded drastically. One should not wish for too easy a life in this world, he insisted, and if one wished others an easy life, one wished them to hell. In these rules Flattich also explained at some length how servants should be treated and how children should be brought up. He pointed out that faithfulness was the foundation of a happy marriage, and that the authority of a father did not depend on his using force and making all the decisions. Mothers, in his view, should refrain from sweets, from laziness, and from complaining constantly. As to the role of 'work', Flattich mentioned in the twenty-fifth rule that one should work at something useful and not spend time doing useless things. One should prefer to do something sensible, he wrote, and earn less, rather than waste time. Therefore, in Flattich's view, simple people were the happiest, as they had useful things to do, even though working hard could be bitter for them.

In a series of reflections on different matters, Flattich discussed the happiness of rich and poor people, remarking that although most people wished to be in a higher social class, persons of higher rank were more enslaved than persons of lower rank, since high-ranking persons depended on even higher persons and thus had no will of their own. Aside from that, Flattich divided the people of the world into two groups: dogs and pigs. The former were those of higher rank, the latter the mob. Flattich added that in the empires of this world the rich and distinguished were in command, while the low and the poor had to fit themselves in, rarely becoming anything of consequence. Flattich concluded that in contrast to the Kingdom of God, the empires of this world esteemed the rich and the distinguished, while the poor and the low were kept in their place. But in Christ's realm the poor and the low were esteemed highly, while a rich man like Nicodemus would seldom rise to recognition.

Several aspects of Flattich's catalogue of rules are underlined, modified, or supplemented by other Württemberg Pietists of his time. Brastberger, for instance, when stressing repentance and conversio in one of his sermons, demanded that repenting sinners should restore and return goods that they had taken from others.[15] Improper property, as defined by Brastberger, was everything taken or acquired from others by cunning, deceit, or force, including most forms of commerce and trade. Brastberger admonished the State not to require too high taxes and asked masters not to pay their workers and servants too low wages. He also rebuked servants for being lazy and stealing from their masters; he chided shopkeepers for selling goods that were not of the quality they declared, and he asked clerks to fulfil their duties. All these and many others acted illegally, Brastberger continued, and ought to repair the damage they had done. Brastberger knew that such illegal practices were widespread and that there was little hope for higher moral standards. Unfortunately, he added, there is no office, no rank, no profession, no business where property is not acquired illegally every day. In his view, poor people did not care about this as they considered it to be a traditional practice. As they could not change the laws of hunting, as they called it, they tried not to concern themselves with it. As for the hunters, Brastberger continued, since they did not want to stop deceiving and stealing, they were not ready for serious conversion. What would become of my office, my business, or my profession as a tailor, a baker, a butcher, or a miller, they would argue, if I would have to give up the way I am used to making money? Rather, they would say, I will stay as I am, because I cannot change the world alone. What a miserable confession, Brastberger commented bitterly. Here one could see how the human soul was put in irons, he went on, and observe the wretched way in which most people died as they fell under

[15] *Die Ordnung des Heils*, pp. 278–300.

Adam's curse. Brastberger would not have been the famous Pietist preacher that he was had he not added a passionate plea for conversion. He warned that unless Christians got rid of the curse, they could not stand in front of God's jury, or defend themselves against the attacks of Satan. If they awakened, perhaps, on the day of their deaths, their souls would be burning, and they would be in despair. As long as there was still time, sinners should try to repent, Brastberger continued, and try to throw the sparks of the devil from their loaded consciences. They should try to discharge themselves of the injustice which they had swallowed like water, or else they would bring eternal death to their souls. As Brastberger portrayed them, true Christians would do best to abstain from any active part in business or commercial life. His plea for conversion was detrimental to economic progress.

In a famous essay written in 1759 Oetinger described the order of things after the return of Christ, thus instructing his fellow Pietists on how to behave when preparing for this glorious period.[16] He wrote that Christ would restore the original harmony of things lost by the Fall of Man, and, as a result, the land would be extremely fertile and yield crops without much effort. Everyone would have enough land, all injustice would disappear, everyone would be content, and there would be general peace and obedience. Oetinger explained that equality, community of all goods, and exemption from all services and all contracts would then exist. Although Oetinger was convinced that princes would be well advised to introduce reforms in preparation for Christ's return and the Golden Age, he was sceptical about whether they would do so. In his view, one could not expect the princes of this world to follow the lesson which he had elaborated and thus prepare for Christ's return. Oetinger did not comment specifically on how the subjects of these princes should prepare for the returning Christ—that was, it seems, all too clear: they should not work for material goods, but should prepare their souls and work towards spiritual renewal.

Eighteenth-century Württemberg Pietists were convinced that time spent climbing the social ladder was time spent in vain. They believed that God expected everyone to remain in the social stratum in which he grew up and to try to live there the life of a good Christian. When asked to accept higher posts themselves, Pietists hesitated to accept. That God needed loyal helpers in all parts of society was one of their standard remarks. Hiller laid down this opinion in one of his hymns, first published in 1762.

---

[16] *Des Wirtembergischen Prälaten Oetinger Ablandlungen von den lezten Dingen*, pp. 30, 39.

The Lord's wisdom is wonderful,
he makes a compound of poor and rich.

If everyone was poor, who would offer something?
If everyone was rich, who would serve at table?
Love is the aim, therefore let us all praise
the Lord's wisdom.

The Lord's wisdom is just.
Everyone has to serve according to his rank.
The servants to the masters, and also the masters to the
servants.
This is what they are accountable for to God.
He is the one who distributes, therefore let us all praise
the Lord's wisdom.

This is how the Lord consoles the poor;
they serve God, even if they are held in villeinage.
This defies the boldness of the rich who are angry
because God does not count the rank of people.
This gives us joy; so let us all praise
the Lord's wisdom.[17]

In a series of fictitious conversations between persons of different professions, Magnus Friedrich Roos tried to demonstrate that Christian faith
could blossom in any one of them.[18] Bad, sinful companions had to be
avoided, just as bad, sinful inns and wicked talk about others had to be.
Injustice had to be suffered without revenge. As Roos understood it, the
Christian belief should add an extra dimension to all kinds of work and all
business transactions in every position of life. In his book, Roos has one
shoemaker say to one of his comrades:

Even if he leads us on uneven paths,
his cross is full of love;
he who ponders about his advantage,
there he will find the best of it,
as if in a course full of thorns
he will be led to roses plentiful.

---

[17] *Geistliches Liederkästlein*, part 1, p. 266.
[18] *Erbauliche Gespräche von wahren Geschichten welche sich unter Handels = und Handwerksleuten zugetragen haben, und merkwürdige Erweisungen der Gnade und Gerechtigkeit Gottes enthalten*, 2nd edn. (Tübingen, 1789), pp. 102–3.

The other shoemaker replied:

Yes, rather, let us go through seven furnaces
than be led away from you, my lamb.
Rather I would be dead than have
the door of my heart locked.

This may seem rather ignorant of the way shoemakers talked in Roos's time and quite unlikely to convince any of them of the advantages of Christian faith. For Roos, however, this might have been exactly the message he wanted to convey: that God's Kingdom was not part of this world.

All eighteenth-century Württemberg Pietists would have agreed that there are good Christians in all social classes, and that members of any social group could gain access to God's Kingdom. There are, however, in the works of Philipp Matthäus Hahn and Machtholf a few hints which reveal that they believed the middle social stratum to be better suited to a truly Christian lifestyle than any other. For Hahn, for instance, neither the socially distinguished nor the socially inferior had the best understanding of spiritual wisdom. The clever world may consider God's things as folly, Hahn said in one of his sermons, and most among the distinguished as well as most among the insignificant are totally blind.[19] There are signs before them, but they don't see them, and many of those who do see them are not willing to leave sin and rid themselves of darkness and heathen behaviour. They are not prepared to accept insult, disgrace, hard work, self-denial, and do not want to carry Christ's cross or accept his way of thinking, because they would lose their worldly way of thinking. When Machtholf asked for his daily bread in a prayer, he asked for an ordinary, moderate portion, not too little and not too much. He recommended asking for a moderate income, bestowing neither poverty nor wealth.[20]

The social conservatism of Hiller, Roos, and other eighteenth-century Württemberg Pietists can still be found in the writings of Christian Adam Dann. Dann was a generation younger than the disciples of Bengel cited thus far, and served as one of the important links between eighteenth and nineteenth-century Württemberg Pietism. The world is like a vineyard, Dann explained in 1809.[21] God hires people at different times and for

---

[19] *Betrachten und Predigten*, p. 15.
[20] *Leben und Schriften des Machtholf*, p. 115.
[21] *Das Nöthigste für Dienstboten, bestehend in guten Lehren und schönen Exempeln* (n.p., 1809), new edn. (Stuttgart, 1838), pp. 6, 8, 9.

different tasks, which correspond most exactly with what individual strengths and abilities allow. Therefore, according to Dann, no part of humankind should despise any other, nobody envy anybody else, or grumble about the good housekeeper in the false notion that the task given him was too hard or too low. It is remarkable, however, that Dann goes on to praise the hidden virtues of servants. This kind of work, he explained, helped to break a person's will, and servants needed such Christian virtues as fidelity, conscientiousness, frugality, justice, happiness, punctuality, childlike attachment, discretion, thoughtfulness, contentment, peacefulness, cleanliness. Blessed are those, Dann remarked about servants, who live unnoticed by men, yet the better noticed by the Lord, who observes even things kept in secrecy. Blessed are those who dwell in the shadow of domestic life and who, seeking heaven, pass through the quiet valley of seemingly unimportant, yet carefully accomplished, tasks. Great will be their reward.

As we know, between 1750 and 1800 the social composition of the Pietist movement in Württemberg changed completely. In 1752, the year of Bengel's death, clergymen shaped the face of Pietism in Württemberg. Together with a few teachers they wrote the edifying tracts read by Württemberg Pietists, and assembled pious Christians in Pietist conventicles. When they left a parish, and a pastor or teacher succeeded who was not a Pietist, the conventicle ceased to exist. In 1800, by contrast, most conventicles were conducted by non-theologians, namely artisans and peasants. By 1800, also in Württemberg, most theologians believed in enlightened theology, and only a few, like Dann, had retained an interest in Pietist conventicles. When Dann praised the Christian virtues of lower-class people such as servants, he acknowledged that Pietism in Württemberg by 1800 had become a cause of these lower classes.[22]

VII 'COMMUNITY' AND 'WORK' IN THE WÜRTTEMBERG PILGRIMS' PROGRESS

Eighteenth-century Württemberg Pietists called 'community' the spiritual union between a true Christian and God as well as the practical union of reborn Christians for the purpose of mutual edification. On the other hand, they considered 'work' to be part of the duties which God

---

[22] About nineteenth-century Württemberg Pietism, see M. Scharfe, *Die Religion des Volkes. Kleine Kultur- und Sozialgeschichte des Pietismus in Fellbach 1750–1820. Zwischen sozial Protest und bürgerlicher Anpassung* (Tübingen, 1985).

expected a true Christian to fulfil. However, eighteenth-century Württemberg Pietists did not believe that 'work' had value in and of itself. Rather, work should not distract from religious obligations and from the path of salvation.

It is only when one takes into consideration the specific political, cultural, social, and economic situation of Württemberg in the eighteenth century, that what Württemberg Pietists said and wrote about 'community' and 'work' gains its real significance. The 'community' with Christ that they asked true Christians to seek then appears as a form of convincing resistance against the policy of the duke and life at his court, both of which attracted and corrupted many Württemberg families: the 'community' they practised in their conventicles would thus appear to be a successful effort to assemble and educate those who resisted and opposed the duke, his court, and their clientele. It should be added that eighteenth-century Württemberg Pietists had given up the older Protestant concept of a covenant between God and a whole people. Therefore they did not work for the conversion of all of Württemberg to their concept of Christian faith. Bengel had taught them that salvation history had progressed too far to accomplish that. What they believed in and what they worked for, however, was the rescue of the remaining few faithful children of God in their country. This could be achieved by assembling in their conventicles, or by emigrating to a place of refuge in a foreign country like Pennsylvania.

Viewed against the historical background of eighteenth century Württemberg, it is quite remarkable how little Württemberg Pietists stressed the value of 'work'. All eighteenth-century Württembergers had to work hard to make a living. They even had—and still have—their own word for hard work: *schaffe*. *Schaffe* means labouring like a slave; not working because it is a joy to take part in the creation of a better world. Neither does *schaffe* mean work as a kind of punishment for sinful human desires. Rather, *schaffe* stands for continuous hard work and sometimes for the almost perverse form of a self-imposed compulsion to work. Certainly, eighteenth-century Württemberg Pietists do appear to us as models of hard-working Christians. It has to be stressed, however, that Flattich and his fellow Pietists did not expect true Christians to work day and night, and they were far removed from the Calvinist concept of a close link between the capacity to achieve something and the efficiency of spiritual life. Where eighteenth-century Württemberg Pietists held responsible positions in business, as, for example in the textile trade of Calw in the early eighteenth century, neither the quality nor the quantity of commercial activities rose.[23] Economics was not the field in which eighteenth-century Württemberg Pietists excelled. In their eyes economics was not the field in which God expected them to accomplish something special.

As we know from seventeenth-century Europe, eschatological thinking was especially strong in those regions where, and at times when, there was significant political pressure and social tension, such as Bohemia around 1620, England from the 1630s to the 1650s, and the Holy Roman Empire in the 1670s and the 1680s.[24] The Duchy of Württemberg—economically poor and socially and culturally divided—may be added to the list as an eighteenth-century example. As there seemed to be no hope for a better life in the near future, the Pietists who wrote on and spoke of the return of Christ inaugurating a better future convinced many of their countrymen. As a result, Pietism remained strong in Württemberg throughout the eighteenth century. When Bengel and his disciples preached the virtues of a simple, modest life and called frugality even one of the preconditions for salvation, they set a new standard. Those who were poor and joined the Pietist conventicles could consider themselves heirs of God's Kingdom. Moreover, by idealizing a life of modesty and simplicity, the leaders of Pietism made it easier for their followers to cope with the harshness of life in eighteenth-century Württemberg.

The persuasive power of Pietism in eighteenth-century Württemberg therefore lies in the ability of Pietist clergymen to combine two elements which their contemporaries were unable to join. They were sure that they were on the path of salvation and reward, and lived in the hope of Christ's return. At the same time, they considered the rigidity of their daily life to be something meaningful. The little they earned and possessed seemed to them to be a guarantee of future riches, and the humbleness of their lives was a sign of future glory. No doubt the conventicles had a key position in this respect. It was here that the faithful were told of the plan of salvation, and where the connection between their daily life, their ethical convictions, and their salvation was explained. In retrospect we see that the ethical and theological positions of eighteenth-century Württemberg Pietists were somewhat problematic. On the one hand, the Pietist clergymen taught that the 'world' was sinful and that true Christians should

[23] H. Lehmann, 'Pietismus und Wirtschaft in Calw am Anfang des 18. Jahrhunderts. Ein lokalhistorischer Beitrag zu einer universalhistorischen These von Max Weber', *Zeitschrift für württembergische Landesgeschichte*, 31 (1972), pp. 249–77.
[24] See H. Lehmann, *Das Zeitalter des Absolutismus* (Stuttgart, 1980), pp. 123–34.

separate themselves from it and seek to save their souls. On the other hand, they were convinced that *all* political changes were caused by God, and therefore should be taken seriously as 'signs'. On the one hand, they left the sphere of politics and economics to others. On the other hand, they depended in many ways on whatever these others did or did not do. In the conditions of the time, a separate Christian 'community' within eighteenth-century Württemberg society—a truly Christian island within the sea of eighteenth-century Württemberg life—was not possible. By contrast, in the nineteenth century most Württemberg Pietists were involved in missionary activities at home and abroad. They tried to change the 'world' in which they lived. As a result of their efforts, nineteenth-century Württemberg was more influenced by Pietist ideas than eighteenth-century Württemberg ever was. A new chapter in the history of Pietism in Württemberg had begun.

With regard to the Weber thesis, some last remarks should be added. As an heir of the tradition of nineteenth-century German liberalism, Weber cherished individual effort very highly—in culture as well as in politics, and in economics no less than in religion. As a result, Weber was unable to give due credit to the element of 'community' which existed in seventeenth- and eighteenth-century religious movements. Correspondingly, he did not pay much attention to Pietist conventicles.[25] In contrast, modern research considers the conventicles to be one of the basic factors which shaped the movement of Pietism. This is also true for Württemberg. What is characteristic for Pietism is the separation from the sinful 'world' and the formation of a new 'community' in the conventicles.

Within the context of religious life in these conventicles, finally, the role of 'work' was less important than Weber had imagined. Of course, for eighteenth-century Württemberg Pietists, outright laziness was not acceptable. What they distrusted, however, was the open and outright eagerness to obtain material goods. On the basis of their own experience in eighteenth-century Württemberg economic life, the notion that a true Christian should try to make a lot of money seemed strange, if not sinful, to them, even if the money was not spent on luxuries but invested in one's business. Certainly the frugality of inner-worldly asceticism appealed to them, especially as this lifestyle was in sharp contrast to life at the baroque courts. Since they hoped for the return of Christ, spending time to make money was almost a waste of time in their eyes, and was, at best, neither

---

[25] See H. Lehmann, 'Ascetic Protestantism and Economic Rationalism. Max Weber revisited after two generations', *HThR*, 80 (1987), pp. 307–20.

harmful nor helpful. For them, other things were more important. For them, being industrious and successful in business was not linked to progress on the path of salvation. While there are some recent studies which confirm the lasting validity of Weber's thesis,[26] eighteenth-century Württemberg Pietism does not seem to be a good case in Weber's favour.

Deutsches Historisches Institut, Washington, D.C.

[26] See, for example, G. Marshall, *Presbyteries and Profits: Calvinism and the Development of Capitalism in Scotland, 1560–1707* (Oxford, 1980).

CATHOLIC REVIVAL IN THE
EIGHTEENTH CENTURY

by SHERIDAN GILLEY

IN his famous essay on von Ranke's history of the Popes, Thomas Babington Macaulay remarked that the 'ignorant enthusiast whom the Anglican Church makes an enemy . . . the Catholic Church makes a champion'. 'Place Ignatius Loyola at Oxford. He is certain to become the head of a formidable secession. Place John Wesley at Rome. He is certain to be the first General of a new Society devoted to the interests and honour of the Church.' Macaulay's general argument that Roman Catholicism 'unites in herself all the strength of establishment, and all the strength of dissent', depends for its force on his comparison of the Catholic Regular Orders with the popular preachers of Nonconformity.[1] As the son of a leader of the Clapham Sect, his witness in the matter has its interest for scholars of the Evangelical Revival, and has been echoed by Ronald Knox in his parallel between Wesley and the seventeenth-century Jesuit, Paolo Segneri, who walked barefoot 800 miles a year to preach missions in the dioceses of northern Italy.[2] More recently the comparison has been drawn again by Owen Chadwick, with the judgement that the 'heirs of the Counter-Reformation sometimes astound by likeness of behaviour to that found in the heirs of the Reformation', and Chadwick's volume on the eighteenth-century Popes contains some fascinating material on the resemblances between the religion of the peoples of England and of Italy.[3] An historian of Spanish Catholicism has compared the Moravians and the mission preachers of eighteenth-century Spain,[4] not least in their rejection of modern commercialism, while an American scholar has traced some of the parallels between nineteenth-century Protestant and Catholic revivalism in the United States.[5] Not that Wesleyan historians have been attracted to study the great movements of revival religion in the Catholic

[1] T. B. Macaulay, 'Von Ranke' (1840) in *Critical and Historical Essays*, 2 vols (London, 1966), 2, pp. 62–3.
[2] R. A. Knox, *Enthusiasm: a Chapter in the History of Religion with Special Reference to the XVII and XVIII Centuries* (Oxford, 1950), p. 423.
[3] O. Chadwick, *The Popes and European Revolution* (Oxford, 1981), p. 159.
[4] C. C. Noel, 'Missionary preachers in Spain: teaching social virtues in the eighteenth century', *AHR*, 90 (1985), p. 888.
[5] J. P. Dolan, *Catholic Revivalism: The American Experience 1830–1900* (Notre Dame, Indiana, 1978).

countries in Wesley's lifetime[6]—a neglect which is hardly surprising. One point of origin of the Evangelical revival was among refugees from Roman Catholic persecution, and for all the popular confusion, encouraged by men like Bishop Lavington, between Methodists and Papists, and for all Wesley's belief in religious toleration and tenderness for certain Catholic saints and devotional classics, he was deeply hostile to the Roman Catholic Church, as David Hempton has recently shown.[7] Yet there are many points of likeness as well as difference between the enthusiasts of Protestant and Catholic Europe, and both these need to be declared if Catholics and Protestants are ever to attempt to write an ecumenical history.

Macaulay describes the sixteenth-century Roman Theatine Order as rather like the Oxford Holy Club: 'The members of the new brotherhood preached to great multitudes in the streets and in the fields, prayed by the beds of the sick', and indeed, had the same 'great object' as 'our early Methodists, namely to supply the deficiencies of the parochial clergy'.[8] That last aspiration in Catholicism went back at least to the friars of the thirteenth century, and it was the Franciscan tradition of open-air preaching that produced both the most popular Italian orator of the first half of the eighteenth century, Paolo Girolamo Casanova, canonized as St Leonard of Port-Maurice, near Genoa, and much of the content of his preaching. The Theatines, however, were the first of the Counter-Reformation Orders of Clerks Regular, of priests with an activist as well as a contemplative spirituality, though bound by religious vows; and it was the Orders of Clerks Regular, of whom the Jesuits were the chief, who often dominated the function of missionary preachers in northern Italy in the later seventeenth century, another clerical brotherhood of sixteenth-century origin, the Oratorians founded by St Philip Neri, being more important in the south. Neri, one of the most attractive saints in the calendar, won the title 'Apostle of Rome', and might be accorded the merit of having converted the pagan Renaissance city back to Christianity; and his Oratories, not houses of Clerks Regular but independent communities of secular priests, were supplemented in the seventeenth century by the French Congregation of the Mission, established by St Vincent de Paul, a saint loved even by Voltaire. The two chief new Italian missionary

---

[6] Thus one of the Macaulay quotations above (comparing Wesley and Loyola) is cited, but misinterpreted for the eighteenth century in E. Gordon Rupp's new *Religion in England 1688–1791* (Oxford, 1986), p. 444.

[7] D. Hempton, *Methodism and Politics in British Society 1750–1850* (London, 1984), pp. 31 ff.

[8] Macaulay, p. 51.

orders of eighteenth-century origin, the Redemptorists and Passionists, founded by St Alphonsus (Alfonso Maria dei) Liguori and by Paul Danei, canonized as St Paul of the Cross, were a part of that tangled web of warring jurisdictions and rival power-houses of the spirit in Counter-Reformation Catholicism which meant that the Roman parish priest, unlike the Anglican parson, had to justify his place in the ecclesiastical sun.

In this, there were points of difference and resemblance between the Methodists and Catholic missioners. St Leonard in northern Italy after 1713, St Alphonsus in the south, were proclaiming the need for conversion and repentance to urban Catholics who were actually immoral in behaviour or were only formally practising their religion, or to peasants in large tracts of underpriested countryside, 'where the church had lost a large measure of its hold over the populace during a long period of economic stagnation (1630–1720)'.[9] The missioners quite as much as the Methodists appealed to the many neglected by the parochial clergy, and were frequently opposed by ecclesiastical vested interests not slow to stir up riot and calumny; most of the parish priests of the town, like Nocera, offered a new Redemptorist house, indignantly presented the authorities with a list of its religious establishments to prove that no new one was required. But the parish mission preached by the clerical itinerant had achieved an established place in the Counter-Reformation Church, and his demand for renewed holiness and for a more faithful attention to Communion and confession was difficult to deny, especially when he came armed with a mandate from pope or bishop. St Leonard of Port-Maurice preached the great penitential mission for the Roman Jubilee of 1750 before the Pope and Cardinals and an audience of 100,000 people. St Leonard's rules for missions included a clause on being 'on good terms with the parish priest',[10] whose permission for a Redemptorist mission was actually required.

There was no class of men whom Liguori was more anxious to convert than the parochial clergy; and though the lives of the missioners could become a tangle of conflict—leading even, in the case of St Alphonsus, to displacement by the Pope from the leadership of the Order he had founded—there was no real sense that Redemptorists were foreign to the

---

[9] M. Rosa, 'The Italian churches', in W. J. Callahan and D. Higgs, eds, *Church and Society in Catholic Europe of the Eighteenth Century* (Cambridge, 1979), p. 72.

[10] Fr. Giuseppe Maria, *Life of Blessed Leonard of Port-Maurice* (London, 1852), p. 166 (with the *Life of Blessed Nicholas Fattore* by Fr. Giuseppe Alapont).

very character of Catholicism as the Methodists were widely considered to be alien to the constitution of the Church of England. The missioner might save some local enterprise threatened by indifference or hostility, as at Rieti, where a group of clerics, anxious to promote 'the glory of God and the salvation of souls', came together 'to catechize the children, instruct prisoners, visit the sick, and labour to reform those who had gone astray', only to be accused of 'ignorance, rashness, and presumption . . . as sectarians and lovers of novelty'.[11] The group was saved from extinction by the intervention at the local bishop's request of St Leonard, who gave them his support and even a name as 'Amanti di Dio'. There is a striking difference between their experience of bishops and their fellow clergy and that of the brothers Wesley.

Yet no more than the Methodists did missioners deny the demands of a strict other-worldliness. Quite as severely as any evangelical preacher, the missioner attacked licentious songs and dancing and hard drinking and gambling, concluding the mission with whole holocausts of playing cards, immoral books, and offensive weapons, and even assailing the citadel of carnival itself. At Sarno, the missioners closed the taverns for ten years, and of the great international port of Leghorn, it was said that at least for a time it 'seemed another Ninive converted'.[12] They were out to renew whole communities, even though the effects were seldom lasting: at Naples, the Redemptorist drive against prostitutes seems to have merely concentrated them in a single suburb. Of course, such moral discipline was also sometimes enforced by official regulation; when St Alphonsus, who had declined the great see of Palermo, had forced on him the little diocese of St-Agatha-of-the-Goths, he would have prostitutes whipped or imprisoned or exiled, though he also saved girls from exploitation by their parents and pensioned or dowered numerous prostitutes who had repented.[13] In short, the mission was a part of a religious world in which the missioner expected a communal rather than just an individual response. One high aim of the mission in villages riven by faction and feuding was to re-establish communal harmony by persuading the families of murderers and their victims to forgive one another. St Leonard's missions to Corsica, which took up six months in 1744, and were patronized by the Genoese governor, included sermons in churches

---

[11] *Life of Blessed Leonard of Port-Maurice*, p. 98.

[12] *Ibid.*, p. 53.

[13] *The Life of S. Alphonso Maria de Liguori* [*sic*], *Bishop of St. Agatha of the Goths*, 5 vols (London, 1848–9), 4, pp. 24–42.

packed with rival bands of banditti; and while the records are replete with individual brands plucked from the burning—the most notable being the well-named robber-chief Lupo d'Isolaccio—the repentances have a community flavour, as a great dam of collective hate suddenly burst in a torrent of general tears and love.

There are, no doubt, parallels to this in the history of Methodism: the difference was that the tensions set up by the call to an other-worldly Catholicism were essentially *inside* the wider religious sytem, and not, as for Methodists, a minority call to a new reality outside it. Though many Evangelical preachers were also Anglican pastors, and though the Methodist societies took half a century to drift from the Church of England and did not complete the parting until after Wesley's death, the hardest conflict experienced by many a Catholic missioner was, like that of St Alphonsus Liguori with his ambitious father, a battle *within* the assumptions of Catholicism over the right of a promising son to abandon marriage and a prosperous secular career for holy poverty and the celibate priesthood. Again, the leaders of the missionary movements tended to be of well-to-do or even aristocratic parentage: St Leonard was educated by a wealthy uncle, St Paul of the Cross was the son of an impoverished nobleman, St Alphonsus's father was Captain-General of the King's Neapolitan Galleys, and even rulers respected the charismata of the holy man: Cosimo III dei' Medici, Grand Duke of Tuscany, was as anxious to solicit the advice of St Leonard as any of his subjects, and three duchesses escorted the Saint's body to its tomb.

This is not to suggest that the missioners' message always found a warmer hearing than the one given to the Countess of Huntingdon. The missioner to a town or parish could be received by its principal inhabitants, and with a public procession and the ringing of bells; but he did not win automatic favour by persuading a gentleman's mistress to enter a convent, or by preaching against dances and balls: St Leonard's life records the many opponents of his missions among those who, from their station in life, 'ought to have promoted' them. There was sometimes an aristocratic reserve to overcome—as among 'the nobles of Pistoja (Pistoia), who previously had seemed ashamed of any external demonstration of religion', but came to the devotions of the mission 'with great fervour and recollection, even kissing the ground'.[14] It may have been that the advent of Jansenist and Enlightenment ideas in the second half of the eighteenth century opened a greater gulf between élitist and popular Catholicism,

---

[14] Giuseppi Maria, p. 43.

and that the very fervour of feeling whipped up by the missioners produced an educated and fastidious reaction against it. In Spain, the preachers won great popularity with the poor by inveighing against the vices of the mercantile rich, but they thereby aroused the hostility of commercially minded and influential Enlightenment reformers, who did not scruple to use the Inquisition against them.[15] But before the Josephist 'reforms' of the Grand Duke Leopold in Tuscany, after 1780, there does not seem in Italy at least to have been anything like the degree of rationalist revulsion from vulgar or heart religion experienced by Methodists in England.

Indeed, the leaders of the missionary movement were, for all their populism, no more like Macaulay's 'ignorant enthusiast' than was John Wesley himself. St Leonard of Port-Maurice had been a professor of theology, while the more than a hundred books published by Liguori have raised him to the hagiographical rank of Doctor and fashioned the moral and doctrinal teaching of the modern Roman Church. Of course, much of their activity was one of vulgarization, of preaching and devotions in the vernacular: St Alphonsus wrote the most popular of Italian hymns, 'Tu scendi dalle stelle', and his converts included the goat-herders and shepherds of the Abruzzi and urban proletarians like the son of a Neapolitan tailor, St Gerard Majella, whose short life of ecstacies, austerities, and miracles have made him 'the most famous wonder-worker of the 18th century'.[16] Obviously, Liguori's social position was sometimes indispensable to his influence, as when his prayer groups among the Neapolitan beggar-*lazzaroni* were raided by policemen who scented sedition. But the Roman Church did not hesitate to raise conspicuous examples of proletarian sanctity to its altars, and there is an obvious contrast with the lack of such recognition in the Church of England.

That is, however, a point of contact between Methodism and Catholicism—that in both, the poor had the Gospel preached to them; and there was also some overlap in the content of the Gospel preached, however different its form. In one sense, that content was mere Christianity. No Methodist could have outdone the Catholic missioners' preaching of repentance; the need for faith; heaven, hell, death, and judgement, the wickedness of Satan and the enormity of sin. St Leonard was famous for his account of the last moments of the dying sinner; Alphonsus, a gifted artist, painted vermin-ridden corpses or would regale a mission by torch-

---

[15] Noel, p. 886.
[16] D. H. Farmer, *The Oxford Dictionary of Saints* (Oxford, 1987), p. 278.

light with a lively picture of the damned. Again, Wesley would no doubt have had some sympathy with the missioners' accounts of the terrible fates of those who resisted their message, some of them persons of fashion: sudden death by thunderbolt or globes of fire, leaving strangely black and blasted corpses behind them. The catalogue of St Alphonsus's victims opens with the lady who accused him of immorality and had her tongue eaten by worms.

There were other inducements to conversion which were more specifically Catholic. In eighteenth-century England, ferocious whippings were imposed on children and convicts and servicemen. Following the medieval flagellant tradition, the missioner would publicly beat himself to call sinners to repent, and, indeed, St Leonard of Port-Maurice secured some of his most dramatic reconciliations of former enemies by lying on his own back with a flail until the contending parties fell on one another's necks, weeping for very shame. For all the colour and drama of the Evangelical Revival, this was not a device to which Protestants could have recourse, but like the public penitential procession which was part of the Catholic mission, led by priests with ropes around their necks, sometimes carrying crosses and crowned with thorns, the flagellant recalled the Scourging at the Pillar, and thereby involved both spectator and participant in the devotional sense which was at the heart of the mission, of repentance and salvation by identification with the suffering and Passion of the Lord. The most memorable of images of St Paul of the Cross in one of his great public assemblies is of his taking the discipline and then dragging his rheumatic body (though he lived to be eighty, as Liguori to over ninety) to the foot of the great mission cross where he intoned the Good Friday sequence *Ecce lignum crucis*. 'He seemed', says his biographer, 'to be dying and laying his soul in the Saviour's wounds'.[17]

The Stations of the Cross, a form of meditation and public prayer on scenes from the Via Crucis between Pilate's house and Calvary, is of late medieval Franciscan origin, and derives from the Franciscan-conducted pilgrimages in Jerusalem, but it was in the eighteenth century that St Leonard established the definitive number of Stations at fourteen, and greatly popularized their extension in non-Franciscan parish churches, introducing them himself in more than five hundred places. In 1749, he set up the most notable of these with the Pope's blessing in the battered Colosseum, which was consecrated in 1756 by the greatest of eighteenth-century

---

[17] H. Daniel-Rops, *The Church in the Eighteenth Century*, trans. J. Warrington (London, 1964), p. 319.

pontiffs, Benedict XIV, as a church and memorial to the Christian martyrs who had suffered there. Public crosses were erected for missions and sometimes left as a memorial to them, and it was the Franciscan influence which shaped the spiritual teaching of St Paul of the Cross as founder of the Passionist Order, and of the Congregation of the Most Holy Redeemer of St Alphonsus. It is true, of course, that their conception of Passion devotion was influenced by their own fierce asceticism, and that it was popularized with other cults unacceptable to Protestants, the adoration of the Blessed Sacrament and devotion to the Sacred Heart of Jesus, and to the Virgin Mary. Again, Wesley would no doubt have been repelled by the role assigned by Liguori to Mary in the economy of salvation, and by his attempts to liberalize the conditions for forgiveness of sin. Yet to some degree these forms of devotion were interfused with that of the Passion. The Confraternity which led the Colosseum devotions was called the 'lovers of Jesus and Mary'. It was a vision of Our Lady which revealed to Paul Daneo the emblem of the Passionist Order, a white heart with the cross above it, and the words JESU PASSIO with the three nails of Calvary. The heart of Jesus embodied the suffering compassion of the Lord and his mercy for sinners; and reverence towards it was bound up with that reverence for his wounds and precious blood through which mankind's salvation had been won. The Anglican *Hymns Ancient and Modern* and *English Hymnal* have given currency among Protestants in this country to only one eighteenth-century Italian hymn, 'Viva! Viva! Gesù', translated into English by one of the ex-Evangelical Cardinal Newman's Oratorians,[18] and its verses may stand for what the missioners taught:

> Glory be to Jesus,
> Who, in bitter pains,
> Poured for me the life-blood
> From his sacred veins.

> Grace and life eternal
> In that Blood I find;
> Blest be his compassion,
> Infinitely kind.

[18] By Edward Caswall. There is another version by another (ex-Evangelical) Oratorian, Frederick Faber. See *The Westminster Hymnal*. There is also an enchanting story of the influence of the hymn in an English country parish in Frederick Brittain's 'Mr. Sweetie', in *Mostly Mymms: Tales and Sketches of South Mymms and Elsewhere* (Cambridge, 1953), pp. 19–24. The Vicar of the village, known as the Patriarch, was an Anglo-Catholic of the evangelical type, who once confounded the Kensitite demonstrators against his incense-bearing annual village procession by borrowing some of General Bramwell Booth's Salvation Army bandsmen.

> Blest through endless ages
> Be the precious stream,
> Which from endless torment
> Doth the world redeem.
>
> Abel's blood for vengeance
> Pleaded to the skies;
> But the Blood of Jesus
> For our pardon cries.
>
> Oft as it is sprinkled
> On our guilty hearts,
> Satan in confusion
> Terror-struck departs.
>
> Oft as earth exulting
> Wafts its praise on high,
> Hell with terror trembles,
> Heaven is filled with joy.
>
> Lift ye then your voices;
> Swell the mighty flood;
> Louder still and louder
> Praise the precious Blood.

Could Wesley have said more? He would no doubt have reprobated St Leonard's penitential cross with its five sharp points pressed against his heart; but he would have rejoiced in St Leonard's first proclamation in one of his early missions, that like a greater before him, he 'only intended to preach Jesus Christ and Him crucified'.[19]

In one of his most famous passages in *A Tale of Two Cities*, Dickens wrote of the eighteenth century that 'it was the epoch of belief, it was the epoch of incredulity ... we were all going direct to Heaven, we were all going direct the other way'. As Professor Ward's *opera omnia*, still incomplete, remind us, the Age of Reason was also an Age of Faith. The Catholic missions can be understood on various levels: as the last attempt by the Counter-Reformation to church and Christianize the inadequately churched and Christianized populations of Catholic Europe; as a movement of resistance to modern instrumental commercial values; and increasingly, towards the end of the century, as a reaction against the onset of 'enlightened' opposition to Christianity from the devotees of

---

[19] Giuseppi Maria, p. 41.

Deism or atheism. There is, however, considerable evidence that just as Evangelical Christianity revivified the English and American Protestant Churches, so the ecclesiastical structures of the Catholic *ancien régime*, shaken by the French Revolution, survived in part because the Church had retained a place in the hearts of multitudes touched by the popular preachers.[20] French scholars have argued that levels of religious practice in modern France have tended to remain high where the mission preachers before 1789 were successful; and that the eclipse of popular religious practice has occurred wherever revivalism failed. The phenomenon may require a more complicated explanation, but illustrates the fact which Reg. Ward has taught us, that the religious movements of the eighteenth century continue to influence our own.

University of Durham

[20] F. Boulard, *An Introduction to Religious Sociology. Pioneer Work in France* (London, 1960).

JOHANN GOTTFRIED HERDER:
THE LUTHERAN CLERGYMAN*

by NICHOLAS HOPE

TO ask the questions how we remember familiar historical figures
and how they would like to have been remembered befits, perhaps,
a collection of essays like this one. For us today, Herder is important
as one of the leading literary figures of the German *Sturm und Drang*. He
made seminal contributions as a philologist and linguistic ethnographer,
as an aesthete and critic. We think of him, too, as a Christian philosopher
who questioned, like his dear friend, Hamann, the sceptical empiricism of
Hume, and, more especially, their own teacher, Kant, who had brought
Hume to their notice. Historians see Herder as the father of the idea of
history as it is experienced and interpreted by each generation, and as the
progenitor of our modern romantic and nationalist movements.

In other words, we prefer to remember Herder for a secular evangelism
which has very little to do with what Herder considered to be his vocation
in life.

Herder officiated as a Lutheran clergyman for thirty-seven years: after
ordination in 1767, at Riga, the capital of Livonia; at Bückeburg, the
capital of the Duchy of Schaumburg-Lippe, and finally, until his death in
1803, at Weimar, the seat of the Grand Dukes of Saxe-Weimar-Eisenach.
There is no general historical account of this activity. Even Herder's
collected writings, published in the nineteenth century in several dozen
volumes: those published shortly after his death by Herder's family, and
edited by Johann Georg Müller, as well as those edited at the end of the
century by Bernhard Suphan, include only a handful of volumes which
record Herder's work as a clergyman and his views about the Christian
faith and tradition.[1] This omission is really as much a reflection of the

---

* This essay's text was finished in early May 1989, fortuitously 200 years to the day Herder was
in Rome. He might smile at that. I thank Dr Horst v. Chmielewski, chief librarian of the *J. G.
Herder Institut*, Marburg/Lahn, and his fellow librarians for being so attentive in providing rare
material on Germany east of Hamburg, the Baltic States, and, of course, Herder in recent
years.
[1] J. G. Herder, *Sämmtliche Werke*, ed. J. G. Müller *et al.*, 2nd edn. (Stuttgart and Tübingen, 1827–
30), 60 vols. J. G. Herder, *Sämmtliche Werke*, ed. B. Suphan *et al.* (Berlin, 1877–1913), 33 vols. I
have used Suphan's critical edition mainly [hereafter *Werke*] unless otherwise stated. Herder's
correspondence, which contains much on his work as a clergyman, is now collected in the
magnificent J. G. Herder, *Briefe. Gesamtausgabe 1763–1803*, ed. K. H. Hahn (Weimar,

seriousness with which Herder took his parish duties as it is of subsequent historical interest. There was little time to keep a record in a century like the eighteenth, where a German prince's Lutheran official religion provided the coping to the social order. Herder knew the limits which his office imposed on him in this century where the Protestant clergy tended to be undervalued, overworked, and as Herder's wife, Caroline, frequently complained, underpaid. She was left to manage his daily finances! But, in a more profound sense, given the Lutheran view he held of his vocation, Herder did not see the value of writing daily details. The spoken word offered as prayer and comfort; as a sermon; in the instruction of children in Christian doctrine; or as a hymn, was what mattered. The clergyman's office meant to Herder the study and everyday practice of his Christian faith in the sense of Luther's Preface to the Wittenberg edition of his writings of 1539.[2] He had, therefore, little time for disputatious Lutheran theology taught in the German university lecture theatre; nor could he be bothered to systematize his theological thoughts, for he believed that the work of Jesus and his disciples, as well as that of his heroes, Luther and Melanchthon, had always been with the living congregation. It is for this reason that Herder eulogized Zinzendorf, one of the contemporaries he most admired. He contrasted the names of the many places where the Brethren had cheerfully established themselves in the world with Zinzendorf's many official titles of nobility expressive of the age in which both men lived, but which both abjured. In doing so, Herder argued, Zinzendorf had significantly broken down the exclusivism and pedantry associated with Lutheran orthodoxy and introspective Pietism in German-speaking lands. Calmness, forbearance, a childlike giving and happy disposition, the will to break with convention and

---

1977–84), 8 vols. Useful commentary thereon: E. Pältz, 'Zur Edition der Briefe J. G. Herder's', *Theologische Literaturzeitung*, 106 (1981), pp. 546–51. The only book to tackle 'Herder: the Clergyman' is the charming collection of essays and documents relating to Herder in office at Weimar: E. Schmidt, ed., *Herder im geistlichen Amt* (Leipzig, 1956), R. Haym, *Herder nach seinem Leben und seinen Werken* (Berlin, 1880–5), 2 vols, is still the best biography of this subject. A challenging, though overstated, case is made by E. Adler, 'Herders Kampf wider den geistlichen Despotismus', *Deutsche Zeitschrift für Philosophie*, 8 (1960), pp. 820–37.

2 *D. Martin Luthers Werke*, ed. J. C. F. Knaake (Weimar, 1883 ff.), 50, pp. 657–61. Herder returned to this Preface repeatedly at Bückeburg and Weimar: see nn. 35 and 62 below. Herder knew Luther as few other clergy in eighteenth-century Germany. He possessed first editions, and the available scholarly texts like J. G. Walch's 24-vol. Halle edn. of 1740–53. See Suphan's comments in *Werke*, 18, p. 543, *passim*; H. Bluhm, 'Herders Stellung zu Luther', *Publications of the Modern Language Association of America*, 64 (1949), pp. 158–82, and H. Bornkamm, *Luther im Spiegel der deutschen Geistesgeschichte* (Heidelberg, 1953), pp. 20–2, 123–33.

decorum, humility, and a sense of light and humour, which Zinzendorf tried to give to German and European Protestantism, were in Herder's opinion infinitely more valuable than more arid volumes of theological exegesis, which, in trying to defend the one true Lutheran faith, served to obscure rather than illuminate the Bible's message.[3]

The influence of Herder's home environment and landscape; what he constantly referred to in his writings as genetic and climatic impressions experienced in childhood acting on temperament, behaviour, and speech, coloured his religious opinions. Caprice, 'the long chapter of chances (which) the events of this world lay open to us', to use Sterne's words in *Tristram Shandy*—Herder's *vade mecum* whilst a theological student at Königsberg and as a curate at Riga—played a major part too in Herder's decision to take Orders.[4] It was like the simple throw of a dice as he wrote on the opening page of his travel diary of 1769:

> Ein großer Theil unsrer Lebensbegebenheiten hängt würklich vom Wurf von Zufällen ab. So kam ich nach Riga, so in mein geistliches Amt und so ward ich deßelben los: so ging ich auf Reisen.

Here Herder was expressing a thought akin to Zinzendorf, who also saw his religious vocation as being shaped as much by a gamble as divine design.[5] But blind chance was close, too, to Linné's theodicy in his *Nemesis Divina*, which Herder had become aware of while at Riga. Beneath the surface confusion of the world there dwells a just God. The numinous in the natural world order demands awe, reverence, and faith in divine providence.[6] Herder put Linné's perception poetically in his essay *Der*

---

[3] *Adrastea* (Leipzig, 1802), 4 = *Werke*, 24, pp. 32–7. Herder praised Zinzendorf's contribution to the congregational hymn. See n. 67 below. Also 'Ein Chor Singender ist gleichsam schon eine Gesellschaft Brüder: das Herz wird geöffnet', in *Lieder der Liebe* (1778) = *Werke*, 8, pp. 404–5). Some of Zinzendorf's more sanguinary hymns Herder rejected for aesthetic reasons. Herder disliked Halle and Herrnhut's tendency to split up in *ecclesiolae*. Wesley and Methodism: *Adrastea*, 4, *Werke*, 24, pp. 149–62.

[4] W. Dobbek, *Johann Gottfried Herders Jugendzeit in Mohrungen und Königsberg 1744–1764* (Würzburg, 1961), pp. 3, 198; Sterne, *ibid.*, p. 191; K. Stavenhagen, *Herder in Riga* (Riga, 1925), p. 10.

[5] J. G. Herder, *Journal meiner Reise im Jahr 1769* = *Historisch-Kritische Ausgabe*, ed. K. Mommsen *et al.* (Frankfurt, 1983), p. 7. 'Du hast einen doppelten Beruf: Du bist ein Priester des lebendigen Gottes. Du bist aber auch ein Pilgrim auf dieser Welt', in *Der freywilligen Nachlese. Bey den bisherigen Gelehrten und erbaulichen Monaths-Schriften vi. Sammlung* (Frankfurt and Leipzig, 1723), pp. 718–36: cited by C. Schmolders, *Die Kunst des Gesprächs* (Munich, 1979), p. 192.

[6] C. Linné, *Nemesis Divina*, ed. K. Hagberg (Stockholm, 1960), p. 7. On these notes, written c.1750–70, and subsequent editions, S. Lindroth, *Svensk lärdomshistoria* (Stockholm, 1978), 3, pp. 236–8. Linné's theodicy and religious views, which had roots, like Herder's, in Bible reading, Arnd, and Scriver, see W. Malmeström, *Carl von Linnés religiösa åskådning* (Uppsala and Stockholm, 1926). Nemesis, *ibid.*, pp. 170–86; U. Cillien, *Johann Gottfried Herder Christlicher*

Redner Gottes (c.1765), when he wrote of God's presence as feeling a drop of that awe which a newborn angel might feel standing before God; of the devotional mood as simply a tone from one's soul, or the soft breath of an evening breeze on a calm lake.[7] He thus took to heart the lines from Ovid's *Ars Amatoria* which Linné had placed above the entrance to his country home, *Innocue vivite: numen adest.*[8] Herder's temperament was tender hearted, with a strong inclination towards a manic-depressive state, which dwelt not only on the Gothic and bizarre, but also sought after religious certainty in a world where Newtonian physics and the French *philosophes* had still failed to account for why man should resort to myth and allegory.[9]

A heartfelt, trusting, Christocentric faith, based on readings from Arnd's *Vier Bücher vom Wahren Christentum* and Luther's Bible; singing Luther's hymns to the accompaniment of the lute—Hamann, a very accomplished lutanist, envied Herder for his ability to retain the words and melodies of most hymns in the hymnal—at family prayers in the single living-room of the little artisan's house beside the medieval parish church of St Peter and St Paul in Mohrungen, where Herder's father was verger and cantor, filled Herder's need of religious certainty and shaped his understanding of the congregation as one which placed liturgical formality, being 'seen' in church, and matters of rank, second to an understanding of Christian doctrine and prayer made alive by reading

---

Humanismus (Ratingen, 1972), pp. 136–41, in her discussion of Herder and Nemesis misses his connection with Linné. Herder's appreciation of Linné's *Nemesis* in *Zerstreute Blätter*. 2. *Sammlung* (Gotha, 1786) = *Werke*, 15, pp. 330–1. Herder was informed by the chemist, and bookkeeper to the Riga orphanage, Jakob Benjamin Fischer (1731–93), a pupil of Linné at Uppsala. He wrote *Versuch einer Naturgeschichte von Liefland* (Leipzig, 1778), and with August Wilhelm Hupel (1737–1819), vicar of Livonia's largest parish, Oberpahlen (Põltsamaa), in the 1760s, and chief pastor at Reval (Tallinn) after 1773, supplied Estonian and Latvian folk-song texts to Herder. Fischer: J. F. v. Recke and K. E. Napiersky, eds, *Allgemeines Schriftsteller- und Gelehrten-Lexikon der Provinzen Livland, Esthland und Kurland* (Mitau, 1827–32), I, pp. 568–9 [hereafter Recke-Napiersky]. See also, H. Schaudinn, *Deutsche Bildungsarbeit am lettischen Volkstum des 18. Jahrhunderts* (Munich, 1937), pp. 134–5.

[7] *Werke*, 32, p. 7.

[8] The full quotation is: 'Innocue vivite; numen adest; / Reddite depositum; pietas sua foedera servet; / Fraus absit; vacuas caedis habete manus': Ovid, *Ars Amatoria*, bk. i, lines 640–2. On the numinous, and *Talio*, see Malmeström, *Linné*, pp. 162–7, 175, 177, 191–3.

[9] A useful discussion of Herder on awe (*Schauder*) is by Mommsen in *Journal meiner Reise*, pp. 244–57. Herder was also influenced by Edmund Burke's, *A Philosophical Inquiry into the Sublime and Beautiful* (1756), German edn. (Riga, 1773). Caroline wrote in her Memoirs of the hidden world of spirits as being always close to Herder's imagination: *Werke*, ed. Müller, 22, pp. 190–3.

Luther's Bible and singing his robust vernacular hymns.[10] The Bible was Herder's childhood book. Job, the Psalms, Ecclesiastes, Isaiah, and the Gospels were listed as favourites, since they coupled in Herder's, as in Linné's, imagination, the natural world of animals, flowers, and fields with the numinous and prophetic.[11] Above all else, his mother's simple stoical belief in Christ our Saviour put the 'touching and edifying' story of Jesus for children at the centre of his work as a preacher, catechist, and schoolmaster.[12] His mother's piety gave Herder the capacity to listen, which Goethe singled out as one of Herder's most likeable traits. In terms of the unsettled religious climate of Lutheran East Prussia between the end of the Great Northern War and the Seven Years' War, Herder's religious upbringing was, however, typical of many artisan Lutheran households. They warmed to the mission and cheap religious devotional literature provided by Halle and a supportive city clergy at Königsberg. Kant, who came from a similar home, summed up this warm neighbourly piety in a way which revealed as much about himself as it did his roots:

> Man sage dem Pietismus nach, was man will. Genug! Die Leute, denen er ein Ernst war, zeichneten sich auf eine ehrwürdige Weise aus. Sie besaßen das Höchste, was der Mensch besitzen kann, jene Ruhe, jene Heiterkeit, jenen inneren Frieden, der durch keine Leidenschaft beunruhigt wurde. Keine Not, keine Verfolgung setzte sie in Mißmut, keine Streitigkeit war vermögend, sie zum Zorn und zur Feindschaft zu reizen.[13]

The presence, also, of a sizeable minority of Calvinists in the East Prussian towns and countryside, who had settled under the benevolent eye of the Hohenzollerns in the seventeenth and early eighteenth centuries as a

[10] Herder's father noted important family occasions on the fly-leaf of his copy of Arnd; E. Gronau, 'Herders religiöse Jugendentwicklung', *Zeitschrift für systematische Theologie*, 8 (1931), pp. 312–13; Dobbek, *Herders Jugendzeit*, p. 23. Hamann was a favourite pupil of the musician and virtuoso lutanist Johann Reichardt (1720–80).

[11] 'Nur der Bibel zu gut ward ich Theolog, und ich erinnere mich meiner Kindheitsjahre, in denen ich Hiob, den Prediger, Jesias und die Evangelien las, wie ich kein Buch sonst auf der Welt gelesen habe und lesen werde. Mein ganzes Leben entwickelt mir nun, was mir meine Kindheit sagte'. Herder to Friedrich Haller, Weimar, 3 Jan. 1783, *Briefe*, 4, no. 248. In common with Linné, Herder retained his childhood need to be out in nature all his life. Saturday summer afternoons in the meadows outside Mohrungen gathering speedwell and cowslips to make herbal tea was one of his more enjoyable experiences as a schoolboy. Dobbek, *Herder's Jugendzeit*, p. 30.

[12] Gronau, *Jugendentwicklung*, p. 313. 'Die Lebensgeschichte Jesu, für Kinder so rührend und erbaulich', *Journal meiner Reise*, p. 43.

[13] Karl Vorländer, *Immanuel Kants Leben*, 2nd edn. (Leipzig, 1921), p. 4.

result of trade with the seaports or religious persecution, acted as a leaven in the Established Church, especially when the main aristocratic families like the Dohnas, Waldburgs, Dönhoffs, Lehndorffs, Finckensteins, Podewils, and Kreytzens embraced this faith.[14] In Livonia, too, during the 1760s, when Herder was at Riga, the exclusive Lutheran church established by seventeenth-century Swedish ecclesiastical law was forced to be more tolerant; first by German ordinands trained at Halle, and by Buddeus at Jena, who had migrated to Livonia to fill over fifty per cent of the vacant benefices left by the Great Northern War and the contemporaneous plague, and then by the Moravian Brethren after Zinzendorf's visit to Riga and Reval (Tallinn) in 1736. Despite the Conventicle Act of 1743, it was the Brethren who built the first bridges between German barons, the German Lutheran clergy, and their subject Estonians and Latvians. They also shaped, after being allowed to settle again in 1764 as part of Czarina Catherine's colonization policy, the new historical interest in Estonian and Latvian culture shown by Herder and his fellow clergy.[15] Herder's superior, Riga's chief pastor, Immanuel Justus von Essen (1719–80), himself a pupil of Buddeus, went further, too, by actively fostering good relations between Riga's Lutheran and Orthodox clergy, and calling for more tolerance to be shown to Riga's small Reformed congregation.[16]

---

[14] E. Machholz, *Materialien zur Geschichte der Reformierten in Altpreußen und im Ermlande* (Lötzen, 1912), pp. 6–7. Mohrungen in Herder's day had a Reformed congregation under the supervision of the Reformed pastor of Reichertswalde. Count Dohna was their patron, *ibid.*, pp. 92–3.

[15] J. Eckardt, *Livland im achtzehnten Jahrhundert* (Leipzig, 1876), pp. 243–4, 434–5. The connection with Halle and Jena is discussed by A. F. Stolzenburg, *Die Theologie des Jo.Franc.Buddeus und des Chr.Matth.Pfaff* (Berlin, 1927), repr. (Aalen, 1979), p. 386. He uses T. Harnack, *Die lutherische Kirche Livlands und die herrnhutische Brüdergemeinde* (Erlangen, 1860), pp. 22, 59. For the new interest in the Estonians and Latvians shown by these German pastors, Schaudinn, *Deutsche Bildungsarbeit*, pp. 112–37. Herder was simply one of the many North German and Saxon clergy who migrated East to Livonia and Estonia after 1721 for the opportunities and better standard of living they offered. See E. Seraphim, *Ostpreußisch-baltischen Kulturbeziehungen im Zeitalter der Aufklärung*, in E. and A. Seraphim, ed., *Aus vier Jahrhunderten. Gesammelte Aufsätze zur baltischen Geschichte* (Reval, 1913), pp. 259–98. Berlin, for Herder, was a remote place on the map before 1769. Dobbek, *Herders Jugendzeit*, p. 189.

[16] Von Essen: Recke-Napiersky, 1, pp. 527–9. He had also tried to make the Swedish service-book more intelligible for Riga's parishioners: see *Handbuch für die Kirchen der Stadt Riga, zum bequemeren Gebrauch etc* (Riga, 1760). Swedish ecclesiastical law was observed until 1832 in Estonia and Livonia. The service-book (*Handbuch, Kirchenagende oder Liturgie*) was translated into German by Superintendent-General Gabriel Skragge in 1708; also into Latvian at Riga, and Estonian at Reval. It remained in use until 1805. In practice, Swedish liturgical uniformity was less than uniform in Herder's day. Only in the cities of Riga and Reval was it observed more assiduously. See, A. W. Hupel, *Topographische Nachrichten von Lief- und Ehstland* (Riga, 1777), 2, pp. 91–2. Relations with Riga's orthodox clergy: Eckardt, *Livland,*

But Herder also experienced the liturgically conservative Reformation Church Order of Königsberg (1568), based as it was on Duke Henry's of Saxony, and the even more conservative ecclesiastical law of Sweden (1686) with its service-book (1693) in use at Riga.[17] These prescribed a liturgy which remained close to the Ordinary and Proper of the Latin Mass and was still fairly rich in liturgical colour. These cities maintained this tradition because they alone possessed the means to fund the 'Latin' grammar schools whose choirs upheld this liturgical tradition. Congregational hymn-singing, whether in church as an integral part of the order of service, or at home to the lute's accompaniment, was a special East Prussian and Livonian tradition in educated circles long before Pietism emphasized the congregational hymn at the expense of the sung liturgy. This liturgical conservatism coupled with worship in a very large number of medieval churches in East Prussia and Livonia; cruciform vaulting and stained glass continued to shape church architecture in East Prussia for a major part of the eighteenth century; served to enhance Herder's curious feeling of simultaneous awe and elevation in church, and his acute sense that sacred music, liturgical tradition, and custom, if they needed reform because of a growing lack of understanding of Latin and the surviving rites of the medieval liturgy, had to be carried out with as little inconvenience as possible to the accepted order of service in public worship.[18] Herder in this sense was an establishment man. All the more so in provinces like East Prussia and Livonia, which had been united as a single church province under the Teutonic knights, and where Catholic survivals like the red-letter days in the almanacs and combined hymnals and prayer-books were still assiduously observed in Herder's day. On the other hand, the overdone pomp and circumstance, the piddling observance of protocol, and a formalized official ritual for the very large

---

pp. 352–4. Suphan also refers to this, and Bishop Platon of Pleskau and Narva's visit to Riga in 1764, *Werke*, 32, pp. 202, 536–7.

[17] The liturgy included in the edition of Königsberg's Church order of 1568 was re-issued separately almost unchanged in 1741, 1780, and 1789. Bishop Ludwig Borowski, Kant's biographer, when he began his cautious liturgical reform in 1789, used the moderate words of the 1568 preface as his guide.

[18] A. Wiesenhütter, *Protestantischer Kirchenbau des deutschen Ostens in Geschichte und Gegenwart* (Leipzig, 1936), p. 41. Herder's reference to local environment as also influencing his decision to take orders: 'Eindruck von Kirch und Altar, Kanzel und geistlicher Beredsamkeit, Amtsverrichtung und geistlicher Ehrerbeitung ... Mein Leben ist ein Gang durch Gotische Wölbungen', *Journal meiner Reise*, pp. 124–5. Or the influence of medieval church architecture: 'Gothisches, dunkles, abentheuerliches Gebäude' etc., 'Sabbath und Sonntagsfeier' = *Werke*, 6, p. 93. W. Dobbek, *Herders Jugendzeit*, pp. 24–5.

number of Sunday and weekday services in the city churches, to which were added the major Christian festivals—the full three days were observed at Riga into the 1770s—and the many saints' days, by the city fathers of Königsberg and Riga, turned Herder into a lifelong critic of churchmanship as mere social convention, and the snobbery associated with social precedence and patronage.[19] The statutory aspect of the Hohenzollern *Rétablissement* confirmed his worst suspicions that Lutheranism was being used merely to police the maintenance of good political behaviour, especially when he heard Hamann pour out his heart after a day's work as a royal tax-inspector about his experience of Prussian political arithmetic practising the parole he called *Glaube–Exerciere–Zahle*.[20]

If Herder's years as a theology student at Königsberg university between 1762 and 1764, and as a curate at Riga until 1769, had brought him into contact with an open-minded seaport culture in cities which were experiencing an economic and cultural upswing, and whose patriciates were eagerly reading the new literature of the British and French Enlightenment, they reinforced, on the other hand, these early doubts Herder was beginning to have about the relationship of Church and State in Lutheran Germany at a time when scepticism in religious matters was becoming fashionable. Herder certainly preferred to listen to Kant on ethics, the cosmos, and human geography rather than another dull lecture of exegesis on the New Testament. He also enjoyed discussing with Hamann over a clay pipefull the latest picaresque book by Sterne (Hamann played 'Uncle Toby' to Herder's 'Yorick'), Richardson, or Swift, and he spent time browsing over the catalogues of the European Enlighten-

---

[19] Observance of the Christian festivals at Riga, Hupel, *Topographie*, 2, p. 83: 'In den rigischen Stadtkirchen wird täglich, aber des Morgens zu früh, gepredigt, wenige, oft nur 6 Zuhörer finden sich ein, die meisten schlafen noch, oder sind des Sommers schon an ihre Geschäfte gegangen. . . . Ueberhaupt ist der öffentliche Gottesdienst in den rigischen Stadtkirchen mit viel alten Zeremonien, und äussern dem Geist des Evangeliums nicht ganz angemessenen Gepränge überladen', *ibid.*, 2, p. 91. Surplices and chasubles were worn over a black cassock with large ruff, *ibid.* There were six Lutheran churches, including the cathedral, within the city walls.

[20] 'Ist aber je ein Jahrhundert reich an Verordnungen, die in Kirchensachen ergangen, gewesen, so ist es das gegenwärtige', was the way the senior Königsberg clergyman D. H. Arnoldt summed up the eighteenth century in his *Kurzgefaßte Kirchengeschichte des Königreichs Preußen* (1769): quoted by W. Hubatsch, *Geschichte der evangelischen Kirche Ostpreussens* (Göttingen, 1968), 1, p. 206. Frederick the Great's reign in East Prussia amounted to a string of emergency laws for church and school, H. Notbohm, *Das evangelische Kirchen- und Schulwesen in Ostpreussen während der Regierung Friedrichs des Grossen* (Heidelberg, 1959), p. 187. Hamann on political arithmetic: J. Nadler, *Johann Georg Hamann 1730–1788. Der Zeuge des Corpus Mysticum* (Salzburg, 1949), p. 380.

ment in the bookshops of Kanter in Königsberg and Hartknoch in Riga. This boosted Herder's sense of the need to break with his provincial frame of mind, and to separate the ethical aspect of religion from external signs embodied in religious rites.[21] On the other hand, Herder quickly realized, certainly in Hamann's Rabelaisian but nevertheless pious household, where Bible reading and family prayers were *de rigueur*, that if the Incarnation is the central Christian fact; if Christianity is a 'taste for signs'; if man is not mind alone and God cannot be managed by reason alone; if popular religious expression has to be respected and accounted for; if religious revelation is necessary for an understanding of the history of creation, an understanding of the vernacular canon of Scripture is fundamental, and has to be defended whatever the cost against theologians who approved of Deism and Natural Religion.[22] On this reading, Herder and Hamann, who fortified each other's religious opinions, since Hamann was one of the very few Herder felt he could open out his heart to on religious matters, were not so much irrationalists or exponents of a 'Counter-Enlightenment' as is sometimes argued, but reasonable, enlightened Lutheran churchmen, who did not rate human reason highly in a world, if religion was left out, which was governed largely by chance; by suspect patronage, which overrode, if it possibly could, humane ideals like the social contract; by human error, and exploitation.[23] You could not knock away the crutches provided by an Established Reformation Church

---

[21] Herder's notes on Kant's lectures are edited by: H. D. Irmscher, 'Immanuel Kant. Aus den Vorlesungen der Jahre 1762 bis 1764. Auf Grund der Nachschriften Johann Gottfried Herders', *Kantstudien, Ergänzungsheft*, 88 (1964). What Herder learnt from Kant is discussed by A. Gulyga, *Immanuel Kant* (Frankfurt am Main, 1981), pp. 68–72. Herder later wrote of Kant in the prime of life as having the 'fröhliche Munterkeit eines Junglings', which he thought would accompany him into old age, *Werke*, 18, p. 324. W. Dobbek, *Herders Jugendzeit*, p. 108. Also *ibid.*, pp. 99–116 for Kant's influence. Herder used the observatory on top of the Fridericianum where he lived and taught part-time. He devoured new travel literature like Thomas Shaw's, *Travels & Observations relating to several parts of Barberry & the Levant* (Oxford, 1738). On Sterne, Richardson, and Swift, R. Unger, *Hamann und die Aufklärung* (Jena, 1911), 1, pp. 405–6. 'Shandysieren' was a favourite expression of theirs.

[22] For Hamann's view of the Incarnation, Revelation, and Scripture, T. J. German, *Hamann on Language and Religion* (Oxford, 1981), pp. 57–9, 83, 132, 156. 'Signs', Hamann to Lavater, 17 Jan. 1778, *ibid.*, pp. 173–5. Also R. G. Smith, *J. G. Hamann 1730–1788. A Study in Christian Existence with Selections from his Writings* (London, 1960), p. 69. The Bible as a fundamental book, Unger, *Hamann*, 1, p. 128. Also W. Leibrecht, *Gott und Mensch bei Johann Georg Hamann* (Gütersloh, 1958), pp. 43, 45.

[23] Herder's confidence in Hamann: Gronau, *Jugendentwicklung*, p. 340. Hamann and Herder as representatives of Counter-Enlightenment: I. Berlin, *Vico and Herder. Two Studies in the History of Ideas* (London, 1976), and I. Berlin, 'The Counter Enlightenment', and 'Hume and the Sources of German Anti-Rationalism', reprinted in *Against the Current. Essays in the History of Ideas*, ed. H. Hardy (Oxford, 1981), pp. 1–24, 162–87.

or by popular religious practices, but you could, in Luther's spirit, try and make the laity understand what Christ stood for by a humane and vividly spoken religious language and vigilant pastoral care within the framework of the local established church. Hamann summed up their reasons thus: 'Es ist mir ein großer Trost, daß ich zu einer Kirche gehöre, welche sowenig gute Werke als Orthodoxie zur Gerechtigkeit macht, die vor Gott gilt.'[24] There is always time for following Christ's example. That is why the texts of Paul in prison, II Corinthians 11. 19–33 and 12. 1–11, the courage with which Paul looked into his spiritual face; Nicodemus, John 3. 1–15; Nathanael, John 1. 35–51, and especially Lazarus, John 11. 1–44—'a story, which is told so gently, sorrowfully, and intimately, that the words seem to drip off like the still morning dew on flowers'—were favourites in Herder's homiletic repertoire.[25]

It was Herder's luck, when he left Riga, despite the hope he had of breaking with German provincialism and being another Reformer within a possibly 'national' framework, to remain a clergyman, albeit one in high office, in the compromising world of the little German states. Herder was twenty-six on appointment as Chief Pastor at Bückeburg in 1771; thirty-two, when he became Superintendent-General at Weimar in 1776. The importance of these posts is the way Herder used them to amplify publicly his scepticism about princely and city-father Lutheranism, and the way his more academic colleagues, in particular those of Halle and Berlin, easily accommodated themselves in their Bible scholarship, in their understanding of Christian doctrine, the Christian ministry, and the structure of public worship, to Enlightenment thinking.

Schaumburg-Lippe represented for Herder all that was worst in *Kleinstaaterei*, coupled with the worst excesses of his own Frederician Prussia. It consisted of a mere 130 square miles of rural poverty, made worse in the 1770s by the press-gang and the highest military expenditure of any Westphalian or Hanoverian territory, given Count Wilhelm's wish to create a second Sparta modelled on Potsdam and the military reforms he had carried out in Pombal's Portugal. It was, therefore, a state with a very

---

[24] Nadler, *Hamann*, p. 429. Respect for liturgical order: Leibrecht, *Gott und Mensch*, p. 258, and *ibid.*, pp. 28, 88, 95.

[25] 'Betrübt' (sorrowful) is a reference to Matthew 26. 38. Sermons on Paul in Prison, Nicodemus, Nathanael, and Lazarus: Sexagesima 1775, *Über den Selbstruhm*, *Werke*, 31, pp. 374–96; Trinity Sunday, 21 May 1769?, *ibid.*, 32, pp. 478–501; *Stille Größe Jesu* 1774, 31, pp. 312–38; *Auferweckung des Lazarus* 1774, pp. 339–74. Caroline wrote of Herder's style of preaching: 'Herder predigte im wahren Sinn der Homilie', *Werke*, ed. Müller, 22, p. 27. Herder's sermons are collected in *Werke*, 31 and 32.

impoverished Lutheran church, run by a ruler of the Reformed faith, but indifferent to religious affairs, who, in his zeal for staffing his court with the brightest and youngest representatives of the Enlightenment like Thomas Abbt, Herder's predecessor, forgot all about the generally poor quality of his Lutheran clergy, or resorted to simony, given his constant need for ready cash.[26]

Herder's bitterness fired him to publicize his thoughts about the Bible and Luther for the first time, using as a guide two books which constantly lay open on his desk: Pascal's *Pensées* and his *Lettres écrites à un Provincial*.[27] He received further encouragement from the devout Countess Maria, a woman close in her religion to Zinzendorf, and from Bach's third son, Johann Christoph Friedrich (1732–95), the court *Concert-meister*, who held similar religious views to his own, and was likewise angered by the Count's indifference to Lutheran public worship and sacred music, and the patronizing attitudes he exhibited to his miserably-paid professional staff.[28]

An Prediger. Fünfzehn Provinzialblätter, published in 1774, was Herder's splenetic ungrammatical reply from the heart of provincial Germany to Johann Joachim Spalding's (1714–1804) elegant common-sense defence of the Lutheran clergy against the criticisms made by Pietists and Hume. His *Gedanken über den Werth der Gefühle in dem Christenthum* of 1761, and his *Ueber die Nutzbarkeit des Predigtamtes und deren Beförderung*, probably the most important homiletic work in late eighteenth-century Germany, which he published in 1772 at Berlin as Provost (since 1764) of St Nikolai and the Marienkirche caused him unwittingly to become Herder's

---

[26] Herder began on the wrong footing with the tall and unbending Count Wilhelm when he arrived late at his first audience in a sky-blue silk cape embroidered in gold with white waistcoat and hat. Having to walk and listen in the park of Count Wilhelm's summer residence, *Zum Baum*, to the Count's views on the folly of all human endeavour once a month in the summer after preaching was agony for Herder, Haym, *Herder*, 1, pp. 459–67. Herder poured out his real feelings to Caroline and Hamann, see *Briefe*, 2 and 3. Herder thought the Count a true Don Quixote of the eighteenth century: Herder to Hamann, 20 July 1776, *ibid.*, 3, no. 253. On simony, and ordinand Karl Ludwig Stock: Haym, *Herder*, 1, pp. 725–9, *Briefe*, 3, no. 188 and *passim*.

[27] Caroline records this in her memoirs, *Werke*, ed. Müller, 32, p. 184. See also introduction to *Werke*, 7, p. viii. Herder was fascinated by Pascal's and Giordano Bruno's view of the Universe as an infinite sphere whose centre is everywhere, and whose circumference is nowhere. Herder constantly returned to the asymptote in his religious writing.

[28] Herder's friendship with Countess Maria is discussed by H. Stephan, *Herder in Bückeburg und seine Bedeutung für die Kirchengeschichte* (Tübingen, 1905), pp. 71–3, 112, 143, 190, and Haym, *Herder*, 1, pp. 719–21, 747–8. J. C. F. Bach: C. Wolff *et al.*, eds, *The New Grove Bach Family* (London, 1983), pp. 309–14. Article too by Rolf Benecke in *Die Musik in Geschichte und Gegenwart* [hereafter *MGG*], 1, pp. 956–60.

Escobar.[29] The anger Herder expressed at the values of Frederick the Great's court, especially its growing influence upon the little German courts like Bückeburg, and the way Berlin's senior clergy, like Wilhelm Abraham Teller (1734–1804) in his *Wörterbuch des neuen Testaments zur Erklärung der christlichen Lehre*, published also at Berlin in 1772, propagated a common-sense approach to Christian doctrine and the preaching office, blinded him unfortunately to an older colleague who had only begun late in life to drew similar lessons from a similar pastoral experience.[30] Spalding, who had spent the early part of his career as a country parson in the Swedish part of Pomerania, like Herder, considered it essential to improve the quality of the local clergy by raising their meagre stipends, and by making them aware of their own worth in helping them to understand their pastoral function in church and parish, rather than a continued adherence to the snobberies associated with university theology. It was time they came down to the level of the man or woman in the pew. Spalding was also close to Herder in his rejection of patronage; in this case that dispensed by the Pomeranian *Ritterschaft*, and urban pomp and circumstance of the kind which, since 1764, had required him to preach at

[29] *An Prediger* (Leipzig, 1774) = *Werke*, 7, pp. 225–312. The important previous draft of 1773 is printed *ibid.*, pp. 173–224. 'Ich predige nicht zum Druck, nicht Spaldingsch, rund und klassisch schön', Herder to Lavater, end of 1773, and 5 Nov. 1774, *Werke*, 7, pp. vii–viii. Hamann had also written a similar provincial letter from the heart of East Prussia to Berlin: *Lettre neologique et provinciale sur l'inoculation du bons sens* (1761), Nadler, *Hamann*, pp. 139–42. For the connection with Herder's historical treatment of the Bible in his other simultaneous writings, *Auch eine Philosophie der Geschichte, etc.* (1774), *Älteste Urkunde des Menschengeschlechts* (1774–6), *Erläuterungen zum Neuen Testament* (1775), and *Briefe zweener Brüder Jesu in unserm Kanon* (1775): see H. Stephan, *Herder in Bückeburg*, pp. 161–7, Haym, *Herder*, 1, pp. 600–54. The best introductions to Spalding are J. Schollmeier, *Johann Joachim Spalding. Ein Beitrag zur Theologie der Aufklärung* (Gütersloh, 1967), and R. Krause, *Die Predigt der späten deutschen Aufklärung 1770–1805* (Stuttgart, 1965), pp. 18–34. Herder soon regretted this outburst against Spalding whom he really admired. See n. 84, below. Both revered the writing of Anthony Ashley Cooper, third Earl of Shaftesbury (1671–1713).

[30] Teller's *Wörterbuch*, *Werke*, 7, p. 209. Teller, *Allgemeine Deutsche Biographie*, 37, pp. 556–8, and *RE*, 19, pp. 475–81. Teller's *Lehrbuch des christlichen Glaubens* (Helmstedt and Halle, 1764) was confiscated in Electoral Saxony. On the Berlin clergy: C. Rathgeber, 'The Reception of the Religious Aufklärung in Berlin at the End of the Eighteenth Century' (Cambridge Ph.D., 1985). Herder was hurt, too, in being upstaged by Friedrich Nicolai's satirical novel written in the manner of Sterne: *Leben und Meinungen des Herrn Magisters Sebaldus Nothanker* (Berlin, 1773–6), 3 vols, which, he thought, concentrated too much on the issue of the clergy's dignity and matters of dress. Herder wore clerical dress only when he had to. See his lines in the *Wandsbecker Bote*, 1774/5: 'Talare hindern freyen Gang, / Reichthümer freye Seele', *Werke*, 29, p. 57. See n. 26 below. Herder was also hurt by Nicolai's criticism of his emotional writing and his interest in folksong: see Herder's epigram on Nicolai: 'Herr Nikkel had gemacht dies Buch / daß jeder grosssen Geist drinn such / und so gemacht, daß jedermann / gar keinen Geist drinn finden kann', *Werke*, 29, p. 540.

solemn *Te Deums* for one or other of Frederick the Great's victories.[31]
What made Herder, however, bracket Spalding's sincere defence of the
clergy with the casuistry employed by Berlin court theology was the way
Spalding, in his unadorned prose, wrote of the clergy as part of the civil
order: as 'depositaries of public morality'. Their vocation was ethical
rather than scriptural. Herder simply glossed over, given what he mistak-
enly assumed was Spalding's support of the Frederician police state he so
despised, Spalding's own serious misgivings about the way Christian ethics
and duties were, and could be, confused with the law. Herder also considered Spalding's didactic use of the Bible in the sermon as one which, in
its insistence on congregational understanding, threw out Lutheran
teaching about the Trinity, Atonement, Justification, and the certainty of
Salvation, in favour of fashionable neo-Stoic views which ruled out
Providence and the means of grace.[32]

Herder's view, despite his similar insistence on the need for a better
clergy, was that the office, in Pascal's sense handed down from Mel-
chizedek and the Patriarchs and Prophets, was one which sanctified the
clergyman rather than the other way round. In Melanchthon's words the
clergy were, 'Custodes librorum Propheticorum et Apostolicorum et
verorum dogmatum ecclesiae'.[33] The purity of the Gospel had to be maintained whatever the cost. You could not, either, in Matthew Prior's words,
'be of your patron's mind, what'er he says'.[34] Herder thus quoted Luther's
Preface of 1539 in support of his argument that 'God's Word' alone is the
essence of the clergyman's office.[35] What the clergyman preached was an
appeal to the heart, intuition, and simple faith in the sense of Pascal's gloss
on Psalm 119. 36: 'incline my heart unto thy testimonies'. Christian
wisdom is a constant return to childhood, Matthew 18. 3, where faith
comes by hearing, Romans 10. 17. Christianity is, in Pascal's sense, a 'fact',
and also, in Hamann's sense, a 'taste for signs'.

---

[31] J. J. Spalding, *Lebensbeschreibung von ihm selbst aufgesetzt und herausgegeben mit einem Zusatze von dessen Sohne Georg Ludwig Spalding* (Halle, 1804), p. 103.

[32] 'Diese sind noch immer die eigentlichen Depositairs der öffentlichen Moralität', Spalding, *Nutzbarkeit*, p. 54. *Ibid.*, p. 66, Spalding wrote of the clergy as religious teachers who should show 'Bereitwilligkeit zu helfen, Redlichkeit im Gewerbe, Fleiß im Dienste anderer, Gehorsam und Treue gegen den Regierenden, Ertragung schwerdrückender Lasten'. *Ibid.*, p. 216, for Spalding's distinction between Christian ethics and the law. On the spread of Neo-Stoic values in Frederician Prussia, G. Oestreich, *Neostoicism and the Early Modern State* (Cambridge, 1982).

[33] *Werke*, 7, p. 252.

[34] *Ibid.*, p. 253.

[35] *Ibid.*, p. 302. See n. 62, below.

> Die ganze Religion in Grund und Wesen ist Thatsache! Geschichte! Auf Zeugniß der Sinne und nicht der Oberkräfte allein; bei dem Empfangenden auf Glaube, der alle Kräfte fasset, gebauet: nach Zweck und Inhalt ans Volk, den größten, sinnlichern Theil der Menschheit und nicht an Grübler gerichtet; in Art und Sprache sie mit allen Trieben umzuschaffen und zu lenken. So predigten die Apostel Jesum und philosophirten nicht: so redeten die Propheten als Stimmen Gottes! Glaube aus der Predigt, die Herz und Sinne und den ganzen Menschen traf. Gott spricht und handelt mit Menschen als Kindern, und Kinder sind sinnlich![36]

We must simply follow Jesus as the 'author and finisher of our faith', Hebrews 12. 2, in the sense of the glory John saw after the Ascension, or in the sense of what Paul wrote in his intimate and local letters to the Greeks and Romans, or in his difficult letter to Timothy and Titus on the qualifications of the preacher.[37] In this journey, 'portrayal of the Bible as it is: each book in terms of time, place, important and less important subjects', should be our guide.[38] As to 'law', matters between Church and State, Herder pointed out that he saw confessions of faith and church orders as religious statements produced in particular historical circumstances. The German Reformation was an arbitrary political and legal edifice. These religious statements, therefore, needed to be adjusted to the standards of his own time. No one demanded that the Lutheran symbols should be the norm of faith and thought, as if one was standing before Charles V in the *Reichstag*. On the other hand, these powerful expressions of faith, produced in turbulent times, which to some extent established the religious freedom, peace, and values of the modern German social order and its welfare, were not to be thrown overboard—by implication oaths taken by the clergyman at ordination had to be respected—simply because philosophic fashion dictated it, or replaced by new more 'dignified' ones graciously authorized by some court or other.[39] Herder

---

[36] *Werke*, p. 265.
[37] *Ibid.*, pp. 310–12. Pp. 307–12 are really a portrait of Christ's person. Herder's Christocentrism is discussed by Stephan, *Herder in Bückeburg*, pp. 227–32.
[38] *Ibid.*, p. 305.
[39] *Ibid.*, pp. 278–81. On the vexing question of orthodoxy and oaths taken to the *Landesherr*, Stephan, *Herder in Bückeburg*, pp. 102–4, 191–3. The public debate about the Anglican Thirty-nine Articles of Religion in England in the 1770s was closely followed in Protestant Germany. 'Orthodoxie, wahre Theologie herzustellen, geradezu dem Strom des deistischen Jahrhunderts unsrer rechtgläubigen Theologen entgegen', Herder to G. F. Brandes, Bückeburg, 5 Jan. 1776, *Briefe*, 3, no. 219, was written apropos the attempt by the 'liberal' Faculty of

concluded that the one uncontroversial point he wished to make was: return to the Bible as the one and only true Reformation source of the clergyman's office.[40]

But to dwell on the rancour Herder expressed at Bückeburg about the misuse of his office by an indifferent Enlightened state and his fashionable colleagues is to pass over what Herder, as a practising clergyman, thought essential in church. These were private and common prayer, to which Bible-reading and preaching belonged organically, and the liturgical and musical order of service.

Prayer, learnt instinctively by the child in the Christian household, Herder felt, remains in our very fibres all our lives. But, as an expression of faith, it should be more than the child's automatic folding of hands and simple lip movements, when a parent says *sey andächtig*, or some godly opiate taken by adults on Sundays in church to satisfy their consciences. Prayer contains no magical properties; nor is it the lukewarm opiate 'improvement' copied from modern Anglican writers by Lutheran pastors who wished to be abreast of fashion.[41] Pleasanter dreams and addiction have little to do with prayer. Prayer does not guarantee that God is on the Lutheran side. Christ died for all. We should understand why we pray. The right devotional attitude, composure in God's presence, are prayer's essence. Before using the official prayer or service-book, think about prayer's contents like grace, righteousness, deserts, judgement, death, and resurrection. Here Herder was thinking of his native East Prussian parishes, where many clergy, like his schoolteacher, Trescho, found how difficult it was for confirmands to grasp the meaning of these theological terms.[42] We should always ask ourselves, can I, may I, am I in a position or not to pray to God? Why do I go to church? To pray is to 'open my thankful little childlike heart', to follow Christ, to examine conscience, to forgive, and to forget personal worries, as Paul did in prison.[43] We should be there standing still by the poor crib in Bethlehem reflecting on what

---

Theology at Göttingen to examine his Christian belief when Herder applied for a professorship in 1775. They had been prompted to do so by George III.

[40] *Ibid.*, 7, p. 281.

[41] 'Sey andächtig', *Werke*, 6, p. 92. Opiates and improvement, *ibid.*, 6, p. 306, and 10, pp. 355–6. Herder was thinking too of Apollinaris when he wrote of the 'lieblichsten Opiumträumen jenes Bischofs aus Laodicea'.

[42] *Ibid.*, 6, p. 93. On comprehension of the Catechism in East Prussia, Notbohm, *Kirchen- und Schulwesen*, p. 179.

[43] Sermon: Sixteenth Sunday after Trinity (1768), *Über das Gebet*, *Werke*, 31, pp. 73–95. *Fassung* is used for the devotional mood in God's presence, *ibid.*, p. 82.

Jesus suffered for mankind. Do we really know him? Do we see the exceptional quality of redemption which Zacharias, Mary, and Joseph saw and trusted in? [44] Have we that necessary inner peace to reflect on the hour of our death and the need to forgive, as Jesus did away from the crowd in the garden at Gethsemane? [45] God is with us always: at dawn, at night, in springtime, during autumn storms. Prayer is a continual daily service we perform to God. Prayer is reading our Bible as a 'calm, continual conversation with You . . . a remembrance of You . . . an intimate calm prayer which both elevates and makes better'. We are in constant need of grace in a world which we should learn to love, but not too much. [46]

What marks off Herder from Halle and Herrnhut piety—his emotional debt to both was nevertheless a large one—was the emphasis he put on the understanding of prayer as an integral element of the Lutheran order of service. Prayer is a common act in a public setting. Co-operation with Johann Christoph Friedrich Bach refreshed Herder's view on the need for sacred music which helped the congregation to find the devotional mood necessary for common prayer. Congregational togetherness could only be achieved, so Herder argued, by trying to understand the correspondence between biblical words and melodies, in both an historical sense of not simply throwing overboard tradition, and paying due attention to modern German idiom and modern polyphonic musical structure. Why was Mozart's *Magic Flute* so often performed in Germany, he asked? Not only because the libretto celebrated the victory of light over darkness and the return of conscience, but also because Mozart's music conveyed this message. [47] In this sense Herder wrote, and Bach set to music, favourite themes of Herder's sermons as oratorios: *Die Kindheit Jesu* (1772), *Die Auferweckung des Lazarus* (1773), and *Der Fremdling auf Golgotha* (1776), and as cantatas for Whitsun (1773), Michaelmas (1775), and Ascension (1776). [48] As important, if not more so, to Herder, was the

---

[44] Sermons: Second day of Christmas 1765, *ibid.*, 32, p. 285, and Christmas Day 1768?; *ibid.*, p. 448. Zacharias, Mary, and Joseph: Third Sunday in Advent (1773); *ibid.*, 31, p. 257, and Fourth Sunday in Advent; *ibid.*, p. 267.

[45] Christmas Day 1768, *ibid.*, 32, p. 454.

[46] God's omnipresence, *ibid.*, 31, p. 88. Bible reading and prayer: *Ueber die Göttlichkeit und Gebrauch der Bibel*, Second Sunday in Advent (1768), *ibid.*, 31, p. 121. 'Dieses Leben soll uns nicht so gefallen', etc., Fifteenth Sunday after Trinity, *ibid.*, 32, p. 331. See also *ibid.*, 10, p. 397.

[47] 'Wirkt die Musik auf Denkart und Sitten?', *Adrastea* (Leipzig, 1801–2), 2 = *Werke*, 23, p. 345.

[48] Texts to Oratorios: *Die Kindheit Jesu*, *Werke*, 28, pp. 28–33; Lazarus, *ibid.*, pp. 34–44; *Fremdling auf Golgotha*, *ibid.*, pp. 84–100; Cantatas: Whitsun 1773, *Werke*, 28, pp. 45–51; Ascension 1776; Michaelmas 1775, *ibid.*, pp. 79–83. Music: Wohlfarth Catalogue J. C. F. Bach: *Die*

provision of up-to-date hymnals which also respected tradition. This, we shall briefly see, was Herder's main concern at Weimar. The church service was thus a musical unity from the first to last note which reflected the Epistle, Gospel, and sermon. Careful attention was to be paid to traditional liturgical form and colour, because congregations were on the whole conservative and visually-minded. But to cling to the ancestral hurdy-gurdy for the sake of custom was simply wrong. The choir and organ took precedence over congregational singing in an undramatic way if antiphonal singing could not be established.[49] To read Herder on this subject is to enter the mind of one of the chief, but sadly forgotten, handful of musical reformers who tried to restore a sense of historical continuity to the Lutheran order of service and its sacred music within the late eighteenth-century movement for liturgical 'decency' in Protestant Germany. Herder shared similar views to Johann Kuhnau and Johann Sebastian Bach, who emphasized the composer's need not only to move the affections skillfully, but also to understand the right sense and scope of the scriptural text.[50] In this sense Herder's musical offering has a profundity which far outstripped even that of his celebrated musical contemporary, Dr Burney.[51]

Twenty-seven years as Superintendent-General, and fame as one of the handful of great men of letters at Saxony-Weimar-Eisenach, suggest that Herder had found at last a home he could enjoy close to the heart of the Reformation.[52] But Weimar, seen through clerical eyes, was a replica of all that Herder had to come to loathe at Bückeburg about the little

---

Kindheit Jesus XIV/2; *Lazarus* XIV/3; *Fremdling auf Golgotha* XIV/7; Ascension 1775 XIV/8; Whitsun 1773 XIV/4. On the merits of the oratorio and cantata see: *Werke*, 23, p. 559.

[49] *Cäcilia, Zerstreute Blätter 5 Sammlung* (Gotha 1793) = *Werke*, 16, pp. 253–67. On the unity of the order of service from first to last note, *ibid.*, pp. 259–61.

[50] A. Schmitz, *Die Bildlichkeit der Wortgebundenen Musik Johann Sebastian Bachs* (Mainz, 1949), p. 26: cited by J. Day, *The literary Background to Bach's Cantatas* (London, 1961), p. 107.

[51] A sensitive appreciation of Herder's musical offering is by Walter Wiora, 'Herder', in *MGG*, 6, pp. 203–14.

[52] Herder's ministry in Weimar is sketched by I. Braecklein, 'Zur Tätigkeit im Konsistorium des Herzogtums Sachsen-Weimar', in Schmidt, *Herder im geistlichem Amt*, pp. 54–72, and H. Eberhardt, 'Johann Gottfried Herder in Weimar', *Amtsblatt der Evangelisch-lutherischen Kirche in Thüringen*, 31 (1978), pp. 198–207. In general: R. Herrmann, *Thüringische Kirchengeschichte* (Weimar, 1947), 2. Herder's work as a schoolmaster was constantly hampered by the Duchy's parlous education system, P. Krumbholz, *Geschichte des Weimarischen Schulwesens* = *Monumenta Germaniae Paedagogica*, LXI (Berlin, 1934), pp. 86–167. In English there is W. H. Bruford, *Culture and Society in Classical Weimar 1775–1806* (Cambridge, 1962). Bruford skates over Herder's conscious debt to Luther and the Reformation.

'enlightened' Lutheran states. Weimar, some 200 square miles, twice as large as Schaumburg-Lippe, under Duke Karl August (1775–1828) was, however, just another little state whose ruler, in his drive for an eminence set apart from the extended family of Thuringian little courts, saw his impoverished rural subjects chiefly as a source of ready cash. He thus showed no respect for his poor-quality country clergy and schoolmasters living in a countryside he ensured could not support them, and he remained away from a church whose rites he believed belonged to one of the many vitrines in his palace. Lukas Cranach's triptych commemorating Luther's preaching in Weimar's late fifteenth-century city church, St Peter and St Paul, which portrayed Luther with open Bible in hand standing beneath the Cross, with blood pouring on to his head from Christ's pierced side, was thus a constant reminder before Herder, as he officiated, of the Reformation Church which continued to suffer in late eighteenth-century Germany. A week spent mostly on consistorial business, which meant working through boxes of parish accounts, hearing grievances about stipends which didn't deserve that name, imposing fines on marital transgressions, and being constantly outvoted by his fellow clergy councillors and lay assessors on what he regarded as essential measures to improve the training of the local clergy or instruction of the young in Christian doctrine and in the classroom, forced Herder to take his pen and expose once again, within the limits of his oath taken to Karl August (though this time with a very much sharper awareness of historical development), the mess and misuse made of the Reformation by *Kleinstaaterei*.[53] Typical was Herder's confidence to Hamann in 1785 that Cranach's portrait of the pallid, sullen, and crestfallen Luther after his rows with Duke George of Saxony in 1528, which hung in his study, fittingly expressed his own mood about the way church order was mocked and the liturgical inheritance squandered in Thuringia:

> (Auf Luthers Bild)
>
> Guter, schwarzer Mönch, mit starkem Arme begannst du abzukehren den Staub, der die Altäre verbarg. Aber schnell entrisen dir andre das säubernde Werkzeug, lasen vom Staube das Gold, hingen den Besen sich auf: Und nun steht der endgüldete Altar in argerem Staube ohne Säuberung; — Gold können sie fegen nicht mehr.[54]

---

[53] *Werke*, ed. Müller, 22, pp. 204–5 and 21, p. 232. Herder wanted to write a biography of Luther to expose the resultant mess made by Saxon princes, but he feared reprisals, see J. G. Müller, *Aus dem Herderschen Hause, Aufzeichnungen 1780–1782* (Berlin, 1881), pp. 31–2.

[See opposite page for n. 54]

Herder wished Luther could be there to see all the rubbish heaped on his grave. The bitter doctrinal rows between Lutheran churchmen of Flacian or Philippist persuasion, which had first adulterated Luther's teaching in post-Reformation Saxony and Thuringia, were simply buried by a mass of arbitrary princely disciplinary edicts, and eventually by Weimar's *Generalpolizeidirektion* of 1770: a typical product of the Enlightenment in its absolute indifference to established religion. Thuringia and Saxony no longer provided a home for the Reformation. Enlightened Weimar considered less the welfare and happiness of its Christian subjects, which it impoverished, than their classification as good citizens according to whether they paid their taxes without needing to be asked. Herder thus saw his congregation, as well as all the others in his diocese, as condemned for life to ignorance and superstition by the official humbug of a state which showed little inclination to support its clergy, churches, and schools.

Herder's parish work provided, however, a contrast to Weimar's political darkness. It was the mellow and refreshing experience of a fine autumn: a time, despite all the anguish high office caused him, when Herder gathered up his views on the Christian ministry and worship in some of his most personal writing: his fifty letters *Das Studium der Theologie betreffend* (1781–2), his additional letters to *Theophron* (1781), and his two-volume *Vom Geist der Ebräischen Poesie* (1782–3).[55]

These were written when Herder was closely involved in setting up local theological seminaries for his ordinands, and was starting to reshape Weimar's liturgy and hymnals. Pastoral refreshment was helped by the visit in 1780 of the young Göttingen theological student, Johann Georg Müller, the brother of the noted historian of the Swiss cantons, who had initially come to seek Herder's pastoral advice, but who soon became the obvious recipient of the letters Herder was publishing, virtually another son, and eventual editor of Herder's papers.[56]

---

[54] *Epigramme* = *Werke*, 29, p. 646. The letter to Hamann, Saturday before Cantate 1785, *ibid.*, p. 756. Cranach's portrait is also described by Müller, *Aus dem herderschen Hause*, p. 36.
[55] These letters are collected in *Werke*, 10 and 11. Commentary by F. W. Kantzenbach, 'Herders Briefe das Studium der Theologie betreffend. Überlegungen zur Transformation der reformatorischen Kreuzestheologie', in J. G. Maltusch, ed., *Bückeburger Gespräche über Johann Gottfried Herder 1975* (Rinteln, 1976), pp. 22–57. *The Spirit of Hebrew Poetry*, *Werke*, 11, pp. 213–475, and 12, pp. 1–308. Commentary H. Robscheit, 'Herder als Ausleger des Alten Testaments' in Schmidt, *Herder im geistlichenAmt*, pp. 26–38.
[56] See especially Müller, *Aus dem herderschen Hause*.

These books summarized all that Herder had uttered so far. They also attempted to reconcile Herder's Christocentric faith with the Enlightenment, however hurtful Reimarus's and Lessing's recent writings were to him.[57] To be a clergyman was to read the Bible as a human document, which, in the sense of Luther's Preface and Lectures on the Psalter, is a garden full of fruitfulness and change rather than the workhouse of the theologians. Theology is a practical, happy, liberal discipline like all the others. Why not feel free to read the Enlightenment? Why distinguish between reason and Scripture? A half of the letters were thus devoted to the Old and New Testaments. Only the last three considered the daily, mundane aspects of the clergyman's office, though a knowledge of ecclesiastical history, law, and local custom Herder regarded as essential too.[58]

Herder's debt to Linné appeared once again in his advice not to shy away from the Elysian fields of old tradition and religious customs; that without a sense of Providence all Christian teaching is useless in a world which Linné shows us is governed by the great unseen scales of deeds and consequences.[59] The Graces and the Furies are at hand in every one of our actions. The powers of human reason, Herder repeated, are thus weak in a world where we have little idea of our origins, and where we possess no physical data about what is to become of us in the future.[60] The clergyman should have constantly before him, like a good shepherd, the situation and needs of his congregation. Herder was glossing a sermon he had preached at Stadthagen installing the new incumbent in January 1776. Herder advised once again to speak directly to the congregation and not to images of them fashioned by university theology. Don't copy from others. Copying, he stressed, was a peculiarly German vice.[61] Do Christ's work.

---

[57] Kantzenbach, *Herders Briefe*, discusses the question of the Bible as a source, accommodation, and prophecy raised by Reimarus and Lessing. In general, K. Aner, *Die Theologie der Lessingzeit* (Halle, 1929, reprint Olms, 1964).

[58] *Werke*, 10, pp. 1–12, 277–83. Caroline in her memoirs records Herder as writing in 1797, 'die tollen Bücher sind für mich oft die Besten: sie zwingen zur Sobrietät', *Werke*, ed. Müller, 22, p. 190.

[59] On the Bible as a garden rather than a workhouse, *Werke*, 11, p. 8. 'Ohne Providenz ist uns die Lehre von Gott unnütz: der Gott der Epikurer, der außerhalb der Welt wohnet, ist uns ein entbehrliches Wesen', *ibid.*, 10, p. 334. *Talio*: 'Christus entdeckt uns nehmlich die moralische Regierung Gottes in der Welt als ein große, unsichtbare Waage der That und der Folgen: Du kannst nichts, weder Gutes noch Böses in die Eine Schaale legen, ohne daß sich die andre, mit gleichem, aber progreßivem Maas der Schwere in guten und bösen Folgen rege', *ibid.*, p. 337.

[60] *Werke*, 10, p. 346.

[61] As the shepherd, *ibid.*, p. 244. Homiletics and conduct in church, *ibid.*, 11, letters 38–46 inclusive. Sermon: Stadthagen, 14 Jan. 1776 in *ibid.*, 31, pp. 408–15. 'Siehe da die Gemeine,

Follow Luther's *Oratio, Meditatio, Tentatio* offered in his Preface of 1539.[62] This was the way to deal with the wretched dried-up words 'edification' (*Erbauung*), and 'devotion' (*Andacht*). Jesus has to do with fact.[63] He certainly did not use modern teaching methods, Weimar's *matinées royales*, or Weimar's police, at Galilee.[64] You will find him at Gethsemane praying alone. Prayer is 'full of confidence, is childish', and in this world we should not love too much.[65]

These letters and the *Spirit of Hebrew Poetry* also reflect Herder's other chief concern at Bückeburg and Weimar: the place of the Bible in church; in particular the Psalms and hymns in their musical setting. The Psalms praise Elohim, the unseen divine breath. The Psalmist makes this visual to the eye. In the words of Psalm 49. 15, the Psalms express God's hospitality in his bright refreshing home and our understanding of it, Psalm 49. 3. Therefore, learn to read the Psalms. Read the Psalms in the original without commentaries. One can imagine that this stern advice might have decimated Herder's audience as it would today.[66]

How did one make the congregation participate in the vivid worship of the Psalmist? Herder put the hymn at the centre of his liturgical order fashioned for the practical clergyman, because he considered the congregational hymn as providing a form of expression, given the level of education in his time, which could vocalize as little else could, the needs and thoughts of the laity. The hymnal was the layman's Bible in verse, in which he found comfort, instruction, refuge, and happiness.[67] The hymn

---

die dir anvertraut ist und die du zu Gott führen sollt . . . Wapne dich also mit Gott, o guter Streiter Jesu Christi', *ibid.*, 10, p. 414.

[62] *Werke*, 10, pp. 327–8 Herder returns here to Luther's Preface of 1539 in his *Provinzialblätter*. See n. 35 above, *ibid.*, pp. 324, 368–70.

[63] *Ibid.*, 31, pp. 409–10.

[64] *Ibid.*, 10, pp. 380–1.

[65] *Ibid.*, pp. 386–7, 396–7.

[66] *Ibid.*, 11, pp. 359–60, 371–3. Music and how to read the Psalms, *ibid.*, 12, pp. 208–11. Herder remembered the contrast he had made between *ruach*, *pneuma theou*, and *l'esprit de quelque chose* in his Latin thesis *De Spiritu sancto auctore salutis humanae* he had presented for ordination at Riga in 1767, J. Kirschfeldt, *Herders Konsistorialexamen in Riga im Jahre 1767* (Riga, 1935), pp. 8–9.

[67] 'Die tiefste Grundlage der heiligen Musik ist wohl der Lobgesang, Hymnus: ich möchte sagen, er sei dem Menschen natürlich', *Cäcilia* = *Werke*, 16, p. 256; 'Mir ists immer rührend, wenn eine Christliche Gemeine mit Herz und Überzeugung Auferstehungs- Geburts- Passionslieder, als Facta und Entschlüsse über Facta singet; in ihrer größten Simplicität ist eine Kraft, die manches neuere Machwerk von gereimten oder ungereimten Raisonnement weder nachahmen, noch ersetzen kann', *ibid.*, *Werke*, 10, p. 171. Congregational participation in sacred music see: *Werke*, 11, letter 46, pp. 63–73.

was a form of prayer as well. It was thus advisable to cherish what was left of the simple Latin hymns of the early Church, or even more recently those of the Moravian Brethren, so hard to come by, which expressed simply, devotion, cordiality, and a sense of brotherhood. Herder thus found it appropriate to give on Whitsun 1781 one of his two Moravian hymnals to Müller to prove his argument.[68] If Klopstock's ideal of anti-phonal singing could not be realized in the average church, the congregation had still to be the focal point of a liturgical unity composed of sermon, Bible-reading, and singing.[69] But good sacred music could not copy the music and instrumentation of the Hebrews and the Greeks, though it was important to try and understand these musical origins as the Erlangen orientalist, August Friedrich Pfeiffer had recently done.[70] Herder felt modern Italian and German polyphony, the organ and the little chamber orchestra, to be the appropriate musical accompaniment. With this in mind, he thus translated the text of Handel's *Messiah*, which was performed at Weimar for the first time in 1780, and then frequently thereafter.[71] Even Goethe, who paid little attention to Herder the clergy-man, noted many years later, in 1824, the joy he had felt at this first performance.[72] Herder also once again composed cantatas, like that for Easter 1781, which the court *Capellmeister*, Ernst Wilhelm Wolf (1735–92), put to music, or started on an entire cycle of cantatas for the Christian Year.[73] On the other hand, Herder moved with caution and discretion, mindful of how difficult it was to introduce new hymns and melodies, while at the same time retaining and restoring old stock, in Protestant Germany, where uncritical compilation, duplication, and rewriting, mocked any sense of a common core of serviceable congregational hymns. This, then, was the tone of the hymnal he authorized at Weimar in 1795, and which was to remain in use until 1882.[74]

---

[68] *Werke*, 10, p. 171; 11, pp. 69–70. Herder's gift to Müller: *ibid.*, 12, p. 441.

[69] Herder was thinking of Klopstock's *Die Chöre*, *ibid.*, p. 441; also *ibid.*, 10, p. 233. Herder's definition of the unity of the order of service: 'Die Anordnung des Gottesdienstes selbst im Innern und Äußern, Sänger, Leser, Prediger, die Gemeine, also ihre Erziehung', *Cäcilia*, *Werke*, 16, p. 261.

[70] A. F. Pfeiffer, *Über die Musik der Ebräer* (Erlangen, 1779): cited by Herder in *Werke*, 12, p. 248. Herder's praise of modern Italian and German polyphony: *ibid.*, p. 253.

[71] Herder's text: *Werke*, 28, pp. 105–14. His appreciation of Handel, *ibid.*, 23, pp. 556–9. Reference to the Messiah and its arias: *ibid.*, 11, letter 46, pp. 72–3.

[72] *MGG*, 14, p. 771.

[73] *Ibid.*, pp. 770–5 for article by Dieter Härtwig. Cantatas for the Christian Year: *Werke*, 28, p. 557, and *Aus dem herderschen Hause*, p. 71.

[74] See Herder's prefaces to two editions of 1778, and the preface to 1795: *Werke*, 31, pp. 707–22. Reprinted in Schmidt, *Herder im geistlichen Amt*, pp. 217–29. K. Ameln, 'Johann Gottfried

To authorize cautious hymnological reform showed Herder how difficult it was in the small state, given the ruler's *Jus liturgicum*, and the
obviously low level of popular education. Herder felt that he was reliving
much of what he had experienced at Riga. Little had changed, if he
excepted the increasingly shrill tones of theological enlightenment in
Germany's Protestant universities like nearby Jena. There was still too
much mindless coercion as well as pecuniary dispensation in spiritual
discipline concerning confession, marriage, and suicide. Thirty years as a
catechist had taught Herder that he was none the wiser as to how best to
explain Christian teaching and conduct to children and their parents. The
twenty to thirty catechisms which lay open on his desk, written in their
opaque theological language, did not give him hope.[75] In liturgical
matters, the large number of Sunday and weekday services, which
required sermons and lessons to follow pericopes virtually unchanged
since those in the Epistolaries and Evangeliaries of the pre-Reformation
church, imposed an intolerable burden on a poorly educated country
clergy who had to officiate usually in several churches. If the pericopes
were the layman's calendar, obscure texts were of no help either. No
wonder there were many empty pews at weekday Matins, in the winter
months especially.[76]

The last decade of Herder's life, which happened to coincide with the
end of the eighteenth century, heightened his sense of melancholy about
the current state of the Christian Church. He took a little satisfaction
from the official end of penance imposed by the Church in 1786 in
Saxony-Weimar, at his new hymnal of 1795, and the new series of

---

Herder als Gesangbuch-Herausgeber', *Jahrbuch für Liturgik und Hymnologie*, 23 (1979),
pp. 132–3. T. Schrems, *Die Geschichte des gregorianischen Gesanges in den protestantischen Gottes-
diensten* (Freibourg, 1930), p. 106, mentions Herder including as nos. 1–3, the *Kyrie summum*,
Paschale, and *Magne Deus*. The 1795 hymnal included 28 of Luthers hymns; Paul Gerhardt
was also well represented, *Werke*, 12, p. 441. Herder disliked his choirboys having to sing also
in the opera chorus in Weimar's theatre. For his row with Goethe: C. A. H. Burkhardt,
'Herder and Goethe über die Mitwirkung der Schule beim Theater', *Vierteljahrschrift für
Literaturgeschichte*, 1 (1888), pp. 435–43. Caroline refers to this also: *Werke*, ed. Müller, 22,
p. 28. Herder was aware, too, of the attempt to provide Riga with a more up-to-date hymnal.
See A. W. Hupel's appendix. 'Gedanken über das Rigische Gesangbuch' in his *An das Lief- und
Ehstländische Publikum* (Riga, 1772), p. 83 and *passim*. Hupel stressed the importance of providing cheap hymnals as Halle had done.
[75] Braecklein in Schmidt, *Herder im geistlichen Amt*, p. 64.
[76] *Ibid.*, pp. 60–2. 'Die Revision der Liturgie', Weimar, 23 Oct. 1797 = *Werke*, 31, pp. 761–74.
R. Bürkner, 'Herder als Liturgiker', *Monatschrift für Gottesdienst und kirchliche Kunst*, 8 (1903),
pp. 387–94.

pericopes and his Catechism, which he authorized in 1798; but his misgivings about his ministry were equally strong. His holiday in Italy between September 1788 and July 1789, particularly his stay at Rome between Advent and Easter as reflected in his letters home, express a sombre mood when faced with almost two thousand years of Christian history and worship.[77] Gibbon's account, which Herder approved of, because it exposed layer upon layer of human distortion of Christ's person and teaching, he thought almost too mild in its criticism.[78] Though it was good to experience Advent, Christmas, Lent, and Holy Week at St Peter's, the outward ceremony and the voices of the castrati depressed him.[79] Seeing the tall, dark, still cypresses, conjured up Rome as a city of the dead. The eighteenth verse of his poem *Spirit of the Cypresses*, which he sent to Caroline on 17 March 1789, sums up his mood:

> Daneben sah ich — darf ich Dich auch nennen,
> Du inhumanes, alt — und neues Rom?
> Doch, wer wird Dich im Namen nicht schon kennen
> du Kapitol und du St. Peter's Dom?
> Du Pfuhl, aus dem die Erde zu verbrennen
> ausging ein alter und ein neuer Strom.
> Von Kriegern einst bewohnt und Senatoren,
> von Pfaffen jetzt bewohnt und Monsignoren.[80]

---

[77] These letters are collected by Hahn in *Briefe*, 6. They are also edited by W. Dietze and E. Loeb, *Bloß für dich geschrieben. Briefe und Aufzeichnungen über eine Reise nach Italien 1788/89* (Berlin and Weimar, 1980). Herder's letters to his children are charming descriptions of landscape, animals, and history. See especially letters 19, 40, and 41, *Briefe*, 6.

[78] Gibbon's influence on Herder and his *Ideen zur Philosophie der Geschichte* (1784–91): Haym, *Herder*, 2, p. 231, also Bruford, *Culture and Society*, p. 230. For Gibbon in the context of the new history in Livonia and Estonia in the 1770s: Schaudinn, *Deutsche Bildungsarbeit*, pp. 124–37, and H. Neufschäffer, 'Die Geschichtsschreibung im Zeitalter der Aufklärung', in G. v. Rauch, ed., *Geschichte der deutschbaltischen Geschichtsschreibung* (Cologne and Vienna, 1986), pp. 63–85. Herder's views on ecclesiastical history: K. Scholder, 'Herder und die Anfänge der historischen Theologie', *Evangelische Theologie*, 22 (1962), pp. 425–40.

[79] To Caroline, Rome, 27 Dec. 1788, *Briefe*, 6, no. 51.

[80] To Caroline, Rome, 17 March 1789, *ibid.*, no. 66, includes Herder's poem, *Spirit of the Cypresses*. The poem is also printed in *Werke*, 29, pp. 568–73. The cypresses are also mentioned in his letter to Caroline, Rome, 21 Feb. 1789, *ibid.*, no. 62. 'Ich habe an Weihnachten gnug, und eine Woche heilige Castratenmusik mehr oder minder wird mir auch nicht der größeste Verlust sein. Im Grunde sind dies alles für mich Pfützen aus einem todten Meer, so sehr sich auch Goethe den Mund aufreißt, ihre Süßigkeit zu loben', to Caroline, Rome 27 Feb. 1789, *ibid.*, no. 64. Compare the final lines of the penultimate stanza of Herder's poem included in no. 66 above: 'Vom ganzen Heer Kastraten-nachtigallen / sollt' Ave! Amen! in die Lieder schallen'.

Only Caroline's letter which reached him on Ascension at Florence could raise his spirits, for it reminded him of their honeymoon, years ago at Göttingen on Ascension, and that soon he would be back over the mountains.[81] Ecumenical thoughts, like his approval of Fritz Stolberg's conversion to Rome, or enthusiasm for Goethe's aesthetic appreciation of Roman Catholicism's genius for making its ceremony popular, were cooled by the way his Roman experience had confronted his historical imagination and sense of justice.[82] Herder was no romantic in spiritual matters. His two little books, *Vom Geist des Christenthums* and *Von Religion, Lehrmeinungen und Gebräuchen*, written a decade later in 1798, in their attempt to answer what Christianity amounted to at the end of the eighteenth century, show us that Herder, despite his genius for painting the religious mood and situation, was a man whose equally strong historical and practical sense constantly struggled with the ceremony for ceremony's sake and murky legalism—what he called the *Stöcke und Blöcke* mentality—of Germany's little Protestant states.[83] The papacy was merely one of these writ large. In this sense he could never fully subscribe to the romanticism of Schleiermacher's *Reden*, which appeared the following year.[84] Herder was a clergyman of his age. But to try to measure Herder's faith with the thermometer of the Enlightenment is an unproductive task too. The historical span of Herder's career as a clergyman shows us that Herder's contribution to the debate about the Lutheran clergyman's office and Lutheran public worship is also a timeless one. The remark made years later by Herder's daughter-in-law to Henry Crabb Robinson over dinner one night at Heidelberg, in 1834, that Herder 'spoke the language

[81] To Caroline, Florence, 21 May 1789, *ibid.*, no. 81.

[82] Herder and Stolberg's conversion: Haym, *Herder*, pp. 560–1. See n. 80, above, for his rejection of Goethe's romanticism. See Bürkner, *Herder als Liturgiker*, pp. 387–9.

[83] His two little books are printed as *Christliche Schriften, 5 Sammlung = Werke*, 20, pp. 1–130, and pp. 135–265. 'Stöcke und Blöcke', *ibid.*, p. 69.

[84] Caroline's sarcastic aside 'mit ihrem Religions-Schleiermacher' to Jean Paul in a letter, 1 Feb. 1800, Haym, *Herder*, 2, p. 555. H. Stephan, 'Schleiermachers "Reden über die Religion" und Herders "Religion, Lehrmeinungen und Gebräuche", *Zeitschrift für Theologie und Kirche*, 16 (1906), pp. 484–505. Herder in his *Religion, Lehrmeinungen und Gebräuchen* came closer to Spalding's view in *Religion eine Angelegenheit des Menschen* (Berlin, 1798), *Werke*, 20, pp. 141–2. Herder also cited the story of the Mirror in Swift's *Tale of a Tub*, Haym, *Herder*, 2, pp. 552–5. On the place of Baptism and Communion in the order of service: *Werke*, 20, pp. 192–5 and 195–210. Their importance is stressed also earlier in his *Provinzialblätter*: *Werke*, 7, p. 232. Herder was critical of what he thought to be the 'authorized' aspect of the Anglican Eucharist. He wrote of this as 'eines Parlamentsgliedes der hohen Kirche vollkommen werth'; *ibid.*, 20, p. 204. On Herder's view of the order of service: G. Carstensen, 'Några drag i pietistisk och rationalistisk Kultkritik och Kultmotiveriung i den tyska Lutherdomen', *Lunds Universitets Årsskrift N.F.Avd 1*, 20, no. 3 (Lund, 1925).

of orthodoxy without being orthodox', is true only up to a point.[85] Herder took his vows very seriously, and he respected the religious customs of his local church. On the other hand, he repeated at the end of his life a Christocentrism which is as relevant today as it was then. We are all members of the one Body of Christ, I Corinthians 12. 12. The person and teaching of Christ cannot be separated.[86] Every institutional form given to Christianity by man ages. Even the first Christians were only mortal. Look at Paul's first Epistles to the Corinthians and Galatians. Don't simply copy.[87] Beware of blind guides who 'strain at a gnat and swallow a camel', Matthew 23. 24. A critical history of Christian doctrine—how much all of us could learn from that. Public worship is not *Gottesverehrung*, or the sadly misused words 'devotion' and 'edification'.[88] To worship is to pray, understanding why and how, and prayer is a common act of Christian fellowship. Prayer is to read one's Bible, and to think constantly of childhood and first impressions.[89] The curious fact is that we do not remember Herder for this.

University of Glasgow

[85] *Diary, Reminiscences, and Correspondence of Henry Crabb Robinson*, ed. T. Sadler (London, 1869), 3, p. 48.

[86] *Werke*, 20, pp. 61–2.

[87] *Ibid.*, pp. 77, 96–7. ' Wir sind keine Hellenen'; *ibid.*, p. 98.

[88] *Ibid.*, p. 245. 'Strain at a gnat'; *ibid.*, pp. 145–6. The need for a history of doctrine, *ibid.*, p. 239.

[89] See Herder's Advent sermon of 1768 where he movingly described Bible reading and prayer, *Werke*, 31, p. 121, and n. 46. Christ's suffering on the Cross at Calvary Herder made vivid by printing the colloquial description by the vicar of Mohrungen, Christian Reinhold Willamovius (1701–63): 'Er hieng Mutter-Faden-nackt am kreuz', *Ueber die neuere deutsche Litteratur, 2 Sammlung 1767 = Werke*, 1, p. 269; another reference, Dobbek, *Herders Jugendzeit*, p. 202. See too Herder's epigram alluding to his own work at Weimar: 'An des Crucifix im Consistorium / "O du heiliger, bleibt dir immer dein trauriges Schicksal, / zwischen Schächer gehängt, sterbend am Kreuze zu seyn?" / Und zu deinen Fußen erscheint das Wort des Propheten / von den Ochsen und Farr'n feisten geselligen Schaar. / Heiliger, blick' auf mich und sprich auch mir in die Seele: / "Vater vergib! denn sie wissen ja nie was sie thun"', *Werke*, 29, p. 647. 'Ochsen', etc. is a reference to Psalm 22. 13, *ibid.*, p. 756.

THE RELATIONSHIP BETWEEN ESTABLISHED PROTESTANT CHURCH AND FREE CHURCH: HERMANN GUNDERT AND BRITAIN

by MARTIN BRECHT

translated by DAVID MELDRUM

THE present-day exchange of British and German research into church history can hardly be described as flourishing. Very seldom are historical topics from the other country ever investigated. This even applies to those areas where the paths of German and British church history have met. One notable exception is Professor Reginald Ward, who has not only striven to establish contacts with German church historians, but has also himself published a number of works on German church history. It is therefore only fitting to express appreciation of such amicable relations through the years by a study of German-British history. The scope for such a study embraces the fields of Pietism, Methodism, and the revival movement.

From the beginning of the nineteenth century, the pastor of the German Savoy Church in London, Karl Friedrich Adolf Steinkopf (1773–1859), had been engaged in establishing many important links between Britain, Germany, and Switzerland in his capacity as co-founder and promoter of the Bible and Mission Societies. Such contacts are at least to some extent general knowledge. On the other hand, however, research into church history has paid scant regard to the further relations which developed between Germany and Britain during the nineteenth century. It is therefore of value to highlight a theme from this domain which, in part, even touches upon the ecclesiastical background of the scholar whom we wish to honour.

Following the publication in recent years of his diaries and some of his writings, several of the typical problems which arose between committed German and British Christians are illustrated in the person of Hermann Gundert (1814–93).[1] Gundert, most undeservedly, is almost completely

---

[1] Hermann Gundert, *Tagebuch aus Malabar 1837–1859* (Stuttgart, 1983) [hereafter *TBM*]: *Schriften und Berichte aus Malabar* (Stuttgart, 1983) [hereafter *SBM*]: *Calwer Tagebuch 1859–1893* (Stuttgart, 1986) [hereafter *CTB*]. See also Hermann Gundert, *Die Evangelische Mission, ihre Länder, Völker und Arbeiten* (Calw and Stuttgart,[4] 1903).

forgotten today. He hailed from a Stuttgart Pietist family. His father was one of the founders of that city's Tract and Bible Society. In the course of his studies, Gundert was periodically exposed to the influences of Hegelianism, as propounded by David Friedrich Strauß, from which he was later to shake loose upon his conversion in 1833. By virtue of his studies, where he was successful not only in the theological examination, but also in a subsequent Ph.D., Gundert, like many of his contemporary Pietist theologians from Württemberg, benefited from a sound scholarly education—one which he never disclaimed and which was later to stand him in good stead in a variety of different ways. Gundert's lifetime work can be divided into two halves. During the period spanning 1836–59 he worked as a missionary in India. This occupation gave birth to, among other things, *A Malayalam and English Dictionary* (Mangalore, 1872), which even to this day is acknowledged as having made a revolutionary contribution to research into Dravidian languages. The Duke of Argyll, to name but one, helped to subsidize its publication. That the Gundert family was deeply rooted in India can still be seen in the works of Gundert's grandson, the poet Hermann Hesse (1877–1962). From 1862 onwards, after returning from India due to ill health, Gundert worked as the head of the publishing house in Calw; a firm which was among the most influential Pietist publishing foundations of nineteenth-century Germany. In attempting to combine Pietist piety with sound biblical knowledge, Gundert was to leave his own personal hallmark on this foundation. It was not coincidental that from 1885 the chief editor of the publishing house was the New Testament theologian Adolf Schlatter. At the same time, Gundert continued to work with the Basel Mission and to promote Pietism within the church. His diary provides documentary evidence of the astonishing vitality exhibited by Württemberg Pietism, together with the resultant problems it encountered during the second half of the nineteenth century. Gundert's own personal British contacts endured in Calw as well. Furthermore, he witnessed there the spread of Anglo-Saxon revival movements into Württemberg. On the basis of his earlier experience, Gundert, for the time being at least, accepted these movements with a certain degree of openness.[2]

In trying to understand the path followed by Gundert, and his outlook, it is important to become familiar with the particular peculiarities of the Württemberg church from which he stemmed. Its profession of faith was

---

[2] cf. *TBM*, IX–XVI. M. Brecht, *'Die gute Botschaft wichtig und deutlich zu machen', 150 Jahre Calwer Verlag 1836–1986. Die Festvorträge* (Stuttgart, 1986).

Lutheran-orientated, but its liturgy was just as plain as that of Switzerland. No ordinations were conducted, only investitures. Only those missionaries who were destined to work in British colonies were ordained, as a result of British requests—for example, Gundert's future missionary colleague, Dr Hermann Friedrich Mögling (1811–81). By virtue of the Basel Christian Society (founded in 1780) and her daughter organization, the Basel Mission (founded 1815), close co-operation had developed with Switzerland, both in the internal and external missions. Such co-operation was not considered to pose any confessional problem to Pietism, which was prevalent in the Württemberg church. It is not surprising that, as a result of this Pietism, there took place no process of reconfessionalization in the Württemberg church, unlike the situation in Bavaria, for example. Gundert rejected the idea of a Lutheran-based mission being run from Württemberg.[3]

Unlike Mögling, Gundert did not decide to enter the Basel Mission upon his conversion. He had been paid a visit by George Müller (1805–98) in 1834, a Plymouth Brother hailing from Germany, who was a pastor in Bristol at the time. Gundert recorded: 'He puts me to the test, admonishes me, fills me with enthusiasm, and is yet another of the voices which convey to me God's compassion.'[4] In 1835, when Müller's brother-in-law, Anton Norris Groves (1795–1853), was endeavouring to appoint a private tutor for his children in Basel, he was referred to Gundert. At that time Groves, a former dentist, was planning a trip to India as an independent missionary, and Gundert was to accompany him. He had originally been an advocate of the Church Missionary Society, but in the light of certain reservations with regard to Anglican Church order, he had no desire to enter its service. He had previously been engaged in an effort in Persia, and now, by this time, he felt drawn towards India, where he had earlier lent support to Karl T. E. Rhenius (1790–1838), a missionary who was working in Madras independently of the Anglican Church. Although the initial contacts with Groves were not exactly trouble free, Gundert was eventually won over.[5]

Prior to his departure for India, Gundert resided in Britain from October 1835 until March 1836. He had launched himself on such an intensive study of English that within a short space of time he initially began writing his diary in English. During this period he had greatly

[3] *CTB*, p. 440.
[4] *CTB*, p. 34.
[5] *CTB*, pp. 45–7, 52–4.

differing experiences with the various church denominations. He was impressed by the robust, upright sermons delivered by George Müller. He admired Groves for the spontaneous and tangible way in which he supported the missionary cause; methods which compared admirably with the cumbersome German approach. On the other hand, however, he was put off by the narrow-mindedness of several Nonconformists, and came to feel isolated. Occasionally he would visit Bristol Cathedral to listen in on the organ recitals; an activity which was frowned upon by the Nonconformists as taboo. One Baptist accused Gundert of not having been properly baptized. As far as Gundert himself was concerned, he had no doubt that he was properly baptized as a child. He side-stepped this problematic issue in order to avoid the intolerable situation of being at variance with his friends.[6]

Gundert, however, was far more aware of his points of difference with the Anglican Church than he was with opinions expressed by a number of Nonconformists. He visited the Church Missionary Society in Islington and took part in an ordination ceremony. Listening to the pronouncements of the bishop during an ordination of priests, he went 'weak at the knees' at the prospect of German missionaries having to conform to such a system.[7] At that time Gundert was particularly sensitive in relation to the problem of ordination. Groves had entrusted him with the task of promoting the independent missionary work conducted by Rhenius by making known in Germany the latter's dissent from the Anglican Church.[8]

Gundert indicated that the missionary work carried out in India had been initiated jointly by Halle missionaries and British Missionary Societies. Even within the Church Missionary Society itself, confessional divergences had been of no initial consequence. From 1820 onwards, however, attempts were made to link German missionaries more closely to the Anglican Church system. Furthermore, the ordination of native catechists was no longer to be undertaken by missionaries but by the Bishop of Calcutta. Rhenius took particular exception to the fact that, in doing so, those who had been ordained were to commit themselves to the Anglican Church order in its entirety. In his eyes, the ordination itself was an 'external consecration', which could easily be dispensed with. Friends

---

[6] *CTB*, pp. 49–52.
[7] *CTB*, p. 51.
[8] *SBM*, pp. 21–71, esp. pp. 24–9 and 71, Gundert's Introduction and Conclusion to the documentation.

such as Groves backed him up in this opinion, and in 1835 the Church Missionary Society and Rhenius parted company, resulting in a division within the blossoming work being carried out in Tirunelveli. The major reason for this rift resided in a publication of one of Rhenius's writings, in which he put forward his point of view in a critical and unabashed fashion. Rhenius considered it his duty to stand up for the freedom of the Christian individual in the face of constraints imposed by the Anglican Church system. In Gundert's opinion it was not really so much an issue of a mere literary battle, but more a matter of the subordination of German missionaries within the Anglican Church system.

The pronouncements made by Bishop Daniel Wilson of Calcutta in this regard were not lacking in lucidity either. A properly constituted Anglican Church ought to be established. Regular church order rather than the content of preaching was to be looked upon as the guarantee of salvation. Seen from a traditionally German standpoint, it is understandable why Rhenius, supported by all manner of exegetic, historical, dogmatic, and practical argument, contested the fact that the Anglican Church had been endowed with the authority of divine law. He called for a unification of the various churches in evangelical truth and for 'the justification and salvation of sinners leading to the building of believers'; thereby revealing the contrast between conceptions centred upon salvation and those upon the teaching of justification.

Under such circumstances, the fundamental question arose as to whether or not German missionaries were in actual fact still in a position to work alongside the Anglican Church. Gundert's documentation of both Rhenius's and his opponents' writings, together with his own introduction, would tend to point to something of a split, in which he himself would side with the Nonconformists. However, having no great desire to see this conflict being transported over to Germany, Gundert's father confiscated his work, thus preventing it from reaching the publication stage in the first place. None the less, this problem remained acutely topical in India, where even Gundert himself was constantly having to come up against it. As a result of his Württemberg origins, and his contacts with Nonconformists, he remained somewhat detached from the Anglican interpretation of office. This ecumenical problem in which he so unwittingly had become embroiled still remains an issue today.

It quickly became apparent that any missionary work under Groves would prove difficult. At very short notice he decided not to work in Calcutta but in Madras instead, with Gundert having to readapt himself to the local language. Moreover, Groves was prejudiced by members of the

Church Missionary Society against Rhenius, and he endeavoured to with-draw support from him. Previous to this, Gundert was to make an assessment of the conditions in Tirunelveli, and when he submitted a positive report of Rhenius's work, he was accused of bias by Groves. In the end, Groves commenced a programme of missionary work in Chittoor, to the west of Madras—the main burden of which was placed squarely on Gundert's shoulders. Despite having to come to terms with the economic difficulties, Gundert also had to contend with mistrust on the part of Mrs Groves, which resulted in some intense animosity between them. It was becoming clear to Gundert that he would have to part company with Groves.[9] A total rift was, however, averted, still leaving the door open for rather more infrequent contact: for example, in 1851 Groves visited Gundert and furnished him with a detailed report of theological developments underway within Plymouth Brethren circles, and of the extended work being carried out by George Müller in Bristol.[10] As in the past, Gundert basically appears to have been in agreement with the activities of the Free Church.

The options open to Gundert were twofold: he could either join Rhenius in Tirunelveli or, alternatively, enter the service of the Basel Mission in Mangalore. Gundert resolved to accept Rhenius's invitation, but the latter suddenly died in the summer of 1838. As Gundert had rightly anticipated, independent missionary work in Tirunelveli could consequently no longer be maintained. The progress of such work necessitated a renewed merger with the Church Missionary Society. However, on the basis of certain ecclesiastical reservations, Gundert was reluctant to be associated with the Society. The differences which existed between the Free Church and the Anglican were constantly being commented upon by those British with whom Gundert came into contact. It would seem, however, that he did not personally become involved, and even celebrated Communion according to the Anglican rite, 'in order to defuse vexation'. However, he could not very well enter the service of the Church Missionary Society. Alternatively, he could have applied to join the Basel Mission, a step he had been urged to take by his friend in Mangalore, Hermann Mögling. It was in October 1838 that Gundert arrived in Mangalore.[11]

In the ensuing years, Gundert built up the missionary station of Tellicherry, to the south of Mangalore, which was originally destined to

---

[9] *CTB*, pp. 37f., 55–65; *TBM*, pp. 17–21, 41.
[10] *TBM*, p. 225.
[11] See n. 8 above.

serve the slaves working on the cinammon plantation of Andjerkandi. Due to the ill-treatment meted out to the slaves and the moral conditions prevalent there, there was frequent tension with the owner, Frank Brown, and his family. The Basel Missionaries came upon extreme elements of colonialism in this area, and were opposed to them. They were very strict in their moral demands, on such matters as telling lies, damage to property, and transgressions of a sexual nature. The constant assertion of Christian ethics helped towards safeguarding their own identity and, in the end, commanded respect for the mission.[12]

In conjunction with our theme, the relations fostered between Gundert and the British he met in India are of particular interest. Unfortunately, these can only be highlighted in part, because the edition of his diaries provides no details pertaining to individuals. There were, naturally enough, constant contacts within a social framework. One would continually come across colonial officers who had pledged generous support to missionary work out of a sense of personal conviction, with Gundert being responsible for the spiritual well-being of several of their number. After he had returned home to Europe, Judge Strange bestowed his house on the mission and remained one of its sponsors thereafter. The Girls' School received furniture from Major Lawes, and one soldier donated 20 rupees. With the consent of the Anglican priest, the Revd Lugard, the missionaries ministered to the British community, being responsible for the administering both of the Sacrament and the British School, which in 1842, however, had to be given up. Having said that, Gundert considered the English sermons as burdensome. A Bible Study for 'gentlemen', undoubtedly referring here to 'Indo-Britons', was instituted. In 1840 moves were afoot to attempt to elbow out missionaries from the Anglican chapel on grounds of 'danger to the barracks from heretics'. In a further instance, another missionary had to perform a baptism since Gundert had not been ordained. For fear of possible unrest, sub-collector Chatfield had prohibited the preaching of sermons at the bazaar; a decision which led to his being branded an 'enemy' of the mission. The missionaries, however, refused to comply with this instruction, confident in the knowledge that they would receive backing from Connolly, who was not only the collector, but also one of their sponsors. When Connolly was transferred to Calicu, paving the way for Chatfield to become his successor, Gundert noted in his diary: 'You, Lord, seem to be intent on robbing us of human support.'[13]

---

[12] *CTB*, pp. 65–74; *TBM*, *passim*.
[13] *TBM*, pp. 44 f., 51–4, 58 f., 63, 73–5, 78, 84, 86, 90–2, 102, 128–30, 198, 217, 307, 395.

Between December 1845 and February 1847 Gundert was on furlough in Germany. Thereafter he continued his work in Tellicherry initialy in very much the same way he had done in the past. Of notable value is, for example, the entry under 20 February 1848: 'I am preaching in Malayalam and English. In the evening I had 9 believers (officers) over for tea.' A short time later mention is made of a 'Ladies Meeting', which both Gundert and his wife attended. Gundert paid a visit to chaplains Taylor and Kinlock in Cananore in a bid to secure from them 'alms for the poor'. They are described as being 'very worldly', Taylor, for his part, bemoaned the fact that to some extent the Basel missionaries had not been ordained. Specific record is made of the fact that not one 'gentleman' attended an English sermon.[14] In 1849, Gundert transferred to the missionary station of Chirak-kal, to the north-west of Cananore. In his capacity as General Secretary of the Malabar mission, Gundert now had to tackle problems which arose beyond his own station. As in the past, there was still some tension with the Anglicans, who, for example, took occasional exception to the considerable influence exerted on British Christians by Gundert's blunt colleague, Samuel Hebich. Hebich had enlisted a group of British workers for the mission, and quite a few officers to support it. This gave rise, however, to a backlash of feelings; such that it was not unknown for the soldiers to be forbidden to attend services conducted by missionaries. However, through the bishop, invitations were made to dine with the missionaries.[15]

Almost every page of the diary offers factual evidence of how lively and colourful relations were with British circles in Cananore, and also to what extent Gundert and Hebich had been making a considerable impression on the British military and their families with their urgent proclamation of recognition of sins and assurance of forgiveness, coupled with pastoral care. Certainly, attendance at church services was, on occasion, rather thin on the ground, with British Christians by no means reaching a consensus of opinion amongst themselves, comprising as they did members with High Church views and Independents of various denominations. Several of the views held by the missionaries met with opposition. In 1852, however, Hebich became marriage Registrar for the British Community in Cananore, while the missionaries, for their part, had to rely on the services of the British doctors.

The talents and potential of the individual missionaries were of varying proportions. Gundert had to report regrettable failings and sexual trans-

---

[14] *TBM*, pp. 16f., 172, 177, 180–2, 184.
[15] *TBM*, pp. 218, 227, 269, 313.

gressions in some instances. Attempts were made to resolve such incidents internally as far as possible, for example, either by sending the wrongdoers back home or despatching them to North America.[16] It was not uncommon for the missionaries to experience personal animosity or differences of opinion against themselves with regard to the tasks to be accomplished. The Basel missionaries had originally enjoyed considerable freedom in the way they structured their work. When Joseph Josenhans, the inspector of the Basel Mission, visited the Malabar mission in 1852, he went to great lengths to try to implement a fixed system of organization and regulations to govern the financial domain or the liturgy. In doing so, he came face to face with hostility on the part of a number of missionaries, who refused to fall in with centralist instructions radiating from the Basel Mission Committee. This was justified inasmuch as not every decision taken at home could be put into practice on the mission field. However it gradually dawned on Gundert that a certain code of discipline was necessary; a realization which also no doubt formed part of his 'ecclesiastical' experience.[17]

However, this new system prevented neither Mögling nor Hebich from conducting mission projects on their own authority, a venture which, in both cases, could almost have culminated in a rift with the Basel Mission. None the less, Gundert dissuaded Josenhans from parting company with Mögling, and justified this in an interesting manner: 'You can say what you like about Mögling, but he is not simply one of a crowd but a special gift from God to our mission; one of the few Basle people who have become public figures in India.'[18] This also applied to Hebich, with his fascinating nature, and the cultured and refined Gundert himself, albeit in a different way. These three individuals represented the prominent personalities of the Basel Malabar mission. Gundert was the one who, directly upon his return to Germany, highlighted in one of his speeches that the mission's work was not being supported by the missionaries and indigenous population alone, but that British officials, officers, and soldiers, together with their families, were also making a considerable contribution towards it. In some instances, it was precisely these men who, in the past, had indulged in improper relationships with Indian women and had then been converted and had gone on to become shining examples.[19]

A project launched by the Church Missionary Society to translate the

---

[16] Cf. Gundert's letters, *SBM*, pp. 167–256 *passim*.
[17] See the record of the visitation, *SBM*, pp. 139–48.
[18] *SBM*, p. 179.
[19] *SBM*, p. 258.

Bible into Malayalam had already been completed when Gundert arrived in India. Gundert did not refuse to acknowledge this translation, but did, however, criticize the fact that too little attention had been paid to the peculiarity of the various biblical literary genres, and that the translators had stuck closely to the English translation of the Bible. An attempt in 1848 at a common revision by the Church Missionary Society, the London Missionary Society, and the Basel Mission ended in failure. Consequently, the Basel missionaries, under Gundert's supervision, made ready their own translation, which was to be based on the original text. The Basel Bible Society was asked to handle the project as it was thought highly unlikely that either the Madras or the British Bible Society would publish this second translation. Gundert's importance as a Bible translator can be evidenced in his reflective deliberations on some problems which had arisen during the course of a translation from English into Malayalam. After the New Testament Epistles had been prepared and gone to print at the Tellicherry Press, in 1853, it transpired that the old translation of the Gospels did not, as had originally been thought, tie in with them.[20] The printers in Tellicherry (Tellicherry Orphan Press) had been instituted as far back as 1839 for the manufacture of school textbooks and 'Bible study guides'. Gundert's knowledge of the Stuttgart Bible Society, passed down from his father, was to prove advantageous to him in this regard.[21] The completion of the Malayalam Bible did not occur until after Gundert had returned to Germany.

The high esteem in which Gundert was held by the British Administration was manifest not least in the fact that ever since 1855 it had been anxious to secure him as Inspector of Schools.[22] He was consulted upon the translation and manufacture of textbooks for government schools. A 'spelling book', together with a book on world history, originally a product of the publishing company in Calw, had already been printed in Tellicherry. Gundert put forward proposals on how they could be adapted to the needs of government schools, and in 1856 presented a manuscript to this end. A book of Malayalam grammar was already available, and Gundert was making plans for the compilation of a geography book and a book outlining the history of Malabar. He was particularly interested in the composition of a reading-book, embracing the best Malayalam literary works. He had personally published a collection of 1,000 Malayalam proverbs

[20] SBM, pp. 98–105, 177–9, TBM, p. 227.
[21] TBM, p. 58. A list of the publications of the Tellicherry Press would be of great interest for the history of Christian journalism in India.
[22] TBM, p. 314; SBM, p. 205.

back in 1850, and was now acting as adviser to the relevant authorities in connection with examination requirements in the realms of higher education. Such standards were of value in the light of the planned establishment of a university in Madras.[23]

It would have been welcome news in Basel for Gundert to accept the position of Inspector of Schools. He himself was also tempted by the position; however, he did harbour some reservations as to the religious impartiality which would then be required of him. The decision dragged out for over a year. Gundert was certainly prepared to maintain a neutral stance in office, and he also set no great store by the title of Reverend; however, he wanted to be able to continue preaching. Furthermore, he would dearly have liked to go on playing a background role in the running of a mission station. In March 1857 Gundert eventually accepted the post on a provisional basis, thus rendering him now responsible for the complete scholastic supervision of government schools, both Protestant and Catholic missionary schools and schools of Brahma.[24] Gundert took his new charge very seriously and his appraisal of the teachers, the standards, and the financial situation of the schools was both sober and to the point.

He made greater demands on curricular teaching standards than the majority of teachers could meet. It is a distinct possibility that, with Gundert's appointment, the Government had its sights set on raising the level of school standards. The resources which had been put at the disposal of the schools had evidently been apportioned on a tight budget.[25] Due to ill health, Gundert was forced to return home in the spring of 1859, and although he had never expressed any dissatisfaction with his office, he was nevertheless pleased to have left government service.[26]

After returning home to Germany, Gundert was still no doubt anxious to uphold his supranational horizons at all costs. Again in his new activities his interest was not exclusively confined to Germany. His personal commitment to missions, for example reflected in attending mission galas, the holding of missionary groups, or the publication of the Calw mission pamphlets, all testify to his interest in world-wide missionary work. Naturally his involvement with India still remained, and contacts there were further nurtured by the exchange of letters and frequent visits being paid to Calw by Indian missionaries.

---

[23] *SBM*, pp. 207, 215–17, 244 f., 253 f.; *TBM*, p. 319.
[24] *SBM*, pp. 220, 248 f., 255; *TBM*, p. 357.
[25] *TBM*, pp. 359, 363 f., 366 f., 372 f., 384, 387–92.
[26] *TBM*, p. 395.

A number of other British guests are also frequently mentioned in his diary. Calw was easily accessible from the spa towns of Liebenzell and Wildbad, which were popular with visiting British. The publishing house in Calw, founded by Christian Gottlob Barth (1799–1862) had by 1836 developed out of a distribution centre for Christian tracts, initially run by the British Religious Tract Society. *Zweimal zweiundfünfzig biblische Geschichten* (Twice Fifty-two Bible Stories), written by Barth in 1832, represents the most successful publication to come from the publisher, and up until 1945 it could boast 482 separate German editions and translations in 68 different languages. Around the year 1860, this work must surely have been by far the most widely used Protestant textbook in the domain of religious education. Translations into the missionary languages of Africa and Asia stemmed in part from the English version of the book, entitled *Dr. Barth's Bible Stories*. In many instances, its distribution was once more financed by the Religious Tract Society. The success reaped by these *Bible Stories* spurred Barth on to produce additional Christian school literature, much of which alongside the *Calwer Bibelwerk* (Calw Bible Publications), was also translated into English and a number of other languages.[27] In 1860, Barth, with Gundert's assistance, envisaged an expansion of the English business contacts within the publishing company in Calw; a venture which, however, scarcely got off the ground. To some extent this could be attributed to the fact that, under Gundert, the publishing company had undergone a process of reorientation, away from straightforward biblicism towards the careful consideration of modern exegetic research. He was more interested in the solid character of the books published than their translation into English.[28]

As a representative of the Basel Mission, Gundert attended the Missionary Conference held in Liverpool in 1860. He was to advocate that a more pronounced Christian direction be lent to the education system in India. He also called on the missionary societies in China to work together towards a simplification of the alphabet. Moreover, he was instructed to level criticism at British colonialism along the Gold Coast and at the immorality exhibited by the officers based there. During this period, Gundert held discussions in the Bible Institute in London pertaining to the Malayalam Bible translation, and, among other things, he also called in on the Church

[27] See M. Brecht, 'Christian Gottlob Barths "Zweimal zweiundfünfzig biblische Geschichten" — ein weltweiter Bestseller unter den Schulbüchern der Erweckungsbewegung', *Pietismus und Neuzeit*, 11 (1985), pp. 127–38.
[28] *CTB*, pp. 149, 438.

Missionary Society, the Malta Mission, and the friends of Groves.[29] In 1862, Gundert conducted talks with the Bible Society in London concerning the translation of the *Calwer Bibelwerk* into English—which, in the end, was financed by the publishing company in Calw—and likewise with the Religious Tract Society regarding the acquisition of the Calw school textbooks. Gundert then undertook a subsequent trip to Glasgow.[30] During the course of both stays in Britain there arose numerous incidental meetings, primarily with people closely involved in missionary work. Gundert's reservations *vis-à-vis* the Church Missionary Society still persisted, and in 1870 he was dismayed at his daughter Marie's decision to take in children who had come under the care of this Society.[31] Gundert himself was later to be engaged in the accommodation of British children at the Christian Boarding School in Korntal, near Stuttgart.

The Calw diaries serve as a documentary not only of the life and work of Hermann Gundert after his return from India, but they also afford an insight into both church and religious life in Calw and in Württemberg. As a result of his enthusiasm for the mission, Gundert came into contact with Pietists in particular. Pietism in Württemberg during the latter decades of the nineteenth century was still considerably more vibrant than is generally appreciated. For decades the majority of its adherents had been closely integrated within the Established Protestant Church and had acquired decisive influence over it. The various so-called Lutheran-based communities lived under the umbrella of the Established Protestant Church but were, however, responsible for their own organization. Certain separatist tendencies continued to emerge on the periphery of Pietism, since the leadership of Lutheran Pietism had no great inclination either to tolerate or to integrate outsiders. People belonging to those circles in which a separatist spirit was alive were at this time becoming somewhat more open to British or American influences. On the basis of his own personal experience of English Free churches, Gundert exhibited a certain awareness and understanding in relation to these undercurrents which were at that time rolling in on Germany. However, here, once more, he was forced to witness the delineation between the Free Church and the Established Protestant Church and he had to take his stand. Incidentally, in 1859 it is stated that the Mennonites sided with the Michelites, that is the society founded by Johann Michael Hahn († 1819).[32] In 1861, people in Stuttgart were

---

[29] *CTB*, pp. 155–9.
[30] *CTB*, pp. 209–14, 216, 225 f.
[31] *CTB*, p. 371.
[32] *CTB*, p. 139.

becoming concerned about the infiltration of 'sects', a phenomenon which was not elaborated upon in any greater detail. Not every minister would seem to have been in agreement with 'the repudiation of everything non-conformist'.[33] Gundert occasionally came into contact with Baptists on whom he did not, in actual fact, pass a negative judgement; indeed, he even liked a certain Baptist minister called Hermann from Heilbronn. Having said this, he did, however, regard some incidents as 'odd'. It would appear that he considered it best not to make too much of a fuss over the 'Second Baptists'. Movements such as these simply came and went, only to make room for new follies.[34] The emergence of the Mormons in 1863 seems to have been nothing more than a brief episode devoid of any lasting success.[35] Even Gundert's own son, David, is described in 1869 as being 'Plymouth-Brethren minded'.[36] In 1889, Gundert took the followers of Irving to task during a Bible Study on I Corinthians 14.[37]

The Methodists were to pose the greatest challenge to the Established Protestant Church during the 1860s. Theirs is a particularly interesting story, as far as Württemberg is concerned. Christoph Gottlieb Müller, a butcher from Winnenden, near Stuttgart, had joined the Methodist ranks in London. Being the first ever Methodist to be sent off to Germany, he had, since 1831, been conducting successful missions from his home town in Württemberg. He avoided, however, a separation from the Established Church and up until his death in 1858, Methodism represented a sort of Lutheran-affiliated community. During his furlough in 1847, Gundert had had dealings with Müller, since the latter's daughter had wanted to enter the service of the Basel Mission against the express wishes of her father.[38] After Müller's death, the process of separation got under way, fuelled by the English preachers Lyth and Barratt, with Württemberg, the centre of German Methodist teaching at the time, being strongly affected by it. In 1862, complaints raised by ministers from Remstal came to Gundert's attention concerning 'Methodist dishonesty; first and foremost only out to win souls; their lack of any church; gradual celebration of communion in the homes of families. There is only a provisional congregation but when they are attacked they constitute themselves into a church.' The preacher

[33] *CTB*, pp. 196, 220.
[34] *CTB*, pp. 206, 231, 256, 266 f., 273, 587.
[35] *CTB*, pp. 235–7, 251 f.
[36] *CTB*, pp. 261 f., 368.
[37] *CTB*, p. 631.
[38] *TBM*, pp. 152 f.

Lyth's visit to the pastor in Winterbach, 'smoking a cigarette and accompanied by a helper' was regarded as provocative.[39]

In 1865, at the request of former Pietists, the Methodist minister named Puklitsch, who is said to 'look intelligent and speak nicely', sought Gundert's permission to use the Pietists' Hall for his meetings—a request which was, however, denied. The Hahn'sche Gemeinschaft (The Hahn Society) hastily banned the participation of its followers at Methodist meetings because the normal strict segregation according to sex was not adhered to at such gatherings. The Methodists went on to organize a further meeting in the neighbouring town of Hirsau. The Pastor of Hirsau and the Dean of Calw attacked the Methodists in sermons. In so doing, the Dean differentiated between a sound, healthy root, affording drive and vitality, and unhealthy outgrowths: for example, importance being attached to inner experience as opposed to the Scriptures and sacraments.[40] The Methodists had quickly assembled a group whose members believed their faith to have been invigorated through their teaching, with some individuals from Calw and the surrounding villages of Stammheim, Alt- and Neuhengstett journeying to Pforzheim for both Communion and agape meals. There was already talk of appointing a Methodist missioner in Calw. In Stammheim there was 'great opposition' towards the Methodists, but in Hirsau the Pietists lost some of their number to the Methodist ranks. By the end of 1866, a meeting convened by Methodists could already muster 500 participants, and shortly afterwards the registration of 84 new members was documented. The Pastor of Hirsau delivered a sermon attacking those who latched on to a preacher and were not content to hear a clergyman preach the Gospel pure and simple. He was not the only one to give vent to such helpless protest. As reflected in his speeches, the Dean of Calw expressed a positive opinion of the Methodists, but did, however, point out that their particular fashion of celebrating Communion—even at that time being attended by some hundred people—would culminate in an ecclesiastical schism. He denounced the idea of mocking the Methodists on the occasion of a masked ball. Gundert also took note at this time of favourable attitudes being expressed with regard to a certain minister named Barratt, which likewise warned of division taking place. Notwithstanding the church's desire to avoid this process of separation setting in, it could not be stopped, and in April 1866 the first 61 notices of withdrawal were submitted from

---

[39] *CTB*, p. 202.
[40] *CTB*, pp. 280, 286, 289f.

Calw and the surrounding area. In this connection the Dean announced that the church was lacking in ecclesiastical discipline.[41]

After the separation process had been completed, the Methodists only made sporadic appearances, giving rise to the assumption that the initial upsurge of the new movement had receded. In later years, Gundert refused to take part in communal gatherings with Methodists, reasoning that 'the threat of proselytisation had not yet disappeared'.[42]

Curiously enough, Methodism met with success in Württemberg precisely because there already were devout circles in existence there, and not because there was any lack of them. The Pietists were bitter at the fact that Methodists were being enlisted from their ranks. Perhaps Methodist teaching satisfied both the community and conversion needs of many spiritual people to a greater extent than Württemberg Pietism, which was, at that time, somewhat airy-fairy.

The publisher of *Schriften und Briefe* (Letters and Papers) asks himself whether or not Gundert might be regarded as a forerunner of the ecumenical movement.[43] This question has no easy or convincing answer. It was as a Pietist from the Established Württemberg Protestant Church—one relatively open in its confessional beliefs—that Gundert opted, together with British Nonconformists, to enter the missionary field. When practical co-operation with Groves turned out to prove impossible, he went on to join the Basel Mission in preference to the Church Missionary Society. In a multiplicity of different ways, his activities in India culminated in co-operation with representatives of the Anglican Church, which was, however, not entirely frictionless. Upon returning to Germany, Gundert took part in many different missionary conferences, where he stressed the need to overcome the bedevilling problem of ecclesiastical divisions. On a personal level he was open in his relations with representatives of other denominations. However, he did not ignore the need to draw the line somewhere at times when the opponents seemed bent on separation, as was the case with the Methodists. Gundert's Christian horizons were broadened considerably by virtue of his experience of the conditions prevalent in Britain. However, at the same time he came face to face in Britain with the model of an ossified church system. Even if, in concrete cases, he made allowances for it, it remained a system to which Gundert was fundamentally unable to relate

---

[41] *CTB*, pp. 296–8, 301, 308, 311 f., 314–17.
[42] *CTB*, p. 469.
[43] *SBM*, on the back of jacket cover.

on the basis of his origins and Pietist-biblical theology. In a note written in 1865, Gundert aptly captures his Pietist relationship to the Church; one of broad yet none the less structured dimensions, characterized by a critical yet not uncaring attitude:

> The Mission is guilty of the fact that we take a somewhat dispirited delight in the old, venerable Halls, to which we by no means have become disloyal, and that we do not expect a revival to sweep through the Church until such time as it goes beyond merely presenting a friendly face to the well-minded outside but also protects itself internally from teachers of false doctrine. Should a teacher remark that we are very broad-minded and hence, as a result, secular, we then have to confess that, when all is said and done, we do feel more drawn toward believers in other churches than to the non-believers currently still belonging to the same church as we and our friends . . . We all return home from the mission field, cured of pride in our church but not of allegiance to it. We do not want to weed out all undesirable elements but we do contend, nevertheless, that a body such as the church should dispose of a number of rules by which those who call its fundamentals into question are expelled.[44]

In conclusion, the question arises as to whether or not Gundert in fact deserves any mention in the narration of contacts between Germany and Britain. This question demands an affirmative response—and this for a number of different reasons. Gundert is representative of those who contributed to the combined expansion of Christianity throughout the nineteenth century. Württemberg Pietism acted as a driving force behind this movement by virtue of the fact that it possessed the necessary degree of openness without, however, sacrificing its own image. The Christian Mission was only able to succeed within a framework of supranational cooperation. At the same time it set in motion a process of mutual acquaintance and exchange between German and British Protestantism. In this regard, the fact that such a process might possibly have been more advanced in the nineteenth century than it is today should give us food for thought: historical research both reminds us and rebukes us today.

Westfälische Wilhelms-Universität, Münster

---

[44] *CTB*, p. 274.

UNITY AND SEPARATION: CONTRASTING ELEMENTS IN THE THOUGHT AND PRACTICE OF ROBERT AND JAMES ALEXANDER HALDANE

by DERYCK W. LOVEGROVE

I N June 1799 the General Assembly of the Church of Scotland issued a Pastoral Admonition to its congregations denouncing the missionaries of the newly formed Society for Propagating the Gospel at Home (SPGH). They were, it alleged, 'a set of men whose proceedings threaten[ed] no small disorder to the country'.[1] In issuing this warning the Assembly brought to public attention for the first time the work of two of the most prominent Scottish leaders of the Evangelical Revival, Robert and James Alexander Haldane. The Haldane brothers, two of the moving spirits behind the offending organization, were wealthy Presbyterian converts to an undenominational activism already much in evidence south of the border. For a decade spanning the turn of the century their religious enterprise challenged Scottish ecclesiastical conventions, provoking strong contemporary reactions and leading to a marked divergence in subsequent historical assessment. From 'the Wesley and Whitefield of Scotland',[2] at one extreme, they have been described less fulsomely as the source of a movement which, though it alarmed all the Presbyterian churches, proved to be short-lived, dying away 'among its own domestic quarrels', 'marred by bitterness of speech, obscurantism and fanaticism'.[3]

Contemporaries seem to have found it little easier to agree on the leaders' personal qualities. In 1796 Thomas Jones, the minister of Lady Glenorchy's Chapel in Edinburgh, commended Robert Haldane to William Wilberforce as 'a man of strickt honour integrity religion prudence and virtue', who being 'possessed of a fortune from £50,000 to £60,000 . . . thinks it is his duty . . . to employ a considerable portion of it in promoting the cause of God'.[4] By 1809 Haldane's former friend and colleague, Greville Ewing, had become so disenchanted with his methods

---

[1] *Acts of the General Assembly of the Church of Scotland, 1638–1842* (Edinburgh, 1843), p. 871.
[2] G. Yuille, ed., *History of the Baptists in Scotland from Pre-Reformation Times* (Glasgow, 1927), p. 55.
[3] A. J. Campbell, *Two Centuries of the Church of Scotland 1707–1929* (Paisley, 1930), p. 160.
[4] Thomas Snell Jones to William Wilberforce, 14 Sept. 1796, Edinburgh University Library, Laing MSS La.II.500. Lady Glenorchy's Chapel was a proprietary building linked to the Church of Scotland.

that, having referred to him scornfully as 'the POPE of independents', he accused him bitterly of 'the greatest effort [he had ever seen] from any motive whatsoever, to ruin the comfort, and the usefulness, of a minister of the gospel'.[5] Though his brother, James, appears to have inspired a more universal affection, the forcefulness of both personalities ensured that mere neutrality would never be easy.

From the fleeting comments offered by historians the most positive evaluation of the Haldanes centres upon their 'undenominationalism' or 'catholicity'.[6] Their obvious dislike of denominational division and their willingness to make common cause in Evangelical ventures with all people of similar sentiments has prompted the most recent work on Scottish Congregationalism to speak of their advocacy of 'ecumenical Christianity'.[7] While this is to some extent misleading, a more wide-spread view is that the diminished emphasis on ecclesiastical distinctions was accompanied by a beneficial release from the tyranny of conventional and external forms of worship.[8] In its best moments the Haldane movement focused upon the more fundamental issues at the heart of religious life.

Negatively, most commentators have noted the link within the new movement between the propensity for innovation and the appearance of a critical spirit leading to division, disenchantment, and ultimately to failure;[9] a tendency to ignore the wider principles of religion in favour of tithing mint, dill, and cummin. In one or two summaries, however, there is an interesting variation on the latter theme, for while the work of the Haldanes is not seen as accomplishing anything significant in its own right, it is regarded as a necessary goad, having the most salutary effect upon a neglectful and complacent religious establishment.[10]

---

[5] G. Ewing, *Facts and Documents respecting the Connections which have subsisted between Robert Haldane, Esq. and Greville Ewing, laid before the public, in consequence of Letters which the Former has addressed to the Latter, respecting the Tabernacle at Glasgow* (Glasgow, 1809), pp. 249–50.

[6] J. MacInnes, *The Evangelical Movement in the Highlands of Scotland 1688 to 1800* (Aberdeen, 1951), p. 128; C. G. Brown, *The Social History of Religion in Scotland since 1730* (London, 1987), pp. 121–2.

[7] H. Escott, *A History of Scottish Congregationalism* (Glasgow, 1960), p. 80.

[8] W. L. Mathieson, *Church and Reform in Scotland. A History from 1797 to 1843* (Glasgow, 1916), p. 69; Campbell, *Two Centuries*, p. 161.

[9] G. Struthers, *The History of the Rise, Progress, and Principles of The Relief Church, embracing notices of the Other Religious Denominations in Scotland* (Glasgow, 1843), pp. 391, 405–7; J. Ross, *A History of Congregational Independency in Scotland* (Glasgow, 1900), pp. 82–4.

[10] J. Cunningham, *Church History of Scotland*, 2 vols (Edinburgh, 1859), 2, p. 577; MacInnes, *Evangelical Movement*, pp. 150–1.

In January 1798, following a lengthy but encouraging exploratory tour to the north of Scotland by James Haldane, John Aikman, and Joseph Rate, an itinerancy which discovered a ready response to evangelism in many places, and especially in the remote county of Caithness, a group of lay-men met in Edinburgh to draw up the constitution of the SPGH.[11] At the heart of the new society was the conviction that many parts of the country were deprived of adequate means of religious instruction.

The founding address set out in unequivocal terms the undenomina-tional character of the new body, declaring: 'it is not our design to form or to extend the influence of any sect. Our sole intention is to make known the everlasting gospel of our Lord Jesus Christ.' It was envisaged that the society would 'be composed of persons of every denomination, holding unity of faith in the leading doctrines of Christianity'. Its agents, both itinerant preachers and catechists, were required 'to endeavour to strengthen the hands of all faithful ministers of Jesus Christ of whatever denomination, and as far as they [could] discourage all bitter party spirit, wherever they discover[ed] it among Christians'.[12]

In adopting these aims the new society stood firmly in the Evangelical tradition of the 1790s, a decade which saw the formation of many similar co-operative schemes from the Village Itinerancy and the Religious Tract Society to the [London] Missionary Society. Against a background of population movement, social and political upheaval, and growing dis-satisfaction with the established forms of religion, the new co-operative Christian spirit suited the needs of the age.

Nor was co-operation merely a matter of expedience. Throughout their careers as church leaders the Haldanes were prepared to work with anyone whose aims were compatible with their own. In their early, Presbyterian phase both brothers gave their support to the Society in Scotland for Propagating Christian Knowledge (SSPCK). James served a regular three-year term on the committee of directors from March 1796 until December 1798, the eve of his ordination as an Independent pastor.[13] From his 1796 tour with Charles Simeon to the welcome he extended at his own pulpit in Edinburgh to ministers of various persuasions, including

---

[11] The wholly lay character of the SPGH was unusual. The long-established Society in Scotland for Propagating Christian Knowledge had always exhibited strong clerical direction, but even in newer bodies such as the Edinburgh and Glasgow Missionary Societies the ministerial element remained prominent.

[12] *An Account of the Proceedings of the Society for Propagating the Gospel at Home, from their commence-ment, December 28. 1797, to May 16. 1799* (Edinburgh, 1799), pp. 8, 11, 14.

[13] Edinburgh, Scottish Record Office, MS GD 95/2/11.

Anglicans, Independents, and Baptists, the former ship's captain displayed an evangelist's disregard for the niceties of denominational distinction.[14] On his preaching tours, while he tended at first to criticize laxity, error, and narrowness wherever he found them, he readily identified with those of similar views, such as the parish minister at Tain in Easter Ross, and George Cowie, the Antiburgher minister at Huntly, who shared the same interest in evangelism.[15]

Although the Haldane movement evoked little response in Scottish Episcopalian circles, apart from the brief itinerancy of William Ward based on the Chapel of Old Deer, in Aberdeenshire,[16] friendly contacts with English Evangelical clergymen were more substantial. In addition to the dubious help of Rowland Hill,[17] a considerable influence came through the correspondence of John Campbell with leading figures in the English revival. Campbell, the 'philanthropic ironmonger' of Edinburgh's Grassmarket, was both an intimate friend of the Haldanes and other Scottish Evangelicals and of the venerable Anglican clergyman John Newton, Rector of St Mary Woolnoth in the City of London.[18] These personal contacts were supplemented by the monthly appearance of the *Missionary Magazine*,[19] an Edinburgh-based periodical which copied the format and content of the English *Evangelical Magazine*.[20] The Scottish publication gave those associated with the SPGH a detailed awareness of the wider scale of Christian expansion, including ventures which received Anglican support.

As the Scottish movement achieved a degree of stability and success, plans were set in motion for the creation in the largest and most strategically sited burghs of tabernacles or preaching centres on the Whitefieldite model; meeting places which the poor could attend freely in order to hear

[14] A. Haldane, *The Lives of Robert Haldane of Airthrey, and of his brother, James Alexander Haldane*, 3rd edn. (London, 1853), pp. 136–44, 219, 232, 298; D. Reeves, 'The interaction of Scottish and English Evangelicals 1790–1810' (Glasgow M.Litt. thesis, 1973), pp. 119–21.
[15] J. A. Haldane, *Journal of a Tour through the Northern Counties of Scotland and the Orkney Isles, in Autumn 1797* (Edinburgh, 1798), pp. 79, 90–1.
[16] John Craigie to William Robertson, 6 April 1799, SRO, MS GD 214/659; Dundee University Library, Br. MS 3/DC/7; *Missionary Magazine*, 4 (1799), pp. 110–11.
[17] Hill's practical assistance was reinforced by the journals of his two Scottish preaching tours which were published in 1799 and 1800, and by his *Series of Letters, occasioned by the late Pastoral Admonition of the Church of Scotland* (Edinburgh, 1799).
[18] R. Philip, *The Life, Times, and Missionary Enterprises, of the Rev. John Campbell* (London, 1841), pp. 79–100.
[19] *The Missionary Magazine, a periodical Monthly Publication, intended as A Repository of Discussion, and Intelligence respecting the Progress of the Gospel Throughout the World* (Edinburgh, 1796–1813).
[20] The *Evangelical Magazine* had commenced publication in 1793.

a succession of Evangelical preachers.[21] Though the new buildings soon acquired a quasi-denominational character, serving as homes for congregations of 'tabernacle people',[22] their existence, especially in the early stages of the movement, represented a genuine expression of the undenominational spirit. The substance of the message preached from their pulpits, as in the open air, was biblical and conversionary, and as such devoted little thought to the weightier matters of church order. While in the longer term the experiment proved unstable,[23] the immediate effect of the tabernacles was to provide a visible focus of unity and achievement.

Despite its essential concern for the common elements of Reformed Protestantism, the initial success of the Haldane movement provoked a strong reaction from the Scottish churches. Unconvinced by its protestations that it had no intention of creating another sect, the opponents of the new Evangelicalism were alarmed precisely by its indifference towards existing forms of Presbyterianism. Within the Established Church the hostility of the dominant Moderate party, with its distaste for any form of enthusiasm, was both predictable and obvious. As the 1799 Pastoral Admonition, Declaratory Act and associated correspondence reveal, leaders such as George Hill of St Mary's College, St Andrews, objected strongly to what they regarded as an attempt by the missionary preachers to alienate the affections of the people from their parish ministers.[24] The smaller Presbyterian bodies, the Antiburgher and Relief synods, reacted against the Haldane preachers with similar proscriptive measures.[25] The very existence and operations of a new and aggressively expansionist body such as the SPGH seemed to imply a measure of criticism and to threaten the future viability of local congregations.

For the Established Church there was the additional fear that this new unitive movement concealed more sinister republican and democratic ideals. As early as January 1797 William Porteous, a Glasgow minister, had voiced this concern in connection with Robert Haldane's contemporary application to the East India Company to go as a missionary to Benares. Writing to Robert Dundas, the Lord Advocate, Porteous stated his belief

---

[21] A. Haldane, *Robert and James Alexander Haldane*, pp. 230, 233; D. E. Wallace, 'The life and work of James Alexander Haldane' (Edinburgh Ph.D. thesis, 1955), pp. 111–12, 121–2.

[22] Struthers, *Relief Church*, p. 387.

[23] Ewing, *Facts and Documents*, Appendix, pp. 257–62; Catherine McNeil to Alexander Haldane, 27 May 1851, Gleneagles, Haldane MSS.

[24] *Acts of the General Assembly*, pp. 868–73; George Hill to Henry Dundas, 30 May 1799, SRO, MSS GD 51/5/427/6–7.

[25] Struthers, *Relief Church*, pp. 404–5; Haldane, *Robert and James Alexander Haldane*, pp. 260–1.

'that the whole of this missionary business grows from a democratical root'.[26] In this, as in the other areas of concern, the substance and force behind the complaint stemmed from the recognition that a new and unprecedented combination of interests had appeared which paid scant regard to conventional norms.

If the confrontation which developed during the late 1790s represented a clash between the opposing interests of religious revival and traditional churchmanship, the Haldanes appeared two decades later in more surprising circumstances: at the heart of a bitter dispute involving one of the primary instruments of Evangelicalism. The new controversy erupted in 1821, when Robert Haldane began investigating the practices of the British and Foreign Bible Society.

In the Apocrypha Controversy, as it came to be known, there were no factors of ecclesiastical polity or ministry to cloud the issue. The debate centred upon the practical expression of Christian unity made possible by the fundamental rule of the Bible Society, the circulation of the Scriptures without note or comment. In August that year it had come to Haldane's notice that Continental versions of the Bible circulated by the Society included the Apocrypha.[27] Not only in his eyes was scriptural purity at stake, but also the clarity and effectiveness of evangelism, for the Bible Society had been created in 1804 as a primary instrument of the Evangelical Revival. Out of the many societies formed in that period, it alone, by virtue of its simple and unexceptionable aim, had been able genuinely to transcend denominational barriers and thereby attract the widest measure of support.[28]

Over the ensuing twelve years Robert Haldane fought a tireless campaign on conjunction with the leading Church of Scotland Evangelical, Andrew Thomson, and the Edinburgh auxiliary of the Bible Society, against what he believed to be the compromising policies of the Earl Street committee of the parent body. In a succession of lengthy tracts Haldane sought to expose the naïvety, expediency, and duplicity of the London directors, the heterodoxy of many of their Continental agents, the hostile attitude of the latter towards evangelical activity, the deficiency of certain translations employed by the society, and the theological harm caused by circulating the Apocrypha with its mixture of 'absurdities' and 'pernicious doctrines'.[29]

---

[26] William Porteous to Robert Dundas, 24 Jan. 1797, EUL, Laing MSS La.II.500.
[27] A. Haldane, *Robert and James Alexander Haldane*, pp. 517–18.
[28] R. H. Martin, *Evangelicals United: Ecumenical Stirrings in Pre-Victorian Britain, 1795–1830* (Metuchen, N.J., 1983), pp. 84–7, 92–3.
[29] R. Haldane, *Review of the Conduct of the Directors of the British and Foreign Bible Society, relative to*

As an opponent of Bible Society policy Haldane did not stand alone, yet there cannot have been many more forthright attacks upon the directors than those which flowed from his pen. If they persisted in their errors, he believed, their clear duty was to adopt a more appropriate name, one which emphasized the inclusion of the Apocrypha. The Society's supporters would then be under no illusion as to the object to which their donations were applied. The published reports, he suggested with unconcealed scorn, should state that

> This is a Society which does *not* confine itself with rigorous exactness to the dissemination of the Holy Scriptures, as they are received by Christians of different denominations in this country, who have all resolved to merge their peculiarities so as to agree in publishing, as the Bible, whatever shall be considered to be the Bible, whether in Christian, Mahometan, or Pagan countries: to all of which it has pledged itself to extend its influence.[30]

Despite the catholicity of his intentions and the interdenominational unity of the Edinburgh committee, a body which included both Churchmen and Dissenters, it is all too easy, given Haldane's developing reputation for controversy, to see his Calvinist and biblical susceptibilities as shibboleths standing in the way of a wider co-operation between Christians of different persuasions. The Scottish controversialist would, of course, have regarded any such collaboration as entirely spurious.

Like many exponents of Evangelicalism operating in a climate of disdain for ideas associated with enthusiastic manifestations of religious revival, the author of *The Evidence and Authority of Divine Revelation* and the *Exposition of the Epistle to the Romans*[31] was fond of emphasizing his wholehearted commitment to the classical doctrines of the Christian faith. In his *Letter to the Editor of the Edinburgh Christian Instructor* (1820) he set his own concern for orthodoxy against various erroneous notions culled from the writings of eminent Churchmen, including William Warburton and William Paley. Four years later, in his reply to strictures made by Professor

---

the Apocrypha and to their Administration on the Continent (Edinburgh, 1825), pp. 50–1, 72–3; *Review of the Conduct of the Rev. Daniel Wilson, on the Continent, as a member of the Society for Promoting Christian Knowledge, and of the British and Foreign Bible Society . . .* (Edinburgh, 1829), cap. 3.

[30] R. Haldane, *Review of the Conduct of the Directors of the British and Foreign Bible Society*, pp. 35–6.
[31] The first editions of these works were published in 1816 and 1835 respectively.

Chenevière of Geneva in the pages of the *Monthly Repository*, he drew an even more powerful contrast between his own affinity with the teachings of Calvin and his fellow Reformers, and the deviation from those doctrines displayed by the Venerable Company of Pastors.[32]

Yet the impressive list of writings published by the Haldanes in their very titles denoted a strong controversial tendency. Repeatedly the authors emphasized their differences with contemporary church leaders on many of the central issues of Christian theology. Moderate parish ministers in Scotland, encountered by James Haldane during his 1797 tour, were castigated for their resort to a pulpit doctrine enshrining the merit of good works, rather than justification by faith alone.[33] The Genevan pastors, led by Chenevière, were rebuked by his brother for their denial of the divinity of Christ, and their rejection of a range of biblical ideas contemptuously dismissed as 'the mysterious points of the Christian religion'.[34] Professor Tholuck of Halle University, quoted elsewhere sympathetically for his negative assessment of the vitality of Continental religion in the mid 1820s,[35] was censured a decade later for his own Neology.[36] Even fellow Evangelicals and Dissenters were taken to task for errors ranging from an overemphasis on the human response to God, and a rejection of limited atonement,[37] to Edward Irving's insistence on the corruptibility of the human nature of Christ.[38] Ironically, this eagerness to criticize the doctrinal shortcomings of others conveys an impression not of mainstream sympathies, but of an outlook essentially sectarian.

The opposition mounted by both writers to the theological errors they detected around them was well argued and logical. Robert Haldane in particular emphasized the destructive effect of false belief on the complex

---

[32] R. Haldane, *Letter to M. J.J. Chenevière, Pastor and Professor of Divinity at Geneva: occasioned by his 'Summary of the Theological Controversies which of late Years have agitated the City of Geneva',* published in the Monthly Repository of Theology and General Literature* (Edinburgh, 1824), pp. 2–8, 24–5.

[33] J. A. Haldane, *Journal of a Tour*, pp. 58, 71.

[34] R. Haldane, *Letter to M. J.J. Chenevière*, p. 22.

[35] R. Haldane, *A Second Review of the Conduct of the Directors of the British and Foreign Bible Society, containing an Account of the Religious State of the Continent* (Edinburgh, 1826), p. 52.

[36] R. Haldane, *For the Consideration of the Ministers of the Church of Scotland. Remarks on Dr Tholuck's Exposition of St Paul's Epistle to the Romans, translated by one of themselves* (Edinburgh, 1837), pp. 4–5.

[37] J. A. Haldane, *Man's Responsibility; the Nature and Extent of the Atonement; and the Work of the Holy Spirit; in reply to Mr Howard Hinton and the Baptist Midland Association* (Edinburgh, 1842), part 2, caps 1–2.

[38] J. A. Haldane, *Refutation of the Heretical Doctrine Promulgated by the Rev. Edward Irving, respecting the Person and Atonement of the Lord Jesus Christ* (Edinburgh, 1829), p. 9.

of doctrines which constituted the Gospel. In his reply to Chenevière he recounted his own systematic use of the Epistle to the Romans to demonstrate to the Genevan theological students, who had gathered in his house in 1817, the principal Pauline teachings concerning the person and work of Christ. He attempted also to show the steps by which he believed the city's pastors had undermined the doctrinal integrity of the faith. In this work, as in the tracts concerning the Bible Society, he displayed a low regard for the theological condition of Continental Protestantism. Many Continental theologians, in his eyes, were beyond the pale of Christian co-operation. Their heterodoxy merely lent eight to a deliberate campaign to subvert, neutralize, and even persecute orthodox Christianity. As can be seen from both the Geneva and Apocrypha controversies, a constant polemical barrage was maintained against the insidious effects of Arminianism. Yet in the end no one error or set of mistakes was regarded as all important. Both writers saw themselves confronted by a shifting network of ideas, not always consistent, but possessing the same debilitating and destructive potential in their effect on vital belief, and, therefore, claiming their best attention as defenders of the faith.

In his 'Summary of the Theological Controversies which of late Years have agitated the City of Geneva', published in 1824, Chenevière had defined his adversary's views as intolerant and partisan. The baneful influence upon the Genevan students he described as:

> A Scotchman, Mr Haldane, a rigid Calvinist, whose theological principles are to be found in print, especially in his Commentary on the Epistle to the Romans, in which those who have the courage to undertake the task may judge of his doctrines.[39]

Assuming a substantial measure of truth in Haldane's own portrayal of Chenevière, the Genevan Professors' description was entirely predictable. Yet even the more sympathetic Ami Bost, himself a participant in the Swiss *Réveil*, had reservations concerning the Scotsman's views:

> On peut admettre qu'il fallait au commencement de l'œuvre, et en présence d'une incrédulité presque absolue, des principes rigoureux: et tous ceux qui ont connu M. Haldane s'accordent, sans exception, à en parler avec un amour, une reconnaissance et un respect également profonds. Quant à moi . . . je ne l'ai pas connu personnellement. Il est

---

[39] *Monthly Repository*, 19 (1824), p. 4.

probable que, même après avoir subi son influence, je l'eusse secouée plus tard dans ce qu'elle avait de trop étroit.[40]

Given the use made of reasoned argument by Robert Haldane in pursuit of his apologetic aims, especially in his approach to the early nineteenth-century quest for convincing evidences with which to supplement, or supplant, revelation, it might be possible to ignore the Swiss evidence and to regard his theological views as a synthesis between traditional Calvinism and more optimistic beliefs stemming from the Enlightenment. Such an interpretation might appear to gain credibility from his unwavering interest in evangelism. Yet his approach to the pursuit of Christian evidences was not characteristic of the genre. In *The Evidence and Authority of Divine Revelation* he declared that he had long been deeply convinced that it was necessary 'to attend not merely to the arguments which can be adduced to prove the Bible to be true, but to the Salvation which it reveals'. He aimed to treat the evidences of Christianity not in the abstract, but in close association with doctrine, and as a means of vindicating 'the full inspiration and unspeakable value of the Holy Scriptures'. Obliquely he criticized many of his eighteenth-century predecessors for portraying natural religion based on evidences as an adequate substitute for a faith dependent upon divine revelation.[41]

At a comparatively late point in his life, Robert Haldane reiterated his firm adherence to Calvinist doctrine. Writing against certain views expressed in Tholuck's *Exposition of St Paul's Epistle to the Romans* he described the 'moderate Calvinism' professed by some of his contemporaries as 'refined Arminianism'. It was, he argued, 'impossible to modify the former without sliding into the latter'. Election, though a doctrine unpalatable to many Christians because of their faulty conception of divine truth, was explicitly taught in Scripture and was essential to the biblical concept of salvation.[42] In the writings of each of the brothers reliance upon reason was ultimately limited by deference to biblical authority. Repeated appeals were made to the obvious meaning of Scripture, and if their Calvinism has to be qualified it can only be so by the addition of a prefix such as 'biblical' or 'evangelical'. Haldaneism was not a resurgence of early eighteenth-century Calvinism, with its gloomy emphasis upon the doctrine of reprobation. Of the two men Robert evinced the greater

---

[40] A. Bost, *Mémoires pouvant servir à l'Histoire du Réveil Religieux des Églises Protestantes de La Suisse et de La France, etc.*, 3 vols (Paris, 1854–5), 1, p. 81.

[41] 2nd edn., 2 vols (London, 1834), 1, pp. i–ii, xvi–xviii.

[42] R. Haldane, *Tholuck's Exposition*, p. 18.

concern for the philosophical aspect of theology, yet even he made little mention of hell or reprobation. In his reply to Chenevière, as in his later exposition of Romans, he treated election as a positive concept, one which was a source of joy to the Christian believer.[43] Ultimate respect was accorded to the idea of divine sovereignty, since every other doctrine was seen to be contingent upon it. In consequence he displayed a marked reluctance to probe the adverse significance of limited atonement, despite his willingness to affirm his belief in the doctrine only days before his death.[44]

Though James Haldane restated his own adherence to the doctrines of the Westminster Confession as late as 1846,[45] his writings display a less formal commitment to Calvinism than that expressed by his brother. While their differences in matters of belief were minimal, James made little if any reference to any inherited system of doctrine, appealing only to scriptural authority and apostolic practice. It was that biblicism which led him, rather exceptionally given the confessional nature of Scottish churchmanship, to reject explicitly as early as 1806 the authority of the Confession.[46] In practice that rejection is not so surprising, for there was in this period a widespread movement away from belief in the covenanted community.[47] His anti-confessional stance was, moreover, far from complete, for although he had withdrawn his formal assent to the Confession, he had not rejected its theology. His objections were concerned with its social and political implications, and with the idea of so much significance being attached to historical and, therefore, ultimately fallible human constructs, in preference to the authority of the divinely-inspired text.

If the first signs of the Haldanes' sensitivity towards civil religion began to emerge, as the testimony of Greville Ewing and James Somerville suggests, in private discussions following their adoption of Evangelicalism,[48] the period prior to the Pastoral Admonition remained one of close

[43] R. Haldane, *Letter to M. J.J. Chenevière*, pp. 36–7, 38, 93–5; *Exposition of the Epistle to the Romans: with Remarks on the Commentaries of Dr Macknight, Professor Moses Stuart, and Professor Tholuck*, 8th edn., 3 vols (Edinburgh, 1859), 2, pp. 302–27, Commentary on Romans 8. 29–30.

[44] A. Haldane, *Robert and James Alexander Haldane*, p. 633.

[45] *Ibid.*, p. 652.

[46] J. A. Haldane, *A View of the Social Worship and Ordinances Observed by the First Christians, Drawn from the Sacred Scriptures Alone: being An Attempt to Enforce their Divine Obligation; and to represent the guilt and evil consequences of neglecting them*, 2nd edn. (Edinburgh, 1806), p. 108; *Observations on Mr Brown's Vindication of the Presbyterian Form of Church Government, As Professed in the Standards of the Church of Scotland* (Edinburgh, 1806), pp. 33, 40–1.

[47] Mathieson, *Church and Reform*, pp. 32–3, 45–6, 57–62.

[48] Ewing, *Facts and Documents*, pp. 7–8; R. Haldane, *Address to the Public concerning Political*

connections with the Established Church. However strongly they felt about the lethargy and theological shortcomings of the Scottish clergy, their new active faith led them to regard themselves as agents of the wider Church, whose duty was to engage with others of similar philanthropic intentions. It was in this spirit that Robert Haldane conceived the plan of selling his estate at Airthrey, near Stirling, and with the proceeds establishing a privately sponsored mission in Bengal. Of his three projected companions, two were active ministers of the Established Church, while the other, though a Dissenter in England because of his non-episcopal ordination, had received his training at the Edinburgh Divinity Hall.[49]

In the stream of importunate letters and the printed *Memorial* directed in turn between September 1796 and the following summer at the Lord Advocate, the Secretary of State for War and the Colonies, and the directors of the East India Company, the Airthrey landowner emphasized his broad Christian concern for the people of India. In an early letter to Henry Dundas he argued that plans in hand to create an extensive religious establishment in India would not be affected by his own proposal: 'My plan does not supersede theirs. The field is by much too ample for us all; & I am sure the Gentlemen will rejoice at any assistance which can be given them.'[50] Writing to the Secretary of State's nephew, Robert Dundas, in a markedly more insistent and less deferential vein, Haldane took care to align his project with the Scottish Establishment:

> Indeed we can scarcely suppose that you will not grant our request, when we are assured that you countenanced the Scotch Society for propagating the Gospel, & expressed your affection for the Christian Religion, your predeliction [*sic*] for the Church of Scotland, & approbation of the general views & objects of the Society—Our views are entirely the same as theirs & therefore they ought also to meet with your Countenance & approbation. At the same time we think it

---

Opinions, and Plans lately adopted to Promote Religion in Scotland, 2nd edn. (Edinburgh, 1800), p. 32. Somerville was the senior parish minister at Stirling from 1793 until 1817†.

[49] Greville Ewing was an assistant to Thomas Jones at Lady Glenorchy's Chapel, Edinburgh until December 1798 when he left the Established Church in order to become a Congregational minister at the Haldane Tabernacle in Glasgow. William Innes held the second parish charge at Stirling until he resigned in 1799 to become the resident minister at the Dundee Tabernacle. David Bogue was pastor of an Independent church at Gosport, Hampshire, a position which he held from 1777 until 1825†.

[50] Robert Haldane to Henry Dundas, 30 Sept. 1796, Edinburgh, National Library of Scotland, MS 2257 fol. 53ʳ.

proper to observe that we are no bigots to any sect. What we wish to propagate is the great Doctrines & principles of Christianity—Modes & Forms of Worship are with us things of far inferiour considera-tion.[51]

When the plans for the Bengal mission were rejected in January 1797 by the East India Company directorate, Robert Haldane turned his atten-tion to another possible means of realizing his aim with semi-official church blessing. At the beginning of February he wrote to the committee of directors of the SSPCK requesting a commission from the Society 'and authority to such as are Ministers among us to preach the Gospel abroad, and to those of us who are not Ministers to assist them as Catechists'. In March a general meeting of the Society, having carefully considered a report from a subcommittee appointed to investigate the matter, approved the request and the text of the commission. The latter stipulated that Ewing, Innes, and Bogue, the ministers involved, should demit their charges in a regular manner, that the expenses of the work should be borne entirely by those commissioned, that a regular report of the work should be submitted to the Society, and that the commission should not in any way be deemed to interfere with the legal rights of any other corpor-ate body or chartered company.[52] Although the plan never came to fruition, Robert Haldane's acceptance by the Society in the relatively humble role of catechist marked the closest the Haldane movement came to a formal expression of its catholic aspirations.

Although, as William Innes later recalled, the source of inspiration for the India project was the first account of William Carey's mission to Bengal,[53] too much significance should not be attached to the Dissenting aspect of that English precedent. The Scottish plan owed more to the zeal of a new convert, and to the undenominational character of the Christianity embraced, than to any consideration of the relationship between religion and the State. When, therefore, the dream of an overseas venture proved impossible and the Haldanes turned to domestic evan-gelism, there is little reason for doubting the sincerity of the non-sectarianism which they expressed in 1799 through the SPGH. Nor is it surprising that two years earlier Robert Haldane rounded indignantly on John Robison for a serious calumny against him. The Edinburgh professor

---

[51] Robert Haldane to Robert Dundas, 28 Sept. 1796, EUL, Laing MSS La.II.500.
[52] SRO, MSS GD 95/2/11 and GD 95/1/6. I am indebted to David Currie for bringing these references to my attention.
[53] William Innes to Alexander Haldane, undated, Gleneagles, Haldane MSS.

in a purported exposé of a sinister international conspiracy had attributed to the would-be missionary, with thinly veiled anonymity, the statement that 'he would willingly wade to the knees in blood to overturn the establishment of the Kirk of Scotland'.[54]

Yet, as the discussions within the Haldane–Ewing circle indicate, doubts existed from a very early stage concerning the validity of religious establishments, a debate which in the form of an untimely leak almost certainly provided the basis for Robison's lurid attribution. After 1797 the force of questioning intensified as relationships between the evangelists and the Established Church began to deteriorate. With the publication of the General Assembly's 1799 Declaratory Act against unqualified ministers and preachers, and a further report investigating the most effective method of regulating 'vagrant teachers and Sunday schools',[55] leading Churchmen openly appealed to the civil power for assistance in controlling the new expansionist religious movement.[56] William Robertson, the procurator of the Church of Scotland, obligingly provided the Lord Advocate with a long and detailed list of relevant legislation already to be found on the statute-book.[57] Nor was recourse to the law only contemplated in Edinburgh. Both the records of the Presbytery of Caithness and private correspondence reveal that prosecutions were brought against the SPGH preachers John Cleghorn and William Ballantine at Inverness justiciary court in September 1799 on the grounds of their unauthorized celebration of marriages. Those who supported the accused feared a sentence of transportation, though in the event no penalty was imposed.[58]

Even before the Established Church had begun to apply formal methods of control the Haldanes' attitude had hardened. On 3 February 1799 James was ordained as pastor of the Congregational church newly constituted in the Edinburgh Circus. What had commenced the previous summer as a means of providing indoor accommodation for evangelistic preaching to the city's poorer inhabitants had begun to evolve into a gathered church. Under the twin influences of practical necessity and scriptural exposition the rationale of the new type of ecclesiastical organ-

---

[54] J. Robison, *Proofs of a Conspiracy against all the Religions and Governments of Europe, carried on in the secret meetings of Free Masons, Illuminati and Reading Societies* (Edinburgh, 1797), p. 485; A. Haldane, *Robert and James Alexander Haldane*, pp. 212–17.

[55] *Acts of the General Assembly*, pp. 868–9, 873–5.

[56] George Hill to Henry Dundas, 30 May 1799, SRO, MS GD 51/5/427/6, fol. 2ᵛ.

[57] William Robertson to Robert Dundas, 10 May 1799, SRO, MS GD 214/659.

[58] Presbytery of Caithness, minutes 8 Jan. 1799 to 12 Jan. 1802 *passim*, SRO, MS CH 2/47/6; William Sutherland to William Robertson, undated, SRO, MS GD 214/659; Catherine McNeil to Miss Haldane, 28 April 1851, Gleneagles, Haldane MSS.

ization gradually developed, with the pastor providing an impetus for the process through his numerous publications setting out the apostolic ideal and the appropriate forms of order and discipline. By 1808 his mature view of the local church, as 'a body of persons collected together by the influence of the truth, and appearing to walk according to it',[59] not only embraced the principle of separation from the world, including the State, but had begun in its quest for purity to discover certain tensions between that goal and the original task of evangelism.[60]

In the gradual emergence of the new form of church community three important elements can be detected. The confluence of Enlightenment thinking and Whitefieldite Evangelicalism had produced an attitude which defined religious life in individual terms. Such an approach allowed the recognition of the essentially secular character of contemporary society. Within the Haldane movement there was from the outset a marked preference for a literal and commonsense treatment of the biblical text. Under the influence of this tendency the earlier Calvinist focus upon Old Testament covenant theology gave way to a simple, pragmatic quest for apostolicity. As the concept of apostolic order developed, so, in turn, the initial practical aims began to yield to more theoretical considerations. In 1807, at Kingsland Chapel on the northern outskirts of London, the pastor, John Campbell, found himself facing solemn warnings and even sarcasm from Robert Haldane regarding the danger of preferring 'usefulness' to 'duty'. Campbell was only able to resist the pressure exerted by his Scottish friend with the help of letters he had received over many years from his non-separatist confidant, John Newton.[61]

By 1808 the transition from national church to radical Independency had been completed. The former willingness to subordinate matters of organization and government to the all-consuming task of evangelism had been replaced by the conviction that any formal link between Church and State was indefensible, being intrinsically harmful to true religion. The earlier insistence upon common action had given way to an equally striking preoccupation with order and discipline. Yet James Haldane, whose writings most clearly illustrate the new focus of attention, steadily refused to advocate any form of resistance to the Established Church

---

[59] J. A. Haldane, *Presbyterian Form of Church Government*, p. 10.
[60] J. A. Haldane, *Observations on the Association of Believers; Mutual Exhortation; the Apostolic Mode of Teaching; Qualifications and Support of Elders; Spiritual Gifts, &c.* (Edinburgh, 1808), pp. 65, 86–8.
[61] Philip, *John Campbell*, pp. 359–61.

other than that of scriptural argument. Instead, he portrayed the later refusal of the Voluntaries to pay the annuity tax, levied for the support of the established clergy, as a rejection of the biblical injunction to be subject to civil government.[62] Though he could not himself support the principle of establishment, he warned in 1832 that the growing enthusiasm for the forcible separation of Church and State marked not a coming triumph for Christianity, but rather the entrance upon an apocalyptic struggle with the forces of infidelity.[63]

Prominent among James Haldane's reasons for disapproving of establishment was his belief that the civil connection exerted a deleterious influence upon the Church's ministry. In a reply to Thomas Chalmers he suggested that worldliness and professionalism were the hallmarks of an established clergy.[64] Although he was able to maintain a lasting friendship with parish ministers who shared his Evangelical convictions, his relationship with others was less satisfactory. Haldane's early strictures against the clergy emerged in the context of his own itinerant preaching. They were concerned not primarily with moral weakness or practical shortcomings, but with the doctrinal and spiritual contribution made by the individual to public worship. Gone was the old respect for clerical learning: in its place a more subjective assessment based upon what was regarded as the only appropriate qualification, a knowledge of 'the doctrine of Christ' necessarily denied to those who had not experienced regeneration.[65] At Kirriemuir in 1797, having attended communion in the parish church, the evangelist told a large crowd assembled in the market place 'that what they had heard was not the gospel'.[66] This aggressive practice directed against individuals aroused widespread ill feeling. It was one of the factors which, in spite of its rapid abandonment, persuaded moderate Evangelical ministers not to denounce the Pastoral Admonition and Declaratory Act.[67]

---

[62] J. A. Haldane, *The Voluntary Question Political, Not Religious. A Letter to the Rev. Dr John Brown, occasioned by the allusion in his recent work to the author's sentiments upon National Churches* (Edinburgh, 1839), pp. 4–5.

[63] J. A. Haldane, *The Signs of the Times Considered; with the Duty of Preparation for the Approaching Crisis; being the substance of Five Discourses* (Edinburgh, 1832), pp. 57–8.

[64] J. A. Haldane, *Two Letters to the Rev. Dr Chalmers, on his Proposal for Increasing the Number of Churches in Glasgow*, 2nd edn. (Edinburgh, 1820), pp. 16–17.

[65] J. A. Haldane, *Two Letters to the Rev. Dr Chalmers*, p. 17.

[66] J. A. Haldane, *Journal of a Tour*, p. 40.

[67] Evangelical parish ministers in Edinburgh had, with the opening of the Circus, a more local cause of resentment. Not only did its preference for Independency accentuate the schismatic tendency within Evangelicalism, but the succession of visiting preachers ensured a constant leaching of support from their own congregations.

Yet this early polemical tone, and the encouragement given to altern-ative forms of ministry, did not indicate a complete disregard for existing conventions. Contrary to the impression created by the Pastoral Admoni-tion, with its denunciation of those who assumed 'the character of missionaries' without the 'advantages of regular education',[68] the new movement did not reject the Reformed concern for adequate theological preparation. Instead, it transferred the balance of emphasis from the moral and intellectual sphere to that of spirituality. There was a recogni-tion that even the new type of itinerant preacher needed not only to be literate, but also to receive appropriate instruction in doctrine, biblical exposition, and homiletics. The English model of evangelical expansion, from which much of the Scottish impetus derived, had already created a prominent role for a revised version of the traditional Dissenting academy.[69] It was this which influenced Robert Haldane in the estab-lishment of a series of seminary classes at Glasgow, Dundee, and Edin-burgh between 1799 and 1808.[70]

Those accepted for training were left under no illusion concerning their sponsor's intentions, nor of the strict limitations they were expected to place on personal ambition. As a former journeyman-printer and member of the 1799 class later recalled:

> Mr Haldane, most distinctly gave us, his students, to understand that by that means we were not to rise above the level on which he found us. He was mistaken, for by the very fact that we had become educated persons, and ministers of religion, without indulging any self conceit, we were raised considerably in the social scale.[71]

Though many of the 300 men trained in the seminary classes spent some while as itinerant preachers, the majority eventually became settled pastors. Several attained prominence within the wider Church, while a few achieved some measure of academic distinction. The intellectual content of the courses may have improved when Haldane extended the training period from twelve months to two years, but disagreements connected with the syllabus revealed the sponsor's somewhat limited aims. In 1800 he acceded grudgingly to Greville Ewing's concern to

---

[68] *Acts of the General Assembly*, p. 872. Contrary also to Mathieson, *Church and Reform*, p. 84.
[69] Reeves, 'Scottish and English Evangelicals', p. 1; D. W. Lovegrove, *Established Church, Sectar-ian People. Itinerancy and the Transformation of English Dissent, 1780–1830* (Cambridge, 1988), cap. 4.
[70] R. F. Calder, 'Robert Haldane's theological seminary', *TCHS*, 13 (1937–9), pp.53, 59–63.
[71] David Sutherland to Alexander Haldane, 7 Nov. 1853, Gleneagles, Haldane MSS.

instruct the students in Greek, but refused to consider Latin and Hebrew on the grounds of time and relative usefulness.[72] The possession of a two-year seminary education was sufficient to expose the weakness of most contemporary allegations of ignorance, but the academic training afforded to Haldane students did not compare with the traditional standards set for Presbyterian ordinands.

The practical estrangement from the parish ministry created by these differences in educational attainment and social status was of comparatively little consequence, however, compared to that which stemmed from the apparently amorphous character of the Haldaneite ministry. With their unregulated band of itinerant preachers, catechists, sabbath school teachers, and peregrinating ministers, the operations of the SPGH outraged the Presbyterian sense of propriety. The blurring of the traditional distinction between lay status and that of the ordained preaching ministry offended many within the Established Church, including the widely respected Evangelical leader John Erskine, who believed that laymen at most should confine their activities to private exhortation.[73] Despite a spirited defence of lay preaching,[74] there is no sign that the passage of time lessened this alienation, and the appearance in 1800 of the first products of the Haldane seminary classes, with their dedication to an itinerant ministry, merely served to emphasize the division.

The ordination of James Haldane as pastor of the Circus church might be interpreted as the first sign of a return to a more conventional view of ministry, but this was not the case. Guided by biblical and apostolic practice and influenced by his reading of the eighteenth-century separatists Glas and Sandeman, he moved steadily to a more radical position. By 1806 he was advocating a form of leadership based on a plurality of elders. These men would not be a reiteration of the Presbyterian concept of the ruling elder, for Haldane had already come to reject the lay-clerical distinction as unscriptural. They were instead a group of members set apart and ordained by the congregation for the task of ministry. Quoting a Presbyterian author, he argued that ordination conferred no special status or honour, conveyed no supernatural character, and signified only an

---

[72] Ewing, *Facts and Documents*, pp. 68–70. Haldane argued that more time should be devoted to reading Church History and Divinity and to 'searching and explaining the Scriptures'.

[73] Philip, *John Campbell*, pp. 139, 223–4.

[74] G. Ewing, *A Defence of Itinerant and Field Preaching* (Edinburgh, 1799); R. Hill, *Journal of a Tour through the North of England and parts of Scotland. With Remarks on the Present State of the Established Church of Scotland, And the different Secessions therefrom. Together with . . . Some Remarks on the Propriety of what is called Lay and Itinerant Preaching* (London, 1799).

appointment to a task within the church. Nor was it correct to associate the practice primarily with the administration of the ordinances, for baptism and the Lord's Supper had wrongly usurped the place of preaching.[75]

In 1808 the quest for an apostolic ministry reached its final stage at the Edinburgh Tabernacle, with mutual exhortation being accorded a prominent place in public worship. The significance of this development lay less in its extension of the ministerial function to all church members than in its implications for conventional attitudes towards selection and preparation for the pastoral office. In a pamphlet commending mutual exhortation as a divine ordinance James Haldane argued that existing methods of selecting pastors depended upon human judgement and learning. The process leading to ordination, even among the new Independent congregations, presupposed at least a formal trial of gifts. More commonly, he suggested, 'Young men are obtained from academies; and if they appear to possess a little learning, and a tolerable facility in speaking, every other pastoral qualification is overlooked'. By contrast, the new practice, when incorporated in congregational worship, provided a natural means for the divine choice of pastoral leadership to become apparent.[76] The implications of his views were obvious. Not only did mutual exhortation have the effect of eliminating the element of rational selection, it also removed the need for theological institutions with their manifest reliance upon human learning.[77] Not surprisingly the new elements of worship at the Tabernacle aroused strong opposition. John Aikman described them as 'destructive, both of the pastoral office and of all order in the house of God'.[78] More generally the Haldanes became identified, even in the thinking of many of their former associates, with a restless desire for innovation.

Accusations of that character were by no means new. Almost a decade earlier opponents of the SPGH had criticized the Society's agents for believing that they possessed 'some secret and novel method of bringing

[75] J. A. Haldane, *Social Worship*, pp. 211–17, 255–62.
[76] J. A. Haldane, *Observations on . . . Mutual Exhortation*, pp. 41–6.
[77] Although his seminary classes ended in 1808, Robert Haldane continued to show an interest in theological education. Apart from well publicized activities at Geneva and Montauban between 1817 and 1819, he provided financial support during the 1820s for the training of Baptist home missionaries at Grantown-on-Spey and for a small institution in Paris. A. Haldane, *Robert and James Alexander Haldane*, p. 331; Robert Haldane to Sergeant Lefroy, 4 Sept. 1822, Gleneagles, Haldane MSS.
[78] A. Haldane, *Robert and James Alexander Haldane*, p. 361.

men to heaven'. The ecclesiastical legislation of 1799 had sought to combat contempt for 'the rules ... for the orderly dispensation of the word and sacraments'.[79] Yet the Haldanes and their disciples, at the outset at least, had shown few signs of renouncing accepted patterns of worship and discipline. Practical itinerancy provided little scope for experiment in either sphere.

During the early preaching tours attendance at parish worship was not uncommon, and while the less congenial sermons were often subjected to public scrutiny, there is no suggestion that the itinerant's presence at the service betrayed any kind of ulterior motive. Where sympathetic clergy were involved the situation was more straightforward. In May 1798 Joseph Rate, an itinerant with the SPGH, attended the kirk at East Wemyss, where he 'heard an evangelical lecture from Mr Gib, the minister there'. A few days earlier another of the Society's agents had preached by invitation in the parish church at Croy, near Inverness.[80] The following summer, before the ban on unauthorized preaching had been imposed by the General Assembly, the English itinerant Rowland Hill not only gained access to pulpits at Paisley and Greenock, but with equal significance chose to remain silent in the town of Dumbarton in deference to the Evangelical parish minister, who had not been warned of his coming.[81]

Though the general state of the Church did not impress the early itinerants little was said concerning the subject of discipline. While presbytery minutes recorded routine cases of sabbath-breaking and sexual impropriety, evangelists' journals passed over such matters in silence. Only James Haldane dealt with the wider issue during his first visit to Caithness. Commenting on the low state of religion in that area he drew a firm parallel between the lack of 'faithful', or Evangelical, preaching in the ten parishes of Caithness and the sharp deterioration in ecclesiastical discipline within the county. In particular, he lamented the contemporary practice of commuting for a fine the public profession of repentance for the sins of adultery and fornication. Still worse in his opinion was the general and unhesitating admission of offenders to the communion table once they had paid their fine.[82]

While his remarks indicated a latent concern, they gave no direct hint

---

[79] *Acts of the General Assembly*, pp. 869, 871.
[80] *Proceedings of the SPGH*, pp. 45, 27, 35.
[81] R. Hill, *Journal of a Tour*, pp. 31–4.
[82] J. A. Haldane, *Journal of a Tour*, p. 76.

of his future doubts concerning the possibility of effective discipline within a national church.[83] In 1797 Haldane still appeared to adhere to the traditional concept of the godly commonwealth, and to accept the need for the effective operation of the ecclesiastical courts as the primary agents of Christian discipline.

There was, therefore, prior to the formation of the Circus church in 1799, a largely uncritical acceptance of the existing forms of order and discipline. Preaching occupied a pre-eminent position in worship. Observance of the Lord's Supper and baptism remained the province of the parochial clergy. The proper exercise of ecclesiastical discipline was expected. And until February that year neither brother formally renounced Presbyterianism. The early use of the Circus building was merely an extension of the semi-detached attitude to established religion exemplified by Lady Glenorchy's Chapel and other similar proprietary places of worship. Even after the new church had been constituted, in January 1799, an element of ambiguity remained, for of the 310 persons who united in communion 30 maintained their membership of the Established Church, seeking admission to the Lord's table only on an occasional basis.[84] More significantly for future developments, James Haldane at his ordination to the pastorate, while indicating his approval of the simple and scriptural plan of the church, 'disavowed any confidence in it as a perfect model of a church of Christ, to the exclusion of all others'.[85]

While the pattern of congregational autonomy adopted by the Circus church permitted a more consistent emphasis on discipline, it did not involve a revolution in church order. The professionalism of the educated ministry had given way to a simpler concept, yet the pastoral function continued to be the responsibility of a single leader. Mutual exhortation appeared but only at informal weeknight gatherings confined to church members.[86] The Lord's Supper, no longer regarded as a sacrament, was limited to monthly observance,[87] while in similar fashion the ordinance of baptism retained its traditional character as a rite of inclusion in the Christian community associated primarily with infants.[88] Although the

---

[83] J. A. Haldane, *The Obligation of Christian Churches to Observe the Lord's Supper Every Lord's Day, stated in a Letter to the Church of Christ assembling in the Tabernacle, Edinburgh. To which are added, Miscellaneous Observations* (Edinburgh, 1802), pp. 48–9.

[84] A. Haldane, *Robert and James Alexander Haldane*, p. 237.

[85] *Missionary Magazine*, 4 (1799), p. 78.

[86] J. A. Haldane, *Observations on . . . Mutual Exhortation*, pp. 42–3.

[87] J. A. Haldane, *Lord's Supper*, p. 4.

[88] J. A. Haldane, *Reasons of a Change of Sentiment & Practice on the subject of Baptism; containing a plain view of the signification of the word, and of the persons for whom the ordinance is appointed; Together*

scriptural ideal had begun to exert its influence, reason and custom continued to be powerful factors. In 1802 the innate conservatism of early Independency was openly acknowledged by James Haldane in a pamphlet which argued for a weekly observance of the Lord's Supper. Reviewing the progress of his own thinking, he confessed to his fellow church members:

> From the time of the formation of the church, I should have esteemed it a privilege to have shewed forth [our Lord's] death as often as I commemorated his resurrection. I thought, however, this would have been inexpedient.[89]

In the transitional period between 1799 and 1808 the ordering of church life and worship had more in common with inherited forms than the new principle of congregational government might appear to suggest.

With a suddenness reminiscent of its origins the Haldane movement in 1808 suffered a serious and permanent setback. A damaging schism, which dislocated the Tabernacle congregations, was precipitated by the adoption of antipaedobaptist views by James Haldane. While the example of English Evangelicalism warns that the divisive potential of baptism should not be underestimated,[90] and personal animosities served to intensify the disagreement, other factors were also involved. Those who clung to the original form of Independency attributed most of the blame to the reckless pursuit of change.

By 1805 the practice of weekly communion had spread beyond the Edinburgh Tabernacle. During a visit to Breadalbane, John Campbell noted its regular observance in that area.[91] Yet frequency of communion did not lie at the heart of the 1808 division, in spite of its place among a list of 'ecclesiastical novelties' to which Campbell and others subsequently showed resistance. Far more damaging to unity were changes involving less familiar or popular elements of church order, most notably the elevation to public prominence of exhortation and ecclesiastical discipline. Both prompted objections based on the mixed character of Sunday gatherings. With little prospect of success James Haldane sought to

---

with a full consideration of the Covenant made with Abraham, and its supposed connexion with baptism (Edinburgh, 1808), pp. 1–9.

[89] J. A. Haldane, *Lord's Supper*, pp. 4–5.

[90] Lovegrove, *Established Church, Sectarian People*, pp. 36–7.

[91] J. Campbell, 'Journal of a tour to the North in ye year 1805', 9 June 1805, Gleneagles, Haldane MSS.

appease his critics by arguing that unbelievers who happened to be present could not fail to be impressed and attracted by the seriousness and integrity of the new proceedings.[92]

The opposition generated by these changes in public worship was merely strengthened by the parallel adoption of a plural eldership. Not only did this further innovation appear to threaten the pastoral office, it also showed little evidence of positive success. According to one observer when either of Haldane's colleagues was scheduled to preach, congregational numbers declined dramatically.[93] More significantly, a permanent difficulty was encountered in finding suitable persons who were willing to assume the pastoral role on a shared basis.

The introduction of the new practices was indicative of a sea change in attitudes. In their quest for purity of order the innovators showed that they were prepared to jettison any realistic chance of harmony for the sake of adherence to the letter of Scripture. Still more destructive was the missionary zeal with which they pursued that goal. In spite of their awareness of the dangers of Glasite intolerance, the Haldanes failed to apply to their own context the historical lesson it offered concerning obsession with detail, and the resulting sequence of strife, debility, and ultimate irrelevance.

Nevertheless, even James Haldane was prepared to set limits on experimentation. He recognized the impossibility of recreating with absolute faithfulness an apostolic model of Christianity. While certain practices were linked to specific circumstances, the meaning and character of other features of apostolic life were no longer evident.[94] In one marginal example, that of salutation, he overturned his own earlier suggestion of cultural relativity only to find that its introduction provoked a further minor schism within the Tabernacle congregation,[95] and a harsh lampoon in an anonymous poem entitled *Hypocrisy Detected* (1812), a work which showed an intimate knowledge of the Haldane movement.

Viewed overall the attitudes of the Tabernacle pastor embodied a curious mixture of idealism and reality; elements that were capable of acting in concert as much as in opposition, and with not entirely predictable consequences. Far from welcoming the later Irvingite movement, Haldane's view of the extraordinary nature of New Testament

---

[92] J. A. Haldane, *Observations on . . . Mutual Exhortation*, pp. 64–5, 88–90.
[93] Robert Kinniburgh to Alexander Haldane, 15 March 1851, Gleneagles, Haldane MSS.
[94] J. A. Haldane, *Lord's Supper*, pp. 20–30.
[95] Kinniburgh to A. Haldane, 15 March 1851.

glossolalia led him to join the majority in criticizing the 1830s outburst of tongues, especially the involvement of women.[96] In similar fashion his own determination at the Tabernacle to revive the principal features of apostolic worship experienced a measure of restraint from a combination of concern to avoid unnecessary confrontation and belief in the Christian principle of forbearance.[97]

With the coming of schism the evolution perceptible in the thought and activity of the Haldanes had reached its final stage. The original lack of interest in forms and organization had given way to a self-conscious insistence on apostolic propriety. At the same time unity had to all outward appearances been ousted by the persuasive logic of separation. Yet subsequent events reveal the existence of a continuing tension between these opposing elements. The new and uncompromising biblicism which lay at the roots of the emphasis on separation was itself a unitive phenomenon; a transdenominational development whose origins owed much to Robert Haldane.[98]

In their relationships with Scottish Churchmen the Haldanes continued to display considerable ambiguity. While the younger brother showed no hesitation in publicly challenging the pro-establishment views of Thomas Chalmers,[99] private correspondence between Robert Haldane and the Evangelical leader expressed a close affinity of interests. In comments accompanying an exchange of publications concerning the Epistle to the Romans the Scottish Dissenter manifested a warm regard for Chalmers as a Christian of kindred sympathies to whom the utmost respect and charity was due.[100] As late as 1842, only a few months before his death, he showed himself willing, moreover, to identify publicly with representatives of the national church when he condemned the Edinburgh and Glasgow Railway Company for introducing a Sunday train service. In his attack on the company directors, his call for the exercise of disciplinary powers by the Presbytery of Edinburgh contained a wistful if somewhat inconsistent reminder of the outmoded concept of the Christian commonwealth.[101]

[96] J. A. Haldane, *Signs of the Times*, p. 31.
[97] J. A. Haldane, *Observations on Forbearance* (Edinburgh, 1811), p. [iii].
[98] D. W. Bebbington, *Evangelicalism in Modern Britain. A History from the 1730s to the 1980s* (London, 1989), pp. 87–8.
[99] J. A. Haldane, *Two Letters to the Rev. Dr Chalmers*, esp. letter 1.
[100] Robert Haldane to Thomas Chalmers, 29 Dec. 1837, Edinburgh, New College Library, Chalmers MS CHA 4.264.46.
[101] R. Haldane, *On the Purposed Desecration of the Sabbath, by the Directors of the Edinburgh and Glasgow Railway* (Edinburgh, 1842), pp. 29–30.

This sustained evidence of unity in the face of separation goes some way towards accounting for the sharply diverging historical assessments of the two Scottish Dissenters. Their essential paradox was that of a curious and antipathetic combination of broad Evangelical aims and over-zealous interest in detail and the apportionment of blame. At one and the same time the Haldanes were both catholic and sectarian, irenic yet controversial. The sentiments engendered by these apparent contradictions, even among those potentially sympathetic, were expressed in contemporary polemic in the form of an open charge of hypocrisy.[102] In the light of this and other complicating factors arising from political tensions and personality some loss of unanimity in historical judgement is not altogether surprising.

St Mary's College, University of St Andrews

---

[102] Anon., *Hypocrisy Detected; in a Letter to the Late Firm of Haldane, Ewing, and Co. With a Preface containing the Narrative of Mr. James Reid, a missionary sent by these gentlemen to Upper Canada* (Aberdeen, 1812), p. 72.

ANGLICAN EVANGELICALISM IN THE WEST OF ENGLAND, 1858–1900

by JOHN KENT

THE Church of England Clerical and Lay Association (Western District) for the maintenance of Evangelical Principles was started in 1858 as part of a 'more comprehensive plan for a general organized association'[1] of Anglican Evangelicals. The case for such an association was graphically made by an anonymous clerical pamphleteer:

> Now that the Church of England seems called upon to choose, whether she will give her allegiance to Christ, or to Anti-Christ either as Roman or Neologian or a compromise of both—now that hundreds have actually passed away to Rome, and also that so considerable a number of the younger Clergy are more or less under the seductive influence of her errors so as to render it difficult to meet with like-minded men as fellow-helpers,—now that the State, hitherto bound up with the Church, apparently either contemplates casting her adrift or reducing her to a conation of political servitude,—under these, our present exigencies, the desire for union becomes more intense and irresistible. We want to know each other's thoughts and feelings. We are in great need of mutual information and counsel. We thirst for sympathy and encouragement. We want to act together as one man.[2]

The sources of anxiety are clear: the Roman Catholic revival and the parallel growth of Anglo-Catholicism; the development of a critical Anglican theology which cut across older lines of demarcation; and the increasing secularity of the State, which in 1858 was exemplified in Goverment's Indian policy. One should certainly add a further anxiety, about what seemed to be the limited success of Anglican evangelism. In its origins, therefore, the Evangelical Association was not an aggressive pressure group but a response to external pressure.

The Association's first Minute-Book has survived. The first meeting

---

[1] These words occur on the title-page of a pamphlet: '*Church of England Clerical and Lay Association . . . A Letter to a Clergyman of the Church of England*, signed Presbyter. Seeley, Jackson and Halliday, London. Second edition, 1860.'

[2] *Ibid.*, pp. 6–7.

recorded took place on 23 March 1858. The President was the Reverend Alan Gardner Cornwall, Rector of Newington Bagpath cum Owlpen for forty-four years, and for thirty-two years Rector of Beverstone cum Kingscote. These were adjoining rural parishes in the southern Cotswolds, worth £1,070 between them, and lying a few miles north of Wotton-under-Edge. Cornwall claimed the idea of the Association as his own, though there was at least one other claimant, the Reverend Daniel Capper, who was Rector of Huntley, some miles west of Gloucester, from 1839 to 1865, and who was also present at the first meeting of the committee.[3] Both men belonged to that vigorous type of mid-Victorian clergyman who worked hard to make the parochial system more efficient by church and school building, and by the encouragement of 'lay agency'.

This first meeting was already able to divide the Association into thirteen districts: Gloucester, Bristol, Cheltenham, Stroud, Wotton-under-Edge, Fairford, Swindon, Chippenham, Wickwar, Newnham, Newland, Stow, and Tewkesbury. By 6 July 1858, the committee had set up four other districts: Derby, Dorset, London, and Ledbury. These local groups were linked to the central committee by 'corresponding members', and the idea was to combine the setting up of Conferences at which the members could discuss the subjects nearest to their hearts, with the organization of common action on national Anglican matters. The standing committee was to meet every quarter, and the second meeting, held at Davis's Library in Gloucester (27 April 1858), discussed a list of forty-one topics, which had already been proposed for an opening Conference, and selected four:

(1) Unity of Action.

(2) How far are we justified from Missionary statistics and Home interest in Missions in supposing our progress as a Missionary Church has been coextensive with our improvement as a National Church in the present century, and further how best and most effectually may Christian Missions be supported?

(3) Has the Church of England in this Diocese that influence among the masses of the population which an Established Church ought to have? If not, how is it to be accounted for, and what remedies may be applied?

(4) The duty and importance of unity and individuality, of diversity

---

[3] Capper was born in Cheltenham; he rebuilt the Huntley church at his own cost, with S. S. Teulon as architect, in 1863.

and uniformity, separately and relatively considered, in relation to the maintenance of Evangelical principles.

The committee also chose two reserve topics, first, the question of the effectiveness of special revivalist services, and second, 'the state after death, and after the resurrection'. These six subjects suggest something of the more subjective anxieties of mid-nineteenth-century Anglican Evangelicals, their concern about the success or failure of their evangelism, their fear that unity of action—which they saw was vital to their influence in the Church of England as a whole—would compel them to compromise their highly individualized sense of principle. Among the subjects not chosen at this stage were those dealing with education, with changes in the forms of service, and with attracting the poor to church. There were two references to recent intellectual controversy: 'What effects might be expected from a more general and earnest investigation of the Old Testament not so much in the way of verbal criticism as with regard to Doctrine and History'; and 'Science and Revelation—in relation to geological discoveries'.[4]

These subjects were discussed at the first proper annual meeting of the new body, which was held at Christ Church School Room, The Spa, Gloucester, on 8 and 9 June 1858. Sixty-eight members dined at the Kings Head Hotel on 8 June, and twenty-one members attended the 8 a.m. Holy Communion at Christ Church on 9 June. From this gathering, and from the meeting of the standing committee in Stroud on 6 July 1858, came the impetus for further discussion of the state of the Church of England, and proposals to prepare either petitions to the legislature or memorials to the Queen. One of these was to be about India, with special reference to 'the omission of all recognition of Divine Providence' in the government measures which had followed the Indian Rising. Other possible subjects were liturgical revision; the Maynooth Grant, the abolition of which had been a constant Evangelical demand in the 1857 General Election; and Church Rates, 'with a view to suggest some plan of compromise and final settlement', an interesting comment, since a Church Rate Abolition Bill had passed the House of Commons on 8 June 1858, to be blocked later by the House of Lords.

Here one sees the force of wider Evangelical anxieties about the survival of the Established Church in a Protestant form, and about a secular drift in British society, for which the obvious evidence had been

---

[4] All this information comes from the Association Minute-Book (hereafter AMB), pp. 1–19.

the passing of a Divorce Act in 1857. A revealing scrap of draft paper retained in the Minute-Book on page 31, and referring to a committee meeting held in Bristol on 26 October 1858, said that 'in addition to cleansing the Church from error we are in the midst of many social reforms', and that the combined national influence of Anglican Evangelicals was needed to foster a 'deeper spirituality in religion through which we believe that our rulers will alone be guided aright'. There were hopes of the formation of other Associations in Derby, Dorset (where nothing seems to have happened), and Carlisle. The members were also encouraged to unite in a general observance of 17 November in commemoration of the tercentenary of the Reformation in England.[5]

All these attitudes came out strongly in the production, between November 1858 and June 1859, of an Address to Sir John Lawrence. This said that the Association rejoiced that Lawrence had been made an eminent instrument in the hands of Providence for the preservation of British Rule in Upper India. He had said—and the Association warmly agreed—that 'having endeavoured solely to ascertain what is our Christian duty, we should follow it out to the uttermost', and that

> Christian things done in a Christian way will never alienate the Heathen—about such things there are qualities which do not provoke nor excite distrust, nor harden to resistance. It is when unchristian things are done in the name of Christianity, or when Christian things are done in an unchristian way, that mischief and danger are occasioned.

Every Christian government should accept these principles, the Association said, because 'the safety of our Empire depends upon the national recognition of those principles in every department of government'. And the argument concluded:

> We regard the withholding of God's Holy Word from the Government Schools in India as one of the greatest sins of which a Nation can be guilty.

Lawrence replied to Alan Cornwall on 25 June 1859, saying that he was grateful for God's guidance and protection.[6]

---

[5] AMB, pp. 33–4. The Archbishop of Canterbury was said to be in sympathy with this demonstration.

[6] *Report of the Second Annual Meeting, held 7 and 8 June, 1859 at the St James' Schoolroom Cheltenham*, Davies and Son, Printers, Northgate Street, Gloucester, pp. 15–16.

This Memorial revealed the tension in mid-thirteenth-century Anglican Evangelicalism between past and present. The post-Simeon generation (say 1830–60) had inherited stories of comparative Evangelical success in influencing British culture, a success of which the campaign against slavery became and largely remains a symbol. The Cheltenham Conference praised Sir John Lawrence because he had preserved the Empire and had also borne his witness (a primary Evangelical virtue) against withholding the Bible from government Schools in India. Lawrence did not reject this description of his views and actions.

India after the Rising was no longer, however, a story of Evangelical Anglican success, though Lawrence himself used the word of his own Indian career when he replied to Cornwall. When the India Bill was going through the House of Lords in 1858, for example, Lord Derby dismissed as dangerous 'any attempt on the part of the State to convert the native population from their own religions, however false and superstitious'.[7] One of the reasons for the formation of the Cheltenham Association was a realization that although the leaders of the Victorian State did not mind ecclesiastical rhetoric about a 'British mission' in India, they intended the mission to remain politically secular. Evangelical Imperialists (there is no contradiction in terms here) wanted not only to sanctify British rule in India, but also to transform this sanctification into a total policy. In a perfect religio-political society, as they envisaged it, the State and the Established Church would have combined harmoniously to christianize India.

Action about India was probably the highlight of the annual meeting in 1859. At this point the printed membership was as follows: Bristol: 29, including 4 laymen; Cheltenham: 36, including 12 laymen; Chippenham: 10, all clergymen; Fairford: 8, including 2 laymen; Gloucester: 16, including 4 laymen; Ledbury: 3 clergymen; Newnham (Forest of Dean): 10 clergymen; Northleach: 7 clergy and 1 layman; Stow (Cotswolds): 5 clergy and 1 layman; Stroud: 24, including 5 laymen; Swindon: 9, including 2 laymen; Tewkesbury: 7, including 3 laymen; Wickwar: 4, 2 of them laymen; and Wotton-under-Edge: 5 clergy. This made a total of 175, of whom 36 were laymen. In the copy of the printed record of the meeting

---

[7] G. I. T. Machin's interpretation of Derby's words as 'an almost identical, if coincidental, repetition of a Liberation Society minute of November 1857' seems to me to misunderstand Derby's intention, which was to distance the Government from *all* missionary societies. See G. I. T Machin, *Politics and the Churches in Great Britain 1832 to 1868* (Oxford, 1977), pp. 294–5. Anglican Evangelicals, however, thought that the Government should support Anglican evangelism and disavow Dissenting (liberationist) religious activity.

which I possess 59 other names have been written in, most of them as additions to the printed entry for Bristol, and this would bring the total to 234. My copy belonged to T. W. Boyce, curate of St Werburgh's, who was local secretary for Bristol, and this explains the way in which it has been used.

In addition to these names, which corresponded to the Western District proper, 16 other names were printed under the heading of Derby, which was soon to become a separate district,[8] and 14 under the heading of Dorset, where a separate organization was discussed, but not finally established. The only other substantial group was at Worcester, which had 8 members, 3 of them laymen. A scattering of individuals over several counties brought the final total to about 300. By March 1860 a separate Carlisle Evangelical Union had also been formed, so that by that time much of the west of England had been organized as far as the Anglican Evangelicals were concerned. A local secretary, the Reverend J. S. Jenkinson, Vicar of Battersea, was also recorded under the heading of 'London' by the Western District in 1859, but for the time being he had no members.

In the following year, 1860, when Bath had become part of the Association with 28 members, the total local membership of the Western District reached 276, to which 42 additional members described as 'residing at a distance' could be added. By 1865, in years when the Church of England was in constant internal conflict, the total had risen to 383 (Bath 74 and Bristol 121) with another 91 'residing at a distance'. This level of interest seems to have been maintained into the 1880s, but there was continual dissatisfaction about the inability of Anglican Evangelicals to combine effectively at the national level, that is, to form a successful pressure group. The situation seemed to have improved in 1882 when a Central Union of Clerical and Lay Associations was finally formed, with a central committee of 'well-known clergy and laymen residing in or near London', whose brief was 'to watch events bearing on Church questions and the interests of the Evangelical body'.

Organization was no substitute for a deeper unity, however, and the

---

[8] I have a copy of the printed report of the first meeting of what called itself the Midland District, of which Sir Matthew Blakiston, of Sandbrooke Hall, Ashbourne, was President. The meeting was held in Derby on the 19/20 June 1860; there were then 111 members, almost all in Derbyshire, but there were 7 in Leicestershire and 9 in Nottinghamshire. Dorset was to remain in the Western District. A Northern Home Counties Association held its first Conference on 30 June and 1 July 1862, under the presidency of Robert Hanbury. In 1863 an Eastern District seems to have been formed in Norfolk.

restriction of the central committee to people in or near London told its own story. The Western District declined, and by 1887, for example, the figures had become Bath 48, Bristol 80, Cheltenham 33, Gloucester 12, Gloucestershire 26, Somerset 23, and Wiltshire 6: a total of 228, with 24 additional 'outside members'. And this fall-off continued: in 1899 the total membership was 209, in 1900 it was 219, and in 1901 it had fallen to 197. In 1900 the membership was divided into Bath 35, Bristol 57, Cheltenham 31, Gloucester 7, Gloucestershire 16, Somersetshire 41, Wiltshire 9, and 'outsiders' 23.

A comparison of the Western District Reports for 1860 and 1900 reveals other points about Evangelical Anglican history in the later Victorian period. In Bristol, for example, there were, in 1860, 96 names on the membership list, of which 12 may be deducted as those of men living in parts of Somerset which were no longer put under 'Bristol' in the list of 1900. There were 47 laymen in the total of 84; in 1900, however, only 16 laymen were to be found in a total of 57.

The residential distribution of the Bristol Evangelicals was also interesting. In the late eighteenth and nineteenth centuries Bristol expanded and virtually split in half: a new residential area, built on higher ground, hitherto untouched, which stretched through Clifton, Cotham, and Redland out to Westbury, became a bourgeois enclave separate from and almost independent of the old town in the river valley, from which the middle classes now drew many of their servants. In 1900, at least 42 out of the 57 members' addresses actually lay in this series of estates, 25 of them in Clifton alone, while in 1860, 66 addresses out of the 96/84 had come from the same part of the city. From this point of view Bristol Evangelicalism was territorially confined. It is also relevant, however, that Clifton was the title of the new Roman Catholic bishopric which presided over the re-emergence of Catholicism in the west of England after 1850, and that Anglicans of a broadly 'liberal' kind established Clifton College as a boys' school in the early 1860s. Other new cultural influences were working in Bristol in this period: the new University College was started on the edge of the Clifton area in the 1870s, and in the old city below Clifton and Redland working-class organizations were slowly separating out from the Liberal/Conservative political culture. Only a small High Anglican group, however, which had some links with Clifton College and with St Agnes, the church which the College built in the area of St Paul's, then as now a depressed part of the city, showed much sympathy for working-class political aspirations in the last quarter of the nineteenth century.

Clifton had only one church in 1800. Eight more were built by 1900, five before and three after 1860, a sign of the rapid expansion of this self-consciously middle-class suburb. When the Western District launched an appeal for an Evangelical day- and boarding-school as a further step in the internal consolidation of the group, the first intention was to site it in Clifton. However, a brisk internal debate between 'Bristol' and 'Cheltenham' ended in a resolution that 'an appeal for a Dean Close Memorial Middle Class School to be erected in the West of England be substituted for the circular asking for assistance towards the renting of a house in Clifton, as authorised, December 1st, 1882'.[9] Dean Close's personal links had been with Cheltenham, and the school was eventually founded there. There is a copy of a letter to the *Record*, pasted into the Minute-Book, which said that

> the Woodard Schools are inoculating the middle classes with a High Church leaven. Shall not we who believe that we have God's truth on our side endeavour to counteract such teaching, and raise schools where the teaching shall be scriptural and in accordance with that of our Reformed Church?

There is a point of comparison here with Bath, where Monkton Combe was opened as another Evangelical Anglican boys' school in the early 1880s. The school campaign was successful elsewhere: other Evangelical Anglican schools were Trent College, Nottingham; South-Eastern College, Ramsgate; and Weymouth. The Principal of Trent College, the Revd J. S. Tucker, told the Association meeting in 1898 that the High Church Woodard schools had already educated 20,000 boys, and were quietly and unobtrusively training a body of laity and clergy who would undo the work of the Reformation. Tucker admitted that the Evangelical schools could not keep pace with this, they were in any case fewer in numbers, but they did (he said) teach definite doctrine to boys who were ripe for it.[10] The Western Association was never as concerned about the English Benedictine boarding-school at Downside, near Stratton, in north Somerset, well within the Association's area, probably because Roman Catholicism proper was still seen as an alien sub-culture with its own fixed boundaries: the real danger came (it was believed) from the insidious presence of Anglo-Catholicism.

---

[9] See AMB, 'Minutes of the Anglican Clerical and Lay Association': 'Committee held in Abbey Church Room, Bath, 1 February, 1883'.

[10] *Report of the Proceedings of the 41st Annual Meeting, held at Bath, 24 and 25 May 1898* (Bath, 1898), p. 17.

In Bath, as also in Bristol, the intensity of Anglican Evangelicalism seems to have declined towards the end of the century. In Bristol, in 1860, 15 out of a possible 40 churches appeared on the Association list, but by 1900 the figure seemed to have declined to 13 out of a total of about 60. (Even so, 6 out of Clifton's 9 churches were Evangelical.) In 1860, 9 out of 11 parishes in Bath were mentioned on the membership list: it was 9 out of 14 in 1900. The three new parishes: St Luke's 1868, St Paul's 1869, and St Stephen's 1881, were all on the list, but three others previously mentioned had lapsed. By 1865 Bath had 74 members, of whom 24 were laymen, the majority of them army officers. In 1900, however, the number of members had dropped to 35, including 7 laymen, of whom only 3 were officers. Bath Evangelicalism, therefore, was still a dominant urban group of a professional kind, in a town which had not recovered from the social decline of the spa.

As for the northern half of the Association, throughout most of the period under discussion Gloucester was the administrative centre of the Diocese of Gloucester and Bristol. Charles Ellicott (1819–1905) became bishop in 1863, and when the see was divided, in 1897, he remained as Bishop of Gloucester until he resigned in 1904. Ellicott was an ardent Tory advocate of establishment, and he was the only bishop to vote against the Third Reform Bill (1884). He supported teetotalism and opposed agricultural trade unionism intemperately when it flickered across the Gloucestershire countryside in the 1870s: he advised farmers to resist the temptation to throw union organizers into the horsepond. That he was also chairman of the New Testament Revision Company from 1870 to 1881 suggests how little enthusiasm there originally was for a new translation. The Western Association had been formed before he entered the area, but the fact that he was essentially Bishop of Gloucester added weight to the northern part of the diocese.

In Gloucester two new parishes were created between 1800 and 1860: St James, 1842, and St Mark, 1846; and two after 1860: All Saints, 1876, and St Paul, 1884. In 1850 Christ Church, St Nicholas, and St James stood on the Association list, making 3 out of a possible 10 parishes; in 1900 St Michael, St Nicholas, and St Mary de Crypt appeared, making 3 out of 12. 5 parishes on the fronge of the town, Hempstead, Hucclecote, Maisemore, Twigworth, and Wheatenhurst were there in 1860, but had disappeared in 1900. There was no sign, that is, of Evangelical growth in Gloucester, a town which in the later nineteenth century had gently rebuilt itself at the public level in the usual eclectic Victorian manner with a College of Art, a library, and some Italianate banks, but remained small, overshadowed by Bristol and by its closer neighbour, Cheltenham.

In Cheltenham itself, Evangelicalism had been given a strong impetus by Francis Close (1797–1882), who dominated the town ecclesiastically as vicar from 1826 to 1856, when he left for the Deanery of Carlisle. Close was a typical Evangelical, a fierce Sabbatarian who opposed Cheltenham's rapid emergence as part of the entertainment industry: he attacked theatre-going, as well as horse-racing. He became increasingly hostile to Tractarianism and Roman Catholicism, which he did not distinguish very much from one another, in the fashion of the first half of the nineteenth century. In 1860, 5 out of the town's 7 churches appeared on the Association list: St Mary and Trinity, 1823; St James, 1830; St Mark and St Luke, 1855; in 1900 this had changed to 5 out of 11: St Mary and Christ Church, 1865; St Luke, St Mark, and St Paul, 1846. One can hardly generalize about the ethos of Cheltenham: Dean Close School and the Gold Cup have both survived two world wars. Like Bath, however, Cheltenham provided room for Evangelical institutions. The two teachers' training colleges, St Paul's (male) and St Mary's (female), grew in prestige because the struggle to found boarding-schools had been only moderately successful, and it seemed more profitable to create a supply of Evangelical teachers. In 1898, for example, the President of the Association, Canon Roxby of Cheltenham, said that 'what we want is not Evangelical schools but Evangelical masters, and to see that they are placed in the public schools of our land'.[11]

In 1860, however, Close had been gone from Cheltenham for four years, and the Association had been formed without him. Its true centre at that time was probably in the slowly deindustrializing Cotswolds, where Alan Gardner Cornwall provided vigorous leadership as the first President of the Association, which did not recover from his death in 1871. Apart from the Association, Cornwall also expressed his fervent Protestantism as secretary of the Tyndale Memorial, a commemorative stone tower erected on Nibley Knowle, where it still stands, now a battered and rather anonymous puzzle to the stranger to the southern Cotswolds and the Vale of Berkeley. This campaign took place in 1866, long after the controversy over the Martyrs' Memorial at Oxford (1838), and in the shadow of the controversies about *Essays and Reviews*, Darwin, and Colenso. The Nibley Monument symbolizes Anglican Evangelical devotion to the Reformation and to the English Bible as the proper standards of Anglicanism as

---

[11] *Report of the Proceedings of the 41st Annual Meeting, held at Bath, 24 and 25 May 1898*, pp. 19–20.

allegedly part of the Protestant tradition. There was a local element in this because Tyndale came from Gloucestershire, and the last ten years of Wyclif's life were connected with Lutterworth. It is true that seizing the Cotswold heights and sanctifying them to Protestantism and the Bible for ever had a touch of Anglo-Catholicism about it; the idea of setting up public symbols in order to affect the public religious ethos came naturally to the 'Catholic' movement. What was typically Evangelical, however, was the Monument's function as 'witness'—there it stood and still stands to testify to Evangelical belief in the Protestant interpretation of the Bible as the fundamental guide to Christian truth—and it also witnesses, as Cornwall would have intended it to do, against any reckless generation of biblical scholars prepared to produce a 'new English Bible'.

In the 1860s, under Cornwall's leadership, the Western Association tried to mobilize regional opinion in defence of 'the distinctive principles of Evangelicalism'.[12] As early as 23 October 1860, the committee agreed to co-operate with the Midland District in a protest against *Essays and Reviews*. The matter was taken up in detail at a meeting at Cheltenham on 22 November 1860. A petition from the Midland District was circulated in the Western area for signatures, but the Association also went ahead, first with a petition of its own, intended to be sent to the archbishops and bishops, and second with its own summary of the errors of *Essays and Reviews*, which were printed in a three-page pamphlet.[13] The petition, which was finally approved at a special meeting in Cheltenham on 5 February 1861, admitted that liberty of opinion was an Anglican tradition, but said that one had from time to time to censure those whose interpretation of the formularies of the Church contradicted their plain meaning. *Essays and Reviews* was said to contain 'doctrines . . . subversive of the christian faith itself'. The petition dismissed the arguments of the book as 'the repeated fallacies and often confuted objections of sceptics of former generations, clothed anew in modern forms of thought, and reinforced by modern speculations, unfairly stated as to their results, or rashly assumed as discoveries'. The book should be authoritatively declared to contain 'doctrines heretical and contrary to the true teaching of the Church'.[14]

---

[12] This was the title of a paper published by the Association after the 1862 Conference; it was written by the Revd H. A. Simcoe from Egloskerry, Cornwall; it was a direct appeal for loyalty to the tradition of Henry Venn and the eighteenth-century Anglican Evangelicals (there was no reference to the Wesleys).

[13] A copy of the Petition is pasted into the Minute-Book opposite the minutes for the meeting of 22 January 1861.

[14] Quotations are from the copy mentioned above.

At the annual conference, held in Bath on 4 and 5 June 1861, the committee reported that approaches about the petition had been made to clergymen in Gloucestershire who did not belong to the Association to see if they would co-operate, but although these overtures had produced strong expressions of abhorrence of *Essays and Reviews* they had failed as far as signatures were concerned. Some Anglo-Catholics would not have wanted to join an Evangelical Anglican protest, and no doubt other Anglicans disapproved of the Association as a source of division. In fact, the Memorial was signed by 871 individuals, of whom 333 were clergymen and 538 laymen. These figures probably suggest the maximum support on which the Association could draw, since signers identified themselves as sympathizers with the Evangelical group. Cornwall and the lay secretary, C. R. Baynes of Minchinhampton, took the petition to the Archbishop of Canterbury, who referred them, in a letter dated 6 March 1861, to the declaration which the bishops had issued unanimously on 12 February 1861, in which they had condemned denials of the doctrines of the Atonement or biblical inspiration as inconsistent in an Anglican clergyman, but in which they had made no mention of *Essays and Reviews*. This omission no doubt explained why all the bishops, including Tait of London, agreed to the declaration. Cornwall also visited the Vice-Chancellor of Oxford, Dr F. Jeune of Pembroke: he reported that the Hebdomadal Council had politely declined to bring the matter before Convocation. The Memorial was sent to all the bishops: the Association's Report quoted approval from Lichfield, Ripon, Bath and Wells, Winchester, Llandaff, Chichester, and Oxford.[15]

The *Extracts from the Essays and Reviews* which the Western Association published gave a clear picture of the Evangelical Anglican case against the book. There was no question, for example, of accepting the view that the ambitious Frederick Temple was somehow less implicated than his colleagues: his vague Hegelianism was neatly illustrated by a single quotation:

> We can acknowledge the great value of the forms in which the first ages of the Church defined the truth, and yet refuse to be bound by them; we can use them and yet endeavour to go beyond them, just as they also went beyond the legacy which was left us by the Apostles.

---

[15] All the material in this paragraph is quoted from the *Report of the Fourth Annual Conference of the Church of England Clerical and Lay Association (Western District)*, held at Bath, 4 and 5 June 1861 (Seeley, Jackson and Halliday, London, 1861), pp. 3–10.

from the Evangelical point of view Temple simply had no right to 'refuse to be bound' or to 'go beyond'; his language itself showed an improper state of mind. Similarly, Baden-Powell was quoted as saying that '*either* development, *or* spontaneous generation (of species) *must* be true': from the Evangelical Anglican point of view, no such choice existed, 'development' was not a biblical idea.

The main attack fell on Wilson and Jowett. The latter was quoted as saying: 'Nor for any of the higher or supernatural views of inspiration is there any foundation in the Gospels or Epistles'; and Wilson's offence was encapsulated in: 'It by no means follows, because Strauss has substituted a mere shadow for the Jesus of the Evangelists . . . that there are not traits in the Scriptural person of Jesus, which are better explained by referring them to an ideal than an historical origin.'[16] What became obvious in the *Extracts* and the Memorial was that the Evangelicals were bound to demand an official repudiation of the liberal Anglican position: their definition of 'Protestant Christianity' made conflict in nineteenth-century Anglicanism inevitable, and this means that historians need a conflict model of the Victorian Established Church.

What was equally true was that there seemed to be no way in which the three-way conflict—between Evangelical, Anglo-Catholic, and Liberal—could be resolved. The Western Evangelicals felt that they could not make their protests effective, and we find the Report of the Annual Conference of 1864 lamenting that so little had been done.

> This inaction, however, has not been produced by absence of causes for anxiety to the advocates of evangelical principles. A year in which the unhappy Bishop Colenso has continued his assaults upon the Pentateuch., a year in which the final judgement on *Essays and Reviews* was delivered, cannot be deemed void of serious and unwonted excitement. Nevertheless, the Committee has perceived no opening for their intervention.

Only a national movement could cope—'effort on a smaller scale, such as this Association could carry out', would not do.

This was almost a counsel of despair. Nevertheless, in 1864 the Association printed three papers which had not been given at its Bath Conference in May: these were 'Prophetic Study, Its Use and Principles of

---

[16] The quotations come from *Extracts from the 'Essays and Reviews'*, no author, a 4-sided pamphlet, published by J. B. Bailey, Printer, 27, Clarence Street, Cheltenham. A copy is pasted into AMB, opposite the entry for 5 February 1861.

Interpretation', by George Fisk, Vicar of Great Malvern; 'Prophetic Study, The Language of Prophecy', by J. B. Clifford, the incumbent of St Matthew's, Kingsdown, Bristol; and 'The Privy Council Judgement', which dealt with *Essays and Reviews*, by E. P. Hathaway, a lawyer from London. Both the prophetic papers depended on what Fisk called 'the fact of Inspiration',[17] and it was significant that Hathaway, summarizing the effect of *Essays and Reviews*, asked:

> How many souls shall 'stumble on the dark mountains' of unbelief, beguiled there by the ignis fatuus of this new heresy—that the Bible is called 'the Word of God', not because it *is*, but because it *contains*, the Word of God.[18]

Clifford was certain that these were 'the last days', and soberly calculated the scale of Armageddon in a Europe which already had three-and-a-half million soldiers, 'without referring to iron-clads, Armstrongs and Whitworths, and other deadly inventions at home or abroad'.[19]

The only public act of the Association was to send an Address to Christopher Wordsworth, then a canon of Westminster, in support of his protest against the appointment of Arthur Stanley, the most distinguished of mid-Victorian liberal Anglicans and a vigorous defender of *Essays and Reviews*, to the Westminster Deanery. Stanley's appointment was never in doubt, and he was installed on 10 January 1864. On 14 January the Association agreed to the circulation of a letter to Wordsworth, which was signed by 114 clerical and 88 lay members, and which it was intended 'should find its way to Lord Palmerston'.[20] 'We have discerned with sorrow', the letter said, 'the encouragement which he (Stanley) has given to that class of ostensibly Christian teaching which disparages the inspiration of Holy Scripture.'[21] Picking up again the eschatological theme, the signatories recognized in this 'the working of that spirit of seduction from the truth which may characterize the last times'.[22]

The national and local campaigns against *Essays and Reviews* had failed,

---

[17] The Revd George Fisk, *Prophetic Study: its use, and principles of interpretation*, J. Elliott, Printer, High Street, Stroud, MDCCCLXIV, p. 3.

[18] E. P. Hathaway, Esq., Barrister at Law, *The Privy Council Judgement*. J. Elliott, High Street, Stroud. MDCCCLXIV, p. 11.

[19] Fisk, p. 12.

[20] See AMB, 14 Jan. 1864.

[21] *Report of the Seventh Annual Conference of the Church of England Clerical and Lay Association (Western District), held at Bath, 31 May and 1 June, 1864*, J. Elliott, Printer, High Street, Stroud. MDCCCLXIV, p. 4.

[22] *Ibid.*, p. 4.

and in 1865 the Association was to fail again at the local level, this time in a trial of strength in the diocese of Gloucester and Bristol over the election of a Proctor to Convocation. A meeting of the Association's committee in Cheltenham on 2 February 1865, received 'a circular of certain clergymen, intimating their intention of nominating Rev J. R. Woodford as Proctor of the diocese'.[23] Woodford, who represented the High to Anglo-Catholic clergy, was Vicar of Kempsford and Examining Chaplain to the Bishop of Oxford. The Association commented that Woodford would 'consider it no reflection upon him to be described as an advocate of theological views strongly opposed to those held by the Evangelical body'.[24] The use of the word 'body' may be underlined as a further sign of the developing sense of a distinct identity.

The Association claimed that its suggestion of a neutral candidate was rejected, and so the 'Evangelical Clergy were reduced to the alternative either of submitting to the imputation of insignificance by quietly accepting Mr Woodford, or of demonstrating their existence and strength by a practical protest against his election'. The President of the Association, Alan Cornwall, agreed to stand 'though with no expectation of success'. The result of the poll was described as satisfactory, given the 'sentiments of the constituency'. Out of 444 beneficed clergymen, 133 recorded their votes for Mr Woodford and 82 for Mr Cornwall. The Association put a brave face on this, claiming that 'in the light of a Protest two-fifths of the votes must be deemed sufficient evidence that the diocese as a whole is not committed to an approval of Mr Woodford's sentiments'.[25]

Alan Cornwall represented the view that the 'Evangelical body' ought to be prepared to sustain an organized struggle for control of the Church of England. This policy ran counter to the deepest instincts of many Anglican Evangelicals, who preferred a policy like that of the early seventeenth-century Puritans, of internal separation from the institutional Church. They put no emphasis on identity-by-organization, and thought that attendance at Convocation, for example, was a variety of worldliness. This point of view was expressed at the Association's annual meeting, held at Cheltenham at the end of May 1865, by Charles Kemble, who was Rector of Bath, and therefore—conveniently—not a member of the Gloucester diocese. Kemble said that 'the work of the Evangelical

---

[23] See AMB, 2 Feb. 1865.
[24] *Report of the Eighth Annual Conference . . . held at Cheltenham. May 30 and 31, 1865*, J. Elliott, Printer, etc. MDCCCLXV, p. 3.
[25] *Ibid.*, p. 4.

body is evangelistic and spiritual—not political and carnal', and he quoted Pusey on the Jewish exiles in Babylon:

> ... a handful of the worshippers of the one only God, captives, scattered with no visible centre or unity, without organization or power to resist, save their indomitable faith, inwardly upheld by God, outwardly strengthened by the very calamities which almost ended their national existence.[26]

In the discussion that followed he was rebuked by General Aylmer (of Widcombe Terrace, Bath) who 'regretted that Mr Kemble had spoken in terms of commendation of Dr Pusey'.[27] Nevertheless, this image of the Evangelicals as the saving suffering remnant, who thought nothing of the assemblies of men, but expected to be summoned in final triumph to 'that celestial synod which shall never be dissolved' (Kemble again), was deeply satisfying to many in the Evangelical body and enabled them to soak up punishment from their Anglo-Catholic and Liberal-Anglican critics, whom they could dismiss as fundamentally in error. This attitude was to gain ground as the nineteenth century continued, and both points of view, Kemble's and Cornwall's, could amount to a policy of 'undeclared denominationalism'.

For the moment, however, Cornwall was able to persist in a more aggressive policy. Changes in the detail of Anglican ritual were quickening up in the 1860s: the use of incense, altar lights and wafer bread, the Elevation of the elements after consecration, the introduction of surpliced choirs, all increased. Eucharistic vestments were introduced in several churches, including St John's, Frome (1865), a church which was well known to the Western Association. Cornwall presumably favoured the formation in November 1865 of the Church Association, which planned to prosecute alleged innovators in ceremonial. The Western District Report for 1866 admitted that legal proceedings and such like were beyond its own scope, but asserted that it was important to swell the volume of public opinion, and said that 'a succession of Testimonies, small it may be if taken singly, produce a considerable effect'.[28]

This was why the Western District committee met on 28 November 1865 with Cornwall in the chair, and decided to send 'a Memorial to the

---

[26] The Revd Charles Kemble, Rector of Bath, *Convocation, Our Attitude Towards It*. Included in *Report of the Eighth Conference*, pp. 16–17.

[27] *Report of the Eighth Conference*, p. 8.

[28] *Report of the Ninth Conference . . . held at Bristol, June 5 and 6, 1866*, p. 4.

Bishops on the subject of Ultra Ritualism, and a Petition to Parliament on the same subject'. A draft petition was already available, and it was agreed that this should not carry the District's name, but simply be signed by Anglicans in the Gloucester and Bristol Diocese. Wording for the Petition was agreed at the following committee meeting, held in Gloucester on 12 December 1865, but the wording of the Memorial proved more difficult, and was not finally decided until after a further meeting on 2 January 1866.

The case made in the Memorial against Anglo-Catholic innovations in ritual was simple but slightly incoherent. The Memorial began by saying that the signatories were satisfied with the existing 'forms and ceremonies which, though not to be found categorically detailed in any one place or document, have virtually, and by the operation of time and custom, come to be considered those of the Church of England'. Some people, however, were reintroducing ceremonies 'which (under whatever plea they may be defended) have long ago and for good reasons fallen into such disuse as to render their revival an offensive innovation'. Moreover, it was clear that those who got a taste for extravagant ritual would pass on to Rome, while those who were offended by the changes would turn to Dissent. So far the argument held together as a broad appeal to usage, itself understood as an accepted interpretation of 'Anglicanism', and thought of as threatened by wilful innovation. This is important, because there is still a tendency to write as though Anglo-Catholic attitudes on ritual were more respectable than those of their opponents. The tone then sharpened, however, asking the bishops for 'some standing rule or direction in the matter of Ritual Observances, by which these outrages upon the Protestant feeling of the country may be prevented, and all pretext be cut off for a mode of celebrating Divine Service, no way distinguishable by ordinary observers from that of the Mass'. The Petition also asked for 'fresh and definite regulations' which would make clear 'what practices, and what only, should be allowed'.[29] This was really an attempt to replace 'usage' with a re-edited Prayer Book, which would be enforced legally, a rather more revolutionary step than perhaps its advocates realized, but one which revealed that their feelings were as intense as those of their opponents. The policy had the disadvantage that it left the English Church Union, the organizing body of Anglo-Catholics, free to deprecate any alteration in the Prayer Book.

The Memorial was signed by 245 clergymen and 148 laymen, and Alan

---

[29] See AMB, 2 Jan. 1866, for a copy of the Memorial.

Cornwall presented it at Lambeth himself on 3 February 1866 as part of a process in which the Archbishop was bombarded with statements by both Anglo-Catholics and Evangelicals. He replied to Cornwall on 16 February 1866, assuring him that he had no sympathy with the Ritualist movement, and he told the English Church Union that those who were violating a compromise which had lasted for 300 years were doing the work of the worst enemies of the Church of England. It was clear, however, that internal authority could not cope with such a passionate outbreak of disagreement: there was no pronouncement from Convocation until 15 February 1867, and the appeal to episcopal sanction made then had no practical force. By the autumn patience had worn out in Gloucester. On 30 October 1866 the committee had met in the city and had discussed the possibility of

> ... producing and circulating some short and simple cheap Tracts upon the Ritualistic question which the clerical and other members of the Association might exert themselves in disseminating among their congregations and those classes of society which are in danger of being misled rather thro ignorance of the bearing of the question than from any intelligent inclination to the doctrines which such practices are intended to cover.[30]

Nothing seems to have come of this, but the Association Report for 1867 said that in the meantime the committee had come to the conclusion that only direct legislation would restrain the Ritualists.

As a result, the committee met at the Deanery in Gloucester on 8 January 1867. It was agreed that 'Memorials and Protests in reference to Ultra Ritualism have been promoted but without success, and that hence the only course now remaining for the Association is to procure, if possible, legislation on the subject'. A special committee was set up, including Cornwall, H. Law (the Dean of Gloucester), Charles Kemble (Rector of Bath), and E. Walker (Rector of Cheltenham), but it seems to have had only one Bristol representative, H. Martin (Vicar of St Nicholas, Berkeley Square), and this reinforces the impression that in these years the Association was led from its northern end. Some indication of the opinions held among the committee members is suggested by a comment by Dr Walker in a discussion at the annual conference in June 1867. Walker said that

---

[30] See AMB, 30 Oct. 1866.

the desire expressed in some quarters for 'attractive' services is not a question of a little more or less ceremonial or ornament, but part of a regular plan for unprotestantising the Church of England and uniting it with Rome.[31]

This statement was neither as extreme or as reliant on conspiracy theory as it may seem: in the minds of people like Walker and Cornwall the appeal to 'Protestantism' was more than an appeal to prejudice; it was an appeal to an Anglican Evangelical dogmatic position which consciously rejected the Ultramontane direction of the nineteenth-century Roman Catholic revival. Anxiety about 'Catholicism' was being further stimulated in the late 1860s by the political plans for disestablishment of the Anglican Church in Ireland, and it is interesting that the Association Conference of 1868 heard a paper from E. A. Litton (Cheltenham) which actually supported the change, partly on the ground that 'there must be in Ireland a considerable and we trust a growing body of prosperous and intelligent Roman Catholic layment who do not sympathise with the Ultramontane manifestoes of their prelates'.[32] Litton was an able Evangelical theologian, but what he said evidently divided the Association, for the committee report specifically declined to offer a summary of the discussion on the ground that it might cause misunderstanding.

The committee produced a sketch of a drastic Church Ritual Bill which set out to cover every aspect of the problem. Vestments were to be restricted to a plain white surplice and black gown, with optional black scarf and cassock; at the Communion the table was to have a white linen cloth without lace, embroidery, or other decoration; gestures were to be limited to those 'expressly directed' by the Prayer Book, apart from bowing at the name of Jesus during the recitation of the Creed, which was 'of common use and long custom'.[33] Similarly, no ceremonies were to be used which were not expressly directed, and finally, 'no such images, figures, devices, pictures' were to be introduced if they would 'plainly

---

[31] *Report of the Tenth Annual Conference . . . held at Bath, June 4,5 1867*, J. Elliott, Printer, etc. Stroud, 1867, p. 15.

[32] The Revd E. A. Litton, M.A., Rector of Naunton, Examining Chaplain to the Lord Bishop of Durham, late Fellow of Oriel College. *The Connection of Church and State with Particular Reference to the Question of the Irish Church, delivered at Cheltenham, at the Annual Meeting of the Church of England Clerical and Lay Association, June 9, 10, 1868*, London: Longmans and Co.; Cheltenham New High Street, p. 32.

[33] *Report of the Tenth Annual Conference*, pp. 6–7. A footnote added that the aim was 'the preservation of a state of things which it cannot be denied has commonly prevailed for the last 300 years': p. 6.

contravene the Act's intention'. This was a declaration of war on all Anglo-Catholic innovation, and also on those who, like Samuel Wilberforce, the High-Church Bishop of Oxford, asserted that the Church of England

> ... embraced within her fold men of every view between those who absolutely denied her primary principles and those who held the doctrines of the Roman Catholic Church which she had expressly condemned; in that comprehensiveness it was that her strength lay.[34]

The Gloucester Evangelicals could see no justification for a church based on what seemed to them such an unscriptural ground, and their mood was expressed in the description (found in the minutes of the committee meeting held in Bath Abbey on 9 April 1867) of the proposed Parliamentary measure as being for 'the repression of Ultra Ritualism'.[35]

This proposal was passed on to London, where it became involved in the conflict over ritual at national level. As early as the beginning of March 1867, Shaftesbury, who believed in legislative action, was prepared to introduce into the House of Lords a modified version of the draft from Gloucester, which omitted from the original the sections on ornaments, gestures, and ceremonies, and concentrated on giving the force of law to Canon 58, which said that ministers taking services should wear 'a decent and comely surplice with sleeves'. This is usually described as 'Lord Shaftesbury's Bill', and no doubt he agreed with it; Samuel Wilberforce, in a letter written to Gladstone on 10 March 1867, said that this bill 'was drawn by A. J. Stephens'.[36] A printed copy of the later version is stuck into the Western Association Minute-Book between the committee meetings held on 8 January 1867 and 9 April 1867. By the end of March, however, the Tory government, anxious to calm the situation down, was insisting on a Royal Commission to consider the problems of Anglican liturgical variety. Shaftesbury, clearly with the approval of the Association, refused to be placated by the setting up of a Royal Commission, and moved his Bill in the Lords on 14 May 1867. He was defeated by 61 votes to 46, with 11 bishops in the minority. At the annual meeting of the Association in June 1867, an Address to Shaftesbury received 185 signatures: it said that the Association was 'especially and deeply sensible of the service you have been enabled to render, in exposing and repelling a mischievous Ritual-

---

[34] R. G. Wilberforce, *Life of Samuel Wilberforce* (London, 1882), bk. iii, p. 212.
[35] AMB, 9 April 1867.
[36] Wilberforce, p. 206.

ism'.[37] The Annual Report of 1867 claimed that 'the movement for ritualistic legislation originated with the Association', and added that 'the move at Gloucester has been most important, although it has led to a smaller Bill than was there contemplated'.[38] The Report of 1868 went further:

> though that measure was not carried further, its utility has undoubtedly been great. It afforded an opportunity to the country of displaying its feeling, and of warning the Ritualistic party that the Protestantism of England was not prepared to allow, without resistance, the reintroduction of scarcely disguised Popery. It created in short a species of evidence which it cannot be doubted produced a salutary impression on the Church Ritual Commission, and a due influence on its reports. The Association therefore may well feel proud and satisfied with the part it was enabled to take in the measure.[39]

The Association's claim to primary responsibility for what historians usually call 'Lord Shaftesbury's Bill' is reinforced by the minutes of the committee meeting of 13 November 1867, at which it was presented with the bill 'for legal expenses connected with the Parliamentary Measure introduced by Lord Shaftesbury'. The bill was made up as follows:

Mr Baxter, journey expenses	2 – 10
Dr Stephens	50 – 18 – 6
Mr Haldane	33 – 1 – 6
Cab Hire etc	2 – 1
	88 – 11 – 0.

The members were circulated for help with this account. It was reported to the committee meeting of 10 February 1868 that 480 circulars had been distributed appealing for contributions towards 'Messrs Baxter's Bill', and that 247 members had responded, providing £75. 13s 3d. There is a letter in the Minute-Book from Robert Baxter (dated 17 March 1868), acknowledging payment, and adding:

> I have no doubt it has done immense good. Nothing so obviously hit the mischievous party as the debate in the House of Lords. They were

---

[37] *Report of the Tenth Annual Conference*, p. 19.
[38] *Ibid.*, p. 5.
[39] *Report of the Eleventh Annual Conference . . . held at Cheltenham, June 9 and 10, 1868.* Printed at the Stroud News Office, 1868, p. 7.

regularly cowed by it and the tone of the Commission I consider to be taken from the debate. Lord Shaftesbury will be at home the end of this month and ready to go to war again if war is necessary.

This was the high point of the policy which Alan Cornwall and his friends had followed since the late 1850s. Cornwall died in 1872, and from about this time the Association declined in importance. What it had done is easily undervalued. The standard account of Anglican history in the 1860s is written from the Ritualists' point of view, and concludes that the various attempts at restrictive legislation, including the Public Worship Regulation Act of 1874, neither slowed nor speeded the development of ceremonial. Even after the Act of 1874 'the statistics show that the increase in the criticised practices continued without a pause'.[40] I doubt if this is the whole of the truth. The mid-Victorian Church of England was a pattern of conflicting forces: Anglo-Catholicism, the movement of the hour, was moving forward, as Owen Chadwick suggested. At that moment the future of 'Protestantism' in the Church of England depended on a clear demonstration that a passionate opposition existed which would not easily be overcome. The moving of the 'Shaftesbury Bill' in the House of Lords was not just a question of Shaftesbury's personal views: he represented, and everyone knew that he represented, a powerful group in a not untypical diocese. The 'move at Gloucester' signalled that Anglo-Catholicism would find its limits, as indeed it did.

University of Bristol

---

[40] O. Chadwick, *The Victorian Church*, pt. 2 (London, 1970), pp. 324–5.

'WE CLAIM OUR PART IN THE GREAT INHERITANCE': THE MESSAGE OF FOUR CONGREGATIONAL BUILDINGS

by CLYDE BINFIELD

IT is religious Nonconformity's fate to be misknown. Where it truly non-conforms the historian of the mainstream must find it an irritant, a tiresomely indispensable footnote to his thesis. For other historians it is its eccentricities which appeal—its Muggletonians and Southcottians, its Ranters too. What is less appealing is its most insistent theme and its chief continuity, the constant fight for due recognition (which means parity) in constant tension with the natural urge to conform. For who is to say when Nonconformity has served its purpose or when conformity is indeed reconcilable with that higher conformity to which each Nonconformist witnesses?

Neither is Nonconformity allowed much drama beyond martyrdom, that occasional thing. Conversion, the soul's drama, is taken for granted since it is the Evangelical norm. The remainder drama of its long littleness of life is seldom celebrated. It is allowed little social and less architectural drama. Yet Nonconformity has all that and more, inevitably so when national life is so instinct with it. For Nonconformity's drama is most characteristic when it runs closest to conformity.

Take, for example, that most accurately misleading title, the Earldom of Oxford and Asquith. The present, and second, Earl fits his title, more Oxford than Asquith.[1] His public service has led from Balliol to the colonial service. His family connections are with the intellectual, professional, proconsular, and landed aristocracies. His roots lie in the manor house possessed by his family since the Reformation. His childhood was cradled in the memory of that Great War which had killed his father and scythed his father's generation, and for which his grandfather as Prime Minister bore prime responsibility. Could there be a finer model of national conformity? Yet this Earl is a Nonconformist, since he is a Roman Catholic. His formation was Ampleforth before it was Balliol. His social circle, and increasingly his family circle, was that of the Roman

---

[1] Julian, 2nd Earl of Oxford and Asquith, b.1916, educ. Ampleforth and Balliol (1st class in Greats): Asst. District Commissioner, Palestine, 1942–8; Adviser to Prime Minister of Libya, 1952; Administrative Secretary, Zanzibar, 1955; Governor of Seychelles, 1962–7: *Who's Who*.

Catholic intellectual revival, all Knox and Waugh. And for all its allure and literary celebration this marks a profound national discontinuity.

So it was, in mirror image, with the first Earl, that Prime Minister more Asquith than Oxford, of whom it might be remarked that none in the past hundred years has been more representative of, or more in conformity with, the contemporary body politic.[2] For though that Earl's uncle and grandfather had failed in their own attempts to enter Parliament, their entrepreneurial-cum-political cousinhood, full of commerce and the intermediate professions, more Boase than Burke, could be stretched over half a century to include some thirty MPs, culminating in at least three peerages and as many baronetcies. But because that cousinhood too was rooted in dissent, Protestant this time, it has been simpler for Asquith's biographers to mark the obvious discontinuity between his career and its formation (and so briskly to dismiss that formation) than to ponder any continuities. They have confused the Nonconformity which nurtured him with the nonconformist connections which formed him. The former soon enough left his stage, save for the occasions when he cared to call its rhetoric to mind. The latter, a network national in scope, generations thick and backed by political muscle, should not be dismissed; Asquith depended on its influence for much of his power.

But this recreation of a cousinhood depends for its thesis not so much on people being related to each other as on people knowing that they were related to each other; and, indeed, *knowing* and not just *knowing of* those relations. And how might that be proved in layers of society which seldom went in for muniment rooms?

There is one such proof: *The Home Circle: A Record of Births, Marriages and Deaths*, a small and rather pretty notebook or album of a sort once common and much used by Victorian women.[3] This one had belonged to the widow of a Congregational minister, whose third wife she had been; a short, stout, active, snappy, marcel-waved woman, with money of her own, autocratic by nature and unpopular with her servants. It contains the names and dates of 206 births, all of them, save for Queen Victoria and a handful of Congregational pulpiteers, the names of kinsmen or intimate friends. There were 31 marriages and 48 deaths. Since their recorder,

---

[2] This is the theme of C. Binfield, 'Asquith: The Formation of a Prime Minister', *JURCHS*, 2, 7 (April, 1981), pp. 204–42, esp. 204–10.

[3] I am indebted to Mrs M. P. Skinner for access to this notebook and information about her grandmother, Edith Hall née Firth, third wife of Revd Frederick Hall (1839–1917) of Bradford, Heckmondwike, Wimbledon, and Scarborough, for whom see *Congregational Year Book* (1918), p. 132.

Edith Hall, lived from 1859 to 1946, some of the births are still alive, while in a few cases the span goes back to the eighteenth century. And since their recorder was a first cousin of Asquith's, her two centuries of home circle contain in their small notebook more positive proof of that particular holding together of several generations of cumulative attitudes than might ever now be recreated in the current vogue for family history.

This community contained within one woman's *Home Circle* might be set beside the community contained by one building. Or to put it another way, one might move from an Oxford earl (that suburban villa dressed to look like Versailles) to an Oxford college (that intrusive dissentery disguised as the most Catholic place in Oxford).[4]

Mansfield College has provided the motive force for twentieth-century English Congregationalism, shaping its theology, directing its polity, determining its accent as it has turned into the United Reformed Church. Its first five Principals have been men of consequence in Oxford, of note in their discipline, of eminence in their Church. It is a success story, even if its lifespan, denominationally speaking, now seems dangerously close to that of a suburban church: thirty years growth, thirty years prime, and thirty years decline. Consequently it illustrates with equal force two quite different interpretations of denominational history. In both it serves as solvent, but in one the process is of active, pace-setting assimilation to re-formed norms, and in the other it is of disintegration. In one, the last barriers are breached as full citizenship finds its religious expression in ecumenism, for when all are nonconformists now, what need is there of Nonconformity? In the other, all defences are down so that old, re-grouped establishments may reassert their hold, for when all are one, what price the awkward individuality of any?[5] Is there anywhere here the soul's necessary drama, the evangelical home circle's chief determinant, conversion?

As stage-set, stone gold tracery on a green ground, Mansfield College is a work of art. It is its architect's masterpiece. That architect's name, Basil Champneys, reflects the variety of his buildings, precious, charm-filled,

---

[4] Alice, Marchioness of Salisbury, thus described Asquith; the 'most Catholic place in Oxford' is ascribed either to Frederick Heiler (A. L. Drummond, *The Church Architecture of Protestantism* [Edinburgh, 1934], p. 293) or to Albert Schweitzer.

[5] The 'disintegrative' thesis has been most recently and persuasively advanced in M. D. Johnson, *The Dissolution of Dissent, 1850–1918* (New York and London, 1987) and the tensions within Mansfield can be followed in E. Kaye, *C. J. Cadoux, Theologian, Scholar and Pacifist* (Edinburgh, 1988), esp. pp. 28–70, 141 *et seq.*

resonant, intelligent.[6] Champneys was a Cambridge graduate, in young middle age, of Evangelical descent rising swiftly through the professions. His grandfather was Paul Storr the silversmith. His father was a slum parson who became Dean of Lichfield.[7] His brother became a medical baronet.[8] Champneys's own career began in the late 1860s with Early French Gothic. Twenty years on he was an established practitioner, whose vigour had been accommodatingly tempered with equal success to those twin outworkings of the Gothic revival, 'Queen Anne' and late English Gothic. Champneys's forte lay in educational and ecclesiastical buildings with some domestic and commercial variants. He was an educated architect, whose sensitive intelligence almost carried him into originality, a major architect less by virtue of his genius than by the aptness of his chief commissions. Newnham College, Cambridge, has been called the Queen Anne revival's 'most complete and successful' building.[9] It must be its aptest and its prettiest. The Rylands Library, Manchester, first astounds by its Gothic liberation of space and then reassures by the efficiency of its appointments. And Mansfield College, Oxford, whose success led to the Rylands commission, convinces by a combination of style, reference, and purpose so excellently suited to its situation that its effrontery quite fades away. Each is a major example of an accepted style adapted to the updated demands of building type. Each also served a radical purpose—higher education for women, the world's wisdom unlocked for Cottonopolis, eternity unlocked for choice Dissenters in a reforming Oxford. The purpose of each was not quite conforming. The genesis of two of them was overtly Nonconforming.

All this is to be read in Mansfield's stone and glass. The style of the college was 'Edwardian Gothic', a phrase at once ambiguous (which Edward?) and English.[10] The style of the chapel was more tentatively than ambiguously ascribed to 'English Gothic of the character which was current towards the close of the fourteenth century, and would be some-what analogous in type to St Cross at Winchester'.[11] We will return to an aspect of this. The craftsmanship of the whole is socially, geographically,

---

[6] For Champneys (1842–1935) see *DNB*; M. Girouard, *Sweetness and Light. The 'Queen Anne' Movement 1860–1900* (Oxford, 1977), pp. 49, 60–76, 84; J. Maddison, 'The Champneys Buildings, Mansfield College, Oxford', *Mansfield College Magazine*, no. 185 (1982–3), pp. 28–32.

[7] For William Weldon Champneys (1807–75) see *DBN*.

[8] For Sir Francis Henry Champneys (1848–1930) see *DNB*.

[9] Maddison, 'Champneys Buildings', p. 29.

[10] *Mansfield College, Oxford: its Origin and Opening* (1890), p. 45.

[11] *Congregational Year Book* (1887), p. 258.

and confessionally catholic.[12] Here, architecturally and historically, is a Free Church treasure-house, whose painted glass and statues must make it an idolatrous building for all instinctive Free Churchmen. Here, none the less, is a building which answers the prime architectural test, for it works on the whole as it was intended to work, with incalculable effect for the development of English Congregationalism. Its stone and glass congregate the Church for those who are to be its ministers.

One enters the chapel by passing Bunyan to pass under Origen and between Athanasius and Augustine into a 'large parallelogram with narrow side-passage aisles'[13] wherein are chairs rather than pews. One sits between Wyclif, Calvin, Cartwright, Baxter, Howe, and Whitefield to the west, and Wesley, Watts, Owen, Hooker, Knox, and Luther to the east. To the north, should it be a Sunday in term, one confronts, along with pulpit and table, an extraordinary arrangement of stalls for those living statues, the Principal and tutors. So much for flesh and stone, exhibited at once in 'their historical and ideal relations'.[14]

Now for the windows: to the north—tobacco, since W. H. Wills of Bristol presented Christ in Glory; to the south—yarn, since Jesse Haworth of Manchester presented the loaves and the fishes. To the east and west, tobacco again, ennobled now, stand sixty-three men and seven women.[15] They represent the New Testament Church, the Latin Church, the Continental Medieval Church, the Continental Reformation Church, the American Church, the Greek Church; and also the Medieval British Church, the British Reformation, Puritanism, and contemporary (that is to say eighteenth- and nineteenth-century) Nonconformity.

Since the point of the windows is their conscious and on the whole successful completeness, the Catholic church looking in on the gathered church, the obvious question to ask is, who is absent? Where are William of Orange or William Ewart Gladstone? Where is Wilberforce? Where is John Henry Newman (a less foolish question than might appear)? Why only seven women, and why Queen Margaret of Scotland and Elizabeth Fry, the mother of Augustine, but not the mother of God? (The probable answer to that is more pragmatic than Protestant: any possible Lady window is obscured by the organ). Where are the Irish, other than Patrick who was not Irish? Or the Welsh, other perhaps than Patrick? Why so

---

[12] 'Mansfield College Chapel. Notes on the Decorations' unpaginated typescript leaflet.
[13] *Congregational Year Book* (1887), p. 258.
[14] *Mansfield College . . . Opening*, p. 48.
[15] 'Mansfield College Chapel. Notes on the Decorations'.

many Scots? Were some centuries quite so faithless as these windows suggest? Were the middle of the fourteenth and fifteenth centuries such spiritual deserts? Why America, but not Canada, Africa, or the Antipodes? And why New England rather than America? None of this is to deny the strength or the catholicity of those saints who are there, though it has to be admitted that the weakest windows are the two contemporary windows: one is at best a job lot of worthies, the other is the most period selection of all, perhaps because it is the most instructively diplomatic.[16]

Of course, these windows, with their accompaniment of statues, are choicest historiography, God's variant of the Whig view of history, but there is more to such historiography than meets most eyes. The aim, to east and west, in stone and glass, accompanying the worshipper, is to demonstrate this building's, and therefore this people's, inheritance—Reformed and Catholic and Orthodox. To north and south, encompassing the worshipper, there is

> the axis on which the whole witness of the College and Christian Church turns ... Holy Scripture as pointing to Jesus Christ, incarnate, risen and glorified ... the content and the end of all the witness of the Church of God.[17]

And obliquely to dot that 'i' and cross that 't' there are Amos and Plato in a small window to the north-east, the Hebrew and the Hellene, that conjunction of prophecy and philosophy which has formed western Christianity. While in a small window to the north-west are a Birmingham widow and a Birmingham alderman, the precise conjunction of English piety and philanthropy, municipal and provincial, without which this college would not have stood a chance. Whatever the exclusions, therefore, the concept is grandly inclusive.

So much for this building's message to the worshipper. What is its message to the less engaged passer-by? The quick answer is tradition-cloaked radicalism. Any Oxford college built on part of Merton's old cricket ground must tend to the traditional, and at Mansfield tradition informs style and disposition as well as setting. But any dissentery in Victorian Oxford must be as radical a thought for Dissenters as for Oxonians. Here are change and pretension. Here is instant ancestry,

---

[16] Elizabeth Fry, Philip Doddridge, Thomas Chalmers, Alexander Vinet, John Brown (of Haddington), and Frederick Schleiermacher can each be justified, but as a collectivity? Similarly with the six Victorian Congregationalists, James Legge, David Livingstone, Thomas Binney, Alexander McKennal, R. W. Dale, and Alexander Hannay.

[17] 'Mansfield College Chapel. Notes on the Decorations'.

pathetic, bracing, irritating. And here, too, is radicalism, less in the conventional audacity of an obvious style than in the completeness of the concept. There was, in fact, nothing new for Nonconformists in style, statues, or stained glass. Gothic had been a dissenting commonplace for college and chapel alike since the 1840s. So had painted glass. Symbolic sculptures had accented dissenting Gothic at least since the 1860s. The point, therefore, lies in none of these. It lies in the conscious completeness, the overview contrived from colour and material to supplement the Word distilled from print and intellect. More modern minds, excited by the audio-visual revolution, should warm to this sensual liberation from cerebral constraints and find here a visual path to faith as catholic as anything which might astound them at Ottobeuren or Wies. More puritan minds will warm to the discipline which such art imposes and be warned by the distortion inseparable from all art. For the exclusions owe almost as much to scholarly doubt about what some past saints actually looked like as they do to any narrow view of history:

> I have hunted for Robinson, Browne, Penry and Barrow through the Hope Collection here and in the British Museum, and have failed to find in either place any portrait. I have also gone over books of portraits, but cannot find anything that can be suggested as a substitute.[18]

Thus Mansfield's first Principal, writing to the Vice-Chancellor of the University of Liverpool as he sought to schematize the Church and so complete his college chapel.

The spirit of this was nicely caught by the celebratory sonnet of indifferent quality which John Stuart Blackie, the intelligent Victorian's representative Scotsman, wrote 'on being witness to the imposing ceremony of the inauguration of Mansfield College, when the heads of the principal old Houses were entertained by the Principal of the new . . . in a festal tent':[19]

> Hail to thee, Oxford, with fair front, and free
> From churchly pride and scholarly conceit,
> And with wide arms of kinship spread to greet
> All eager souls that seek a sign from thee!

[18] A. M. Fairbairn to A. W. W. Dale, 23 May 1908. W. B. Selbie, *The Life of Andrew Martin Fairbairn DD, DLitt, LLD, FBA, etc.* (London, 1914), p. 430. The windows were by Powell and Sons, Whitefriars.

[19] *Mansfield College . . . Opening*, p. IX. For Blackie (1809–95) see *DNB*.

Too long, too long men saw thee sit apart
From all the living pulses of the hour
Glassing thyself in thy peculiar dower
Like a vain beauty with a loveless heart
But now God taught thine eye to look abroad
On this rich pomp of things, and recognize
In changing forms and ever new disguise
The radiant face of one unchanging God,
And in the complex play of great and small
See how all live for each, and each for all.

It is not a comfortable poem. The new college's freedom from churchly pride and scholarly conceit is as questionable as the glassed-in quality of its peculiar dower. And the invocation of team spirit in the sonnet's last line is at once too spirit-of-the-age and too accurate an encapsulation of the dilemma of Independent parsons trained for ministry in gathered churches to sit easily with the seamless continuities of the Church catholic. Certainly the building's inaugural addresses grappled significantly with that discomfort.

The tone was set by R. W. Dale, minister of Carr's Lane Congregational Church, Birmingham, whose statesmanship had largely brought the college to Oxford. Dale was too rare among ecclesiastics and theologians for being also a working minister, in lifelong pastoral charge. The massively anchored and disciplined Protestant theology of his sermon provided the evangelical dynamic which let him stake a claim in the Catholic Church. Here was vital religion, giving life to the discipline:

> The theologian . . . must first of all be a saint. It is not enough that he has mastered the theories of conflicting theologies . . . He must know for himself the greatness of the Christian redemption. His own consciousness that in Christ, and through the death of Christ, he has received the remission of sins, must find an explanation in his theory of the Atonement. His joy in the discovery that Christ's relations to God determine his own relations to God must be explained in his theory of Justification. . . . He must be vividly conscious that in the power of a new life he has passed into a new world, if he is to be able to give any true account of that Divine regenerative act in which the new life is imparted. He must have trembled at the judgement to come if he is to speculate to any purpose on the principles and issue of the judgement.
> His science is the science of God. . . .[20]

---

[20] *Mansfield College . . . Opening*, p. 66. For Dale (1829–95) see *DNB*.

Here were grounds for sharing in Christendom:

> . . . we claim our part in the great inheritance; the fathers and martyrs of the Early Church are ours; and the doctors and saints of the East and of the West; and the mystics and the Reformers; devout Anglicans and devout Puritans; the leaders of the Evangelical revival—Calvinistic and Arminian; and those who in later times have renewed the faith and rekindled the sinking fires of zeal in our own and other lands. They are our elder brethren in Christ. . . .[21]

And here were grounds for striking out in liberty, for while 'Truth itself is not the truth to the man who has been false to his intellectual conscience in the formation of his belief . . .':

> The substance of the faith delivered once for all to the saints of the first age has been verified in the experience of the saints of every succeeding generation. . . . Theologians have not to create new heavens and a new earth, but to give a more exact account of that spiritual universe whose mysteries and glories have environed the saints from the beginning. A theology which quenches the fires of the sun and the splendour of the stars . . . is destined to failure. It is an account of another universe than that in which the saints are living, and the faith of the Church has authority to reject it.[22]

For those who listened, renewing their own verification in experience, there were both life and reason in the new chapel's statues; and its windows were bound to follow. But more yet. The thoughtless visitor might, on giving thought, wonder why John Henry Newman is nowhere to be seen in these catholic Oxford windows. No participants at the opening would have wondered, but Newman was most certainly to be savoured in, of all occasions, the first Communion service. Here the address was given, an occasional gleam through mannered latticework, by the President of Cheshunt College, Henry Robert Reynolds, he whom Matthew Arnold had proposed for the Athenaeum.[23] One gleam must certainly be noted.

Reynolds should have been an Oxford man. His father had been at Oriel in the 1800s, but while in the United States on a remittance man's diplomatic posting he had turned to Congregationalism, catching, as his

[21] *Mansfield College . . . Opening*, p. 69.
[22] *Ibid.*, pp. 74, 76–7.
[23] In 1869. *Henry Robert Reynolds D.D His life and Letters Edited by his Sisters* (London, 1898), p. 226. For Reynolds (1825–96) see *DNB*.

son put it, 'that sense of the value of each soul of man and the superb hope that a man alone with God might find his calling and election sure'.[24] Reynolds's own ministry began in the 1840s at a time when Puseyites, where not the rage, were the cause of rage. But now, in 1889, in Oxford at least, this Congregationalist inevitably reflected on the great religious movements associated with the place as he annexed the Oxford Movement, that 'wonderful step in the right direction', to his vision of the Christian mainstream:

> May we not cherish, and in this very service . . . express, our profound conviction that the great Evangelical movement of the last century, and the Anglo-Catholic movement of this century, are cooperating to produce a greater movement than either? . . .
>
> This enterprise of ours is but one involuntary expression of a vast force of sanctified judgement, without which our action would have been impossible, and it bids fair to transcend the conception of Wiclif and of Cranmer, the burning breath of Wesley, the far reaching ideal of Newman and Pusey, and will be, in fact, the supplement and the complement, and eventually the realisation and the co-operation of them all.[25]

That broad annexing of the catholic spirit into a system which had, as Dale had put it that same day, so consciously 'broken with the polities of the great Churches of Christendom',[26] became denominational orthodoxy. It would have been effrontery had it not been expressed by so transparent a gentleman-saint as H. R. Reynolds, and it was reworked in the third major utterance of that festal inaugural.

The new college's first Principal, Andrew Martin Fairbairn, had come to Oxford from Bradford, which was something of a Congregational heartland.[27] His formation, however, had been in the significantly different atmosphere of Scottish Dissent, and while Oxford, like Cambridge, confronted every Nonconformist with the allure of Establishment at its least endurable, forcing each to fashion his own apologia or conform, Fairbairn's Scottishness in large measure protected him. Shortly before he crossed the border he wrote that 'a national church is the ideal church, concentrating the state and connecting religion with all the forms and

---

[24] *Mansfield College . . . Opening*, p. 87. For John Robert Reynolds (1782–1862) see *Congregational Year Book* (1863), pp. 256–60.
[25] *Mansfield College . . . Opening*, pp. 88, 90, 91.
[26] *Ibid.*, p. 68.
[27] For Fairbairn (1838–1912) see *DNB*.

phases of its life'.[28] He never lost that ideal sense. He found the word 'non-conformist' to be 'foolish and insolent, the symbol of civil intrusion into a sphere too high for it'.[29] '. . . I deeply resent the terms Nonconformity and Dissent. They . . . are used as if they denoted an attitude to the Catholic Church of Christ, when all they denote is an attitude to a civil institution . . .'.[30] Consequently Fairbairn's lecture was a diplomatic *tour de force*. It celebrated some of his new college's statues, and it explained what would fill some of its windows. Part history and part apologetic, it surveyed the academic enterprise and Theology's place in it. There was a gracious section on Cambridge Puritanism and Neo-Platonism. There was a charming section which aligned new Mansfield with old Merton. Two sections in particular demand present comment.

Fairbairn's most loving lecture portrait is of John Wyclif. Here his strokes were at their broadest. Wyclif was

> a true son of his university: it made him, shaped him, believed in him . . . he was honoured and supported by his university. But the Church condemned him . . . and the point where the suppression was most jealous and most rigorous was the university. Now mark the result . . . Oxford . . . ceased to produce men, and began to erect buildings. It was a century of munificent Churchmen, great in architecture, in the sovereignties of high office, in statesmanship even, but not in the region of reason and spirit. The cycle begins with William of Wykeham, runs through Chichele, Waynflete, and Fox to Wolsey; in their *regime* New College, All Souls', Magdalen, Corpus Christi, and Christ Church rose. . . . But who will say that a city of imperial marble is better than a city of free and independent men?[31]

Here Fairbairn runs close to catastrophe, for who is to say who wins at Mansfield, the *spirit* of Wyclif, so carefully recreated by the Principal, or the *stone* of William of Wykeham, so deftly encapsulated by the architect? For just down the road and just a year or so previously, Basil Champneys, of all architects, had been extending New College, of all colleges, making a particular study of William of Wykeham, of all patrons, from whom he believed he was collaterally descended.[32] In Mansfield's library and gatehouse tower there are Wykehamist references

[28] Selbie, *Fairbairn*, p. 75.
[29] *Ibid.*, p. 368.
[30] *Ibid.*, p. 257.
[31] *Mansfield College . . . College Opening*, pp. 113–14.
[32] Maddison, 'Champneys Buildings', pp. 30–1.

which would be coincidence, or perhaps unconscious plagiarism, in any architect less educated than Champneys.[33] Perhaps Fairbairn's evangelistic spoon was too short for supping with Oxford devils. What price concept when it is pretension which tells?

The second section worth attention takes one from Oxford particularities to the general theme. Fairbairn needed at some public stage to answer the questions, 'Why this college and why this place?' He did so in the opulent manner of Edwardian Nonconformity's Liberal Imperialism:

> We dare not, even were we able, deprive ourselves of our inheritance, with all its responsibilities, dignities and duties. We are neither a recent nor a feeble nor an exhausted race. The Puritan and Evangelical churches contain by far the majority of the English-speaking peoples. They reared the men that expanded our empire, founded our colonies, created the will, the spirit, the education, the foresight, and the faith that, in spite of all the forces of misrule thrown by wild and outcast Europe on her shores, still hold the splendid West in order in happy and progressive peace. We represent men who in days of tyranny loved liberty, obeyed conscience, and achieved for others freedom denied to themselves . . . we belong to the larger and greater Church of England. . . . And so we cannot act as if we had no part in the past, no share in the present, no hopes in the future of the English people and the Christian Church.[34]

That passage is so grandly of its time that later readers might too easily underestimate its sense of historic community and continuity, Whig history notwithstanding. The concern for credibility and respectability is not just with Oxford (and therefore current society), but with the Church, truly Catholic and inevitably apostolic. It is also, and no less so, with historic Nonconformity. The buildings and fittings and rhetoric express the first two continuities, and for the third there is the college personnel. Or rather, there are the college's three living communities, immediate, proximate, and extended.

The college's *immediate* community consisted in October 1889 of five tutors and twenty-eight students, with six others.[35] Three of the staff were Oxford graduates, two were Cambridge. The Principal was Scottish. Four of the students were graduates of two universities. Seven were Oxford,

---

[33] Maddison, 'Champneys Buildings', pp. 30–1.
[34] *Mansfield College . . . Opening*, pp. 133–4.
[35] *Ibid.*, p. 241.

four were Cambridge, six were London, with two Welsh (both Aberystwyth), six Scottish (Glasgow, Edinburgh, and Aberdeen), a German (from Bonn and Berlin), and three from the white Dominions. Of the eight who had already left college, four had Scottish degrees, two had American ones, and one was from Cambridge, while two of them were in China, and one each in Portugal, Germany, and America. Since their significance lay in the future, pace-setters for their churches, no more need here be said, save for the light they cast on their Principal's Liberal Imperialism. So much for the college's immediate community and the continuities thus set in motion.

The college's *proximate* community extended to its effectual foundation in 1838. For Mansfield College, though new in name and new in Oxford, was not new in fact. It had existed for nearly fifty intellectually respectable years as Spring Hill College, in Birmingham, where it had already been rebuilt in full collegiate Gothic. There it produced several generations of that key type in British social, Dissenting, and intellectual life, the Nonconformist minister. Ministers, where they stayed the course, were the focal points of a national complex of autonomous local communities, their social lightning conductors, shaping the faith, conserving the tradition, reconciling the fundamental discontinuities of a religious network based on *vital* religion with the continuities imposed by social constraints and common adherence to an *historic* faith. They reconciled their continuity with the Covenant and the discontinuity between one person's conversion and the next. R. W. Dale caught continuity and discontinuity together with his sermon text: 'Contend earnestly for the faith which was once for all delivered unto the Saints' (Jude 3). Reynolds and Fairbairn alike in their different styles tried to contain it within a grand comprehension. Thus the college's proximate community.

The college's third community, its extended community, was there in force on inaugural day, the equivalent of Edith Hall's two centuries of *Home Circle*.[36] Her husband was there, of course, and several others of the *Home Circle*. The husband of one of her birthday connections was on the building committee, while most suggestive of all, flanked by eight deacons representing the cream of Congregational commerce, was the London minister, new and young and freshly Hampstead, who assisted Dr Reynolds at the Communion service. He was R. F. Horton of New College, a past President of the Oxford Union and the first Fellow of an Oxford College since the Commonwealth to have been also in full

[36] *Ibid.*, pp. 230–6.

pastoral charge of a Congregational church. He was also, though tenuously by now, the minister under whom Edith Hall's cousin Asquith, already in his last Herbert years, still sat.

Congregationally speaking, that inaugural gathering reflected the four parts of the British Isles, most sections of the middle ranks of British Society, and a cumulative thickening, both Whitefieldite and Wesleyan, from the eighteenth-century Revival. There were also enough individuals present whose natural points of religious reference were in the seventeenth century for there to be more than merely a snobbishly pious antiquarianism in the day's rhetoric. The strong Cambridge contingent (with one and another of whom Fairbairn had had some anxious moments)[37] may make the point and move us outwards.

The new college had no direct Cambridge equivalent. When dissenteries moved to Cambridge their impact was significantly different. There was, however, an equivalent display of rhetoric in stone, glass, and flesh in the new Congregational Church on Trumpington Street. Emmanuel Church was a monumental statement, flush with the pavement, muscling in on Pembroke, between Peterhouse and the Pitt Press, its thick tower dominant on the Cambridge skyline, its dumpy spire firmly refusing to dream, looking down on Little St Mary's. Emmanuel had been there since May 1874, in much stone though with no statues, to demonstrate a practical reworking of the architectural form best suited to Christian worship, a scholar's early Gothic, Free but French accented, liberated by its architect's discipline. Emmanuel's architect too was a parson's son, manse rather than vicarage, Baptist rather than Low Church. No Champneys he, James Cubitt remained more faithful to the tough High Gothic with which he too had begun. Cubitt's Cambridge determination was to build a church both Congregational and congregational, designed 'to exhibit rather than to conceal such individuality as it may thus become possessed of, and to do this, if possible, with some regard to impressiveness'.[38] As at Mansfield, most of the windows came later; six of them, in the apse, from the William Morris firm. They were completed in January 1906, the year in which W. H. Wills, now Lord Winterstoke, delighted Fairbairn by promising to extend Mansfield's stained glass.[39]

Emmanuel's windows spoke volumes with discreet abrasiveness. They

---

[37] Selbie, *Fairbairn*, pp. 194–7.

[38] *Congregational Year Book* (1874), p. 414. For a full account see *ibid.* (1873), pp. 424–6. For Cubitt, see C. Binfield, 'Towards an Appreciation of Baptist Architecture', in K. W. Clements, ed., *Baptists in the Twentieth Century* (London, 1983), pp. 121–6.

[39] Selbie, *Fairbairn*, p. 426.

were weak on catholicity but strong on churchmanship, innocent of sentimentality and relentlessly authentic in detail. Their six subjects were infinitely suggestive. Here, in the centre, were two laymen, on the right two ministers, on the left two martyrs, one a minister, one not. Here, again, were five Cambridge men (two Clare, one Corpus, one Christ's, and one Sidney Sussex), while the sixth had been taught by Cambridge men and was for nearly thirty years resident in Cambridge. Or, again, here were 170 years of history encompassed by 6 lives (1550–1720), during which the churchmanship to which they supposedly testified and certainly drew attention was formed. Or yet again, here, from January 1906, are Milton and Cromwell to provide the focal point whenever the church members, gathered for Communion, should lift their eyes above the table.

Naturally there was rhetoric to match this coloured glass. Emmanuel's minister inaugurated his church's new windows with a sermon brave in Christian constitutionalism. As he passed from one to another of the six, he came to Milton, mindful that

> The great work of Puritanism was the making of men. By its teaching as to the right of the free access of the soul to God, and its untrammelled liberty of the conscience, by insisting ... that all alike were kings and priests unto God, Puritanism gave a new nobility and strength to human nature, and produced men who were at once cool in judgement, fiery in devotion and strong in action. Milton's writings give us the philosophy of this renewed human nature....[40]

This rhetoric, too, is as characteristic as that at Mansfield, and though Emmanuel was no college (and had no connection with Cambridge's Emmanuel College) it too set its cap at the University. One of its previous ministers still lived in Cambridge, where he had become Professor of Moral Philosophy, and its present minister had been the first student admitted to Mansfield, whose second principal he would shortly become.[41] And the constitutional resonances of his sermon in January

---

[40] W. B. Selbie, *Remember the Days of Old* (Cambridge, 1906), p. 8. Sermon preached 21 January 1906. In addition to Milton and Cromwell, the windows commemorated the Separatist martyrs Barrow and Greenwood and the Cambridge pioneers Francis Holcroft and Joseph Hussey. Selbie and his deacons took as much care over their accuracy as Fairbairn was taking at Mansfield. The Cambridge windows replaced a set of 'figures illustrative of the more important epochs in Scripture history, among them one representing the Crucifixion' (*Cambridge Chronicle*, 23 May 1874).

[41] For James Ward (1843–1925) minister 1870–72, see *DNB*. For W. B. Selbie (1862–1944), minister 1902–9, see *DNB*.

1906 are readily understood in the special light of that election year, and a congregation which included the next Downing Professor of the Laws of England and the Master of Trinity Hall, to whose father's memory those windows were dedicated, and whose namesake, also Master of Trinity Hall, had been ejected in 1662.[42]

Emmanuel's concern to demonstrate its continuity within the University's context is easily explained by the relative strength of that University's Free Churchmanship. For obvious reasons this strength was new and socially, though not intellectually, *parvenu*. In town terms, however, as opposed to gown, Cambridge's Dissent was long established and more substantially so than Oxford's. Cambridge Baptists went back as Baptists to 1721, Cambridge Congregationalists went back as Congregationalists to 1694, and both communities went back as Presbyterians to 1687 and as Independents, less directly but none the less decidedly, to 1662. Emmanuel's consciousness of being the oldest, continuously surviving, Nonconformist organization in Cambridge went deeper than modish antiquarianism. The church retained records unbroken from 1691. Its seventeenth-century covenant was renewed with each fresh ministry well into the eighteenth century, and it remained a lively recollection thereafter. Each new church meeting minute-book was prefaced by a list of past ministers. Here was a natural tradition, memory kept alive, constantly re-presented, by personality, connection, and coincidence. In 1874, when the church moved site and changed name, there were probably no direct descendants in membership of those who had called the first stated minister in 1691, but there was a real overlap of memory.

To give one example. In 1879 Girton's undergraduates included a manse daughter from Leeds via Cheltenham Ladies' College.[43] She worshipped at Emmanuel, and her father would be among the denominational elder statesmen at Mansfield's inaugural. Her great-great-grandfather had ministered to the Cambridge church from 1739 to 1754, moving on to London as Principal of a Dissenting academy.[44] His father, grandfather, and great-grandfather had performed literally yeoman service as pastors of the village congregations nurtured by one of the six

---

[42] For Courtney Kenny (1847–1930), see *DNB*. For Henry Bond (d. 1929), son of William Bond (1818–1904), see *Who Was Who*.

[43] Ethel Mary Conder (1859–1942), second headmistress of Milton Mount College, the school for Congregational ministers' daughters; daughter of Eustace Rogers Conder (1820–92), who had succeeded Henry Robert Reynolds as minister of East Parade Chapel, Leeds, and for whom see *Congregational Year Book* (1893), pp. 214–16.

[44] For John Conder (1714–81), see *DNB*.

men in Emmanuel's windows: a tradition which seems to have begun in storybook fashion in 1633 by a conversion experience when the reading of the Book of Sports turned the farming progenitor of this prolonged piety from football to souls, the 'grace of God ... making that to be an ordinance for my salvation, which the devil and wicked governors laid as a trap for my destruction'.[45]

Such links are the contours of attitudes naturally and widely held through the generations and across society, earthed at a significant stage by such a church as that at Emmanuel, Cambridge, so conscious of its past and of its present responsibility, with its extraordinary amalgam of new gown and old town, the whole held in six apse windows commemorating a wholesale grocer based on Market Hill, whose son was Master of Trinity Hall, and at whose open house for nonconforming students the parents of Maynard Keynes first met.[46] We are back to home circles. Cambridge was a very ordinary place, after all, as a town.

It is this which makes such buildings as Emmanuel Church or Mansfield College representative rather than idiosyncratic, which connects them with other apparent *folies de grandeur*, and which holds them all within the evangelical paradox of vital religion continuously rediscovered.

Dr Fairbairn's nine years in Bradford were an invaluable introduction to some of English Congregationalism's industrial realities and urban possibilities, northern side up. In September 1899 he was in Lancashire to lecture on John Milton to the Literary Society and Women's Guild of Albion Chapel, Ashton-under-Lyne.[47] He also preached in aid of Mansfield. Albion's magazine considered further this Oxford mission in the cause of Protestant truth and true scholarship. It quoted from the college circular:

> The Free Churches are to attempt to prove their fitness to deal with the new Sacerdotalism in the place of its birth, to cultivate a scholarship that will silence it, to evoke spiritual activities and qualities that will rebuke its pride and answer its claims. And this is to be attempted not by methods polemical, but by reason, reasonable speech, seemly living and veracious teaching. ... We have built a

---

[45] *Evangelical Magazine* (October 1795), pp. 393–4; see also M. Spufford, 'A Note on the Conder Family', *TCHS*, 21, 3 (1972), pp. 77–9.

[46] Florence Ada Keynes, *Gathering Up the Threads: A Study in Family Biography* (Cambridge, 1950), p. 39.

[47] C. Binfield, 'The dynamic of grandeur, Albion Church, Ashton-Under-Lyne', *Transactions of the Lancashire and Cheshire Antiquarian Society*, 85 (1988), p. 179.

Chapel, considered beautiful even amid the beautiful Chapels of Oxford; and a College, adapted to . . . the many-organed activities of a varied intellectual and religious life . . . ambitious . . . of penetrating the University with spiritual religion. . . . So to open Mansfield will crown our Churches with dignity, our College with grace, our future with hope.

Fairbairn knew Ashton's Albionites. They were rich, inter-connected, and hungry for education; one of their younger generation shortly married into Oxford Egyptology, which greatly benefited from her family's money.[48] They were also building. Fairbairn preached to them at the point when they, too, their building committee infected with a Gothic contagion, had decided to rebuild. Gothic was reality, healthily imperfect, without disguise, evasion, or exaggeration.[49] Albion's Gothic, thanks to John Brooke, Albion's architect,[50] was early perpendicular of the fifteenth century. And it had stained glass: painted windows to Burne Jones designs from Morris and Co. in chancel and transepts. So (at a distance, since the church held a thousand) figures from the Old and New Testaments accompanied the congregation, while the virtues and graces of the Christian character (that is to say, Justice, Temperance, Hope, Charity, Faith, Providence, and Humility) braced by an unusual septet of saints (Martin, Michael, George, Margaret, Theresa, Lucia, and Dorothy), led from the front, and the minister's daughter allegorized them all for the church magazine.[51]

Perhaps they protested too much. Perhaps truly congregational buildings should not need such careful explaining. Certainly the discovery that the language of art is no more universal than those of the mind or the soul is a hard one for the newly educated to bear. And certainly Albion, like Emmanuel and Mansfield, was the issue less of masterful minds than of masterful minds in committee, that is to say, in community. It was congregational. It was as much a people's choice as the rantingmost hall.

As a fourth Congregational building might suggest. Late Edwardian visitors travelling for the first time from Blackpool to Lytham by 'electric car' would be startled to find

---

[48] *Transactions of the Lancashire and Cheshire Antiquarian Society*, 85 (1988), p. 188. Kate Bradbury, of Ashton, married Francis Llewellyn Griffith (1862–1934) for whom see *DNB*. It was Bradbury money which made possible the Ashmolean's Griffith Institute.

[49] Thus Albion's minister, J. Hutchison, argued in October 1896: *ibid.*, p. 184.

[50] For Brooke (1853–1914), see *R.I.B.A. Journal*, 21 (1914), p. 653.

[51] *Ashton-Under-Lyne and District Congregational Magazine* (February 1896), pp. XV–XVII, quoted in Binfield, 'Albion', pp. 190–1.

rising in front of them in the distance a white campanile, which flashes in the sun.... In a very short time the whole building is before their eyes, its white domes and walls presenting an imposing, dignified example of Byzantine architecture.... While it was building the voice of local criticism was very loud and not always kind; the Fairhaven people had done what is still an unpardonable sin in the eyes of many—something unusual. They had chosen neither brick nor stone, but a new preparation, a sort of glistening white tile-brick; they had departed from the Perpendicular Gothic, which is the style of the two finest churches in the district, and had reared a white sister—though a small one—to Westminster Roman Catholic Cathedral.[52]

This was Fairhaven Congregational Church, a deceptively spacious building designed in the shape of a Greek cross to hold 500. An octagon with three towers capped by little domes and clad in white tiles is a striking concept for a quiet seaside resort, even as a winter-garden concert-hall. Inside, this Lancashire Byzantium gives way to Central Hall baroque. The shape brings preacher and choir close to the people, sharing in worship with them rather than reaching out to them. Winter congregations need not look lost, and summer late-comers might take in the situation at a glance, helped by the raked floor. There is an immediacy about the interior. There are two other things about it. One is the completeness and good sense of the fittings, down to the vestibules, with their space for cloaks and heating pipes for the top coats of a wet congregation. The other is the church's lightness. Here is a Protestant room. It is quite unmysterious.

Fairhaven had no traditions, only associations. It was a place 'to sit without throng by the lapping wavelets on a summer day',[53] a scattering of cottages and large villas south of the railway, the beginnings of a select development promoted by Lancashire businessmen. Its associations, however, were almost apostolic. The parish church was St Paul's, the roads were called Myra or Derbe, with Pollux Gate, Cyprus Avenue, and Melita Place. Its Congregationalism began in 1902, with a church formed in 1904, and its buildings (a touch, perhaps, of the Damascus Road rather than the Golden Horn?) completed in 1912. The membership was

---

[52] G. Stanley Russell, 'The New Church at Fairhaven', *Supplement to the British Congregationalist*, 17 (October 1912), p. 748.
[53] L. S. Walmsley, *Fairhaven Congregational Church, Lytham, Lancashire: the Story of the Stained Glass Windows: A Handbook* (St Anne's-on-the-Sea, 1920), p. 13.

prosperous, their subscriptions never unbalanced by extremes: Rams-bottom, Birtwistle, Crook, Cauthery, Wolstenholme, Kershaw, Briggs, Meadowcroft, Kenyon, an extension of home circles from Blackburn, Bolton, Bury, Rochdale, Oldham, Ashton. From the start they struck a note of pronounced Congregationalism:

> To persons unattached to any of the local Churches we offer the hospitality for which Congregationalists are everywhere esteemed. A warm welcome is promised to any worshippers who will let us make them at home. Visitors will find an open door, free and unappropri-ated seats, and hearty Christian fellowship. . . . Fairhaven Congrega-tional Church is an Independent Free Church, that is, it is free from all external ecclesiastical control; under the Lord Jesus Christ it is a self governing society in all matters relating to its own worship and work. It invites and welcomes to its membership all disciples of Jesus Christ. It holds that beyond the simple or separate assembly, or 'Con-gregation of Faithful People', the only true and catholic unity consists in the recognition (without formal alliance with them) of all Christian Churches of every name as sections of the one Universal Church. We unchurch none who name the name of Jesus Christ in sincerity. . . .[54]

It is clear from church records that the extraordinary building which housed this spirit issued faithfully from the congregational dynamic. Each twist of plan and change of fitting was tested in committee and in plenary. The architects (Briggs, Wolstenholme and Thornely, of Blackburn and Liverpool) reflected Fairhaven's clout.[55] So did the openers, a London pulpiteer, two college principals, and a Mansfield tutor, Moffatt the Bible translator:

> The general reader knows him as the Captain of a fleet of pearl ships, each with a scarlet sail, which he has launched on the broad sea of Holy Scripture. Puritans know him for his 'Golden Book of John Owen', literary men know him for his Introduction to George Meredith.[56]

---

[54] *Fairhaven Congregational Church: Souvenir and Programme of the Opening, October 1912*, pp. 2, 3.
[55] For F. G. Briggs (b. 1862) and (Sir) Arnold Thornely (1870–1953), see W. J. Pike, ed., *Liverpool and Birkenhead in the Twentieth Century: Contemporary Biographies* (Brighton, 1911), pp. 249, 273. For Thornely, see also A. Service, *Edwardian Architecture* (London, 1977), p. 210. For H. V. Wolstenholme (1863–1936); see *R.I.B.A. Journal* (23 May 1936), p. 768.
[56] *Fairhaven . . . Souvenir*, p. 15. For James Moffatt (1870–1944), see *DNB*.

The opening had one marked feature to it. The congregation entered the church where, to the anthem ' What are these', the windows were unveiled.

The windows, like most other aspects of what was none the less a truly congregational enterprise, were the inspiration of Luke Slater Walmsley, of Deanley, a retired Blackburn art dealer.[57] This 'happy example of Christian geniality' was clearly a communicator of genius, since he was not a millionaire. His church's exterior promised tricks and mysteries. Its interior dispelled such fancies. Yet it was alive with art, thanks to the four great windows which lighted it.

From the outset Walmsley had determined to fill his church with painted glass in 'reverent pageant, a crowning of Liberty and a holy offering of thanksgiving and praise', the movement of faith caught in the meeting of daylight and stained glass.[58] Since the cost would lie beyond his means, each window section would be given by members of the church and congregation, who thus shared in telling a story which would so 'appeal directly to a living work-a-day world, and be understood by the common people and evoke their sympathy and emotion' as to lead them to 'the life in God'.[59] There were fifty-eight windows to be followed in natural sequence, scripture and history encompassing eternity. In the chancel, the first to be seen by visitors and the theme most constantly in view for forward-looking worshippers, was the Day of Pentecost. Opposite Pentecost, and never out of the preacher's sight, were the scripture windows. These portrayed the life and ministry of Jesus, Calvary, Resurrection, and Ascension: 'He who has eyes for symbolism will note that a stray lamb is grazing while a red poppy bends over its innocent head'. History streamed to east and west. Here, in the lower parts, were the figures of Wyclif, Savonarola, Luther, Tyndall, Barrow, John Robinson, Milton and Cromwell, George Fox and John Bunyan, Watts and Wesley, William Carey, John Williams of Erromanga and David Livingstone, and John Knox, each a 'worthy who has ... given of his best, even of his life's blood, for the spread of the Gospel and the onward march of religious liberty': and over the head of each 'a winged cherub who brings the symbol of special call'.[60] In the large upper spaces

---

[57] For L. S. Walmsley (1841–1922) see *Blackburn Weekly Telegraph* (29 April 1922). I am indebted to B. Dean Walmsley, Esq. for information about his father.

[58] L. S. Walmsley, *Fighters and Martyrs for the Freedom of Faith* (London, 1912), pp. 13–14.

[59] Walmsley, *The Story of the Stained Glass Windows*, p. 8. The windows, designed by Charles Elliott, were executed by Abbott and Co. of Lancaster. The supervisory eye of Walmsley was as relentlessly correct as those of Fairbairn and Selbie.

[60] *Ibid.*, p. 14; *Congregational Year Book* (1906), p. 185.

were stirring events: Wyclif's trial, Luther at Worms, Latimer and Ridley at the stake, the Mayflower, the Ejectment of 1662, and, for the special pride of Cromwellian Independents, a window wherein a 'Cromwellian Ironside personifies St. George, England's patron saint, who, "For England and Liberty", is spearing to death the Stuart dragon—"Absolutism"—The divine right to govern wrong'.[61]

In sum, 'the spirit of the project is large, catholic, and comprehensive; it is designed to show forth the recovery of the pure truth of Jesus.' As to colour, 'charm . . . has been secured, and pure primaries used with judgement and taste. Historic truth has been the supreme consideration' and a 'restrained suggestiveness' the ruling motive.[62]

Walmsley's own account of his inspiration is a revealing study of the cultural evolution of Victorian Nonconformity, prospering, articulate, Ruskin-bred, Browning-weaned, George Macdonald-flavoured, and home encircled, applying to its setting the sanctified passions once fulfilled in psalmody ('Our windows are not separate songs, but one great oratorio'):

> In the Old Chapel of my childhood there was not one inch of flaming glory of colour to help me to make my angels. I could and did create ghosts in troops from an erratic gas light in the farthest dark corner under the gallery. For all, but especially for the children's sake, I plead that the sweet passion of art, through the haunting beauty of stained glass, may have its place.[63]

Walmsley could not imagine art's sweet passion without liberty for its base, and he had a lively sense of the positive virtues of tradition, 'impregnated by a living intelligence. By a manly sanity, it is the function of living art to do this, as it is also to save nature and realism from the commonplace.'[64] Now, in retirement at Marine Drive, he had a Protestant mission to fulfil:

> The Free Churches have never yet risen to the opportunity of their liberty. They do not realise its potential greatness. Especially is this seen in their neglect of appeal to the reverent imagination in the environment of their fabrics and worship. The Roman Church lives upon it . . . It is quite wrong to think that the Free Churches are

---

[61] *The Story of the Stained Glass Windows*, p. 81.
[62] *Ibid.*, p. 14, 15, 22.
[63] *Ibid.*, pp. 16, 22.
[64] *Ibid.*, p. 15.

cramped as to range for this appeal; indeed anti-sacerdotal by tradition, they, in an especial way, may avail themselves of it with absolute safety. . . . A strong liberty will not fear to give a yard of stained glass to a sweet legend, or to an old medieval saint, if there be some deed or teaching of love to tell us.[65]

This was Edwardian optimism, a recall to the catholic values of Reformed Christianity, rounded by a refusal to stand upon old awkwardnesses now that Reformed Christianity was on the verge of becoming national once more. Walmsley seized on this in his description of the Calvary window:

This inclusive, this more spacious and heavenly, more pure and spiritual ideal of the Passion of the Cross is felt around us as an atmosphere, as the gentler voice of the Christian conscience, of its literature and pulpit: it breathes in a new hymnology, more sweet and gracious, on a more humane plane of truth, tenderness and love, less coarse and fleshly in symbol, more cultured and finely spiritual in appeal. It lives and moves in that subtle thing, the spirit of the age and the national conscience, and it is being translated into legislation.[66]

Few concepts of living are further removed from our own than those of Fairhaven's seaside fusion of the baroque and the Byzantine or Albion's restrained riot of Burne-Jones and the perpendicular, or Emmanuel's large-boned Gothic or Mansfield's merger of Wykehamist and Wyclifite; yet Walmsley was right. Each was oratorio. Each was a celebration of congregational art. Each was popular. Each indeed skimmed along the margin of conformity, but each also made space for conversion, the soul's necessary drama, that chief determinant of the evangelical home circle.

If this seems perverse, as it must, to that most iconoclastic of evangelical historians, W. R. Ward, one can only point to his own Methodism, for though it may be far from such Congregationalism as is here described, it too has survived in creative tension with Oxford and Manchester, and in Durham as now in Petersfield it has sat down in spired Gothic. Where, then, are its truest continuities, its most telling discontinuities?

University of Sheffield

[65] *Ibid.*, p. 16.
[66] *Ibid.*, p. 19.

'FOR GOD AND ULSTER': EVANGELICAL PROTESTANTISM AND THE HOME RULE CRISIS OF 1886*

by DAVID HEMPTON

The churches know by intimate neighbourhood with the people in every part of Ireland the true aims of those who clamour for separation. They see the effects of so-called Nationalism on morals, on character, on society, on the rights of property, and not least, on Christian institutions. Their estimate of Home Rule is the product of many influences. Observation, experience, intuition, historical facts, and facts of daily life—all contribute their part toward that fulness of conviction which they alike own and maintain. Such a solidarity of opinion does not exist on any other public question.[1]

THE geographical distribution of Irish Protestantism was shaped initially not by a complex process of religious change, but by settlement patterns dating back to the sixteenth and seventeenth centuries. In particular, the migration of Scottish Presbyterians to the north-east of Ireland ensured that the Province of Ulster had a higher density of Protestants than any other part of Ireland. The general effect of the Evangelical Revival, pioneered in the 1740s by the Methodists and the Moravians, was to reinforce that geographical pattern, despite repeated attempts to convert Roman Catholics in the south and west of the country. By the middle decades of the nineteenth century the growth of Evangelicalism in all the major Protestant denominations had not only confirmed the geographical concentration of Protestantism in Ulster, but had contributed much to the distinctive religious, social, and political ethos of the Province. Ulster had also emerged as the most developed industrial and commercial part of the country and had experienced less population decline as a result of the famine. This cultural differentiation of Ulster from the rest of the island, though by no means complete, was a stumbling-block in the way of establishing political and religious structures acceptable to an increasingly potent Irish Catholic nationalism

* The research for this article was made possible by a grant from the Economic and Social Research Council. I am also grateful to Dr Myrtle Hill, who was employed as a research assistant on this project, for helping to gather and organize much of the material.
[1] *The Christian Advocate*, 15 Jan. 1886.

in the second half of the nineteenth century. By the 1880s neither the disestablishment of the Irish Church nor various attempts at land reform had quietened Ireland, and Gladstone reached the conclusion that only a considered measure of self-government offered any prospect of long-term peace and stability. Not surprisingly, such a bold constitutional proposal helped crystallize the differences between Irish Catholics and Protestants, and between Ulster and the rest of the country, despite the insistence of those opposed to Home Rule that Gladstone's scheme would bear heavily on the population as a whole. Nevertheless, in a remarkable way the Home Rule crisis brought into sharp focus an Irish Protestant *mentalité*, centred in Ulster, which had been forged over a quarter of a millennium of turbulent history. Moreover, the resistance to Home Rule in Ulster in the period 1885–1920 cemented a Protestant identity which subsequent events have done nothing to undermine. The inability of either the British State or Irish nationalism to coerce or accommodate this sturdy and peculiar minority has resulted in one of the most intractable problems in the modern world. The purpose of this essay is to use the Home Rule crisis of 1886 as a window through which to view the Irish Protestant tradition at a decisive moment in its history. This will be accomplished in two parts. First, there will be an assessment of how the main Protestant churches in Ireland—Episcopalian, Presbyterian, and Methodist—responded to Gladstone's proposals within the setting of a wider British Protestantism. Second, there will be an attempt to explore the Ulster Protestant mind both from the standpoint of those within the tradition and those Irish Protestants who vigorously repudiated it.

Most members of the Church of Ireland had regarded the disestablishment of the Church in 1869 as the end of a cycle of concessions to Irish Roman Catholics which had begun with Catholic Emancipation in 1829. All legitimate grievances had been met, a position of religious equality had been reached, and the Church of Ireland had been painfully reconstructed to suit its new circumstances.[2] Within this mental framework all subsequent agitations on behalf of Irish Catholics—educational, agrarian, or constitutional—were viewed not as legitimate attempts to secure fair treatment, but as unjustified actions designed to take advantage of Irish

<hr/>

[2] The standard treatments of the Church of Ireland in this period are D. H. Akenson, *The Church of Ireland: Ecclesiastical Reform and Revolution, 1800–1885* (London, 1971) and R. B. McDowell, *The Church of Ireland, 1869–1969* (London, 1975). See also A. J. Megahey, 'The Irish Protestant churches and social and political issues' (Belfast Ph.D. thesis, 1969).

Protestantism's relative weakness. In his presidential address to the special meeting of the General Synod in March 1886 the Archbishop of Dublin stated that

> I have carefully considered the statements put forward by those who advocate Home Rule, and I cannot for the life of me discover where the grievance is to be found. If any of our fellow-countrymen were living under the tyranny of penal laws, as they were, unfortunately, some years ago, if Catholic emancipation had not become a fact, if they were able even to complain of the ascendancy in this land of a State Church, or if they were able to persuade us that, owing to some fault in the limits of the franchise . . . they have not a voice in the Imperial Parliament upon questions such as education or the land . . . I would look at the matter in an entirely different light. It is no use trying to trample out a real grievance. But if there be no grievance, then we must trace these demands for Home Rule to one of two causes . . . sentiment or . . . ulterior aims. . . . Undoubtedly, behind the claim for Home Rule—and we should be fools if we did not believe it—there lurks the demand for entire separation, and for a very advanced form of socialism.[3]

What lies behind this speech is the sincere conviction that the old pattern of agitation, coercion, and concession had come to an end; what was therefore at stake in 1886 was the future destiny of the nation, and who was to have the power to shape it.

An examination of the voluminous pamphlet literature of the Church of Ireland between disestablishment and the Home Rule crisis shows that just under half (over 200) were devoted to Prayer Book revision and ritualist controversies, a further third were concerned with educational debates, and about a fifth addressed matters of finance and property.[4] This reflects the determination of many within the Church to maintain its essential Protestantism, to resist Catholic educational encroachments, and to protect the Church's remaining endowments. As a result of the structural changes consequent upon disestablishment, the northern laity, who were generally speaking more evangelical, had achieved more representation, if not necessarily more power, owing to the checks and balances

---

[3] *Journal of the General Synod of the Church of Ireland* (Dublin, 1886), Special Meeting (23 March), pp. liv–lxii.

[4] Calculations are based on the rich pamphlet collection of the Representative Church Body Library, Dublin.

in synodical voting arrangements. The requirement of a two-thirds majority of each order—bishops, clergy, and laity—present and voting, subjected the Church, according to the Protestant Defence Association, to the 'absolute control of a minority, whose Romanising tendencies are patent to all men'.[5] Ritualism, the PDA contended, had corrupted the Church of England, damaged the Protestant missionary movement through its influence on the Society for the Propagation of the Gospel, and, if unchecked, would ruin Protestantism in Ireland.[6] The theology of the Irish High Church Party was, of course, anything but Roman, 'but the simple fact that it moved away from an evangelical position, settling upon more sacramentarian thought, was enough to stir a fear of Rome's potential presence in the Church's fold'. The campaign for the revision of the Prayer Book on more Protestant lines was, therefore, the 'defensive reaction of a Church which knew the enemy to be without, and to be formidable and aggressive. It was that of a Church which feared that the enemy on the outside might enter through even what the Prayer-Book permitted, and that in the process everything would be lost'. As it turned out, the Prayer Book revision was achieved relatively agreeably due to the fear of schism, the openness of the debates, and the voting system of the Church, which put a brake on hasty legislation. But the recurring ritualistic controversies within the Church put Episcopalian Evangelicals on their guard against the 'murky whirlpool of superstition' which threatened to deliver them into the hands of Rome.[7]

For many within the Church, Home Rule threatened to do the same thing by another route. Even the normally controlled *Irish Ecclesiastical Gazette*, in the midst of the crisis, detected a conspiracy of 'a foreign and Ultramontane Church, worked by the Jesuits' to overthrow the Protestant religion in Ireland: 'If we and Rome cannot live together on terms of peace, we must do so with the sword in our hands. No surrender!'[8] Despite such opinions, the leadership of the Church of Ireland was slower to respond to the possibility of Home Rule than the other churches. Resolutions against a separate Parliament from the ultra-Protestant Dr Craig at the Dublin Synod in 1885 had been ruled out of order on the

---

[5] The Protestant Defence Association of the Church of Ireland, *Revision of the Prayer-Book* (Dublin, 1875), pp. 3–4.
[6] See the *Reports of the Protestant Defence Association of the Church of Ireland* which were published annually in Dublin.
[7] P. J. Fahey, 'Ritualism, the revision movement and revision theology in the Church of Ireland 1842–1877' 2 vols (Doctor of Sacred Theology, Rome, 1976), pp. 31–3, 59.
[8] *Irish Ecclesiastical Gazette*, 27 March 1886.

grounds that it was a political matter outside the competence of the Church.[9] The situation in Ulster was rather different. There were reports in the *Gazette* of sermons against Home Rule in the Diocese of Down and Connor and of enthusiastic Episcopalian contributions to the meetings surrounding the visit to Belfast of Lord Randolph Churchill.[10] There was considerable pressure from the north for the bishops to do something, and they agreed to convene a special synod of the Church to debate the issue in late March 1886. Debate is a slight misnomer, for despite the Archbishop of Dublin's assurances that the Church of Ireland was one of the most representative bodies in the world, and despite his political disclaimers, the resolutions against Home Rule were prepared in advance and were moved by the bishops and other dignitaries within the Church. The resolutions were predictable enough, with imperial themes close to the surface.[11]

Although Irish Episcopalians opposed Home Rule on essentially the same grounds as the other Protestant churches, a number of distinctive themes do emerge from the Church of Ireland's records. As befitted the only Protestant church in Ireland with a considerable amount of its property and personnel located outside Ulster, there was an understandable reluctance to allow that Ulster was a distinct entity which might require special treatment. Indeed, Leinster Episcopalians argued a similar case as Ulster Protestants in suggesting that the Protestant parts of the south of Ireland, notably the old Pale, were wealthier and more progressive than the Catholic west, and were therefore specially worth listening to by British politicians.[12] The Church of Ireland's opposition to Home Rule also reflected its social status. In terms of social class the Church of Ireland had the most eclectic membership of any of the churches, but it also had a higher percentage of the gentry and the landed aristocracy.[13] The landed lay leadership of the Church was more at home with the more sophisticated tactics of the Irish Loyal and Patriotic Union[14] or the Irish Unionist Alliance[15] than with the more populist styles of urban Orangeism, but there was still an old paternalist, aristocratic, and

---

[9] *Irish Church Records* (compiled and collected by Robert Walsh D.D.), 8, p. 110.

[10] *Irish Ecclesiastical Gazette*, 16 Jan. and 27 Feb. 1886.

[11] *Journal of the General Synod of the Church of Ireland* (Dublin, 1886), p. lxiii.

[12] *Irish Church Records*, 8, pp. 122–3, 130.

[13] Megahey, 'The Irish Protestant Churches', cap. 1.

[14] See The Irish Loyal and Patriotic Union, *The real dangers of Home Rule* (Dublin, 1887) and *Union or Separation?* (Dublin, 1888).

[15] Belfast, The Public Record Office of Northern Ireland, Irish Unionist Alliance MSS (1887–1914), D989A/8/1–33.

crypto-militarist tradition which saw it as its duty to muster the troops in a national emergency.[16] There was also more hard-headed talk within the Church of Ireland over the precise impact Home Rule would have on Episcopalian endowments, investments, loans, and bonds.[17] There was a general consensus that the Church's wealth would be alarmingly reduced, and there was also unease about what a nationalist Parliament would do to the Church's more attractive endowments, such as Trinity College. Such fears introduced an element of *realpolitik* into many churchmen who were concerned to conduct opposition to Home Rule in a manner not too prejudicial to their vested interests should they be defeated. Generally speaking, then, the Church of Ireland tried to lead with a high hand and had nothing but contempt for the riotous element within Ulster Protestantism who acted like 'fools and madmen'.[18]

The Church of Ireland was also glad to have the numerical support of other Irish Protestants in resisting Home Rule.[19] In Ulster, common cause was made with Presbyterians and Methodists in the great protest rallies,[20] but traditional animosities were not entirely forgotten. The fact that the Church of Ireland insisted on retaining its old name, despite disestablishment, was a constant thorn in Presbyterian flesh.[21] This superficially trivial contention was symbolic of more substantial grievances. There was, for example, an overwhelming preponderance of Episcopalians in official positions in law and local government. Moreover, the Church of Ireland took a particularly tough stand on agrarian outrages, which many Presbyterians regarded as more of a reflection on the behaviour of Irish landlords than on Catholic criminality. The Church of Ireland was also less enthusiastic about the Evangelical Alliance than the other churches, particularly the Methodists.[22] As a church organized on territorial units, it felt itself peculiarly vulnerable to the conversionist ideology of the smaller evangelical churches. Allegations of poaching were common, and the Church of Ireland was prone to dismissive comments on 'tasteless evangelicalism'. The Salvation Army, for example, was condemned as 'ribald sanctimoniousness'.[23] One similarity between the Church of

---

[16] D. C. Savage, 'The origins of the Ulster unionist party, 1885–6', *IHS*, 12 (1961), pp. 185–208.
[17] *Irish Ecclesiastical Gazette*, 23 Jan. 1886.
[18] *Irish Ecclesiastical Gazette*, 12 June 1886.
[19] *Irish Church Records*, 8, p. 132.
[20] *Irish Ecclesiastical Gazette*, 27 Feb. 1886.
[21] *Irish Church Records*, 8, p. 43; *Minutes of the General Assembly*, 4, (1871), p. 134.
[22] *Irish Ecclesiastical Gazette*, 16 Oct. 1886.
[23] *Irish Ecclesiastical Gazette*, 25 Sept. 1886.

Ireland and the other churches is the speed with which opposition to Home Rule became the badge of true churchmanship. At the General Synod Richard Bagwell stated that

> there are some Protestant M.P.s who have taken the oath of allegiance to Mr Parnell; but they in no way represent Protestant feeling. Not one of them . . . would have the slightest chance of election by any Synod, or any council or vestry, of the Church of Ireland, throughout the length and breadth of the country.[24]

By the time of the second Home Rule Bill in 1893, 1,190 vestries out of 1,218 gave their approval to a protest against the measure.[25] Those who were out of step were regarded either as weak in faith or strong in self-interest.

Gladstone could not be regarded as the Church of Ireland's most respected politician. Episcopalians were the least troubled of any Irish Protestants by residual loyalty to the Grand Old Man. In 1886 they repudiated Home Rule and got on with their business of repairing glebes, overseeing church investments, protecting church education, and endowing the Clergy Good Service Fund. But they derived particular pleasure from planning the enthusiastic Jubilee celebrations for Queen Victoria in 1887.[26] The imperial crown still mattered, regardless of the perceived abominations of distrusted politicians, confusing justice for Ireland with concessions to Catholic nationalism.

The long struggle for political, religious, and social equality with Episcopalians had endowed Ulster Presbyterians with a heightened perception of their prominence in the liberal-dissenting tradition. They were therefore concerned to articulate their opposition to Home Rule within the wider forum of British Nonconformity, and were well represented on the liberal-unionist platform. However, like other denominations influenced by Evangelicalism, nineteenth-century Presbyterianism's understanding of progress in Ireland was intricately bound up with its resistance to an increasingly Ultramontane Catholicism. Evangelical missions to Roman Catholic areas became more aggressive than in earlier periods,[27] while annual reports on the state of popery, resolutions on the invalidity of papal ordinances, and expressions of concern over persecutions in

---

[24] *Irish Church Records*, 8, p. 131.
[25] McDowell, *The Church of Ireland*, p. 99.
[26] *Journal of the General Synod of the Church of Ireland* (Dublin, 1887).
[27] *Minutes of the General Assembly*, 2, p. 891.

Spain indicated awareness of the wider dimensions of the Catholic threat.[28] Throughout this period anxiety over Romish influences at home and abroad continued to preoccupy the General Assembly. Its most prolonged and contentious internal controversy, for example, was the debate about instrumental music which paralleled the anti-ritualist campaign within the Church of Ireland in the same period. Such music was presented as 'owing its admission into Christian worship to the innovating spirit of Popery in the dark ages, when altars, images, prayers for the dead, and Latin masses were introduced'.[29] Such preoccupations boded ill for the reception of Home Rule, which was all too easily dismissed as Rome rule.

This new crisis once more provoked a reaction based on the perception that political, religious, and social concerns were inextricably interwoven. The immediate response, therefore, was the calling of a special meeting of the General Assembly, 'to consider the present serious state of the country'. While there was general agreement that the land question needed to be settled equitably, proposals for 'a separate parliament for Ireland, or an elective National Council, or any legislation tending to imperil the legislative union between Great Britain and Ireland' were seen as 'disastrous to the best interests of our country'.[30] While proclaiming their continued support for civil and religious equality, Ulster Presbyterians feared that, given demographic realities, a Home Rule government would lead to 'the ascendancy of one class and creed in matters pertaining to religion, education, and civil administration', while leaving no satisfactory safeguards for minorities.[31] Thus anti-Catholic and anti-Home Rule arguments were not seen to mark any departure from traditional Presbyterian liberalism. On the contrary, the Bill was thought to be giving in to forces which were themselves illiberal—namely, the Irish Parliamentary party and agrarian outrage. To submit to such extremes would, it was feared, produce a denominational system of education and threaten Protestant freedoms.[32]

[28] *Minutes of the General Assembly*, 3 (1861), p. 52; (1862), p. 178.

[29] A. Robinson, *Facts for Irish Presbyterians* (Broughshane, n.d.). See also *Purity of Worship Defence Association in connection with the Irish Presbyterian Church. An Address presented to the Ministers, Elders, and Members of the Church* (Belfast, 1875).

[30] *Minutes of the General Assembly*, 7 (1886), pp. 12–13.

[31] The *Report on Religions and Education, Census of Ireland (1861)* had shown that Roman Catholics made up 77.7 per cent of the total population. Even in so-called 'Protestant Ulster' Roman Catholics accounted for 50.5 per cent of the population.

[32] *Ibid.* See also An Irish Presbyterian, *Ulster and Home Rule* (Belfast, 1886), p. 23; Revd D. Manderson, *How an Irish Nonconformist Views the Question of Home Rule with Regard to the*

The main priority of the General Assembly was to circulate these views throughout Britain so that the basis of its opposition was clearly understood, and kept separate from the more visible and alarming actions of the 'Orange' populace. This was the main thrust of the annual meeting, convened three months later. By presenting Gladstone's latest proposals as out of step with British Nonconformist liberalism, and placing themselves firmly in the reforming tradition, Ulster Presbyterians claimed the support of liberal dissenters on the mainland. Copies of the Assembly's resolutions were sent to MPs and to Scottish and English Presbyterian ministers, and a deputation was sent to London to canvass other influential figures.[33] Dissent from this majority view was strictly limited, in official reports at least, but it was by no means absent. A 'sturdy' minority of the General Assembly supported the second Home Rule Bill in 1893, and its supporters were able to present Gladstone with a petition signed by a 'cross-section of society', containing 3,535 signatures, in favour of its passage.[34] The papers of the Reverend J. B. Armour, converted to the Home Rule side in the late 1880s, make it clear that, apart from the small minority prepared to articulate their opposition, many more ministers only supported the Assembly resolutions because of congregational pressure.[35] With boycotts and exclusions resulting from failure to comply with majority opinion, it is certainly conceivable that some ministers would opt to set aside their political views in the interests of congregational harmony. However, while this qualification serves to modify the view of a united ministerial front against Home Rule, it also illustrates the strength of community pressure, which was both more pervasive and ultimately more effective.

Representing the voice of the professions and of trade and commerce, and with the nucleus of its support in Belfast itself, Presbyterianism represented a powerful interest group, which linked its relative prosperity with its religious identity. The Revd R. M. Edgar of Dublin, editor of the *Presbyterian Churchman*, stated in 1886 that:

Peace and Prosperity of Ireland (Dungannon, 1893); Revd R. J. Lynd, *The Present Crisis in Ireland, A Lecture Delivered at a Meeting of the May Street Literary Association, January 5, 1886* (Belfast, 1886).

[33] *Minutes of the General Assembly*, 7, pp. 105, 146.

[34] Belfast, P.R.O.N.I., Armour Papers, D1792/A2/25, J. B. Armour to W. E. Gladstone, July 1893. The letter accompanied copies of the Protestant Home Rule Address.

[35] *Ibid.*, Revd D. Houston to J. B. Armour 3 Aug. 1892. See also J. R. B. McMinn, *Against the Tide: J. B. Armour, Irish Presbyterian Minister and Home Ruler* (Belfast, 1985).

Ulster, least favoured of the provinces by nature, has become the leading province, mainly through Presbyterian industry and energy. It is our Presbyterian base of operations, and we who occupy the advanced posts beyond Ulster, hope to hold them and extend our pickets and do our best to transform the people into an integral and loyal portion of the greatest Protestant Empire that has as yet existed in the world.[36]

His article on 'Catholic versus Protestant Nations! A Contrast for the Times' clearly reflected the widely-held view that the choice was between Imperial Protestant glory and a tyrannical impoverished Catholic state. A survey of the material, mental, and moral status of the nations of the world suggested that 'all the Protestant countries march at the head'. Thus, one of the central arguments of anti-Home Rulers was that a Dublin government's protectionist policies would 'empty their mills, clear their rivers and shipyards, would stop their looms, would make the voice of their spindles silent and would cause a complete destruction of the industry that has made the province so prosperous'.[37]

With such fears easily converted into discrimination and job losses, there were violent sectarian street riots in Belfast in the summer of 1886, and the fiery preaching of some Evangelical Presbyterians, such as Hugh Hanna, further inflamed local tensions.[38] One particular sermon, preached to his congregation on Sunday 13 June 1886, after a period of rioting, was critical of the part played by the police force, and plainly asserted the right of resistance:

> We stand for right and truth and liberty against the forces of error and tyranny, and we are resolved to resist them in whatever form they may appear. Our safety for every interest that is dear to us lies in the union existing with the sister kingdom—with our kith and kin across the narrow seas that separate us from our Scottish and English brethren. We shall enter into no political partnership with the apostles of sedition and outrage, in Ireland or anywhere else, and we shall defend ourselves against all domination of such kind.[39]

---

[36] *Presbyterian Churchman* (1886), p. 96.
[37] Quoted in F. Holmes, *Our Irish Presbyterian Heritage* (Belfast, 1986), p. 134. See also *Presbyterian Churchman* (1886), p. 95 and R. Anderson, *Sidelights on the Home Rule Movement* (London, 1906), p. 218.
[38] See, for example, A. Boyd, *Holy War in Belfast* (Belfast, 1969), cap. 8.
[39] *Report of the Belfast Riots Commissioners* (1886), Appendix D, p. 587.

This sermon was reprinted in local newspapers, and Hanna's words were subject to close questioning from the commissioners sent to Belfast to investigate the riots. Claiming to represent the opinions of 'practically the whole Protestant community', Hanna's defence was vigorous. Loyalist resistance to the triumph of the separatists had to be seen in the light of a province on the 'brink of civil war', the authorities' 'gross mismanagement' of the crisis, and the actions of a constabulary which had 'changed its front along with Gladstone'. His exhortations to his congregation were, he claimed, 'not only true but expedient', and the sermon as a whole 'social, ethical and pacific'.[40] Hanna clearly felt that it was the duty of the clergy to give counsel in times of trouble, and that it should be appropriate to the seriousness of the threat posed to Ulster Protestantism, however irresponsible it might seem to outsiders. Such zealous language was rarely heard within the calmer confines of the General Assembly, and the meeting on the morning following the riots was held behind closed doors.[41] Nevertheless, whether proclaimed from the platforms of Liberal-Unionist meetings, or expounded from Belfast pulpits, the strength of Presbyterian resistance to Home Rule was undoubted. The Reverend Edgar quite rightly judged that 'the agitators have reckoned without their host'.[42]

The response of Irish Methodists to Home Rule has to be seen in the light of their attitudes throughout the nineteenth century to demands from the Roman Catholic Church and its alleged political representatives.[43] With near unanimity Irish Methodists had opposed in turn Catholic Emancipation, national education, the Repeal campaign, the Maynooth Grant, and the disestablishment of the Church of Ireland. The ideology behind such opposition was based not so much on political partisanship or economic self-interest as on a settled religious conviction that the Roman Catholic religion was the primary cause of all other Irish problems. Thus, political remedies whose effect was to undermine the Protestant foundations of Church and State could only perpetuate the very evils they were designed to remove. Only religious conversion from Catholicism to Evangelical Protestantism, however implausible that had become by the late Victorian period, offered the prospect of long-term peace and stability in Ireland. The anti-Catholic strand in Irish Methodism,

---

[40] *Ibid.*, pp. 345–61; *Speeches Delivered at the Meeting of Belfast Constitutional Club 17 August 1886*, reported in *Belfast Newsletter*, 18 August 1886.
[41] 'The General Assembly', *Presbyterian Churchman* (1886), pp. 193–7.
[42] *Ibid.*, p. 96.
[43] D. Hempton, 'The Methodist crusade in Ireland 1795–1845', *IHS*, 22 (1980), pp. 33–48.

however, was not simply a product of its Evangelical theology, but arose naturally from the peculiarities of its own history. Methodism in Ireland had taken strongest root in areas settled by English Episcopalians and had always regarded itself as culturally integrated into British Protestantism.[44] It was, moreover, the sister church of England's largest Nonconformist denomination and was held to have a special place in the worldwide missionary contest, or so it was perceived, between Irish Catholicism and British Protestantism. As late as 1883 the British Methodist Conference stated that Irish Methodists were in a 'position of danger and of supreme importance', because 'Irish Romanism supplies the main strength of the papacy in every English-speaking nation'. With undisguised self-interest it went on to suggest that 'our chief political, municipal, and social difficulties would become far less serious if the Irish race were Protestantized. Few things could so materially promote the highest and best intentions of England and Scotland as the conversion of Ireland to the pure Christianity of the New Testament.'[45] Irish Methodism was, of course, in no position to effect this transformation, not least because it had become by the 1880s as much an Ulster-based denomination as its Presbyterian Nonconformist counterpart,[46] but its religious diagnosis of Ireland's miseries remained as unimpaired as its commitment to the union between Britain and Ireland.

In an officially endorsed letter to the Queen in 1881 the Irish Methodist Church had already condemned agrarian terrorism and deprecated any attempt to dissolve the union as a palliative to militant nationalism.[47] It came as no surprise therefore that the *Christian Advocate*, the denominational newspaper, entered 1886 in a determined mood. 'Home Rule for Ireland', it stated in the first of many uncompromising editorials, 'means not only war against the Crown rights of England, but war against the Crown rights of Christ ... its inspiration is religious antipathy, its methods plunder, its object Protestant annihilation'.[48] Apart from reflecting the hostility of Irish Methodists to Home Rule, the *Advocate* gave more attention to the forging of a united Protestant front than any of the other denominational periodicals. It gave extensive coverage to the anti-Home Rule activities of the Episcopalian, Presbyterian, Moravian, and

---

[44] David Hempton, 'Methodism in Irish society 1770–1830', *TRHS*, ser. 5, 36 (1986), pp. 117–42.

[45] *Minutes of the Irish Conference*, the answer of the British Conference to the address of the Irish Conference (1883).

[46] Megahey, 'The Irish Protestant churches', cap. 1.

[47] *Minutes of the Irish Conference* (1881).

[48] *The Christian Advocate*, 8 Jan. 1886.

secession churches,[49] and through its advocacy of the Evangelical Alliance it envisaged not only a pan-Protestant resistance to Home Rule, but a pan-Evangelical campaign as well.[50] Home Rule was thus seen not as a debatable political strategy for the government of Ireland, but as an attack on the whole Protestant way of life.[51] Part of the Protestant way of life, according to the *Advocate*, was a stake in Britain's imperial greatness, to which the Methodists were particularly entitled as a result of their heroic contribution to the international missionary movement.[52] The *Advocate*'s editorials bemoaned the corrupting political influence of Romanism in American cities, extolled the benefits of English government and culture in India (in crudely racial terms), and claimed that 'where missionaries go education goes, and the extent to which our English language with all its glorious freightage of terms for liberty, purity, honour and humanity, has been spread among the nations, is a cause for profound gratitude to every enlightened and far-seeing mind.'[53] With such benefits in mind the *Advocate* stated quite categorically that 'Ulster will not submit to anything even seeming to be connected with the tactics of those who would dismember the Empire.'[54]

The most interesting aspect of the *Advocate*'s editorials in 1886 is not so much the ideology behind its opposition to Home Rule, predictable as it was, but its reflection of the obvious tensions within Methodism in the British Isles caused by Gladstone's Irish policy.[55] The paper was at least open enough to print letters from Irish Methodists, mostly from outside Ulster, who either supported Home Rule or who regretted that the official agencies of the Church, including the Committee of Privileges, should take such an uncompromising position on a purely political matter.[56] This dissident minority alleged that its interests were being ignored and that there was both subtle and not so subtle pressure exerted on Methodist Home Rulers either to keep quiet or come into line. In response the *Advocate* stated that it was better to lose anyone, better to 'lose any number than at such a crisis be false to our country, our posterity, our Church and our God'.[57] One particular thorn in the *Advocate*'s

[49] *Ibid.*, 12 Mar., 4 June, and 18 June 1886.
[50] *Ibid.*, 19 Feb. 1886.
[51] *Ibid.*, 15 Jan. 1886.
[52] See N. W. Taggart, *The Irish in World Methodism* (London, 1986).
[53] *The Christian Advocate*, 19 Mar., 9 Apr., and 4 June 1886.
[54] *Ibid.*, 11 June 1886.
[55] *Ibid.*, 22 Jan. 1886.
[56] *Ibid.*, 22 Jan., 29 Jan., and 5 Feb. 1886.
[57] *Ibid.*, 4 June 1886.

flesh was the Methodist MP for West Clare, Jeremiah Jordan, who was a rural merchant of tenant farming origins. In his maiden speech in the House of Commons, in a debate on Home Rule, Jordan delivered a blistering attack on landlordism, clericalism, and Orange bigotry. Of Ulster Protestants he stated that 'property is very largely their religion' and that although they claimed to put their faith in providence, they relied just as much on 'powder and ball'. According to Jordan, the nub of the problem was that 'these people have been pampered all their lives up to the present time; they have been in the ascendancy and they have monopolized power in the country. What they fear is that they will now have to be placed on an equality with other people.'[58] The *Advocate*'s response to Jordan was not to discuss his opinions, but to cast doubts on his Methodism.[59]

A more serious problem confronting Irish Methodists in 1886 was the stance taken on Home Rule by their English brethren. The *Methodist Times* under the editorship of Hugh Price Hughes supported Gladstone's proposals, as did much of the rest of English Nonconformity, despite having no history of sympathy for the cause of Home Rule. By 1886 English Nonconformity's commitment to Gladstonian Liberalism was more important than its loyalty to Protestantism in Ireland, though for many the Home Rule episode occasioned a painful choice between the two.[60] Had anyone other than Gladstone sponsored the Home Rule cause, the position taken by English Nonconformists would have been very different. Their loyalty was primarily to the man, not the issue. This was cold comfort to Irish Methodists, whose estimation of Gladstone's statesmanship fell as rapidly as had their support for Peel during the Maynooth crisis forty years earlier. For them the issue was immeasurably more important than the man or his party. Irish Methodists were acutely aware that 1886 witnessed an important change in their relationship with the rest of British Protestantism. The *Christian Advocate* saw it as the culmination of a new 'English Revolution' in which, for a period of twenty-five years, English Protestants had gone soft on Romanism:

---

[58] *Hansard*, ser. 3, 205, cols 651–61.
[59] *The Christian Advocate*, 26 Feb. 1886.
[60] The resultant divisions disturbed English Methodism at least until the end of the century. See, for example, *The Methodist Times*, 8 July 1886; *The New Review*, 7, no. 38, July 1892; *St. Stephen's Review*, no. 31, 3 Sept. 1892. For a more general analysis, see D. W. Bebbington, *The Nonconformist Conscience: Chapel and Politics 1870–1914* (London, 1982), pp. 84–105; and 'Nonconformity and electoral sociology, 1867–1918', *HistJ*, 27 (1984), pp. 633–56.

The old safeguards of legislation have been demolished one by one. Act after Act has been effaced, which had been regarded as essential to the Protestant character of the empire, and this has gone on until the Protestant succession to the throne is scarcely safe. The duty of opposing Rome has altogether disappeared from quarters where it used to be paramount.[61]

In their address to the British Methodist Conference in 1886 the Irish Conference tried to maintain the old relationship by appealing to a shared history. 'In 1802', the address stated, 'your fathers challenged our loyalty to a united Methodism by referring to "the new and glorious compact" by which the British Isles had just been united. We hold you to that challenge.' The response of the British Conference was, however, an impeccably bland mixture of providentialism, spiritual sympathy, and pious words.[62]

The events of 1886 had come as a shock to Irish Methodists, not only in the sense of having to come to terms with Home Rule, but also in having to accept that English Nonconformist opinion was less reliable than they had supposed. Gladstone's defeat in Parliament and at the polls brought some comfort, as did their view that English Methodist opinion had been unduly influenced by the 'dictatorial centralization' of Hugh Price Hughes and his supporters.[63] In the years ahead, many Irish Methodists made the trip to England to re-educate English Nonconformist opinion on the unchanging character of Irish Catholicism. Within Ireland only a tiny minority of Methodists repudiated the official opposition of the Church to Home Rule, and for some of the preachers life was made deliberately uncomfortable by their congregations.[64] Generally speaking, support for Home Rule came from Methodists in the south and west for whom landlordism was regarded as the real cause of their misery, and from those whose commercial security had been based on good relations with their Catholic neighbours, and who consequently had little to fear from Home Rule.[65] The older more evangelical Ulster-based Methodists, and those with little contact with the land, were the most implacable

[61] *The Christian Advocate*, 7 May 1886.
[62] *Minutes of the Irish Conference*, 7, pp. 87–91.
[63] *The Christian Advocate*, 18 June 1886.
[64] Belfast, Irish Wesley Historical Society MSS (temporarily stored in P.R.O.N.I.), W. Nicholas to C. Crookshank, 25 Feb. 1889. See also P.R.O.N.I., Jordan Papers, D/207/3/2/1/13, A. Duncan to J. Jordan, 4 May 1886.
[65] Jeremiah MacVeagh, *Religious Intolerance under Home Rule. Some Opinions of Leading Irish Protestants* (London, 1911).

opponents of Home Rule. By 1888 Dr Evans, an eminent Irish Methodist, was able to tell his London audience that the Vice-President of Conference (the highest office in Irish Methodism), the Secretary, all the District superintendents, the presidents of the Methodist colleges, all Irish members of the Legal Hundred, and the overwhelming majority of the preachers had signed a declaration against Home Rule.[66] The official position had been established and would not easily be changed. All that remained was to determine the tactics of opposition.

Dr Evans's speech on Methodist solidarity against Home Rule was made at a banquet hosted by the Nonconformist Unionist Association to present Lord Salisbury and Lord Hartington with an address against Home Rule signed by Irish Nonconformist ministers. The Whitehall Rooms of the Hotel Metropole were specially decorated for the occasion with a harp and crown over the chair, and underneath these symbols were the inscriptions *Tria Juncta in Uno; Quis Separabit?* and *Libertus in Legibus*. Apart from serving the interests of the Nonconformist Unionist Association, the aim of the banquet was to persuade influential British politicians that Gladstone's estimation of the views of Irish Protestants was badly mistaken, and that Irish Nonconformists were united in opposition to Home Rule on more noble grounds than mere Orange bigotry. The event was highly stage-managed and had been meticulously planned over a period of six months by W. E. Ball, the secretary of the Nonconformist Unionist Association.[67] Ball's unlikely chief contact and political adviser in Ireland was the Duke of Abercorn, an Episcopalian landowner and member of the Irish Loyal and Patriotic Union.[68] He wrote letters of introduction for Ball to Irish political and religious leaders and defended his position by stating that

> fancy if I in my humble position in the north of Ireland, instead of bringing all parties together, had taken a different course and had proclaimed the Presbyterian Ministers to be a Radical class of men

[66] *Irish Nonconformists and the Unionist Leaders: Speeches of the Irish Protestant Ministers on Home Rule*, 14 Nov. 1888 (London, 1888), p. 14.

[67] Belfast, P.R.O.N.I., Nonconformist Unionist Association Papers, D/2396/1/1–24 and D/2396/5/1–3, S. K. McDonnell to W. E. Ball, 3 Aug., 14 Aug., and 30 Oct. 1888; Lord Wolmer to W. E. Ball, 25 July, 7 Aug., 10 Aug., 5 Nov., 6 Nov., and 9 Nov. 1888.

[68] *Ibid.*, D/2396/3/1–13, Duke of Abercorn to P. E. W. Sykes, 30 Apr., Abercorn to W. E. Ball, 23 June, R. Ross to Abercorn, 26 June, Abercorn to W. E. Ball, 28 June, R. J. Lynd to Abercorn, 30 June, Abercorn to Mr Cox, 29 Aug., Abercorn to Mr Henderson, 29 Aug., Abercorn to Sir Thomas Butler, 29 Aug., Abercorn to Mr Patterson, 29 Aug., Abercorn to W. E. Ball, 14 Nov., Abercorn to W. E Ball, 2 Dec., and Abercorn to W. E. Ball, 4 Dec. 1888.

not worth relying upon—why, it would have made every Body hostile to each other and would have done no end of mischief.[69]

Abercorn canvassed opinion among Presbyterian and Methodist ministers and personally invited R. J. Lynd, the Presbyterian Moderator and 'most ardent defender of the Union', to the London banquet.[70] On the eve of the great day, Ball's brother wrote to him with pardonable fraternal enthusiasm:

> There is no doubt that your political strategy is admirable, I seem to perceive a touch of genius in it. You will have perceived from the G.O.M.'s speech at the Bingley Hall here that your Association galls him bitterly. There can be no question that it strikes him on a side where he had hitherto seemed impregnable, but where in fact he is most vulnerable. I was not at the Bingley Hall, but those who were present say that his references to the Nonconformist ministers of Ulster were much more passionate than the newspaper reports would lead you to suppose. His face, gestures, and voice added an intensity of vitriolic hatred that evaporated in the process of reporting. I enclose a letter printed in the Birmingham Daily Post which will indicate the sort of effect which Gladstone's speech is having upon Nonconformists generally. I imagine all this will greatly strengthen your Association. Surely Nonconformists ought to perceive that this man is more interested in Irish Roman Catholics than in them.[71]

The aim of the banquet was not to persuade Gladstone to think again, but to convince wavering English Nonconformists that their loyalty to Gladstone had led them to ignore the unanimously expressed wishes of their Irish co-religionists. The tone of the meeting was all important Episcopalians were discreetly urged not to attend, Orangeism was not to appear, opposition to Home Rule was to be expressed in liberal humanitarian, not sectarian, terms, but not too liberally lest the conservative members of the Nonconformist Unionist Association (including Chubb, its Vice-President, and Ball himself), and, of course, Lord Salisbury, should be given unnecessary offence. All went to plan.[72] The leaders of the

[69] *Ibid.*, D/2396/3/11, Duke of Abercorn to W. E. Ball, 2 Dec. 1888.
[70] *Ibid.*, D/2396/3/3–5, R. Ross to the Duke of Abercorn, 26 June, Abercorn to W. E. Ball, 28 June, R. J. Lynd to Abercorn, 30 June 1888.
[71] *Ibid.*, D2396/5/10, J. L. Ball to W. E. Ball, 13 Nov. 1888.
[72] *Ibid.*, D2396/5/5,8,14, Charles Adeane to W. E. Ball, 22 and 24 Nov., Lord George Hamilton to W. E. Ball, 10 Dec. 1888.

Irish Presbyterian, Methodist, Congregational, and Baptist Churches took it in turn to show why 864 out of 990 Nonconformist ministers throughout Ireland had signed an address against 'a separate Parliament for Ireland, or any legislation tending to imperil the Legislative Union between Great Britain and Ireland, or to interfere with the unity and supremacy of the Imperial Parliament'.[73] Lynd, on behalf of Irish Presbyterians, denied that their rejection of Gladstone was a rejection of Liberalism, and stated that Presbyterian support for tenant farmers, the civil and religious liberties of Roman Catholics, and for a well-thought-out measure of local government remained undiminished. In a clear appeal to English Nonconformist values he stated that Home Rule would lead to the effective endowment of the Roman Catholic religion, the end of the principle of united secular and separate religious education, and would require coercion on an unprecedented scale against the loyal Protestant minority.[74] Evans, who had clearly been stung by Gladstone's disparaging remarks about Irish Nonconformists in his Bingley Hall speech, repeated the Irish Methodist appeal to the loyalty of the English connection and stated that Home Rule would accelerate the speed of Protestant emigration which had eroded Methodist strength throughout the nineteenth century. The Congregationalist and Baptist spokesmen came closest to importing Protestant religious prejudices into the debate, and, according to the printed record, the audience was less impressed with this approach than with the others. McCaig, the Baptist representative, denied that there was coercion in Ireland, stated that the priests would be the real beneficiaries of Parnellism in Ireland, and accused nationalists of desecrating the Sabbath. 'Sunday is the great day for League meetings', he stated, 'members of Parliament choose that day for displaying their oratorical powers, with the accompaniment of bands playing political and party tunes—often to the annoyance and disturbance of worshipping Protestants.'[75] All the speakers were at pains to point out that Irish Protestants of whatever party or creed were united in their hostility to Home Rule. Protestant Home Rulers were dismissed as an insignificant minority whose genuine Protestantism—in the religious sense—was suspect, and whose principles were regarded as thinly disguised self-interest. Zealous Christianity and worthy citizenship were thought to be incompatible with Gladstone's version of Liberalism.

[73] *Irish Nonconformists*, pp. 4–5.
[74] *Ibid.*, pp. 7–12.
[75] *Ibid.*, p. 21. For the Baptist position, see J. Thompson, 'Baptists in Ireland 1792–1922: A Dimension of Protestant Dissent' (Oxford D.Phil. thesis, 1988).

The banquet of November 1888 was an encouragement to those English Nonconformist leaders such as Spurgeon, Dale, and Newman Hall, who had doubted the wisdom of Gladstone's Irish policy, but it was only one aspect of the work of the Nonconformist Unionist Association in Ireland. W. E. Ball was equally keen to exploit the electoral potential of using Irish Nonconformist ministers as platform speakers in English constituencies.[76] Fiery Irish orators had been doing this throughout the nineteenth century, but by the late Victorian period English provincial Nonconformity required rather more sensitive nurturing. Ball found it difficult to attract men of the 'right calibre' at the right price, and the whole scheme was littered with disputes over the cost of hospitality and recriminations about unsatisfactory speakers.[77] The educated leadership of the Irish Nonconformist churches were either too busy with church affairs or too unwilling to become political preachers to be of much use to the Nonconformist Unionist Association. The less able were both more willing to be of service and more likely to appeal to religious prejudice than political economy. Despite these teething-troubles, Irish ministers appeared frequently during British elections to urge Protestant solidarity and imperial unity in the period after 1886. Anti-Catholicism was well capable of transferring Nonconformist voters into the unionist camp, particularly in the Methodist strongholds of Lincolnshire and the southwest, and in areas with a significant Irish Catholic population, such as Lancashire. Generally speaking, the more evangelical and theologically conservative wings of British Nonconformity were the most susceptible to appeals from their Irish co-religionists. Thus Bebbington concludes that many Nonconformists deserted Gladstonian Liberalism not because their economic prosperity weakened their chapel allegiances, but because they had a genuine religious motive for voting unionist:

> Those who responded to unionist appeals for solidarity with protestant Irishmen were not allowing their own interests to prevail over their chapel loyalties: their very chapel loyalties drove them to

---

[76] Belfast, P.R.O.N.I., N.U.A. Papers, D/2396/1/1–24, Lord Wolmer to W. E. Ball, 20 Sept., 24 Sept., 9 Oct., 10 Oct., 22 Oct., 23 Oct. (two letters) 1888. English Liberal Unionists also spoke against Home Rule on national platforms and in local constituencies, see G. J. Goschen and Lord Hartington, *The Disruption Bill* (London, 1886); G. J. Goschen, *The Cry of 'Justice to Ireland'* (London, 1886); G. J. Goschen, *Address to the Electors of the Eastern Division of Edinburgh* (London, 1886); Lord Hartington, *Address to the Electors of the Rossendale Division of Lancashire* (London, 1886).

[77] *Ibid.*, D/2396/3/13 and D/2396/1/1–24, W. E. Ball to Lord Wolmer, ? Oct. 1888, and Lord Wolmer to W. E. Ball, 3 Nov., 5 Nov., 27 Nov., 1888.

consider the unionist appeals. This, then, was a populist, classless style of politics.[78]

The coming together of Irish Nonconformist churches against Home Rule was significant within both Ireland and Britain. In Ireland it offered an apparently more worthy medium of expressing opposition to Gladstone than either Ulster Orangeism or mere economic self-interest.[79] It was also a way of tapping into the strong Presbyterian liberal tradition, which could nevertheless still claim to be true to its dissenting and liberal heritage. But it also had the unintended effect of Ulsterizing Protestant resistance to Home Rule by concentrating on the geographical area in which Nonconformity was strong. Morever, the coming together of the churches on an agreed platform further marginalized those who had an alternative vision of Ireland's future. Opposition to Home Rule had become, within the space of a few years, the test of the virility of an Irishman's Protestantism. The effect of the Home Rule issue on British Nonconformity was equally important. It introduced a fierce partisanship into Nonconformist politics, which divided churches and damaged old friendships.[80] Within Methodism, Hugh Price Hughes and Sir George Chubb sniped relentlessly at each other, while other churches tried unsuccessfully to draw boundaries between religion and politics. The trouble with the Irish Question was that no such boundary existed. Over the longer term the initial Nonconformist support for Gladstone's policy weakened. Parnell's moral frailties and the educational objectives of English Roman Catholics were unexpected bonuses for the unionist cause. Under such relentless pressure the English Nonconformist press sometimes gave way to the crudest forms of anti-Catholicism that would not have been out of place half a century earlier. Ireland had once again shown that there were limits to the liberality of liberalism.

---

[78] Bebbington, 'Nonconformity and electoral sociology', pp. 633–56.

[79] For the range of Irish Nonconformist arguments against Home Rule see William Arthur, *Shall the Loyal be Deserted and the Disloyal set over them? An appeal to Liberals and Nonconformists* (London, 1886); Thomas Webb, *Ipse Dixit or the Gladstonian Settlement of Ireland* (Dublin, 1886); Robert MacGeogh, *Ulster's Apology for being Loyal* (Belfast, 1888); *The Society of Friends in Ireland and Home Rule* (Dublin, 1893); Manderson, *How an Irish Nonconformist views the Question of Home Rule*; Archibald McCaig, *Reasons Why Nonconformists should Oppose Home Rule* (Dublin, 1886); *Irish Baptist Magazine*, May 1887, pp. 70–1.

[80] *The Methodist Times*, 8 July 1886; D. Bebbington, 'Gladstone and the Baptists', *BQ*, 26 (1975–6), pp. 224–39; Bebbington, *The Nonconformist Conscience*, pp. 84–105. For a revealing insight into the confusions of English Liberalism occasioned by Gladstone's Irish policy, see *The Pilot Balloon. A Calm Exposé of the 'Manchester Guardian' consisting of Verbatim Extracts from the Editorial Columns 1884 to 1886, on the Home Rule Question* (Manchester, 1889).

The response of the Irish Protestant churches to Home Rule was no mere example of institutional posturing, for their opposition rested on a cultural bedrock of Protestant assumptions and values which were central to the emergence of a Protestant identity in Ulster. A recent survey of some thirty Ulster Unionist speeches against Home Rule in 1886, for example, shows that in descending order of priority the arguments employed were as follows: the representatives of an ascendant Roman Catholicism would persecute the Protestant community; Ulster Protestants would be deprived of their imperial heritage and would thus have a reduced status in the world; Catholic nationalists had no respect for law and order and would deliver Ulster into social and economic ruin; Home Rule was a betrayal of loyalism; and Ulster would be forced to shoulder the fiscal and economic burden of Ireland under Home Rule.[81] The disproportionate number of reported speeches from Protestant ministers may partly account for the high profile given to religious fears in this survey, but there can be no doubt that the above issues were indeed dominant in the manifold pamphlets, speeches, and meetings against Home Rule.[82] What is striking about this Ulster Protestant *Weltanschauung* is the extent to which it was a self-referentially coherent ideology, embracing past, present, and future as well as religion, politics, and society. The only chink in its armour was its perceived inability to sustain itself against an imperialistic Catholic nationalism without the continued support of the rest of the United Kingdom. That was the frailty exposed by Home Rule, and it was made harder to bear by Gladstone's and Parnell's persistent but erroneous belief that the eighteenth-century Patriot tradition was a stronger force in Irish Protestantism than Ulster loyalism.[83] The belief persisted, against formidable evidence to the contrary, because both men wished it were so.

Ulster Protestants had an alternative view of Irish history which was relentlessly rehearsed at Orange, church, and political meetings throughout the nineteenth century. The Great Protestant Meeting in Belfast against the Irish Church Bill in 1869 is a good example of its kind.[84]

---

[81] James Loughlin, *Gladstone, Home Rule and the Irish Question 1882–93* (Dublin, 1986), appendix 2, pp. 295–6.

[82] For other interpretations of early Ulster Unionism see P. Buckland, *Ulster Unionism and the Origins of Northern Ireland 1886–1922* (Dublin, 1973); J. F. Harbinson, *The Ulster Unionist Party 1882–1973* (Belfast, 1973); A. Jackson, *The Ulster Party: Irish Unionists in the House of Commons, 1884–1911* (Oxford, 1989).

[83] Loughlin, *Gladstone*, pp. 123–52.

[84] *The Irish Church Bill: The Great Protestant Demonstration in Belfast* (Belfast, 1869). For similar events, albeit on a smaller scale, see *The Great Protestant Demonstration at Hillsborough,*

A huge crowd, optimistically estimated at 100,000 people, crammed into the Botanic Gardens on a bright summer's day. The platform dignitaries were in their place, the music was played by the Conservative Amateur Band, and the catering was in the able hands of Miss Johnson of the Abercorn Arms Hotel. At the heart of the day's entertainment were the speeches, many of which were populist history lectures about the struggles and triumphs of Irish Protestants against an unchanging and disloyal Catholicism. As events and heroes were recalled, to the cheers of the crowd, the virtues most admired were staunchness and unchanging principles, the evils most railed against were betrayal and accommodation. These appeals to forefathers, faith, and the settlement of the land not only foreshortened the past, but helped even the most impious to believe that they were part of a tradition protected by divine Providence for a quarter of a millennium. Here was a memorial and celebratory culture resonant with providential turning points and rich in symbols. The most expert platform orators knew exactly how to manipulate their audience for the maximum applause, and the crowd knew exactly how to manipulate platform orators to tell them what they most wanted to hear. It was not only a great day out for all, but soon took its place in the tradition it was called to celebrate. As with many such meetings since the passage of Catholic Emancipation in 1829, it was a protest against British government policy, and that characteristic also became central to the tradition. But in making their protests Ulster Protestants were not so much giving expression to a contractual view of their relationship with the rest of the United Kingdom, as demonstrating their belief that the pragmatic liberalism of much government policy in Ireland in the Victorian period was based on mistaken assumptions about the real causes of Ireland's difficulties.[85] Hence the suggested remedies, culminating in Home Rule, were not only betraying Irish Protestantism, but were guaranteed to perpetuate the very problems they were designed to solve. In such circumstances the right to resist depended upon the seriousness of the threat to Protestant life, liberty, and property.

The part played by evangelical religion in stiffening the resolve of Ulster Protestants against Home Rule should not be underestimated. For

October 30, 1867; and *Proceedings of the Great Presbyterian Demonstration in Belfast in favour of Protestant Endowments in Ireland*.

[85] The notion of a contractual relationship between Ulster loyalists and the United Kingdom is developed by D. W. Miller, *Queen's Rebels: Ulster Loyalism in Historical Perspective* (Dublin, 1978), pp. 65–80.

over a century old Reformation polarities had been given new social meanings in a province sufficiently divided on grounds of religion to sustain the crudest forms of stereotyping sanctified by theological principles. Protestants believed that having access to the 'Open Bible', being free from priestcraft and superstition, and adhering to a progressive and enlightened faith were at the heart of Ulster's cultural and economic superiority over the rest of Ireland, and, equally important, of Protestant Ulster's superiority over Catholic Ulster.[86] The hotter the Protestantism, in terms of its evangelical zeal, the firmer was this belief and the sharper the antagonism against the 'whole system' of Roman Catholicism. In assessing the power of evangelical religion in Ulster Protestant ideology, Frank Wright perceptively notes that 'defence of the socialization process of evangelical protestantism is more of a universal concern than an actual belief in evangelicalism itself '.[87] He means by this that Ulster Protestants, in the mass, have been more committed to the *right* to preach the Reformed religion and to maintain its influence in education, culture, and society than to the essence of religious belief itself. Hence the religious heroes of Ulster Protestantism have not been theologians or Pietists, but rather those who have most resolutely defended the rights of Ulster Protestants to adhere to the Reformed faith against the unwelcome encroachments of the Roman Church. From this perspective any concession made to Roman Catholics was by definition a weakening of historic Protestantism. The one could only make progress at the expense of the other.[88]

One of the great strengths of evangelical ideology in Ulster was the way in which it could simultaneously narrow the focus to a contest between Reformed religion and Catholic superstition in Ireland and widen it to an international conflict of major proportions. This was facilitated by the late Victorian expansion of the British Empire and by the post-famine migrations of Irish Catholics. Here was a clash of two world empires, one of commerce, Christianity, and civilization as exported by Great Britain, and the other a sordid, embittered, and disloyal Irish Catholic migration, particularly to the United States, where it created another culture in its own image. The corruptions of Tammany Hall and the ill-fated invasion of Manitoba merely confirmed the unchanging character of the Catholic

---

[86] *The Home Rule 'Nutshell', examined by an Irish Unionist* (Belfast and Dublin, 1912).

[87] F. Wright, 'Protestant ideology and politics in Ulster', *Archives européennes de sociologie*, 14 (1973), pp. 213–80.

[88] For the survival of this view into contemporary Ulster fundamentalism see S. Bruce, *God Save Ulster! The Religion and Politics of Paisleyism* (Oxford, 1985).

Irish, even when thousands of miles from home. 'The Home Rule movement', stated the Revd Gilbert Mahaffy to the YMCA, 'has been, from first to last, a movement hostile to British rule. And fostered as it has been on American soil, and supported by American dollars, it is essentially republican.'[89] Thus, depending on circumstances, Ulster Protestants could think of themselves as either a faithful remnant of righteousness in a pagan land or as part of a great and civilizing world empire. They were equally comforting and culturally reinforcing ideas. The Revd Thomas Ellis, for example, told the loyal Orangemen of Portadown in 1885 that 'we have sacrificed our duty to God and to each other too often on the altar of Popish compromise, worldly expediency and carnal selfishness'. He called upon them, as 'the faithful few among the faithless many—the loyal Sons of Judah amid the faithless men of Israel', to abandon their lax Protestantism and follow in the steps of their glorious forefathers.[90] Others, more impressed by Ulster's commercial vitality than depressed by its religious worldliness, simply wanted protection against a Roman Catholic ascendancy so that 'we shall be allowed to continue our triumphant march of Prosperity under the protection of the British flag, a United Parliament, and the Imperial Crown'.[91] Such a framework was watertight. Ulster's success was due to the blessings of Providence and the energy of its people, its failures were attributable to enemies on all sides pressing in on a loyal but vulnerable remnant. It is perhaps surprising that such ideas did not give rise more often than they did to racial notions of the inherent superiority of Ulster Protestants to Irish Celts. It is, of course, possible to find references to such arguments, but they appear mostly in academic journals not in popular speeches.[92] The reason for this is that the ethnic stereotyping indulged in by most Ulster Protestants was based more on religious and cultural assumptions than on scientific or racial observations. Irish Catholics were economically and culturally inferior, not primarily because of their racial pedigree, but because of their religion. Thus, some of the greatest heroes of the Protestant missionary movement in Ireland were converted Catholics. The Irish did not choose the Catholic religion, therefore, because they were racially inferior; they became inferior because they followed the Catholic religion, as was the

---

[89] Gilbert Mahaffy, *The Attitude of Irish Churchmen in the Present Political Crisis* (Dublin, 1886), p. 12.
[90] Thomas Ellis, *God and the Nation. A Sermon preached to the Orangemen of the District of Portadown in St. Mark's Church Portadown* (Armagh, 1885).
[91] *The Home Rule 'Nutshell'*, p. 99.
[92] Loughlin, *Gladstone*, p. 160.

case with many other European nationalities. The extent to which the undeniably common ideas of Anglo-Saxon racial superiority contributed to diagnoses of the Irish problem has probably been exaggerated in both Britain and Ireland. Tom Dunne has shown, for example, that even intensely nationalistic English intellectuals resorted not so much to full-blown race theories about Irish Celts as to historical and cultural arguments for the retarded growth of Irish civilization.[93] Since Gaelic society had bequeathed the political instincts and habits of tribesmen, not citizens, the Irish were simply not ready for the responsibilities of self-government. Hence stereotypes based on impressions and chauvinistic historical comparisons were probably more influential in shaping attitudes than the kind of race theories prevalent in the United States, where the problems were more urgent.

Ultimately, the most important contribution of evangelicalism to Ulster Protestant ideology was the sheer vigour of its anti-Catholicism. The Roman Catholic Church in Ireland was regarded as all pervasive in influence, monolithic in scope, imperialist in intention, persecuting in its essential nature, and impoverishing in its social effects. No state in which its representatives were in control could offer any credible safeguards for the rights of religious minorities. Faced with such a possibility, Ulster Protestant theology had the capacity to adapt to new circumstances. The view that all Christian citizens had a sacred duty to support lawfully constituted authorities was capable of being transformed into a sacred duty to resist religious tyranny. As with English Puritanism on the eve of the Civil Wars, the anti-Catholicism of Ulster Protestants was a potentially radical force, and was, of course, more capable of mass realization than was sacrificial piety. It was propagated by a resurgent Orangeism whose rank and file of agricultural labourers and dock workers was led by the Fermanagh gentry and baptized by the churches. Depending upon the seriousness of the crisis, Orange excesses, including pseudo-military drilling, came to be less feared than Protestant apathy. Even the licence of the Belfast Protestant mobs was defended by some religious leaders, who apparently saw no incongruity between this and their earlier attacks on Fenian agrarian outrages.

Evangelicalism also helped to build bridges between denominations, between clergy and laity, and between churches and voluntary associations. It sustained links between Irish and British organizations, from the

[93] T. Dunne, '"La trahison des clercs": British intellectuals and the first home-rule crisis', *IHS*, 23 (1982), pp. 134–73.

staunchly Protestant, such as the Scottish Protestant Alliance and the Protestant Institute of Great Britain, to the politically mild, such as the Evangelical Alliance and the YMCA. Although most of the prolific evangelical societies devoted to Christian morality and self-improvement operated a 'no politics' principle, their very ethos contributed much to an Ulster Protestant identity. When addressing itself to the issue of Home Rule, for example, the YMCA journal stated that

> The bulletin is not a political journal, but a grave national crisis such as this concerns young men, as well as other. It concerns Christian young men very specially. If carried, this bill would change the entire character of our national life. It would alter the prospects of many of us who are preparing for trades, or commercial life, or for the professions. It would have the most material influence on the religion of the nation ... but perhaps the worst feature of the proposed measure is the tremendous leverage it would give to Romanism—the curse of Ireland for generations.[94]

The formidable array of both denominational and inter-denominational improvement societies in late nineteenth-century Ulster helped to create an ethos of godliness and good citizenship which was inextricably bound up with loyalty to the British way of life. When the Home Rule crisis awakened the slumbering unionist associations in provincial Ulster, therefore, they found themselves lying on an easily politicized bed of respectable Protestant culture.[95] By then evangelical religion had thrown up successive generations of political preachers who unashamedly used their clerical influence on behalf of popular Protestant causes. Their contribution further united religion and politics in a way that boded ill for statesmen called upon to disentangle the threads. As the Reverend Thomas Ellis told the Portadown Orangemen, he had never been able to understand how any man 'with the Bible in his hands and who believed in the moral government of the World by God' could separate religion from politics. Ironically, Gladstone, who provoked much breast-beating among Ulster Protestants, was one of a dwindling number of English statesmen to put much store on such sentiments.[96]

Important though the influence of Evangelicalism was in forging an

[94] YMCA, *Bulletin* (Belfast, 1885).
[95] D. Hempton and M. Hill, ' "Godliness and Good Citizenship": Evangelical Protestantism and Social Control in Ulster, 1790–1850', *Saothar, Journal of the Irish Labour History Society*, 13 (1988), pp. 68–80.
[96] Ellis, *God and the Nation*.

Ulster Protestant identity, it would be misleading to present late nineteenth-century Irish Protestantism in crudely monolithic terms. Not only were there important denominational and class differences, but there was also a Protestant nationalist tradition which supported Home Rule. Mainly religious moderates and liberal reformers, the Protestant Home Rulers were not ideologically committed to any specific Home Rule proposal. Their major unifying factor was the desire to dissociate themselves from the bigotry of the majority Protestant community. Regarding a Protestant Home Rule movement as the 'outcome and true essence of true liberalism', these Gladstonian loyalists were committed to a political rather than a religious tradition.[97] Their tolerance towards those of other religions reflected their lack of commitment to the more dogmatic varieties of Protestant faith, thus ensuring that the antagonism of their less forbearing co-religionists carried the usual overtones of religious and political apostasy.

For a Protestant minister, of whatever denomination, active support of Home Rule in the 1880s carried consequences of varying seriousness. The hostility of congregations, colleagues, or superiors was expressed both verbally and physically, and could mean preaching to an empty church-hall, or the termination of a budding clerical career.[98] Such pressures, apart from the hardships caused to the individuals concerned, made it difficult for activists to rally public support and has probably led to an underestimation of the extent of Protestant support for Home Rule. Even with this in mind, however, any readjustment would simply be to the size of a minority which was never in any position to make its influence felt. In general terms the Protestant Home Rulers thought of themselves as an enlightened minority whose traditional opposition to landlordism and Episcopalian ascendancy helped forge a bond with their Catholic counterparts. Confident of Gladstone's ability, from which they had benefited in the past, and given the alternatives of coercion or minority domination, they believed Home Rule would have beneficial effects for both religious communities in Ireland. A democratically-based self-government, it was felt, would not only bring material gains, but would end sectarianism and diminish the role of priests in Roman Catholic culture.[99] Such views were

[97] Dublin, National Library of Ireland, Irish Protestant Home Rule Association Papers, MS 3657, Press cutting from the *Freeman*, 23 June 1886.
[98] Committee Minutes of the Irish Protestant Home Rule Association, 13 Oct. 1886. See J. Loughlin, 'The Irish Protestant Home Rule Association and nationalist politics', *IHS*, 24 (1985), pp. 341–60.

[*See p. 252 for n. 99*]

251

shaped, as were those of their opponents, both by experience and by a particular interpretation of Irish history in which the Presbyterian reformers of the late eighteenth century were accorded a prominent position.

It is clear that most members of the Irish Protestant Home Rule Association represented the prosperous and successful side of Nonconformity, and there was undoubtedly an element of pragmatism in their political assertions. Merchants, shopkeepers, barristers, doctors, and Members of Parliament scattered throughout rural Ireland were, after all, dependent on the patronage and goodwill of their Roman Catholic neighbours. And while they were aware of their religious isolation, their position as an integrated minority determined that their perception of Catholic Ireland would differ from that of more cohesive Protestant communities in the north-east. It was also, of course, because they were in such a minority that these individuals felt they could most legitimately speak to the fear of Catholic intolerance which, in their opinion, had been scurrilously magnified by Orange bigots in Ulster. They were, nevertheless, completely unrepresentative of mainstream Protestant opinion. Despite claims of its growth and influence, the reality of I.P.H.R.A.'s ineffectiveness was reflected in its predilection for caution and compromise, and while such vagueness facilitated the membership of liberal reformers, it militated against the active involvement of ardent Home Rulers. Anxiety not to antagonize Protestants on the one side or Roman Catholics on the other had a negative influence on strategy. Plans to hold public lectures were rejected for fear of rousing the anger of Catholic clergy, and visits of Liberal cabinet ministers were viewed as 'inexpedient'. Perhaps more serious in the long run, the divergence between the Belfast and Dublin branches of the movement revealed basic differences in the interpretation of a nationalism which was only slowly developing a cohesive ideology.[100] The emerging distinctions between the general political liberalism of the north and the more robust southern nationalism reflected inherently different cultural experiences and expectations. The optimism which comes across in the correspondence is therefore more an expression of the liberal outlook of prosperous, forward-looking individuals than of a

---

[99] Dublin, N.L.I., I.P.H.R.A. committee minutes, 20 Oct. 1886; J. MacVeagh, *Religious Intolerance Under Home Rule: Some Opinions of Leading Irish Protestants* (London, 1911).

[100] *Ibid.*, I.P.H.R.A. committee minutes, 5 June 1886 and July 1887. See also Loughlin, 'Irish Protestant Home Rule Association', p. 343.

united political party, and was not in any case unconditional. The unacceptably violent tactics employed by some nationalists, for example, eroded their belief in the capacity of Irishmen to accommodate their traditional differences without bloodshed.

From the mid-nineteenth century, according to Professor Ward, churches and their theologians in the British Isles, Western Europe, and North America struggled to construct a social policy which took account of market forces and national aspirations while maintaining the Christian ethic of love and self denial.[101] As State support for religious establishments inexorably waned, Christian socialism, Tory paternalism, and liberal individualism were all tried and found wanting in region after region. Churches could neither win the ear of governments nor establish a secure foothold in the world of labour, and were thus condemned to enter the twentieth century in search of ever more desperate and futile remedies for a disease they had never properly diagnosed. In the nineteenth century such social policy as there was was developed by voluntary associations who forced moral and social issues together and campaigned unremittingly for a more godly and hence more prosperous society. But ultimately this was not so much a social policy as an unsuccessful tug of war against the mighty forces of industrialization, class consciousness, and secularism. While some sought in vain for ways of maintaining Christian values in a *laissez-faire* world, Ulster Protestants, who scarcely thought about these matters at all, had a solution thrust upon them. Persuaded by the revival of 1859 that God was still on their side, forced to accept in 1869 that the State would no longer shore up Irish Protestantism, and faced with the defeat of their national and cultural aspirations in 1886, Ulster Protestants dug deep into their historical tradition and once again found strength in adversity. Their remarkable unity of purpose has confounded the British and Irish States for over a century and was constructed with unlikely materials. The sheer vigour of Irish Ultramontanist Catholicism provided them with a far more visible and comprehensible enemy than mere secularism. The concessionary policies of successive British governments persuaded them that the State itself offered no ultimate guarantees at the same time as utilitarians and socialists in Britain placed hopelessly unrealistic faith in the capacity of the State to bring in their millennium. Evangelicalism, which in Britain had undermined the old denominational

---

[101] W. R. Ward, 'The Way of the World: The Rise and Decline of Protestant Social Christianity in Britain', *Kirchliche Zeitgeschichte*, 1 Jahrgang, Heft 2 (1988), pp. 293–305.

order, but which had little else to offer after its own religious zeal had declined, in Ulster strengthened denominational co-operation on the big, if not the little, issues, and offered a perfect theological rationalization of Ulster Protestants' innate sense of their own superiority. At the same time that many theologians and intellectuals became aware that expanding market forces threatened the traditional framework of Christian ethics, Ulster Protestants claimed the market as their own, not only as beneficiaries of the greatest market in the world, the British Empire, but in response to the protectionist noises made by Catholic nationalists.

The Protestant solidarity effected by such forces transcended—but did not entirely eliminate—the denominational, class, and urban/rural tensions which helped undermine the churches in the rest of western Europe. In Ulster the platforms of the great Protestant 'Monster meetings' were dominated by men of landed and commercial property, the clergy, and the educated professionals. They played oratorical games with their hearers, safe in the knowledge that any excesses of the mob would be directed not against them but against their shared religious enemy. Relatively safe from erosion from within, and reinforced by enemies from without, Ulster Protestantism, by comparison with many other religious communities in the late nineteenth-century world, was in a good position to maintain its religious identity, even if its political future was still contested territory. The price paid for this religious success was considerable, not least in terms of the nature of religion itself, but except in the writings of a small band of Protestant idealists the cost was scarcely ever considered. There were simply far more urgent matters to address.

The Queen's University of Belfast

THE EMERGENCE OF THE
NONCONFORMIST SOCIAL GOSPEL
IN ENGLAND

by DAVID M. THOMPSON

ANYONE who sets out to examine the theology behind Noncon-formist social thought and action in the late nineteenth century has to answer two questions: Did such a theology exist? and Was it important? The second question is more fundamental. Twenty years ago John Kent argued that the realities of politics put an increasing strain on the late Victorian claim to a Christian conscience in public affairs, and that in any case Nonconformists did not enjoy a monopoly of moral concern in politics. Like other Liberals, they 'found themselves trying to reconcile the older Cobden-type ideals of liberty, peace, arbitration and anti-militarism with a new belief in the positive values of an allegedly Christian British Empire'. The result was that 'the struggle for political power coarsened their moral sensibility'.[1] In such an analysis the emphasis falls on action rather than thought, and in domestic affairs particularly on the political campaigns for social purity, temperance, or against gambling, where they are easily dismissed as the result of evangelical pietism, class moralism, or social reaction. David Bebbington deliberately eschewed theology in his study of the Nonconformist Conscience. 'Because the focus is on political issues that concerned Nonconformists *en masse*', he wrote, 'the theological views of their leaders, and even their versions of the social gospel, do not loom large.'[2] In his thesis he also commented that 'theology was largely unfashionable, even in sermons', citing Charles Berry, a leading Congregationalist, as an example.[3] Nevertheless, he did not deny that there was a theology.

More recently Richard Helmstadter has criticized the new Noncon-formist theology for failing to provide specific political guidance. 'The theology of Fatherhood and Incarnationism stressed the importance of humanitarian activity, but it provided no political blueprint for

---

[1] J. Kent, 'Hugh Price Hughes and the Nonconformist Conscience', in G. V. Bennett and J. D. Walsh, eds, *Essays in Modern English Church History* (London, 1966), pp. 195, 204.

[2] D. W. Bebbington, *The Nonconformist Conscience: Chapel and Politics, 1870–1914* (London, 1982) p. x.

[3] D. W. Bebbington, 'The Nonconformist Conscience: a study of the political attitudes and activities of Evangelical Nonconformists, 1886–1902)' (Cambridge Ph.D. thesis, 1975), p. 1.

establishing the Kingdom of God on this earth.' So he claimed that 'their vague theology encouraged vague humanitarianism'.[4] That criticism has also been made of Anglican social thought in the same period.[5] Since, however, Helmstadter's focus was also on politics, no extended theological analysis was provided, although he did acknowledge Nonconformist commitment to the Incarnation, unlike Peter Jones, who regarded Nonconformist Socialism as lacking a clear or well-defined dogmatic core, even though penetrated by the doctrine of divine immanence. 'By its very nature, immanentalism (as opposed to sacramentalism) imparts a diffuseness and a vagueness to Nonconformist thinking in this period.'[6]

The present essay argues that there is more to the theological basis of Nonconformist social thought than some of these verdicts suggest. Long ago Troeltsch began his historic study with the assertion that

> the churches and Christianity, which are pre-eminently historic forces, are at all points conditioned by their past, by the Gospel which, together with the Bible, exerts its influence ever anew, and by the dogmas which concern social life and the whole of civilization.[7]

This provides a more balanced perspective from which to begin. In the twentieth century it is clear that social policies cannot be devised simply by reading off solutions from the Bible. One of the most significant movements in the nineteenth century was the practical recognition of this. All Christian social commentators in the late nineteenth century recognized the rightness of the abolition of slavery; they also recognized that slavery was condoned by Scripture. Here, even before biblical criticism has had any significant impact, is the kernel of the Christian social theorist's dilemma. The accusations of vagueness levelled at late nineteenth-century theology often depend for their force on the assumption that it is easier to be specific than it really is.

To explain why attitudes could change in the way they did, it is necessary to set these theological developments in their broader intellectual context. Boyd Hilton has argued that the theological underpinning of early nineteenth-century political economy, particularly in Evangelical-

---

[4] R. Helmstadter, 'The Nonconformist Conscience', in P. Marsh, ed., *The Conscience of the Victorian State* (Hassocks, 1979), p. 167.

[5] E. R. Norman, *Church and Society in England, 1770–1970* (Oxford, 1976), pp. 1–14, 180–6.

[6] P. d'A. Jones, *The Christian Socialist Revival, 1877–1914* (Princeton, 1968), p. 307.

[7] E. Troeltsch, *The Social Teaching of the Christian Churches*, trans. O. Wyon (London, 1931), I, p. 25.

ism, is more significant than has often been supposed.[8] It is therefore important to see how evangelical thought could be brought to a different social and political understanding later: evangelical Nonconformists are thus a particularly interesting group to study.

In his stimulating study of the German Protestant social conscience between 1890 and 1933, Professor Ward remarked that most of the characters in his plot either preserved their faith but lost touch with political reality, or maintained contact with political reality but lost their faith, or the faith in which they had been raised; and he noted that 'not only was social-christianity in this period the politics of churches losing touch with the levers of political power . . . but churchmanship was itself one of the barriers to understanding'.[9] In Germany the Roman Catholics were the pioneers, with the work of Bishop Ketteler of Mainz; and Protestant social Christianity tended to be both anti-Catholic and anti-Semitic. In England there was no anti-Semitism to speak of, but there was a strong anti-sacerdotalism in Nonconformist social Christianity.

There is no doubt that the 1880s saw 'a ripple of socialism' passing over England—'at least, if it is Socialism to take a quickened concern in the condition of the poorer orders and to propound all manner of demands for State help in the matter'.[10] The most obvious churchly manifestation of this was Stewart Headlam's Guild of St Matthew. Originally formed in 1877 to ensure that there would be sufficient communicants for the eight o'clock service at St Matthew's, Bethnal Green, it was subsequently transformed from a purely parochial society when Headlam went to Shoreditch in 1881. Headlam regarded F. D. Maurice and Henry George as the chief influences upon his thinking, and felt that the Guild's most flourishing period was around 1884.[11] But the Guild was never very large and remained exclusively Anglican; so historians have had difficulty in explaining exactly why demands for social reform should have found receptive ears more widely in the churches in this period. One event which focused attention on social problems was the publication of *The Bitter Cry of Outcast London* by the Revd Andrew Mearns on behalf of the London Congregational Union in 1883. The publicity given to this by W. T. Stead in *The Pall Mall Gazette* helped to secure the establishment of a Royal Commission on the Housing of the Working Classes, which

---

[8] B. Hilton, *The Age of Atonement* (Oxford, 1988).

[9] W. R. Ward, *Theology, Sociology and Politics: The German Protestant Social Conscience, 1890–1933* (Bern, 1979), p. 14.

[10] J. Rae, 'Social Philosophy', *Cont. Rev.*, 45 (1884), p. 295.

[11] F. G. Bettany, *Stewart Headlam: A Biography* (London, 1926), pp. 39–40, 79–87.

included the Prince of Wales. Some of the changes demanded could only be achieved by legislation, so the demand for State intervention as such is unsurprising; but the willingness to accept environmental causes for poverty marked a move in a new direction. Even in the churches, however, a divergence of view remained between those who still believed that individual conversion was the only way in which social amelioration would take place and those who argued that the churches had a duty to act, or to persuade the State to act, in other ways for the betterment of society. Even Lord Shaftesbury, pioneer of factory legislation, wrote that State provision of housing at nominal rents for the labouring classes would 'utterly destroy their moral energies'.[12] Behind this view lay a justification for philanthropy which depended as much upon theology as political economy.[13] What was the theology that justified the new view?

The two phrases most regularly used in church circles to describe this social concern are 'Christian Socialism' and the 'social Gospel'. The discussion of Christian Socialism has often been dogged by a tendency to use Marxism as a critical norm by which to judge its truly socialist character in a way which is historically arbitrary. This may delight Marxists, but it should dismay historians of thought who are trying to understand how and why individuals believed the particular combinations of ideas which they did. Socialism is seen today as a political programme: to many Victorians it was seen as a stage in history.

The social Gospel is often regarded as American in origin, and in the early twentieth century the phrase was increasingly used by conservative evangelicals to describe the position taken up by liberal evangelicals.[14] But the origin of the term in church usage is obscure. Visser't Hooft thought it would be interesting to discover when it was first introduced, but did not try to do so. C. Howard Hopkins found it used by a Congregational pastor in Iowa in the spring of 1886, but it is now clear that it is wrong to see it as a peculiarly American phenomenon.[15]

[12] Lord Shaftesbury, 'The Mischief of State Aid', *The Nineteenth Century*, 14 (1883), p. 935; see also, A. S. Wohl, ed., *The Bitter Cry of Outcast London* (Leicester, 1969); A. S. Wohl, *The Eternal Slum* (London, 1977), pp. 200–49.

[13] Hilton, *Age of Atonement*, pp. 73–114.

[14] D. W. Bebbington, *Evangelicalism in Modern Britain* (London, 1989), pp. 211–14; R. C. White, jr. and C. H. Hopkins, *The Social Gospel: Religion and Reform in Changing America* (Philadelphia, 1976), pp. xvi–xvii; J. H. Dorn, *Washington Gladden: Prophet of the Social Gospel* (Ohio, 1966), pp. 182–6.

[15] W. A. Visser't Hooft, *The Background of the Social Gospel in America* (Haarlem, 1928), p. 14; White and Hopkins, *Social Gospel*, pp. 150–2, 167; W. R. Hutchison, 'The Americanness of

A particular phrase should not be emphasized at the expense of the broader framework of thought, but a brief study of it is illuminating. It first occurs in the *Communist Manifesto*, when Marx distinguishes between revolutionary and non-revolutionary Socialism. Saint-Simon, Fourier, Owen, and others, he wrote, 'wish to attain their ends by peaceful means, and endeavour, by small experiments, necessarily doomed to failure, and by the force of example, to pave the way for the new social Gospel'.[16] This is from the 1888 translation. Earlier English translations had appeared in London in 1850, in New York in 1872, and two further translations, described by Engels in his preface to the English edition of 1888 as 'more or less mutilated' appeared in America subsequently. Whilst churchmen may have taken the phrase from Marx, it does not seem very likely: the American Congregational minister in 1886 was referring to Henry George.

The classic distinction between the social and the individual Gospel was first made in England by the Wesleyan minister, Samuel Keeble. He was an admirer of Hugh Price Hughes and wrote for his *Methodist Times*. His book, *Industrial Day-Dreams* (1896), consisted of addresses or articles written in the previous few years, and in a chapter on 'Christian Socialism' he wrote:

> Against Christian Individualism, which demands 'the simple Gospel', Christian Socialism maintains that the Christian Gospel is twofold—individual and social . . . The social Gospel is as sacred and as indispensable as the individual Gospel—the two are complementary, and the neglect of either always brings its penalties. . . . That Gospel, contends Christian Socialism, is far from being 'simple'—it is profound and manifold—and is bent upon saving not only the individual, but also society; upon setting up in the earth the Kingdom of Heaven.[17]

The phrase 'social Gospel' by itself was used at least three times in England between 1886 and 1896, once by an Anglican and twice by Nonconformists. B. F. Westcott, in a sermon in Westminster Abbey on

---

the Social Gospel: an inquiry in Comparative History', *ChH*, 44 (1975), pp. 367–81; A. Mann, 'British Social Thought and American Reformers of the Progressive Era', *Mississippi Valley Historical Review*, 42 (1955–6), pp. 672–92.

[16] K. Marx and F. Engels, 'Manifesto of the Communist Party', in *Selected Works* (Moscow, 1962), 1, p. 62.

[17] S. E. Keeble, *Industrial Day-Dreams* (London, 1896), pp. 62–3.

Advent Sunday 1886 (28 November) on the Kingdom of God, said, 'I pray that we may, God helping us, shew, so that men may see, what the Gospel of the Kingdom, the social Gospel is.' That this was not just a passing phrase is indicated by the fact that in the Preface to the published version of the series he wrote that 'of all the places in the world "the Abbey" . . . proclaims the social gospel of Christ with the most touching eloquence.' [18] Secondly, on 26 June 1887, W. C. Coupland delivered an address on 'Aurora Leigh' at the Unitarian South Place Chapel in Finsbury. Coupland was a Unitarian minister, who became Professor of Mental and Moral Science at Bedford College, 1881–6. In praising Elizabeth Barrett Browning's realism and hopefulness, by comparison with Shelley's idealism and Newman's pessimism, Coupland said of Newman that his Gospel 'is no *social* gospel at all. It is a lesson for the soul in its silent solitude. His vision is of personal redemption alone, the perfection of the sequestered saint.' [19] Thirdly, the phrase was used in the title of John Clifford's second presidential address to the Baptist Union at Huddersfield on 3 October 1888: 'The new City of God; or the Primitive Christian Faith as a Social Gospel'. The text of the address contained no amplification, explanation, or even use of the phrase as such; but it did not appear in inverted commas, suggesting that the usage would not be unfamiliar. [20]

These examples are unlikely to be the only uses of the phrase between 1886 and 1896; a thorough examination of the newspaper literature would probably reveal more. But they illustrate the emergence of a generally accepted distinction from an initially tentative phrase. How and why did this come about, and what ideas lay behind it? What relation, if any, does this have to that other phrase of this period, 'the Nonconformist Conscience'? Since Hugh Price Hughes and John Clifford are usually discussed in this context, this essay will pay more attention to three Congregationalists—J. B. Paton, R. W. Dale, and A. M. Fairbairn—who have received less attention. The reasons for this neglect are obscure; but none of them ministered in London, and Fairbairn was essentially a theologian. Dale may have suffered because he became a Liberal Unionist after the Irish Home Rule crisis of 1886 and was therefore somewhat distant from other leading Nonconformist ministers. The neglect of Paton is strangest of all, because the contemporary evidence suggests that he enjoyed a con-

---

[18] B. F. Westcott, *Social Aspects of Christianity* (London, 1887), pp. 96, v.

[19] W. C. Coupland, *Aurora Leigh*, South Place Religious Society Discourses no 17 (London, 1887), p. 101.

[20] J. Clifford, 'The New City of God', *Baptist Handbook* (1889), pp. 66–95; see also D. M. Thompson, 'John Clifford's Social Gospel', *BQ*, 31 (1986), pp. 199–217.

siderable reputation; but he too was initially against Home Rule, though his biographies do not mention his later views.[21] Both Paton and Fairbairn were Scots and received a Scottish education.

Paton was the first Principal of the Congregational Institute in Nottingham, which was intended to recruit men from the working classes for evangelistic work at home or overseas, from 1863 to 1898. He is important partly for his ideas and partly for his vital role in the life of the *Contemporary Review*. In the history of ideas it is always difficult to judge the impact of the books which usually constitute the main source material. For example, W. H. Fremantle's Bampton Lectures of 1883, *The World as the Subject of Redemption*, attracted little attention in England until they were taken up in America; and copies of S. E. Keeble's *Industrial Day-Dreams* of 1896 were hawked around by members of his young people's department in Sheffield after its cool reception in Wesleyan Methodism.[22] Yet both these books would be regarded as seminal by any modern student. The periodical literature, even though it represents the estimates of a literary or theological establishment, is helpful here for an indication of responses to what is published, and occasionally vigorous controversy. In the later nineteenth century the *Contemporary Review* stands out in its coverage of social questions. In 1876 Paton was approached by Alexander Strahan, publisher of the *Contemporary Review*, for advice about its future. Strahan had founded it in 1866 as a church equivalent of the secular and liberal *Fortnightly*. From 1870 to 1877 it was edited by J. T. Knowles, founder of the Metaphysical Society, and Strahan became anxious about the equal space given to sceptical as well as Christian views.

Paton had been editor of the *Eclectic Review* between 1857 and 1862, with his college friend, R. W. Dale, as a sleeping partner. He brought new life to it by extending the range of topics considered, giving a prominent place to the discussion of social questions, and also securing the financial assistance of Samuel Morley, the Congregational philanthropist, and others in setting it on a new footing.[23] Paton sought Morley's help again. He wrote that he had been pleading with Strahan to use the power of the *Contemporary Review* and his other magazines more emphatically for Christ and Christianity. 'I cannot endure the thought of the

[21] Bebbington, *Nonconformist Conscience*, p. 85.
[22] [W. H. Draper], *Recollections of Dean Fremantle* (London, 1921), pp. 101–2; M. L. Edwards, *S. E. Keeble* (London, 1949), p. 26.
[23] J. L. Paton, *John Brown Paton: A Biography* (London, 1914), pp. 67–71; J. Marchant, *J. B. Paton* (London, 1909), pp. 47–8; A. W. W. Dale, *Life of R. W. Dale of Birmingham* (London, 1905), pp. 125–8.

"Contemporary Review" becoming, like the "Fortnightly", another and the ablest organ for distributing infidelity among our cultured people— all our own sons and daughters.'[24] So with the help of Morley, Francis Peek, and others (including Bishop Lightfoot), Paton raised the money to form a new company to take over publication. Peek was Chairman of the Howard League for Penal Reform and a keen supporter of the Charity Organisation Society. Shortly afterwards Knowles resigned and started the *Nineteenth Century*. In 1882 Peek took over complete responsibility and appointed Percy Bunting, a grandson of Jabez Bunting, as editor, with Paton remaining as consulting editor.

Bunting took a much more definitely Liberal line politically. He was a member of the executive of the National Liberal Federation from 1880 onwards, and was a leading figure in the social purity campaign. He was also a founder, with Hugh Price Hughes, of the West London Mission in 1887, and served as its treasurer. Under his editorship the *Contemporary* earned a reputation for 'broad, evangelical, semi-socialistic Liberalism', as the American *Review of Reviews* put it in 1891.[25] Paton renewed links with French and German writers, and managed most of the correspondence with Germany himself. There were regular articles from Professor F. H. Geffcken on German affairs, and there were also articles on France and Italy. Bismarck's Socialist Law of 1878 was carefully noted in England. Churchmen were in any case following the course of the *Kulturkampf*, and the Socialist Law was related to the political necessities of that conflict. There was therefore considerable attention to the Socialism which Bismarck feared so much. Many of the chapters in John Rae's *Contemporary Socialism* (1884) first appeared as articles in the *Contemporary*, including discussion of the role of Lassalle and Marx in the origin of the Social Democratic Party, and of Christian Socialism, both Catholic and Protestant. Later in the 1880s Bismarck's own attempts at State Socialism were discussed. Paton also invited Herbert Spencer to write the articles on Socialism which were subsequently published as *The Man versus the State* (1884).[26]

Two changes of emphasis were fundamental for the emergence of the social Gospel. One was a broader concept of the State and its purposes;

[24] Paton, *J. B. Paton*, p. 175.
[25] *Review of Reviews*, American edn., 3 (1891), p. 510, quoted in W. S. Houghton, ed., *Wellesley Index to Victorian Periodicals, 1824–1900*, 1 (Toronto, 1966), p. 212. For Bunting, see *DNB*, 2nd Supplement, li, pp. 256–7; Bebbington, *Nonconformist Conscience*, pp. 44–5, 64–5.
[26] Paton, *J. B. Paton*, pp. 174–7; Marchant, *J. B. Paton*, pp. 268–71; *Wellesley Index*, li, pp. 210–13.

the other was a broader concept of the redemption wrought by Christ. In these ways a greater shift was required in the thinking of the Old Dissent than of Methodism, though the effect was seen in both. For this reason the Congregationalist trio are particularly interesting. The focus of the change was the relationship between Church and Kingdom.

Dale described the older Nonconformist view of the State in an obituary of John Bright in the *Contemporary Review* for 1889. Bright's political beliefs were the result of what Dale called 'the moral austerity in his conception of God'. He regarded with apprehension anything which was likely to enfeeble 'the industry, the providence, and the self-reliance of the individual citizen'. The State needed to deal with the people as adults not as children, and therefore 'should do nothing for them that they could do for themselves':

> He opposed the Factory Acts, because he believed that, whatever temporary evil they might check, they would not only interfere with the freedom of manufacturing industry, but would also induce among the people the habit of relying on the State rather than on themselves for the protection of their interest. . . .
>
> He was not indifferent to human misery; he was profoundly affected by it; and when it was apparent that the misery was the result of injustice, he was moved to passionate indignation. But the organization of the State was, in his judgment, too coarse and too rigid to be an efficient instrument for the gracious works of charity. The State is incapable of carefully discriminating between the suffering which is the result of improvidence, indolence, and vice, and the suffering which comes upon the best of men through misfortune. Legislation intended to afford direct relief to large masses of people it would be his instinct to regard with distrust, as likely to lessen the penalties of recklessness and wrongdoing, and so to diminish the motives to virtue.[27]

It was, therefore, for churches or voluntary organizations or individuals to undertake the tasks for which the State was incompetent.

Dale suggested that neither the nation nor the two great political parties shared Bright's view of the State. He felt that Bright had contracted too narrowly the function of the State and had too little confidence in what might be accomplished by legislation. Although

[27] R. W. Dale, 'Mr Bright', *Cont. Rev.*, 55 (1889), pp. 646–7.

263

there was a certain nobleness in the more austere conception of public policy, he wrote:

> We are repelled rather than attracted by what I have called the moral austerity which characterized Mr Bright's political faith. . . . We are so distressed by suffering that, whatever may have been its cause, we are impatient to remove it. . . . To some of us the individual is always innocent and society always guilty.[28]

Dale had discussed some of these issues in an article on 'Positivism and Christianity' in 1883, responding to an earlier one by Frederic Harrison on the death of Leon Gambetta, Prime Minister of France, 1881–2. Harrison had written that 'there will be no complete religion until religious men have just as keen an interest in the progress of the commonwealth as they now profess in the welfare of the soul'.[29] Dale shared Harrison's admiration for Gambetta. He referred to his sermon at Carr's Lane, Birmingham, on 7 January, in which he had been 'protesting against that ignoble conception of human life which attributes to circumstances an omnipotent power over character, and finds the chief explanation of human virtue and vice in our environment'. Whilst he agreed that environment counted for much, he had cited Gambetta as an example of the fact that the personal life which environment solicits and provokes into activity counts for more. But he argued that it was not a function of religion to impose any ideal social order or political constitution with divine sanctions. Religion was intended to strengthen the national life of individuals: 'it must give them a law for the regulation of their personal conduct, and must inspire them with strength to obey that law'. More significantly, Dale argued that the Christian statesman had additional reasons for hope to those on which the secular politician relied—the hopes 'derived from his faith in Christ's sovereignty over the human race', which was 'a redemptive sovereignty': 'His sovereignty over nations—like His sovereignty over individuals—is not a sovereignty of mere authority, but of redemption'.[30]

Hence, although at first sight Dale's argument looks like a traditional evangelical one, he was able in the succeeding paragraphs to claim that the introduction of wise laws to prevent exploitation of farmers and labourers, and the removal of irritants in industrial relations are part of the redemptive work of Christ. Thus he wrote:

---

[28] Dale, 'Mr Bright', *Cont. Rev.*, 55 (1889), pp. 647–8.
[29] F. Harrison, 'Leon Gambetta: a Positivist Discourse', *Cont. Rev.*, 43 (1883), p. 311.
[30] R. W. Dale, 'M. Gambetta: Positivism and Christianity', *Cont. Rev.*, 43 (1883), pp. 476, 490, 493.

All municipal laws that improve the health of a town, reduce the death-rate, promote cleanliness, give fresh air and pure water to the people, are as truly part of that redemptive work which the Church has to carry on in the name of Christ, as the preaching of the remission of sins, or the establishment of Churches and Sunday Schools. He, himself, cured the diseases of men, and we continue His work when we build hospitals; but we do better to remove the causes of disease than to cure it.[31]

Dale's arguments are also important because more than anyone else he stands as a defender of the doctrine of the Atonement in the later nineteenth century. His Congregational Lecture on the Atonement, of 1875, became a classic, and drew an admiring letter from Newman. However, as Fairbairn pointed out, Dale elaborated Maurice's emphasis on the primary place and normative influence of the Person of Christ in language and along lines derived from his evangelical theological inheritance. So he understood sin as something which affected the whole race, and in his final chapter he expounded the significance of the Atonement in terms of the redemption of the race. Hence his exposition of the Gospel could never be purely individualistic; just as his understanding of the Atonement was actually centred in the doctrine of the Incarnation.[32]

Dale's ideas were echoed, if anything more trenchantly, by A. M. Fairbairn. Whereas Dale's background was mainly in English-speaking theology, Fairbairn had been decisively influenced by a year he spent in Berlin in 1865–6, following a crisis of faith during his first pastorate at Bathgate. His main teachers there had been I. A. Dorner and E. W. Hengstenberg. He rediscovered the significance of the Sonship of Christ, which gave new significance to the doctrine of the Fatherhood of God. As he later wrote:

Man too was so interpreted as to be invested with a fresh majesty as an individual, and as a race he had a unity which made his fall and his redemption at once more possible and more reasonable. . . . Nor could the old narrow notion which made salvation rather an affair of a future state than of this life survive on the face of those larger ideas. Redemption concerned . . . the whole as well as the parts. . . . Man had collectively suffered loss and collectively he could be saved. Hence his

---

[31] *Ibid.*, p. 494.
[32] Dale, *Life of Dale*, pp. 325, 707; R. W. Dale, *Christian Doctrine* (London, 1894), pp. 213, 215–17; *The Atonement* (London, 1897), pp. 410–40.

social as well as his personal recovery followed as a matter of course: only the rebuilding of the City of God which had fallen down could satisfy Him who had made the citizen, had planned and built the city.[33]

Although he had regularly preached on social questions on Sunday evenings before he went to Germany, and was a keen student of Ruskin's *Unto This Last*, after his return the theological basis of his position was deepened considerably.

Fairbairn became Principal of Airedale College, Bradford, in 1877, and he was Chairman of the Congregational Union in 1883. His addresses to the Assembly in that year were both concerned with the Church. In the first, he related the preaching of the Cross to the fact that Christianity was a religion without a priesthood—instead, there was direct fellowship between redeemed humanity and God. This was a recurrent theme in his writings. It was found in the Preface he contributed to the Congregational Union Jubilee Memorial Lectures in 1882: 'No one of His apostles was a priest, or exercised a single priestly function, or uttered a word that hinted at actual or possible priestly claims.' [34] Jesus realized the ideal which had been outlined by the Hebrew prophets. Linked to the anti-sacerdotalism is an emphasis on the Kingdom: 'His most familiar idea is the kingdom, His least familiar the Church'.[35] These ideas were developed in an article in the *Contemporary Review* for March 1884 on 'The Churches and the Ideal of Religion' and in a paper to the 1884 Assembly on 'The Sacerdotal and the Puritan Idea'.[36] They found classic expression in *The Place of Christ in Modern Theology* (1894). Noting that the word 'kingdom' is used 112 times in the Gospels and 'church' only twice, he said that the Church must be construed through the Kingdom, not the Kingdom through the Church:

> The idea of the kingdom, then is primary. He comes to found or create it . . . It is ethical in character; to seek it is to seek the righteousness of God, to pray for its coming is to ask that the will of God may be done on earth as in heaven.[37]

[33] A. M. Fairbairn, 'Experience in Theology: A Chapter of Autobiography', *Cont. Rev.*, 91 (1907), pp. 568–8; quoted in W. B. Selbie, *Life of Andrew Martin Fairbairn* (London, 1914), pp. 40–1.

[34] *Jubilee Lectures* (London, 1882), 1, p. xix. This introductory chapter was subsequently expanded by Fairbairn as chapters 4–6 of *Studies in Religion and Theology* (London, 1910).

[35] *Ibid.*, 1, pp. xxvi–xxvii.

[36] A. M. Fairbairn, 'The churches and the ideal of religion', *Cont. Rev.*, 45 (1884), pp. 368–9; Fairbairn, *Studies in Religion*, pp. 132–4.

[37] A. M. Fairbairn, *The Place of Christ in Modern Theology* (London, 1894), pp. 516–17.

His autumn address in 1883 considered contemporary problems, both intellectual and social; and he broadened the concept of the Church's mission to go beyond evangelistic missions. Indeed, he suggested the upper classes were even more in need of conversion than the lower, illustrating this by a discussion of the problems of capital and labour. The more general point he expressed as follows:

> Religion ought to feel that social and industrial questions are peculiarly its own, and cannot be wisely or justly determined without its help. . . . Eternity is now; the man who is, is man the immortal, and the aim of religion ought to be to realize the ideal of God in every man and in all his relations.[38]

The Spectator noted the significance of the Sheffield address as an indication of 'the change in the modern religious temper', and remarked that such an address could not have been delivered in a dissenting gathering thirty years before.[39]

Fairbairn summarized many of these ideas in his *Contemporary Review* article. He drew attention to 'the small degree in which the Christian ideal has been the constitutive and regulative idea of the State and society in England'. Hence he suggested that people were right to feel disappointed with the churches, but wrong to revolt against religion. The important question was what sort of religion was needed. Fairbairn suggested that the determinative idea in religion was the idea of God, and that God's relation to human beings was primary, not vice versa. The primary duty of the churches was to the individual; but saved men were means, not ends: 'they are saved that they may save, work out the moral regeneration of the race'. So the churches needed to be 'the mothers of strenuous philanthropists', 'the teachers of statesmen', 'the weightiest preachers of economic doctrine', and 'the great mothers and guardians of social purity'; they should demand 'that the nation in all its legislation and in all its conduct, home or foreign, follow the righteousness that alone exalteth, recognizing no law as good, no action as honourable, that denies or offends Christian principle'.[40]

Fairbairn made his mark on English Congregationalism by his year as Chairman of the Union in 1883–4. But his influence was confirmed by his appointment as Principal of the new Mansfield College, Oxford, in

---

[38] Fairbairn, *Studies in Religion*, pp. 99–100.
[39] Quoted in Selbie, *Life of Fairbairn*, pp. 143–4.
[40] Fairbairn, 'The churches and the ideal of religion', pp. 354–5, 375–6.

1885. This gave him an unrivalled position of influence, and his partnership with Dale was vital for getting Mansfield off the ground. He did not get involved in the political battles over Irish Home Rule in 1886, and only reluctantly became involved in the later educational agitations. But his influence was clear in a number of ways. He was the main force behind the establishment of Mansfield House, in Canning Town, in 1890—a Congregational equivalent to Toynbee Hall.[41] He was warmly spoken of by Clifford, who recalled his 'mental and spiritual force', particularly his mighty intellect. Washington Gladden, one of the pioneers of the American social Gospel paid tribute to the significance of Fairbairn's emphasis on the Kingdom, and also delivered some of his Lyman Beecher lectures *Tools and the Man* at Mansfield after their initial delivery at Yale in 1887.[42]

J. B. Paton was more influenced by German church life than by German theology. From 1860 he regularly spent part of his summer holiday in Europe, first in Paris, where he helped to start a mission church, and then increasingly in Germany. He regularly visited F. A. Tholuck in Halle, and was particularly impressed by the work of J. A. Wichern's Inner Mission. The phrase 'Inner Mission' was originally coined in Germany to contrast with 'Foreign Mission', and referred to the work of the Church at home, but with a breadth not normally conveyed by 'Home Mission' in English. The German Inner Mission had been a product of the 1848 Revolution. Wichern persuaded the Wittenberg *Kirchentag* to set up a central committee to co-ordinate work in several areas, especially prison visiting, bible societies, and colportage, the alleviation of prostitution, corrupt literature, and drunkenness, the relief of poverty and the care of children. For him the protection of the family, of property, and of labour were central. Wichern's hope that the Inner Mission might form the basis of a united church was no more fulfilled than the other hopes for national unity in 1848, and provoked reaction from confessional Lutherans. Professor Ward's verdict was that the Inner Mission 'institutionalised a peculiarly uninspired form of charity'. Instead of framing a new policy 'the Inner Mission together with the greater part of the conservative pietists who sustained it, lost the hope of social redemption with which they began.'[43]

[41] Selbie, *Life of Fairbairn*, pp. 297–304.
[42] J. Marchant, *Dr John Clifford* (London, 1924), pp. 59, 83–4; R. T. Handy, ed., *The Social Gospel in America, 1870–1920* (New York, 1966), p. 102; W. Gladden, *Recollections* (London, 1909), pp. 323–4, 357; W. Gladden, *Tools and the Man* (London, [1893]), p. iii.
[43] Ward, *Theology, Sociology and Politics*, p. 26.

Paton, however, was enthusiastic to communicate the original vision behind the Inner Mission. In September 1873 he and his friend, Francis Morse, vicar of St Mary's, Nottingham, organized a conference on 'Christianity and the Well-Being of the People', at which a wide range of papers was read. James Stuart spoke about 'Christianity and the higher education of the people', and Dr Barnardo talked about his work for destitute children. Paton read a paper on the significance of the German Inner Mission for England. Most of the paper was descriptive, but the key section was the conclusion. Christianity, he said, was 'a religion which saves society as well as individual man':

> Accordingly we believe ... that the true Church of Christ has to assert and carry out the redemptive work of Christ in society, and that its grand, if not its supreme, object is to build up a true Christian nation, the whole atmosphere of whose social and public institutions, shall be distinctively Christian.[44]

All personal efforts, therefore, should be publicly united, so that the Church might reveal to the world Christ's compassion for the people. Everyone should join in these practical ministries to demonstrate the universal priesthood of believers; and the social work of the Church should be done systematically. The conference resolved to form a union of the representatives of all Christian charities and societies in Nottingham.

Paton also drew a clear distinction between Church and Kingdom when he read a paper on 'The Inner Mission of the Church' at the twenty-first birthday celebrations of the Congregational Institute on 23–25 November 1884. 'The Church then is not the kingdom.' Its purpose was to form the kingdom of God, and to extend it on earth: and this was done 'just in the measure in which, in the hearts of individual men, and in the social relationships of men—the home, friendship, business, the State—the will of God is done here on earth as it is in heaven.' Moreover, Christianity was 'the true religion for individual men, because it is a religion for human society. A man is saved not only by Christ, but into Christ.'[45] This presumably reflects the influence of Fairbairn and Dale, and probably also that of Maurice; and once more the years 1883–4 provide a peak for addresses of this kind.

The evidence for changing attitudes is therefore clear. What was

---

[44] J. B. Paton, *The Inner Mission* (London, 1888), pp. 26–7.
[45] *Ibid.*, pp. 51, 61; see also Paton, *J. B. Paton*, p. 338.

causing the change? Dale's presentation of the Atonement was broadened by the influence of men like Maurice, McLeod Campbell, and F. W. Robertson; Fairbairn's Christology was obviously affected by Dorner; Paton knew Tholuck, and also Dorner, Ritschl, and Harnack.[46] But their advocacy of the social character of Christianity was also a response to another challenge, more often neglected by historians, that of Comte. Dale's article on 'Christianity and Positivism' has already been referred to, but it is not unique. Comte was criticized by John Stuart Mill for having an inadequate understanding of English institutions and of the positive side of Protestantism, and his lack of sympathy for Liberalism was not calculated to win him friends in England.[47] But his philosophy of history did have a considerable appeal. R. K. Webb has noted that 'to the increasingly unsatisfactory answers which orthodox religion gave to mid-Victorian problems, Comte provided a solution which was heightened by a belief in progress and a passion for serving humanity.'[48]

The significance of Comte for English Christian soial thought in the 1880s is most clearly seen in the case of Westcott. There is, in fact, an interesting link between his incarnational emphasis and his response to Comte. In the first sermon he preached at Westminster, in 1884, he indicated the line of teaching he wished to pursue, taking the truth of the Incarnation as 'the revelation of the purpose of the Father for the world which He made'. Westcott believed that 'in this view of life realised among us, of life as individual in its responsibility and social in its aims', would be found 'the sure hope of a solution to the terrible riddles of existence which meet us on all sides'.[49] In the Preface to *Social Aspects of Christianity* he acknowledged his gratitude to Comte.[50] He had studied Comte's *Politique Positive* in the summer of 1867, and in an article in the *Contemporary Review* in July 1868, reprinted as an appendix to *The Gospel of the Resurrection*, he argued that a Positivist in philosophy might be a Christian in religion. A perfect religion needed to take account of three elements—the individual, the world, and God: whilst some Christians were inclined to leave out the world, Comte left out God. Hence, 'by dwelling on the relations of man to humanity and to the world, Comte

---

[46] See C. Welch, *Protestant Thought in the Nineteenth Century, i, 1799–1870* (New Haven, 1972), pp. 194–6, 218–19, 274–82.

[47] J. S. Mill, 'Auguste Comte and Positivism', in F. E. L. Priestley and J. M. Robson, eds, *Essays on Ethics, Religion and Society* (London, 1969), pp. 300, 321.

[48] R. K. Webb, *Harriet Martineau: A Radical Victorian* (London, 1960), p. 308.

[49] Westcott, *Social Aspects*, p. vii.

[50] *Ibid.*, p. xii; see also A. R. Vidler, *F. D. Maurice and Company* (London, 1966), pp. 272–4.

has again vindicated for religion its social destination.' The ideas of continuity and solidarity, Westcott claimed, were not only compatible with Christianity; they were essentially Christian:

> Doctrine which is based upon the Incarnation or the Resurrection must be progressive, organic, and total. . . . They contain a principle of continuous life, a principle of social unity, a prospect of 'the restoration of all things'.[51]

Westcott's social thought was not derived from Maurice, as some have supposed; though reading Maurice's *Epistle to the Hebrews* in 1846, which emphasizes Christ as the embodiment of all humanity, was a help in Westcott's crisis of undergraduate faith.[52] What Westcott and others did was to develop the idea of the progressive revelation of God's purpose reflected in Hebrews 1. 1–2 and echoed in Galatians 4. 4: 'in the fulness of time God sent his Son'. Both texts support a salvation history centred on the Incarnation.

Nonconformists also argued that Positivism did not replace Christianity but was fulfilled by it. Dale had discussed Comte's philosophy in his Chairman's address to the Congregational Union in 1869, and criticized its exclusively rational character. 'The moral and spiritual faculties must be appealed to. The conscience must be awakened.'[53] This came at a period in Dale's life when he had freshly discovered the significance of the fact that Christ was alive. Fairbairn referred to Comte's theory of religious development in an essay in the *Contemporary Review* for October 1871, reprinted in his first book.[54] John Clifford in 1872 admired the insistence of Positivism on 'the unity of history, . . . the total oneness of all human interests, . . . the necessity of self-sacrifice, . . . the subjection of merely national welfare to the larger welfare of the world', but he also distrusted the emphasis on intellectual progress alone. 'Positivism has no moral power'. Christ was 'the true regenerator of society, . . . our atonement'.[55] In 1879 Edward Caird published four articles in the *Contemporary Review* on Comte's social philosophy and religion, in which he linked German and French thought. He suggested that, through the struggle with the

[51] B. F. Westcott, *The Gospel of the Resurrection*, 5th edn. (London, 1884), pp. 250–1, 253–4, 263, 266–7, 272.
[52] A. Westcott, *Life and Letters of Brooke Foss Westcott* (London, 1903), I, pp. 43, 71, 75, 78.
[53] R. W. Dale, *Christ and the Controversies of Christendom* (London, 1869), pp. 18–19, quoted in Dale, *Life of Dale*, p. 233.
[54] A. M. Fairbairn, *Studies in the Philosophy of Religion and History* (London, 1876), pp. 1–57.
[55] J. Clifford, *Jesus Christ and Modern Social Life* (Leicester, 1872), pp. 20–6, 29.

individualism of Hume and Rousseau, Kant and his successors in Germany, and Comte in France, 'were led to that higher organic idea in which the individual and the universal cease to be opposed to each other as reality to fiction, and come to be regarded as different but complementary aspects of reality'.[56] But he suggested that the synthesis was best embodied in Christianity not Positivism:

> The idea of the unity of the Divine and the human—an original unity which yet has to be realized by self-sacrifice—and the corresponding idea that the individual or natural life must be lost in order to save it, were set before humanity, as in one great living picture, in the life and death of Christ.... and the Cross became the symbol of an atonement and reconciliation between God and man, which has been made 'before the foundation of the world', yet which has to be made again in every human life.[57]

Both Paton and Fairbairn were prepared to claim that Christianity was the true 'religion of humanity'. In an address to the Evangelical Alliance meeting in Southport in 1879, Paton declared:

> The spirit of our age is socialistic. Individualism is accounted to be selfishness. Men place before themselves the glory of the commonwealth—the larger interest and greater good of the society of which the individual is a member—as the noblest end of life. Even Materialism preaches this doctrine; it is the very gospel of Comtism. The great movement on the Continent which has the title of the 'Social Democracy', though infidel, is inspired with this generous sentiment. English Secularism is touched with the same elevated thought. Now, we believe that only the *mighty impulse* of GRACE—i.e., of self-sacrificing love, which seeks the righteousness of God, and to establish His righteous law everywhere—will suffice to achieve any true social reform among men. Christianity is the true Secularism.[58]

Similarly, Fairbairn said in 1884 that 'religion ought to be secular, and would be all the more spiritual and eternal for so being'.[59] In his *Contemporary Review* article that year he had concluded that the abstractions of positivism were only for 'the studious enthusiast', whereas the moral energies of religion were for all.[60]

---

[56] E. Caird, 'The social philosophy and religion of Comte II', *Cont. Rev.*, 25 (1879), p. 533.
[57] Caird, 'Social Philosophy IV', *Cont. Rev.*, 26 (1879), p. 80.
[58] Paton, *Inner Mission*, pp. 112–14.
[59] Fairbairn, *Studies in Religion*, p. 99.
[60] Fairbairn, 'The Churches and the Ideal of Religion', p. 377.

Nevertheless, Frederic Harrison, the leading English spokesman for Positivist religion, continued to present Christianity as individualist and other-worldly. In an address at the South Place Chapel, on 1 November 1885, he said that 'the organic weakness of the Gospel is in the world, in public life, in politics, and the higher righteousness of the wise and brave citizen.'[61] Similarly, in an article in the *Contemporary Review* in February 1886 on 'The Radical Programme', he said that the distinctive contribution of Positivism to politics was the formation in public life of what Comte called 'the spiritual power', better rendered in English as 'moral force':

> The true justification of Positivism, in its attempt to find a human base for religion, is this—that in all forms of theological religion, worldly affairs are left to the world and to worldly men. . . . Hence worldly things and practical things, and especially politics, economy, and social institutions, are now regarded as out of the sphere of any organized Moral Force of any sort, either scientific or religious.[62]

Hugh Price Hughes, in the Preface to *Social Christianity*, quoted at length from Harrison's New Year's Address to the Positivist Society in 1889. Hughes commented that Harrison realized that 'what Europe needs above everything else is social religion'. Moreover,

> the power of Christianity for the moral life of the individual was one which Positivism had always recognised; but the power of Christianity for the intellectual, scientific, or political life of nations in a revolutionary age, or for the industrial life of the present generation, was the problem of the day.[63]

Hence Hughes was representing a growing trend when he suggested that 'the social failure of Christianity is not the fault of Christianity, but of Christians who have been selfishly individualistic'.[64]

Until the 1880s Nonconformist political action had been primarily directed towards the redress of grievances. Now this began to change, and campaigns to change the law were justified by the emphasis on righteousness and a Christian nation. The change was bound to be significant,

---

[61] F. Harrison, *Politics and a Human Religion*, South Place Religious Society Discourses, no. 4 (London, 1885), p. 2.
[62] F. Harrison, 'The radical programme', *Cont. Rev.*, 49 (1886), p. 265.
[63] H. P. Hughes, *Social Christianity* (London, 1889), pp. xi–xii.
[64] *Ibid.*, p. xii.

especially when supported by people such as Dale. These themes run through his book, *The Laws of Christ for Common Life*, which consisted in large part of articles published in *Good Words* and the *Congregationalist* in 1883–4. In a sermon delivered as early as 1873, reprinted in that book, Dale had a bitter passage against a 'good little book sent me a little while ago by some simple-minded, devout person' on which were written the words, 'There are no politics in heaven: there is where your life should be; sad, sad, that it is otherwise.' Having pointed out that there were many earthly things, such as hospitals, railways, tea-meetings, gaols, paupers, agricultural labourers on low wages, which were not in heaven, he went on:

> Politics un-Christian! Why, the emancipation of the slaves in the West Indies was a political act, and it was done mainly by Christian people in direct obedience to the authority of Him who, according to the old prophecy, was to listen to the cry of the oppressed, and to break in pieces the oppressor. The repeal of the Corn Laws was a political act, and it was almost a repetition of the miracle of Christ when he multiplied the loaves in the wilderness, because the people were faint from want of bread.[65]

Dale's main political activities were at municipal level, though he was active in the campaign against Forster's Education Bill of 1870, which was probably the context for the receipt of his little book. The Irish problem effectively put an end to his political action, and he was sceptical about the Free Church Council movement, in part because he feared that it would be used for party purposes. The story of moral agitations in the 1880s is well known. The social purity campaign secured the suspension of the Contagious Diseases Acts in 1883 and their repeal in 1886. The suggestion that overcrowding produced incest, though not made by Mearns himself, may have fuelled the publicity for *The Bitter Cry of Outcast London*. Dr Bebbington and others have described how Nonconformist agitations extended into the areas of temperance and mass gambling.[66] A characteristic sermon by Hughes in December 1887 rebutted the suggestion that 'you cannot make men moral by Act of Parliament':

> I never heard anybody say that, except when he was trying in some way to hinder the kingdom of God. . . . At any rate, whether you can

---

[65] R. W. Dale, *The Laws of Christ for Common Life* (London, [1884]), pp. 267–8.
[66] Bebbington, *Nonconformist Conscience*, pp. 38–53.

make men moral by Act of Parliament or not, it is quite certain that you can make them immoral. Behold the liquor traffic as it now exists, created and stimulated by many Acts of Parliament—the supreme curse of our country! Think of the Contagious Diseases Acts, which for so many years dragged some of our military centres to the very verge of hell. . . . The statute-book, be it ever remembered, is the national conscience.[67]

The passage quoted is virtually an extended paraphrase of the opening paragraph of the first chapter of Francis Peek's book, *Social Wreckage* (1883), entitled 'The influence of a nation's laws on its moral character'.

The concern for social righteousness was also one of the forces behind various ecumenical moves in the late 1880s and 1890s. Here Paton was very active, and his ecumenical concern sprang directly out of his understanding of the Inner Mission. He was involved in the Langham Street Conference, between leading representatives of the Church of England and the Congregationalists, which met for two years in 1888–9 under the chairmanship of Lord Nelson, President of the Home Reunion Society of the Church of England. Westcott and Gore were among the Anglican representatives, and Henry Allon was the leading Congregationalist.[68] Earl Nelson's article on 'Christian Union' in February 1889, summing up the work of this group, asked 'whether a council could not be formed in every town or district, and, at some future time, a central council, to meet in London, of wise, sound, large-hearted men, chosen by each denomination as their representatives'. The purpose would be to study social problems and co-ordinate practical work.[69] In view of Nelson's conclusion, it is interesting that the Christian Social Union, which was formed in June 1889, was an exclusively Anglican body. Scott Holland, whom Gore regarded as the prime mover, wrote that they did not wish so much to exclude the 'excellent Nonconformist' as the 'fervid Socialistic Nothingarian', but he admitted that some did not like the narrow basis.[70] Paton undoubtedly would have preferred a more broad-based body. In his retirement he was the moving spirit behind the formation of the Scottish Christian Social Union in 1901. Unlike the Christian Social Union in

---

[67] Hughes, *Social Christianity*, pp. 139–41.
[68] Paton, *J. B. Paton*, pp. 377–8; J. B. Paton, *The Inner Mission of Great Britain* (London, 1895), p. 6.
[69] Earl Nelson, 'Christian Union', *Cont. Rev.*, 55 (1889), pp. 281–2.
[70] S. Paget, ed., *Henry Scott Holland* (London, 1921), pp. 170–1, 243.

England, the Scottish Union was open to members of all churches—following the pattern of the Inner Mission.[71]

Co-operation in social action was one of the driving forces behind the establishment of the Free Church Congress in 1892 and the formation of the National Council of Evangelical Free Churches in 1896. Paton drafted a circular urging the formation of local councils, which was sent to all Nonconformist ministers in May 1891 and signed, among others, by Hughes, Clifford, R. F. Horton, and Scott Lidgett. Whilst Paton's son may have been over-enthusiastic in claiming that 'the circular . . . drawn up by the English Apostle of the Inner Mission' *initiated* the Free Church Council,[72] social concern was certainly a dominating force. In 1895 Paton explained the establishment of local Free Church Councils by saying that it had been felt that 'as a step towards a larger and catholic union between the free churches and the Church of England, it would be well for the free churches to organize themselves for the promotion of similar objects'.[73] As signs of hope for the coming together of the churches he cited the appeal for Christian co-operation in annual services for Christian unity, the formation of social unions as in Glasgow and Manchester, and co-operation in missionary work, which arose from the meetings held at Grindelwald and Lucerne in 1892 and 1893. The Anglo-Catholics were absent from those gatherings, but they did include socially active Anglicans like Samuel Barnett, F. W. Farrar, and Canon Fremantle.[74] Paton's ecumenism was certainly not anti-Anglican; indeed, this would be true of other Nonconformists too. Sacerdotalism, rather than the Church of England as such, was the enemy.

By the 1890s, therefore, a new view of the State has emerged. It can be illustrated from the writings of men as different in other respects as Dale and Clifford. In an 1884 article on political and municipal duty, Dale presented a high theological view of the State:

> When the Son of God became flesh, He revealed the sacredness of human life; its sacredness, not merely in its direct relations to God, but in its relations to that natural order and social environment by which it is disciplined and developed, and in which it exercises its affections and virtues. . . . He affirms the sacredness of civil authority,

---

[71] Paton, *J. B. Paton*, pp. 437–46.
[72] *Ibid.*, pp. 190, 488–93; see also E. K. H. Jordan, *Free Church Unity* (London, 1956), p. 25; Bebbington, *Nonconformist Conscience*, p. 63.
[73] Paton, *Inner Mission of Great Britain*, p. 12.
[74] *Ibid.*, pp. 16–17.

and enforces civil duties with new and Divine sanctions. As there is no conflict between the Divine Kingdom and the Family, neither is there any conflict between the Divine Kingdom and the State. . . . He makes loyalty the religious duty of subjects, and under penalty of the Divine displeasure requires rulers to be just.[75]

Dale therefore argued that the duty of the Christian citizen was 'not to forsake municipal and political life because it is corrupt, but to carry into municipal and political activity the law and spirit of Christ'.[76]

In an article on 'Religion and the State' in 1895 Clifford reflected the same shift. The context of his discussion was disestablishment, but he suggested that there were four new factors in the situation, resulting from changed conceptions of the State, religion, Christianity, and the relation of the churches to one another, which were remaking the world: 'Ideas are the builders of States. They make and re-make institutions.'[77] The State was no longer regarded as 'a mere Parliamentary machine', but rather as 'an organic unity, with a character of its own, with qualities that are more than the total of the qualities of the individuals composing it, and with duties and responsibilities springing out of those qualities'. So,

> like the home, or the village, or the city, it is one of the organs by which the individual realises himself, attains his full development as a man, and at the same time aids the whole organism, inclusive of home and village and city, in reaching its appointed goal; and its real greatness is not simply in the splendid qualities of its individual citizens, but also, and chiefly, in its capacity as a whole for unselfish effort; its enthusiasm for justice, for ordered liberty and progress, and its impartial devotion to the public good.[78]

Religion likewise was being seen not as 'a matter of rules and forms, but of spirit and truth; not of the terminology of doctrines and the accuracy of symbols, but of habits of mind towards justice, towards men, and towards God'. The reason for this change, he thought was the 're-discovery, in these later days, of the teaching of Jesus concerning "the Kingdom of God", and of the relation which that kingdom bears to Christian societies or churches'. For centuries it had been forgotten that the mark of Christ's teaching was the rule of the Father in the life of people; and they had

---

[75] Dale, *Laws of Christ for Common Life*, pp. 187–8.
[76] *Ibid.*, p. 204.
[77] J. Clifford, 'Religion and the State', *Cont. Rev.*, 67 (1895), p. 435.
[78] *Ibid.*, p. 436.

become sectarian and intolerant, and 'blind to the divinity of the State, to the service of the laws, of the Press, of civic activity in establishing the rule of God'. Now, however, new light was shining, 'and in it the "secular" is seen to be not in "things" but in souls, in low aims and selfish motives and unworthy ideals; the disunion of Christians is held to be a discredit, and disagreement a sign of defective vision or of self-seeking'. Clifford went on to suggest that the change taking place was not that the State was losing its religious character, but that the ways in which it could contribute to the religious life of the nation were being rethought. 'The State', he said boldly, 'is essentially a spiritual organism.' He believed that Arnold's vision of the relation of Church and State had now been accepted as the working model. There had been an increase in national and civic ministry. The old liberalism had gone or was going; the alliance of religion and the State was not regarded as an 'unnatural monster'; *laissez-faire* was not regarded as the last word in political economy; personal liberty was not so securely entrenched against the invading State as when the Factory Acts were introduced. 'The State is seeking first the kingdom of God and His righteousness, as though assured that, according to the divine order, "other things" must follow.'[79]

It is difficult to find a more enthusiastic affirmation of the changed view, even though Clifford still maintained that disestablishment and disendowment would be helpful to the Established Church and to the State. Fremantle gave an Anglican response two months later and warmly welcomed Clifford's exposition of the religious attributes of the nation, and noted the significance of this change in a leader of Nonconformist opinion. He observed

> that the unity of human life now being recognised was that which the Reformation settlement distinctly aimed at. The Royal Supremacy (as Dr Clifford admits) was the assertion of this unity. . . . It was the creed of Burke, of Arnold, of Maurice, and of Stanley, and we hail in a great Nonconformist leader the acceptance of what we have always held and have striven to impress.[80]

Fremantle therefore suggested that if 'the idea that the nation is a godless entity' had been abandoned, and it was accepted that 'its direction is to be Godward till it becomes a veritable kingdom of God', disestablishment did not make sense. However, rather than end on a divisive note he

---

[79] Clifford, 'Religion and the State', *Cont. Rev.*, 67 (1895), pp. 437, 438, 439, 442.
[80] W. H. Fremantle, 'Dr Clifford on Religion and the State', *Cont. Rev.*, 67 (1895), pp. 715–16.

emphasized that the changed view of the State was the most important thing, and he devoutly hoped

> that the mass of Nonconformist opinion may go with Dr Clifford in his whole-hearted acceptance of the principle that the nation is the prime organ of Christian righteousness, and is capable of acting effectively as a branch of the Christian Church.[81]

In the event, Welsh disestablishment did not happen, and the education controversy after 1902 made it more difficult for Nonconformists to move in the direction laid out for them. But important moves had been made. It may be more helpful to look at the Nonconformist Conscience in the light of these more general trends in theology and political philosophy than to isolate it as a particular political phenomenon. How widely was the shift accepted? R. F. Horton certainly did not hesitate to preach about politics, even in comfortable, suburban Hampstead, but his *Autobiography* does not suggest that he did this on any particular theological basis. Even though Fairbairn preached at the opening of Lyndhurst Road Church, on 3 July 1884, his voice was almost unintelligible because of the acoustics of the building![82] But Horton never went to a theological college, and his theology was essentially that available to an Oxford Anglican in the 1870s. F. J. Powicke's memories of Spring Hill College, Birmingham, at the same time give an interestingly different picture, showing the influence of Maurice's theology, particularly as mediated through J. Baldwin Brown, on the students of his generation.[83] Maurice's impact on Dale has already been noted. Spring Hill became Mansfield, and Mansfield influenced the attitudes of the generation after Horton.

The movement which took place was regretted by some, and was articulated by the anonymous author of *Nonconformity and Politics* (1909), who claimed that political absorption, particularly in the Free Church Council, was secularizing Nonconformity. If, as is possible, the author was H. W. Clark of Harpenden, it is interesting that his *History of English Nonconformity* (1913) does not include Fairbairn or Paton in the index. But the ambiguity remained. Although 'A Nonconformist Minister' denied that social and political activity were part of the Church's constitutive idea, and claimed the support of Dale for this view, his final chapter did

[81] *Ibid.*, pp. 716, 720.
[82] R. F. Horton, *An Autobiography* (London, 1917), pp. 63, 81–3; A. Peel and J. A. R. Marriott, *Robert Forman Horton* (London, 1937), p. 155.
[83] F. J. Powicke, 'Frederick Denison Maurice (1805–1982): A Personal Reminiscence', *Congregational Quarterly*, 8 (1930), pp. 169–84.

not consider that 'the formation of a definitely Christian party in the State is altogether the visionary thing that some hold it to be'.[84] In any case, it was only corporate Church involvement in politics that he objected to; he strongly believed in individual Christian involvement. So in England, as in Germany, the question of policy remained open. In England, some Nonconformists at least managed to retain both their faith and their political realism; what they lacked in the end were the battalions.

Fitzwilliam College, Cambridge

[84] A Nonconformist Minister, *Nonconformity and Politics* (London, 1909), pp. 177–85, 198–220 (the quotation is on p. 220); see also Bebbington, *Nonconformist Conscience*, pp. 157–8.

ON PROPHECY AND POLITICS:
SOME PRAGMATIC REFLECTIONS*

by KEITH ROBBINS

PROPHECY is inescapably controversial; tension is always in the air. Prophetic utterance, no doubt properly, is apt to make many historians irritable and uncomfortable. Preoccupied with the past, the last thing they want to be saddled with is any responsibility for discerning the future or even seeking to make sense of the present. When Hugh Trevor-Roper, as he then was, attacked the writings of Arnold Toynbee in a savage article in *Encounter* in 1957, the gravamen of his charge was that Toynbee was not a historian at all, but a prophet, and, for good measure, a false one at that. Decent historians should not bother with the ten volumes of *A Study of History* because they were not history.[1] The charges, in detail, may well have been justified, but the asperity went deeper. The caste of mind of historians, if they were truly professional, should make 'prophetic history' an impossibility. Prophets were indifferent to 'facts', or cavalier in their treatment of them, in pursuit of a grand vision. Historians, on the other hand, were obsessively fussy about details and were relatively unconcerned about grand theory. Indeed, historiography had 'come of age' precisely to the extent that it emancipated itself from prophecy.

It has to be said that even W. R. Ward has displayed a certain impatience with prophets in print, notably with the writings of Paul Tillich, widely thought in some circles to be a 'prophet'. Ward, as a Professor of History, is undoubtedly glad to have found a kindred spirit in a contemporary of Tillich who, in 1924, accused his friend of succumbing to the 'demonism of concepts'. Tillich's *Grundlinien des religiösen Sozialismus* (1923) endeavoured to move beyond both the sacramental-historically unconscious and the rational-historically critical attitudes to life in a spirit of prophecy. 'The sacramental and the critical attitude', wrote Tillich, 'unite

---

* I am grateful to Dr R. P. Carroll, Mr G. B. A. M. Finlayson, and Professor G. Newlands for their advice and comments on an earlier draft.

[1] W. H. McNeill, 'Toynbee and the Historical Profession', in J. K. Burton, ed., *Essays in European History* (New York and London, 1989), pp. 77–84; H. R. Trevor-Roper, 'The Prophet', *New York Review of Books*, 12 Oct. 1989. Trevor-Roper was reviewing McNeill's biography of Toynbee.

in the consciousness of the *Kairos*, in the spirit of prophecy.' However, as Ward's exposition of Tillich's thought proceeds, he is unable to detect what precisely is the new content which Tillich seeks to insert in what the German theologian-philosopher otherwise dismisses as the empty abstractions of freedom and equality. Ward speculates on whether the call for the application of a 'universal religious Eros' to the rational economy amounted to anything more than a routine call for 'a new spirit in industry'. By the mid-twenties he believes that even Tillich was coming to recognize that history was not going the way his grandiose concepts suggested it should.

Tillich's response was not in any way to study history, but to adapt the concepts. Thus, he wrote that to observe a period as *Kairos* meant 'to observe it in the sense of inescapable decision, unavoidable responsibility, to observe it in the spirit of prophecy'. All of this did not have much connection with day-to-day politics: 'a venture into the ultimate depth and the whole breadth of what is human is to be the socialism we serve'. Tillich believed that historical periods were categorized by content and form. The modern era was bourgeois-capitalist and its form was democracy. He was not moved to defend democracy. Ward is scathing about the language of a man 'blinded by concepts to the facts of life'. Tillich had embarked upon an 'openness to culture' in 1919, but had merely 'ended in insulation from political existence'. After the Second World War, Tillich continued to assert that if the prophetic message was true, there could be nothing 'beyond religious socialism', though it was not applicable in the foreseeable future. One had to endure a period of living in a vacuum which might be deepened into a 'sacred void' of waiting. Ward comments tartly that a 'sacred void' is not a luxury available to a practising politician—and passes on to a consideration of marginally more congenial thinkers.[2]

The encounter between Tillich and Ward can be considered at various levels. We see on the one hand an Oxford-trained historian, who spent most of his professional working life in the robust atmosphere of northern English universities, and on the other hand a philosopher/theologian of a very different stamp and cultural ambience. We have a problem of language, though Ward readily concedes that the 'dismally unfruitful character' of the Protestant-social enterprise, as he calls it, cannot be ascribed to the peculiar seductions of the German language.

[2] W. R. Ward, *Theology, Sociology and Politics: the German Protestant Social Conscience, 1890–1933* (Bern, 1979), pp. 208–16.

More fundamentally, however, there is the problem of 'prophecy' itself in the modern era. What is the historian to say about utterances 'in the spirit of prophecy', whether in German or any other language? What is meant by the attribution of 'prophetic insight' or a claim to 'prophetic status'? What is the relationship between 'prophecy' and the political process? Can 'prophet' and 'democrat' be reconciled? If God had formerly spoken through the prophets, did he come to favour the secret ballot in the nineteenth century? Do 'prophetic statements' come into the category of the 'great texts' of political or social philosophy whose interpreters have been excoriated by Quentin Skinner? Skinner argues that we should not regard the 'classical works' as attempts to set down universal propositions of perennial importance. Perhaps, therefore, we have to recognize that even a 'prophetic' statement 'is inescapably the embodiment of a particular intention, on a particular occasion, addressed to the solution of a particular problem, and thus specific to its situation in a way that it can only be naïve to try to transcend'.[3] Yet, of course, throughout its history the Church has resisted any such rigid contextualization. Plausibly or not, in particular instances, theologians have constantly engaged in what might be described as 'creative transcription'.[4] These are difficult questions which cannot be resolved in one article, but they permeate all that follows.

The church historian will be well aware of the fact that 'prophecy' poses problems not only for the historian, but also for the Church. The tension between 'prophet' and 'priest' is a perennial aspect of ecclesiastical history. In his study of Lamennais, for example, Alec Vidler directly reflected on this relationship. The encounter between Lamennais and Gregory XVI was not between a good 'prophet' and a bad 'priest' but between a good 'prophet' and a good 'priest', both of whom displayed the characteristic shortcomings of 'priest' and 'prophet' respectively. Gregory had a responsibility to maintain the ecclesiastical system intact and was not disposed to allow a 'prophet' an area of autonomy. Lamennais, however, believed that he was more accurately reading the signs of the times. He made no allowance for the Church as a social institution. The compromises and intrigues of papal diplomacy were odious to him. The mission of the Church was to

---

[3] Q. Skinner, 'Meaning and understanding in the history of ideas', *History and Theory*, 8 (1969), and the debate and discussion in J. Tully, ed., *Meaning and Context: Quentin Skinner and his Critics* (Cambridge, 1988).

[4] J. Barton, *People of the Book? The Authority of the Bible in Christianity* (London, 1988), pp. 12–23, 76–8; R. Morgan and J. Barton, *Biblical Interpretation* (Oxford, 1988).

return—immediately—to its pristine poverty. The priest, Vidler argues, drawing upon Congar, is primarily concerned with the maintenance of traditional doctrine and discipline in the Church, and its hierarchical structure and cultus. The prophet, on the other hand, has a sense of being directly charged by God with a mission to declare the divine judgement on ecclesiastical or worldly corruption or to urge the Church into new paths in changing circumstances.[5]

As in this instance, the relations between priest and prophet may become particularly acute in the Roman Catholic Church because of the nature of its discipline and its centralized authority. It would not be difficult to give many more examples of Roman Catholic prophets. However, it would be quite misleading to suppose that 'prophecy' has posed no problems in the world of Protestant Evangelicalism. It is a question of balance and emphasis. In most instances within Roman Catholicism the priestly conception has been paramount, whereas within Protestant Evangelicalism there has been a reluctance, in many cases, to employ the term 'priest' at all. The 'sacerdotal spirit' has been looked upon with extreme suspicion, because all too often it had issued in 'priestly despotism'.[6] It is the 'prophetic mode' that has been most appealing and normative. Nevertheless, whatever precise nomenclature has been employed within the diversity of Protestant Evangelicalism, an ordained 'ministry' has remained with a major responsibility for cult. Hence a tension between minister/pastor and prophet has been present, too, on the Protestant side, if not in such an acute form, and it has been demonstrated on innumerable occasions in the life of Christian congregations. A 'prophet' who has moved too far away from the views of his congregation has been apt to find himself out of a job; a 'pastor' who has merely pandered to its prejudices has been apt to sink into sterility.

Given an emphasis upon the 'centrality of the Word', therefore, it is not surprising that Protestant Evangelicalism has conceived itself to be in a constant and creative relationship with the prophet tradition of the Old Testament. In successive generations, preachers have uttered 'prophetic' words against the self-image of the age. Recent works have given us a fresh understanding of the importance of prophecy in the first half of the nineteenth century in Britain.[7] It engaged the sustained and systematic

---

[5] A. R. Vidler, *Prophecy and Papacy: a Study of Lamennais: the Church and the Revolution* (London, 1954), pp. 275–8.

[6] J. P. Parry, *Democracy and Religion: Gladstone and the Liberal Party 1867–1875* (Cambridge, 1986), p. 205.

[7] W. H. Oliver, *Prophets and Milennialists: the Uses of Biblical Prophecy in England from the 1790s to*

attention of minds as diverse as James Hatley Frere and John Henry Newman, amongst many others.[8] There remained a confidence in prophecy as prediction. Post-millennialists and pre-millennialists eagerly canvassed their views and found support for their particular interpretations in varied parts of Scripture. At Albury Park, his Surrey country estate, the banker Henry Drummond had a series of prophetic conferences in the late 1820s, not entirely to the liking of Charles Simeon.[9] The date of the millennium itself was naturally a source of continuing interest. Living in what he called the age of expediency and prudence, Edward Irving attempted not only 'prophecy', but stimulated 'prophesying', with unsatisfactory results. The Prophecy Investigation Society began its work in 1842. E. B. Elliott, a Fellow of Trinity College, Cambridge, produced four volumes of *Horae Apocalypticae* in 1844. These scholarly prophetic studies pointed to the arrival of the millennium two-thirds of the way through the nineteenth century. However, when it failed to arrive, good scholarly reasons were found why a later date should be preferred. This was the kind of world in which the Earl of Shaftesbury felt at home.[10] Every political crisis could be illuminated precisely by prophetic interpretation—for example, *The Eastern Question. Turkey, its Mission and Doom. A Prophetical Instruction* (1876).[11] Similarly, I possess a pamphlet which is able to explain the Kaiser's behaviour in 1914 with the help of 'prophecy'.

However, John Harrison has tried to distinguish between 'respectable millennialists' and 'popular millenarians', though he admits that the dichotomy cannot be applied rigidly. Anglican parsons and Dissenting ministers who possessed a penchant for prophecy were not in the same camp as Joanna Southcott, either in their own estimation or in that of the society in which they moved. His work, and that of other scholars, discloses a millennial world of great diversity, populated both by 'prophets' and 'madmen'. He admits that there are 'no neat conclusions to be drawn, only the record of an exploration into largely unknown

the *1840s* (Auckland, 1978); P. J. Korshin, *Typologies in England 1650–1820* (Princeton, 1982), particularly 'Typology and Prophecy', pp. 328–68.

[8] S. Gilley, 'Newman and Prophecy, Evangelical and Catholic', *Journal of the United Reformed Church History Society*, 3, 5 (March 1985), pp. 160–88.

[9] D. Rosman, *Evangelicals and Culture* (London, 1984), pp. 24–6; D. W. Bebbington, *Evangelicalism in Modern Britain* (London, 1989), pp. 85–6.

[10] G. B. A. M. Finlayson, *The Seventh Earl of Shaftesbury, 1801–1885* (London, 1981), esp. cap. 7, 'Prophecy and Protestantism, 1841–1846'.

[11] R. T. Shannon, *Gladstone and the Bulgarian Agitation 1876* (London, 1963), pp. 161–2.

territory' in seeking to describe and explain strange people with strange ideas.[12]

Thomas Arnold did not think himself a strange person. He addressed himself to the interpretation of prophecy in two sermons in 1839. Prophecy, he believed, should not be confused with history. Prophecy was 'God's voice, speaking to us respecting the issue in all time of that great struggle which is the real interest of human life, the struggle between good and evil'. Prophecy did not 'forecast' the coming of Jesus, and if he fulfilled prophecies it was because in him the struggle between good and evil (the heart of all prophecy) was perfectly exemplified. Arnold knew some German scholarship, and there are some emphases in his writing which are similar to German writers. For Bunsen, for example, 'Prediction was the least important aspect of prophecy. What mattered more was the ability to see behind the outward course of events that divine government of the world that had the unity of mankind and the recognition of God as its goal.'[13] For many writers in the world of biblical scholarship, in Britain and Germany, it was 'the religion of the prophets' which achieved the greatest insights and, in the eyes of Wellhausen and his immediate successors, enabled Israel to rise above its surroundings. Prophets, it was supposed, stood apart from, and were often antagonistic to, cultic acts and ritual worship. The crime of Caiaphas, in the eyes of Dean Stanley, was 'the last culminating proof that the opposition of the Prophets to the growth of the Priestly and Sacrificial system was based on an eternal principle, which carries with a rebuke to the office which bears the name of Priesthood throughout the world'.[14]

It is not surprising, therefore, that Evangelical scholars were particularly attracted to the investigation of the world of the prophets and an exposition of their message. The major and minor prophets were subjected to intense scrutiny. The young Robertson Smith, who was later to write so brilliantly on Israelite prophecy, wrote in 1868 that

in Prophecy there was provided a certain supernatural *matter* of thought in vision, etc., probably by supernatural action on the nervous system. This fitted into the natural matter present to the prophet's mind, and the two thus combined were moulded into a thought by the action of the Prophet's mental powers guided by the

---

[12] J. F. C. Harrison, *The Second Coming: Popula Millenarianism 1789–1850* (London, 1979), p. 230.

[13] Cited in J. W. Rogerson, *Old Testament Criticism in the Nineteenth Century: England and Germany* (London, 1984), p. 127.

[14] Cited in Rogerson, *Old Testament Criticism*, p. 241.

formative influence of the Divine Spirit. The double divine action below and above the Prophet's own activity sufficed perfectly to control the result without interfering in a magical manner with the laws of human thought.[15]

Robertson Smith wrote the *Encyclopaedia Britannica* article on 'Prophet'. Prophets were very remarkable people, but for him no purely naturalistic explanation of their message was acceptable.[16]

It scarcely needs to be said that these issues were intensely controversial for Protestant Evangelicals. There were general problems associated with critical scholarship *per se* and particular problems relating to the structures and meanings of individual prophetic books.[17] Once a critical methodology had been accepted, British Nonconformists were poised to make a contribution to Old Testament scholarship on a far greater scale than would be suggested by their numerical strength. In successive generations, for example, Baptists were to produce such scholars as Wheeler Robinson, H. H. Rowley, and D. S. Russell.

These developments in scholarship, and their reception in the churches, have been placed in historical context in several recent studies, but no attempt seems to have been made to assess the relationship between the changing understandings of the prophetic on the one hand and broader political developments on the other.[18] We now pass on to consider this third area of tension.

---

[15] J. S. Black and G. W. Chrystal, eds, *The Life of William Robertson Smith* (London, 1917), pp. 96–7; William Robertson Smith, *The Prophets of Israel and their Place in History to the Close of the Eighth Century BC* (London, 1882); R. A. Riesen, *Criticism and Faith in late Victorian Scotland* (London, 1985).

[16] Of course, prophecy came to be seen in many quarters as capable of purely 'secular' interpretation, and there were many contemporary Victorians who were anxious to be regarded, or were regarded, as 'prophets'. Froude described Carlyle as 'a prophet, in the Jewish sense of the word' and Matthew Arnold, in his Introduction to *Culture and Anarchy* did not like to be referred to as an 'elegant Jeremiah'. Ruskin similarly springs to mind. See G. Landow, *Elegant Jeremiahs: the Sage from Carlyle to Mailer* (Ithaca, 1986), and his *Victorian Types, Victorian Shadows: Biblical Typology in Victorian Literature, Art and Thought* (Boston and London, 1980). P. Keating, *The Victorian Prophets* (London, 1981).

[17] W. B. Glover, *Evangelical Nonconformity and Higher Criticism in the Nineteenth Century* (London, 1954).

[18] N. M. de S. Cameron, *Biblical and Higher Criticism and the Defense of Infallibilism in Nineteenth Century Britain* (Lewiston, N.Y., 1987); D. C. Smith, *Passive Obedience and Prophetic Protest: Social Criticism in the Scottish Church 1830–1945* (New York, 1987), pp. 254–5, explicitly suggests that the greatest contribution of Old Testament criticism was to awaken the Church to the 'central message of the great prophets'.

Prophets remained sources of inspiration for Protestant Evangelicals, perhaps all the more so as emphasis shifted to an understanding of prophecy as judgement on the present rather than prediction of the future. 'New-style' prophecy is a neglected element in the crystallization of the 'Nonconformist Conscience' in the 1870s and 1880s. The belief that there was no valid or meaningful distinction between the spheres of 'religion' and 'politics' was itself presented as 'prophetic'. Prophets thought that attempts to delineate the sacred and the secular were fundamentally misconceived. If Amos had been alive in the last decades of the century he would have been a Nonconformist standing for the House of Commons—or he might have been Mr Gladstone.

In February 1877 Gladstone was informed by Newman Hall that a fellow Nonconformist described him in these terms: 'How grandly Gladstone carried himself last night. He becomes more & more a prophet of the most high God. We ought to be devoutly thankful to God for having called to the side of truth, righteousness and humanity, the most splendidly gifted man in Europe.'[19] Perhaps, indeed, 'prophecy' is a vital clue to understanding the liaison between Gladstone and the Nonconformists. They both believed, in Parry's words, that God spoke with equal force to all mankind, rather than primarily to the 'thinking classes'. Gladstonians saw the purpose of the politician was 'not to direct but to inspire. If he succeeded in maintaining the public mind in a state of alertness against manifestations of evil, those manifestations might be checked: if not, prospects were dark.' In effect, the politician was prophet. It was James Bryce who invited Gladstone to dinner on 12 July 1878 to meet Robertson Smith, and it is perhaps no surprise to find Gladstone reading Leathes on *Old Testament Prophecy* on 12 June 1880.[20] It was because he believed that the people could be infused with a thirst for righteousness that the Liberal leader could approve of the proverb *Vox populi vox Dei*.

The political mobilization of Nonconformity, largely in the form of Gladstonian Liberalism, was at once a crusade against certain specific 'evils' and the expression of the particular sense of injustice felt by a variegated but substantial section of the Anglo-Welsh population. Successive extensions of the franchise in the nineteenth century meant that this segment could now participate in the political process to a degree that had

---

[19] Shannon, *Gladstone and the Bulgarian Agitation*, p. 163.
[20] Parry, *Religion and Democracy*, p. 451; H. C. G. Matthew, ed., *The Gladstone Diaries IX 1875–1880* (Oxford, 1986), pp. 330, 539. Boyd Hilton, 'Gladstone's Theological Politics', in M. Bentley and J. Stevenson, eds, *High and Low Politics in Modern Britain* (Oxford, 1983), p. 53 speaks of Gladstone's 'prophetic admonitions'.

not been possible before. Deep-seated suspicions of the world of politics were replaced by a desire to participate. The 'democratization' of politics in ninetenth-century Britain, in so far as it had occurred, was put forward as a good in itself. Baptists and Congregationalists, in particular, were apt to see in their own ecclesiastical polity a model of democratic government. It was prophetic to be a Liberal.

But there was a problem. Nonconformists had been accustomed to see themselves as 'outsiders', yet they now appeared to be seeking to become 'insiders'. They could only enter Parliament by taking part in elections as members of a political party. The proportion of Nonconformist MPs could steadily mount, but Nonconformists were not a majority in the electorate pre-1918. At the heart of the evolving system of British government was the majority principle. Governments were made possible by winning a majority in a General Election, and then proceeded on the basis of majority support in Parliament. Old Testament prophets, on the other hand, appealed particularly to Nonconformist communities which felt themselves excluded, in a certain sense, from society. The notion of a 'remnant'—a group by definition minoritarian and 'against the stream'—had a haunting biblical basis. It was difficult, however, to sustain such a conviction when majorities were now sought and required as 'democracy' expanded.

The problem could only be 'solved' on the comforting assumption that the majority in an electorate could be brought to support or accept the policies and programmes which flowed from the prophetic insights which Nonconformists believed they brought to late Victorian politics. The career of John Bright was an initial illustration that this assumption was not well founded. His convictions on many public issues reflected his own understanding of the biblical message, but he had to face the fact that his opposition to the Crimean War had brought him a certain respect in some quarters but had no political consequence. He was emphatically in a minority and was seen by his admirers to be a voice in the wilderness. His admirers in Manchester diminished and he lost his seat there at the next General Election. It was possible to draw the conclusion that the role of prophet and the role of parliamentarian were incompatible, and indeed Bright was at times almost persuaded of that himself. When he did return to the Commons, as MP for Birmingham, he deliberately distanced himself from Birmingham Quakers who wanted him to espouse policies on war and peace in particular, which he deemed unacceptable to his electorate. Compromises with conscience, Bright seems to have concluded, were incumbent on parliamentary prophets, although he would not have expressed himself as bluntly as Lord John Russell did in the 1841 debate on whether Jews could be admitted to municipal office. Prophecy, he had then declared, was of doubtful interpretation, and legislative deliberations could not take cognisance of prophetic Scriptures.[21]

Bright was not a democrat in the sense of believing in one man, one vote, and he vehemently opposed the notion of female suffrage. He had played a major part in winning the Second Reform Act, but he thought universal suffrage a dangerous concept. He supposed that to empower 'the poor' or 'the residue' by giving them the franchise could be disastrous, not merely for his own bourgeois prosperity, but for the progress of society as a whole. He seems to have believed that 'the residue' were xenophobic and warlike. Peace, but perhaps not justice, required their exclusion from power.

That was not a conclusion which would have commended itself to the generation after the turn of the century which saw fresh opportunities for 'prophetic action'. Silvester Horne can serve as an example of this new confidence. A Congregational minister, he successfully stood for the Commons in the January 1910 election. He interpreted the result as a victory for 'the people' against 'the peers' and saw no conflict between his two roles as minister and politician. The Congregational way was itself democratic, and he certainly did not see himself as a priest living apart from the world. To campaign against poverty, cruelty, and disease was a Christian duty and authentically prophetic.[22] Horne's theme was echoed in many Nonconformist pulpits during this decade. Texts from Isaiah and Jeremiah were pressed into service to urge righteousness and justice and to castigate corruption and conspicuous consumption. Yet Horne's own parliamentary career, brief though it was because of his early death, was not a 'success'. What made a big impression in Whitefield's Tabernacle did not go down so well at Westminster. Perhaps it was true, as the *Methodist Recorder* suggested on Horne's election, that a man could not do everything. There was a tendency for ministers to speak words of much heat and little judgement. They should learn that there was a time to keep silence.[23]

The intense politicization of Nonconformity provoked a modest backlash in some quarters. The anonymous author of *Nonconformity and Politics*

---

[21] K. G. Robbins, *John Bright* (London, 1979) and 'John Bright—Quaker politician: A Centenary Appreciation', *Journal of the Friends' Historical Society*, 55 (1989), pp. 238–49.
[22] D. W. Bebbington, *The Nonconformist Conscience: Chapel and Politics 1870–1914* (London, 1975), p. 107.
[23] S. E. Koss, *Nonconformity in Modern British Politics* (London, 1975), p. 107.

(1909) was one of a number of voices to protest about the extent to which it appeared that all Nonconformist meetings were being given up to political discussion. Ministers were ready to produce *ex cathedra* pronouncements on any and every political argument of the day. This political activity was in turn held to explain the decline in Nonconformist denominational membership which was becoming apparent. Such claims, however, were vigorously contested by proponents of the 'social Gospel'. It was argued that the working classes were indifferent to the churches, because the churches were indifferent to social justice. It was also suggested that if denominational membership was indeed falling, because certain people could no longer tolerate the political messages to which they were subjected from the pulpit, that was even a cause for satisfaction. What was such a trivial thing as membership statistics as compared with the salvation of the world?

The coming of war in 1914 raised the old issue in a new form. Somewhat optimistically, John Clifford's New Year message of 1914 proclaimed that militarism belonged to the Dark Ages and had to go. In August, however, he had to say something specific. This time the prophet had a new song to sing. He diagnosed a struggle between the forces of freedom and the forces of slavery. 'We believe', declared the Baptist Union Council in September, 'the call of God has come to Britain to spare neither blood nor treasure in the struggle to shatter a great anti-Christian attempt to destroy the fabric of Christian civilization.'[24] Prophecy in the pulpit came to have a certain similarity of sentiment and expression. The President of the Primitive Methodist Conference 1916–17, who declared that he was born to declaim, was able to preach to the text, 'And David went on, and grew great, and the Lord God of Hosts was with him' (II Samuel 5. 10), in politically suitable circumstances.[25] George Adam Smith, author of *Modern Criticism and the Preaching of the Old Testament* (1901) and many other books on the prophets, and at the time Principal of Aberden University, saw it his prophetic duty to go on a speaking tour of the United States to proclaim the justice of the British cause there.[26] Perhaps *Vox populi vox Dei* as conceived by the Gladstonians was perfectly exemplified?

There were, however, smaller voices who were apt to believe that such

---

[24] Cited in A. Wilkinson, *Dissent or Conform? War, Peace and the English Churches, 1900–1945* (London, 1986), p. 24.
[25] Wilkinson, *Dissent or Conform*, p. 30.
[26] S. Wallace, *War and the Image of Germany: British Academics 1914–1918* (Edinburgh, 1988), pp. 172–3; L. Adam Smith, *George Adam Smith* (London, 1943), pp. 169–76.

men did not have a monopoly of prophecy; indeed, in all likelihood they were false prophets. Turning swords into ploughshares was a task for Christians in time of war, even if it should result in unpopularity and criticism. Pulpit prophets of 1914–18 were telling the people what they wanted to hear, whereas the prophetic message of pacifists was of such a challenging character that its veracity was almost established by its rejection. Yet there was no doubting that the war was popular, even if the moral claims made for it were rejected as ill founded. That could mean that *vox populi* was at loggerheads with *vox Dei*. God was more likely to speak through a 'remnant' than through a parliamentary majority at Westminster. Prophecy and democracy pointed in different directions.

The post-war climate was suspicious of prophecy, whatever its precise content. The nature of the war, as it had turned out, seemed to make a mockery of the claims which had been made concerning its ultimate significance. Indeed, it was becoming increasingly difficult to find space for 'the prophetic'. Pragmatic politicians, often of Nonconformist stock, became somewhat ashamed of the rhetoric they had employed and confined themselves to less ambitious statements about their behaviour and objectives. Pulpit prophets also in some cases came to regret their own language and the uncomplicated way in which they had applied their understanding of the Old Testament to Europe at war.

In this respect, the First World War is perhaps a watershed. The surfeit of supposedly prophetic utterance left many contemporaries after 1914 wondering whether the term 'prophetic' was useful or even meaningful any longer. It is a problem which remains in the present. The use and abuse of prophecy raised fundamental issues of hermeneutics. In what way, if at all, was it possible to 'apply' the insights of the Old Testament prophets to the political and economic structures of a very different mid-twentieth century world? The difficulty and even the absurdity of a simple-minded 'translation' from the one to the other had become apparent. And, after 1918, the further extension of the franchise, and the subsequent extension to all women, confronted Nonconformists in particular with the political reality of a democracy which they had latterly pressed for, but whose consequence was to deprive them, over time, of the political influence they had managed to achieve under Liberal auspices before 1914.

The disintegration of the Liberal Party led to a three-way distribution of the Nonconformist vote and its collapse as a coherent entity. A symbol of this dissolution was that it was a Conservative Prime Minister, Stanley Baldwin, who addressed a National Free Church conference in March

1925 on the theme of 'Christian Ideals'. He treated his audience to seasoned reflections on the respective responsibilities, and spheres of operation, of the politician and the churches. It was quite right for politicians to be told, and to be told emphatically, that the Christian churches should give themselves to helping in the elevation of the social condition of the country. Yet, in moving to this objective, he pointed out that the politician had to deal with the mass of the people as they were. Parliament represented all the citizens in a way that religious bodies could not.[27] Neither in this address nor in others to similar gatherings did he make reference to Old Testament prophets. Parliamentary democracy, he implied, required a restraint and mutual respect if it was to function effectively as a system of government. The inspiration to which prophets laid claim could issue in tyranny and an insensitivity to the opinion of others.

Within a few years it had become apparent in Europe just how difficult it was to make a democratic system of government function effectively. It was against the background of Hitler's advent to power in 1933 that A. D. Lindsay addressed himself to *The Churches and Democracy* in lectures before a Methodist audience in 1934. Was Christianity specifically concerned with any particular system of government? He noted that Barthians did not appear to concern themselves with this form of government rather than that. It was as wrong, apparently, on their analysis, to identify the Church with Liberalism as it was to identify it with National Socialism. Lindsay himself, however, went on to analyse contemporary trends and concluded (p. 38) that if the 'economic mass forces win the day and democracy, as we have known it, disappears, the Churches will disappear along with it'. It was therefore right for Free Churchmen to play their full part in a democracy and, by implication, to be prepared to defend it by force if need be against the threat of external aggression. Of course, democracy had its limitations, and there was always room for improvement, but as a system for Protestant Evangelicals it could not be bettered.[28] It could be further argued, though Lindsay did not specifically make the point, that Hitler, as a kind of prophet, was not the model to follow.

Over the next few years, however, as the European crisis deepened, the tension between the claims of 'prophecy' and 'democracy' became more acute. Many 'prophets' in the churches renounced war and would not

[27] S. Baldwin, *On England* (Harmondsworth, 1937), pp. 208–9.
[28] A. D. Lindsay, *The Churches and Democracy* (London, 1934).

support another. The Peace Pledge Union attracted many into its ranks who were convinced that they were prophets for their times. It comes as no surprise, for example, to find Charles Raven described as 'an electrifying and prophetic preacher'. It has rightly been noted that 'Christians on the left charged those on the right with wilfully neglecting the Old Testament prophets and their passionate denunciations of the rich and social injustice'.[29] It remained the case that the prophets were attractive models for various types of dissenter. It was still the case that biblical scholarship, in general, saw the prophets as individuals who were in rebellion against the cultic and social establishment.

The prophetic message of peace was attractive in many quarters in the 1930s. It could indeed be said for a time that 'prophecy' and 'democracy' walked hand in hand. But was 'democracy' asleep? There was a 'voice in the wilderness', but one 'the people' did not wish to hear. Churchill's 'prophecy', however, was secular. It did not root itself in biblical insights. Its specific content, indeed, appeared to be the direct antithesis of what was being offered as 'prophecy' within the churches. Churchill and some of his associates were denounced in various ecclesiastical gatherings as 'warmongers'. Church leaders signed their peace pledges and sought, with some success, to influence opinion against rearmament. Baldwin would have risked electoral defeat in 1935 if he had openly campaigned for rearmament.[30] By 1939, however, the tide of opinion had turned. 'Democracy' was prepared to support another war. There were many people who believed that it was a struggle for 'Christian civilization'.[31] In the reaction against 'appeasement', there was strong criticism of those pacifists who had allegedly placed 'democracy' in danger by a supposedly prophetic obsession with 'peace' to the exclusion of almost all other political and ethical considerations. From this perspective, prophets were not merely tiresome, they were anachronistically dangerous. They threatened the 'democracy' they professed to admire. This was the kind of paradox that appealed to Reinhold Niebuhr, whose stock as a 'true prophet' accordingly rose.

In the post-war world in Britain, discourse about prophecy and its alleged relevance continued to be heard, but the cultural climate in which it was uttered became ever more agnostic. The steady decline in basic

---

[29] Wilkinson, *Dissent or Conform?*, p. 127.
[30] K. G. Robbins, *Appeasement* (Oxford, 1988).
[31] K. G. Robbins, 'Britain, 1940, and Christian Civilization', in D. Beales and G. Best, eds, *History, Society and the Churches: Essays in Honour of Owen Chadwick* (Cambridge, 1985), pp. 279–99.

biblical knowledge in society at large meant that references to the word of the prophets evoked less and less resonance with each succeeding decade. The growth of religious pluralism made it increasingly unlikely that politicians in a democracy, whatever their own personal beliefs and desires, could allow the 'prophetic' voice, as perceived by a minority, to be a major determinant of policy. Even so, there has been a continuing concern within the churches for what is considered to be a 'prophetic' witness.[32]

It has become increasingly difficult, however, to suppose that there is a sufficiently coherent, single prophetical tradition in the Old Testament from which even to make a start in 'applying' the message. The thrust of biblical scholarship has been to draw out the diversity and complexity of the prophetic world.[33] It has also largely discounted the polarity between 'the prophet' and 'the priest' so dear to Protestant Evangelicalism.[34] It is a moral theologian who writes that 'The Old Testament prophets provide dangerous models of black and white denunciation which can hinder Christians from perceiving the ambiguities and ambivalences involved in moral discernment in relation to detailed situations and policies.'[35] It is a contemporary Archbishop of York who has written of the way in which close contact with decision-makers and the complex problems they face can have 'a devastating effect on prophetic certainties. And actually to share responsibility is even more devastating'.[36] At the same time, there has been a fresh emphasis on the extraordinary subtlety of the language and imagination of 'the prophets' in the Old Testament.[37] Their insights were by no means as 'black and white' as some latter-day prophets, presuming to interpret them, have supposed.

Biblical scholarship, on the one hand, and the exigencies of the conduct of democratic politics, on the other, have therefore combined to render 'the prophetic' problematic in twentieth-century Britain. Dr Carroll argues that since it is impossible objectively to differentiate

[32] R. Gill, *Prophecy and Praxis* (London, 1981); R. Ambler and D. Haslam, eds, *Agenda for Prophets* (London, 1980).

[33] J. Bowden, *What about the Old Testament?* (London, 1964), pp. 86–90; J. F. A. Sawyer, *New Perspectives in Old Testament Study* (London, 1977); G. Newlands, 'The Old Testament and Christian Doctrine', *The Modern Churchman* (1973), pp. 238–44.

[34] T. Ling, *Prophetic Religion* (London, 1966).

[35] R. H. Preston, *Church and Society in the Late Twentieth Century: the Economic and Political Task* (London, 1983), p. 107.

[36] J. Habgood, *Church and Nation in a Secular Age* (London, 1983), p. 105.

[37] J. Davis McCaughey, 'Imagination in the Understanding of the Prophets' in J. P. Mackey, ed., *Religious Imagination* (Edinburgh, 1986), pp. 161–73.

between prophets 'mediated truth will not be apparent to people outside the discipleship of a particular prophet'. Yet it would be misleading to suppose that this is an entirely new situation. He himself suggests that the vexed question of who was a 'true' and who was a 'false' prophet was never resolved in biblical times and is most unlikely to be settled in a modern secular society.[38]

Naturally, the framework of democracy, as understood in twentieth-century Britain, was not present in the Old Testament, but the tension between statecraft and prophecy was endemic in the history of Israel. It was and is ultimately a debate about the nature of power and our apprehensions of the working of God in the world. It is often suggested that the relationship between 'the prophet' and 'the statesman' is one of simple incompatibility, whether we explain that incompatibility theologically or psychologically. It then appears to be a matter of taking sides with the prophets or the statesman.[39] A historian, however, brooding on the choice he is asked to make, may well conclude that the incompatibility is not simple but dialectical. And he may decline to make it.

University of Glasgow

[38] R. P. Carroll, 'From Amos to Anderton: Reflections on being a prophet', *Theology* (July 1987), pp. 256–63.

[39] W. McKane, *Prophets and Wise Men* (London, 1965), pp. 128–30.

BAPTISTS AND FUNDAMENTALISM IN INTER-WAR BRITAIN

by D. W. BEBBINGTON

THE history of Evangelicalism, as Professor Ward has taught us,[1] is greatly illuminated by international comparisons. Britain and America in particular have shared a form of conversionist Protestantism with a common origin and many parallel developments. The study of popular religion in each sheds light on similar phenomena in the other. Comparison also helps our understanding of the differences between the two. Fundamentalism is a case in point. The assertive defence of the faith in inter-war America had echoes in Britain, but the echoes were much softer. The series of booklets called *The Fundamentals* (1910–15) that gave the movement its name had British as well as American contributors. Yet the militant temper, the polemic in defence of biblical infallibility, and the urge to save Christian civilization from decadence were much more salient in America.[2] Fundamentalism of this kind did exist in Britain, but it was a much weaker force than in the United States.

Baptists were part of the evangelical world and so shared in its vicissitudes. Although certain Baptist groups—the Strict and Particular Baptists in Britain and the Anti-Mission Baptists in America—had resisted the effects of the Evangelical Revival, the great bulk of the denomination on both sides of the Atlantic had been swept along by its tide. Like the Congregationalists, they remained distinguished from most other evangelicals by their insistence on the independence of the local congregation from all external ecclesiastical authority. Like the Brethren movement and the incipient Pentecostalists, they were also distinguished by their practice of believer's baptism.[3] Neither distinctive mark, however, prevented close co-operation with others who upheld the characteristic evangelical emphases on conversion, evangelistic activity, the teaching of the Bible, and the doctrine of the Atonement.[4] Within those

---

[1] For example, W. R. Ward, *Religion and Society in England 1790–1850* (London, 1972), pp. 1–3; 'The Baptists and the Transformation of the Church, 1780–1830', *BQ*, 25 (1973–4), pp. 167–84.

[2] G. M. Marsden, *Fundamentalism and American Culture: The Shaping of Twentieth-Century Evangelicalism: 1870–1925* (New York, 1980).

[3] For an international survey of Baptist history, see H. L. McBeth, *The Baptist Heritage* (Nashville, Tenn., 1987).

[4] For evangelical characteristics, see D. W. Bebbington, *Evangelicalism in Modern Britain: A History from the 1730s to the 1980s* (London, 1989), cap. 1.

boundaries, British Baptists exhibited a range of opinion virtually identical to that existing among Baptists in the northern United States. While Southern Baptists were organized in a separate convention that cultivated an intense form of revivalism, northerners embraced urbane respectability as well as populist vigour. It was in the north that, by the end of the First World War, liberal and conservative theological trends had diverged sufficiently to permit the outbreak of sustained hostilities between the two. A World's Christian Fundamentals Association, inter-denominational in basis, but led by a Baptist, W. B. Riley, was launched in 1919. Some of its promoters held a 'General Conference on Funda-mentals' immediately before the Northern Baptist Convention annual meeting in the following year. They eagerly denounced liberal tendencies as Modernism, a surrender of Bible truth for the mess of pottage of modern thought. The future of Christianity and of civilization itself seemed at stake.[5] The denomination was riven with cantankerous disputa-tion for five years.

There were similar developments among Baptists in Britain. At an All-Day Bible Demonstration sponsored in February 1922 by the Baptist Bible Union and two similar bodies at the Metropolitan Tabernacle, a leading London Baptist church, there were speeches criticizing departures from fidelity to Scripture, punctuated by a choir singing 'Bible Battle-songs'.[6] The journal of the Baptist Bible Union, *The Bible Call*, carried a message identical to that of the American Fundamentalists. 'The Modernist move-ment', it thundered later in 1922, 'is the religious wing of anarchy, revolu-tion and Bolshevism. Lawlessness and rebellion against authority is [*sic*] a characteristic of the last days.'[7] The evils threatening the Church were so great that charitableness towards error was dismissed as Laodicaean luke-warmness.[8] In March 1923 at Raleigh Park Baptist Church, Brixton Hill, in London, there was a significantly named 'Bible Convention to uphold the Fundamentals of the Faith and to deepen the Spiritual Life'.[9] In the following year *The Bible Call* added a subsidiary title: '*and Fundamentalist Advocate*'. 'We are in hearty sympathy', explained the editor, 'with the Fundamentalists of America and hope to work in co-operation with them.'[10] Although it may not have been as strong as in the United States,

---

[5] Marsden, *Fundamentalism*, pp. 157–61.
[6] *The Bible Call* [hereafter *BC*], Mar. 1922, pp. 18, 24.
[7] *BC*, June 1922, p. 41.
[8] *BC*, Jan. 1923, p. 12.
[9] *Life of Faith* [hereafter *LF*], 14 Mar. 1923, p. 301.
[10] *BC*, July 1924, p. 102.

there can be no doubt that Fundamentalism of the American variety was present among British Baptists.

It was fostered partly by disputes in other British denominations. Between 1906 and 1910 the New Theology controversy disrupted Congregationalism. R. J. Campbell, Minister of the City Temple, propounded a version of idealist philosophy which, he claimed, gave theological sanction to the rising aspirations of the Labour movement.[11] Because the central issue was not the status of Scripture, there was a significant difference from later Fundamentalist debates. The opinions of Campbell were so extravagant that the liberals, not the conservatives, were marginalized for the time being within Congregationalism. Nevertheless, conservatives among the Baptists were alarmed. Campbell, according to John Thomas, later a president of the Baptist Bible Union, was 'substituting the abstract ideas of philosophy for the concrete message of the living Person . . .'.[12] Men like Thomas were on their guard in 1913 when a dispute arose in Wesleyan Methodism about the acceptability of higher critical teaching in the Church's theological colleges. George Jackson, who held moderate critical views, was confirmed in office, but his proto-Fundamentalist opponents formed an ongoing Wesley Bible Union.[13] Conservatives among the Baptists were still censuring Jackson in 1919. H. C. Morton of the Wesley Bible Union was often a speaker on the Baptist Bible Union platform, and the very name of the Baptist organization was modelled on that of its Wesleyan counterpart.[14] Equally important for Baptists was the controversy within the Church Missionary Society, an evangelical Anglican body, in 1922. Opponents of the higher criticism tried to impose a test of loyalty to biblical authority on the society and, on recognizing that they would fail, withdrew to form the Bible Churchmen's Missionary Society (BCMS).[15] A simultaneous campaign against the Baptist Missionary Society led to the creation of an alternative Missionary Trust Fund. Bible-believing Christians, it was said, could now support either the BCMS or the Trust Fund.[16] Resistance in other evangelical traditions to the progress of looser theological views stimulated similar Baptist mobilization.

[11] K. Robbins, 'The Spiritual Pilgrimage of the Rev. R. J. Campbell', *JEH*, 30 (1979), pp. 261–76.

[12] *Yr Efengylydd*, II, p. 19: quoted by B. P. Jones, *King's Champions* (n.p., 1968), p. 99.

[13] D. W. Bebbington, 'The Persecution of George Jackson: A British Fundamentalist Controversy', *SCH*, 21 (1984), pp. 421–33.

[14] *BC*, Oct.–Dec. 1919, p. 7; July–Sept. 1919, p. 3; Jan.–Feb. 1921, p. 9.

[15] G. Hewitt, *The Problems of Success: A History of the Church Missionary Society, 1910–1942*, I (London, 1972), pp. 467–71.

[16] *BC*, March 1923, p. 40.

The immediate precipitant was a scheme for closer ties between the Free Churches of England, chiefly the Baptists, the Congregationalists, the Presbyterians, and the various branches of Methodism. Its promoter was J. H. Shakespeare, Secretary of the Baptist Union since 1898. Shakespeare had urged a United Free Church in 1910, the year of the Edinburgh Missionary Conference that is normally reckoned the start of the modern ecumenical movement. He repeated his plea six years later, contending that the enormities of war must put an end to preoccupation with denominational niceties. 'We may be called by God', he declared, 'to turn our back on our own past.'[17] Some were unprepared to do so. There were suspicions of an attempt to create a creedless church.[18] By 1918 a practical plan for federation of the Free Churches came before the denominational decision-making bodies. A doctrinal basis was proposed, but it was inadequate for the conservatives. At the head of the list of objections were two concerns: the Bible was said to contain the word of God rather than to be identical with it; and there was no affirmation of the essential deity of Christ.[19] An amendment referring the statement of faith back to the churches for consideration was put to the annual assembly of the Baptist Union in April 1918, but gathered very little support.[20] Free Church Federation became a reality in the following year. Apprehensions about where it was all leading were fed by a book published by Shakespeare in 1918, *The Churches at the Crossroads*. While primarily commending the federation project, the author went so far as to advocate reunion with the Church of England. As Shakespeare was to discover, that was more than the denominational mainstream could tolerate.[21] The extreme wing went into blank opposition. A Baptist Bible Union (BBU) was launched to rally the troops.

There were five main categories of supporter. First there were several moderates, men who identified with the BBU in its early stages, but who rapidly became restive at its belligerent tone and soon withdrew. One such was Dr J. W. Thirtle, a deacon at Major Road Baptist Church, Stratford, in London, an Old Testament expositor, and later editor of the popular weekly *The Christian*.[22] Thirtle chaired the first annual meeting of the

---

[17] *Free Church Year Book*, 1916, p. 9: quoted by E. K. H. Jordan, *Free Church Unity: History of the Free Church Council Movement, 1895–1941* (London, 1956), p. 129.

[18] *Journal of the Wesley Bible Union* [hereafter *JWBU*], Aug. 1917, p. 173.

[19] *JWBU*, July 1918, pp. 174–6.

[20] Jordan, *Free Church Unity*, p. 134.

[21] R. Hayden, 'Still at the Crossroads?: Revd J. H. Shakespeare and Ecumenism', in K. W. Clements, ed., *Baptists in the Twentieth Century* (London, 1983), pp. 38, 46–9.

[22] *The Christian* [hereafter *C*], 28 Nov. 1935, p. 12.

BBU on 1 May 1919, but took no further public part in its affairs and by 1925 was publishing editorials expressing dismay at the Fundamentalist controversy being imported to Britain from America.[23] Likewise, C. T. Cook, Minister of Tollington Park Baptist Church, Holloway, another speaker at the first annual meeting of the Bible Union, quickly became disillusioned with its approach. He remained resolutely opposed to Modernism, but by 1926 he was criticizing in the Christian press those who released 'a poisonous cloud of suspicion'.[24] Crucially for the BBU, its first president, Pastor F. E. Marsh of Bristol Road Baptist Church, Weston-super-Mare, took the same course. Marsh was a man of some standing, with over thirty years of ministry behind him.[25] In the autumn of 1919 he was holding a Bible conference under BBU auspices, but within a year he had been superseded as president.[26] He was still zealous for a conservative attitude to Scripture,[27] but his defection from the Bible Union is explained by a painful experience. He had once been condemned for advocating a liberal view he did not in fact uphold.[28] Initial support from these and other moderates was essential for the successful launching of the Bible Union, but their early departure proved a major weakness.

A second category consisted of the immediate associates of James Mountain, Minister Emeritus of St John's Free Church, Tunbridge Wells. The spa town in the years between the wars was a sleepy backwater, peopled largely by well-to-do professionals, people of private means, and the dependants of both.[29] Change—any change—in the outside world tended to occasion anxiety, dismay, or even the proverbial disgust. That was particularly true of the strong evangelical community that bound together many churches and chapels. At times of national emergency thousands thronged the Common for open-air prayer meetings.[30] In April 1925 an after-church public meeting passed resolutions affirming faith in the Scriptures and traditional doctrines.[31] The town was home to a number of angular evangelicals, including Barclay Fowell Buxton, Vicar of Holy Trinity from 1921 and formerly a pioneer missionary of the Japan

[23] *BC*, July–Sept. 1919, p. 3; July 1925, p. 110.

[24] C. T. Cook to editor, *LF*, 3 Feb. 1926, p. 120.

[25] *The Baptist Handbook* [hereafter *BH*], 1920, p. 189.

[26] *BC*, Oct.–Dec. 1919, p. 12; Sept.–Oct. 1920, p. 8.

[27] *The Advent Witness* [hereafter AW], p. 170.

[28] F. E. Marsh to editor, *LF*, 18 Apr. 1923, p. 439.

[29] R. Cobb, *Still Life: Sketches from a Tunbridge Wells Childhood* (London, 1983).

[30] B. G. Buxton, *The Reward of Faith in the Life of Barclay Fowell Buxton, 1860–1946* (London, 1949), p. 218.

[31] *BC*, May 1925, p. 79.

Evangelistic Band, and Major E. B. Liebenrood, converted as a young man in the 1870s through reading an essay on 'The Blood', and a zealous dabbler in prophecy.[32] The atmosphere prevalent in the town of profound pessimism about the tendencies of the times contributed to the Baptist Bible Union. Alderman Caley, a Tunbridge Wells architect, was one of the two foundation vice-presidents, and a colleague, Alderman Elwig, was the first treasurer.[33] Other lay council members of the BBU probably came from the same town.[34] And the prime mover in the creation of the Bible Union was James Mountain himself.

Mountain was an erect, patriarchal figure with a massive white beard, not unlike General Booth of the Salvation Army in appearance. He went about the town in a dated shovel hat and was already seventy-five when he set about founding the BBU.[35] To the like-minded he seemed lovable and gracious, but a Yorkshire upbringing had given him a capacity for plain speaking. His mother, an Irish Roman Catholic, had embued him with a love of poetry, and as a young minister he wrote hymns.[36] Trained as a Congregational minister, he had served at the Countess of Huntingdon's Church in Tunbridge Wells. Just as he was about to become President of the Countess of Huntingdon's Connexion, a small denomination closely allied with Congregationalism, doubts about infant baptism culminated in his being baptized in 1893 by F. B. Meyer. He persuaded a proportion of his congregation into Baptist convictions and founded St John's Free Church in the scene of his former ministry. A man of broad horizons, he had travelled round the Empire as a mission preacher for nearly seven years.[37] Two years had been spent, during a period of recuperation, at the universities of Heidelberg and Tübingen, and so he could speak with some knowledge on German higher criticism of the Old Testament.[38] He possessed a certain amount of Hebrew learning, and had received a D.D. from America.[39] Freed from the active ministry since 1908, he had remained as Pastor Emeritus in St John's manse.[40] If his experience gave

[32] Buxton, *Buxton*. H. S. Blackwood, *Some Records of the Life of Stevenson Arthur Blackwood, K.C.B.* (London, 1896), p. 361. E. B. Liebenrood to editor, *LF*, 19 May 1926, p. 534.

[33] *BC*, July–Sept. 1919, p. 8.

[34] Especially the long-term officers W. J. Bailey, G. S. Coverley, and C. C. Wright, who are likely to have been members of Mountain's church. *BC*, Oct. 1923, p. 153; June 1924, p. 86.

[35] Information from Mrs D. H. Lacey. *BC*, Aug. 1923, p. 128.

[36] *The Record* [hereafter *R*], 21 July 1933, p. 423. *C*, 6 July 1933, p. 12.

[37] J. Mountain, *My Baptism and What led to it*, 2nd edn. (London, n.d.), pp. 1, 6–7, 9, 187–8.

[38] *JWBU*, June 1915, p. 130.

[39] J. Mountain, *Rev. F. C. Spurr and his Bible* (n.p., 1922), p. 2.

[40] *BH*, 1920, p. 191. *AW*, June 1920, p. 104.

him some claims to respect from other members of the denomination, he undoubtedly believed that more was his due. In the last months of the First World War he criticized Shakespeare's federation scheme at the 1918 Baptist Union assembly, and then, in the early months of 1919, he set out on tours to the north of England and into south Wales, drumming up more opposition.[41] Tunbridge Wells was the place where organized Baptist Fundamentalism was born.

A third constituency from which the Bible Union drew strength was composed of the heirs of C. H. Spurgeon, the immensely popular preacher who was Pastor of the Metropolitan Tabernacle in the later nineteenth century. Spurgeon's assault on incipient theological liberalism in the Downgrade Controversy of 1887–8[42] still seemed to sanction similar decisive action thirty-five or so years later. Repeatedly his name was invoked.[43] The pastor of the Metropolitan Tabernacle in the 1920s, Harry Tydeman Chilvers, wrote of an imminent struggle in which his readers must stand by the old paths, and published a sermon on 'The Coming Conflict'.[44] Chilvers, however, lacked standing in the denomination because he had transferred as recently as 1919 from a ministry with the Strict and Particular Baptists, amongst whom were all his family connections.[45] The Principal of the Pastors' College, Spurgeon's other major institutional legacy, was Archibald McCaig, who was nearing the end of a term of office extending from 1898 to 1925. A solid but uninspiring teacher, McCaig did oppose Free Church Federation,[46] but he was unlikely to take a lead in militancy. It is nevertheless significant that when he made a protest against the higher criticism in 1920, four out of five letters of support in *The Baptist Times* came from Pastors' College men.[47] One speaker at the annual conference of ministers trained at the college in 1923 spoke of the Baptist denomination as 'dying', but Spurgeon's men, he contended, would save it from extinction.[48] Such exaggerated claims were grist to the BBU mill.

[41] *BC*, July–Sept. 1919, p. 8.

[42] E. A. Payne, *The Baptist Union: A Short History* (London, 1958), cap. 7. M. Nicholls, 'The Downgrade Controversy: A neglected protagonist'; M. T. E. Hopkins, 'Spurgeon's opponents in the Downgrade Controversy', *BQ*, 32 (1988), pp. 260–74, 274–94.

[43] E.g., *BC*, Jan.–March 1920, p. 2; Nov. 1923, p. 164.

[44] *BC*, May 1923, p. 80; Feb. 1924, p. 17.

[45] *The British Weekly* [hereafter *BW*], 20 Nov. 1919, p. 162; 27 Nov. 1919, p. 197; 4 Dec. 1919, p. 217. See also, H. H. Gladstone, *Harry Tydeman Chilvers: A Modern Puritan* (London, 1964).

[46] *BC*, July–Sept. 1919, p. 7.

[47] John Wilson, William Cuff, and F. A. Jones: *The Baptist Times* [hereafter *BT*], 16 Jan. 1920, p. 41. John Bradford: *BT*, 23 Jan. 1920, p. 57.

[48] *BT*, 11 May 1923, p. 336.

Laymen, too, were inspired by memories of Spurgeon. W. J. Ervine, of Messrs Garstin & Co., Aldersgate Street, and an elder of the Metropolitan Tabernacle, was President of the BBU from 1922.[49] His style of controversy was evident from an article of 1921, 'Shall names be given?' Paul, he pointed out, had cited the names of erring brethren; so should they.[50] Benjamin I. Greenwood was an even doughtier Fundamentalist campaigner. Greenwood was a member of Shoreham Baptist Church on the Sussex coast, but was the son of a Metropolitan Tabernacle deacon.[51] He delighted to recall that in 1886 Spurgeon had given him a set of commentaries by the Puritan divine Matthew Henry. '. . . I cherish the thought', he wrote, 'that in my Christian faith I stand where my friend C. H. Spurgeon stood.'[52] As 'a tried friend and generous helper of the College', he presided over the Pastors' College annual meeting in 1920 and roundly denounced the higher criticism.[53] Three years later he contributed £1,000 towards the transfer of the college to a new site.[54] He believed it was possible to distinguish a Fundamentalist from a Modernist by a short test. Could the candidate affirm '(A) The Holy Scriptures are the truth. (B) Every utterance of Christ recorded therein is the truth'? If so, he was a sound Fundamentalist.[55] In the Primitive Methodist biblical scholar A. S. Peake he recognized a Modernist. 'I regard your teaching concerning the Bible as pernicious', he wrote privately to Peake, 'and I believe that it has wrought incalculable harm both within and without the Christian Churches, but I hope I have never questioned the honesty of your motives, however incomprehensible they may be to me.'[56] Publicly he wrote a critique of Peake's Bible commentary,[57] and in September 1921 arrived, in the company of Mountain, at a meeting to be addressed by Peake on 'The Evangelical Faith and Modern Views of Scripture'. The chairman wisely told the pair that it was a private meeting and asked them to withdraw.[58] Greenwood never accepted office in the Bible Union, but, on this and other occasions, he was drawn into its activities.[59] The name of Spurgeon still held its ancient power.

---

[49] BC, June 1922, p. 44. LF, 7 Oct. 1925, p. 1158.

[50] BC, Mar.–Apr. 1921, p. 8.

[51] BC, July 1925, p. 112.

[52] B. I. Greenwood, The Contradiction of Christ (London, 1932), p. 6.

[53] BT, 10 Dec. 1920, p. 815.

[54] BT, 6 Oct. 1922, p. 638.

[55] LF, 13 Aug. 1924, p. 970.

[56] Quoted by J. T. Wilkinson, Arthur Samuel Peake: A Biography (London, 1971), p. 130.

[57] BC, July–Aug. 1921, p. 16.

[58] BC, Nov.–Dec. 1921, p. 4.

[59] For example BC, July–Aug. 1921, pp. 7–8.

A fourth source of supporters for the BBU was the Bible League. Founded in 1892, the League was an undenominational body designed to organize opposition to the higher criticism. It included men of moderation, including particularly Henry Wace, Dean of Canterbury, but it also encompassed fire-eaters.[60] Prominent among them was A. H. Carter, Minister of Hounslow Undenominational Church, former secretary of the League and in the post-First World War years editor of its journal, *The Bible Witness*.[61] Carter, a speaker at the first annual meeting of the BBU, undertook a campaign of systematic sniping against any utterances in the evangelical world he considered unsound.[62] By 1926 he was assaulting the biblical loyalties of the staunchly conservative China Inland Mission, a campaign from which even James Mountain drew back.[63] Another former secretary of the Bible League, John Tuckwell, who had retired from the Baptist ministry in 1913, was an early castigator of 'Free Church Quackeries' such as federation or Germanized criticism.[64] The League's secretary since 1912 had been Robert Wright Hay, who had studied (but had not graduated) at the University of Edinburgh and had served with the Baptist Missionary Society in India from 1894 to 1901.[65] Wright Hay was an effective organizer who turned the Bible League into the primary motor of British Fundamentalism. His Baptist allegiance made him particularly attentive to liberalizing tendencies within the denomination, and his missionary background meant that developments on the foreign field were specially subject to Bible League censure. Thus Benjamin Greenwood dedicated himself 'to stem the tide of error' after hearing evidence at a Bible League meeting of the woeful effects of the higher criticism amongst missionaries.[66] Of the twenty-two vice-presidents of the Bible League in 1923, nine were Baptists. Three were overseas: A. C. Dixon in America, T. T. Shields in Canada, and J. W. Kemp in New Zealand. Four represented the Spurgeon tradition: Charles Spurgeon, a son of the great preacher, William Cuff, one of his ablest students, Tydeman Chilvers, and Benjamin Greenwood. Two, Principal Edwards of Cardiff and Graham Scroggie of Edinburgh, were more moderate figures.[67] But it is clear that the Bible League was a stimulus to Fundamentalism among the Baptists.

[60] Bebbington, *Evangelicalism*, pp. 187, 189–90.
[61] *LF*, 7 Mar. 1923, p. 269.
[62] *BC*, July–Sept. 1919, p. 3. *JWBU*, Apr. 1919, p. 87.
[63] *BC*, Feb. 1926, p. 32; Mar. 1926, pp. 36–8; May–June 1926, pp. 70–1.
[64] *C*, 13 Feb. 1896, p. 26. *BC*, Oct.–Dec. 1919, p. 7.
[65] *BH*, 1920, p. 178.
[66] *BC*, Mar.–Apr. 1920, p. 8.
[67] *LF*, 12 Dec. 1923, p. 1535.

A fifth group was a knot of Welshmen around Rhys Bevan Jones, Minister of Ainon, Ynyshir (1904–20), and of Tabernacle, Porth (1920–33), both in Glamorgan. Jones was a dynamic Welsh-language preacher who had helped to fan the flames of the Welsh Revival in 1904–5. He was capable of extravagant exegesis: on one occasion the man of lawlessness in 2 Thessalonians was expounded as 'a combination of higher criticism, cubism, radical politics and jazz music'. Yet he also made an early recommendation of Karl Barth to a fellow minister.[68] As a vice-president of the BBU, he contributed a resounding article for the first issue of *The Bible Call* on 'Wales and Federation': 'I dare to declare', he wrote, 'that the Baptist Churches of Wales are solid for orthodoxy, and that they will have nothing to do with Federation on the doctrinal basis which has been proposed.'[69] It was no doubt Jones who arranged for a free copy of *The Bible Call* to be posted to nearly every Baptist minister in Wales.[70] Contributors to Jones's bi-monthly magazine, *Yr Efengylydd* [The Evangelist], were drawn as vice-presidents or as district secretary into the BBU: Charles Davies, Minister of Tabernacle, Cardiff, since 1888; W. S. Jones, Minister of Jerusalem, Llwynypia, since 1904; and W. Trevor Jones, Minister of New Dock, Llanelli, since 1893.[71] Another contributor, John Thomas, exiled from his homeland as minister at Sutton, Surrey, resigned his pastorate in 1920 in order to travel in vindication of the faith. Later that year he became President of the BBU and shortly afterwards co-editor with Mountain of its magazine.[72] He held the presidency, however, for less than two years. From 1922 his energies were redirected into the Victorious Life League, an ephemeral body launched in co-operation with F. E. Marsh and Principal McCaig to 'stand for the infallible authority of the Word of God and a victorious life in Christ'.[73] Perhaps Thomas preferred the new organization because it was intended to be interdenominational;[74] perhaps, like many others, he found the BBU ineffectual. He was to go on to speak at the Fifth World's Fundamentals Association conference at Fort Worth in 1923.[75] Welshmen, whose land was more impregnated with the revivalist temper than England,[76] were more readily

---

[68] Jones, *King's Champions*, pp. 176, 271.
[69] *BC*, July–Sept. 1919, p. 3.
[70] *BC*, Oct.–Dec. 1919, p. 12.
[71] *BC*, July–Sept. 1919, p. 8. Jones, *King's Champions*, pp. 102, 109, 120; 35–8, 262–9; 98.
[72] *BC*, Apr.–June 1920, p. 4; Sept.–Oct. 1920, p. 8; Jan.–Feb. 1921, p. 1.
[73] *BC*, Jan. 1922, p. 6.
[74] *BC*, Nov.–Dec. 1921, p. 14.
[75] *BC*, Nov. 1923, p. 160.

[See opposite page for n. 76]

recruited to the Fundamentalist cause. Of the twenty-nine who sat on the Bible Union council in 1919–20, eight were from Wales.[77] Support from R. B. Jones and his circle greatly strengthened Mountain's hand.

Behind the classes of people that contributed to the Baptist Bible Union were a number of common conditioning factors. It was these circumstances that were largely responsible for the Fundamentalism that emerged. Among them, a deep-seated element in the evangelical psyche, was anti-Catholicism.[78] In the 1920s J. A. Kensit of the Protestant Truth Society could still rouse popular support for the time-honoured demand that all convents should be open to public inspection.[79] In that decade the society, which received most backing from Anglican evangelicals, but also attracted a little from among the Baptists, added criticism of the Bible and evolutionism to the catalogue of Romanist errors it opposed.[80] When, in 1927–8, parliament considered a new Book of Common Prayer containing revisions favouring Anglo-Catholics, there was a Protestant outcry that gathered extensive Free Church support.[81] What particularly troubled Free Churchmen just after the First World War was the emergence within their own ranks of liturgical practices as Roman in inspiration as those of the advanced Anglo-Catholics. W. E. Orchard at the Congregationalist King's Weigh House, who was eventually to enter the Roman Catholic Church, was distinctly provocative in his approach.[82] At an early BBU meeting Kensit gave a list of Free Church ministers and churches adopting Romish customs. The hostility of the meeting to Free Church Federation was grounded on fears that the aim was incorporation into a Church of England stained by sacerdotalism.[83] The ultimate dread was of being swallowed up by Rome. Similar apprehensions ran deep among contemporary Baptists in Ireland. In the early days of the Bible Union four ministers and two laymen were recruited for the council from the Irish Baptists.[84] Although the Baptist Union of Ireland was to take a

---

[76] R. Carwardine, 'The Welsh evangelical Community and "Finney's Revival"', *JEH*, 29 (1978), pp. 463–80.

[77] *BC*, July–Sept. 1919, p. 8. *Baptist Bible Union Manifesto*, 3 Nov. 1920.

[78] G. F. A. Best, 'Popular Protestantism in Victorian Britain', in R. Robson, ed., *Ideas and Institutions of Victorian Britain* (London, 1967). E. R. Norman, *Anti-Catholicism in Victorian England* (London, 1967).

[79] *R*, 5 Mar. 1925, p. 162.

[80] *R*, 9 Oct. 1924, p. 658.

[81] A. Hastings, *A History of English Christianity, 1920–1985* (London, 1987 edn.), pp. 203–8.

[82] W. E. Orchard, *From Faith to Faith* (London, 1933).

[83] *BC*, July–Sept. 1919, pp. 2–3.

[84] *Baptist Bible Union Manifesto*, 3 Nov. 1920.

conservative path during the 1920s, resolving, for instance, its adherence to verbal inspiration in 1924,[85] its members played no active part in the Bible Union. Distance no doubt prevented involvement. The popish spectre nevertheless stalked the minds of the Baptist Fundamentalists. When a Roman Catholic representative was discovered among the guests at the thirtieth anniversary of the ministry of Charles Brown, a denominational leader targeted for criticism by the BBU, there was condemnation of 'such reckless hobnobbing with the followers of the Pope of Rome'.[86] Anti-Catholicism remained a powerful spur to militancy in defence of the Bible.

So did the holiness tradition. In Methodism, the distinctive teaching about entire sanctification, though not fully exploited, was potentially fertile ground for the cultivation of Fundamentalist attitudes.[87] Outside Methodism, the equivalent was the message of the annual Keswick convention, a version of holiness doctrine more acceptable to those in the Reformed wing of evangelicalism. The possibility of holiness by faith— 'the victorious life'—was especially attractive to evangelicals in the Church of England, but three prominent Baptist exponents were F. B. Meyer, W. Y. Fullerton, and Graham Scroggie.[88] Upholders of Spurgeon's doctrinal position and Bible League men rarely embraced Keswick teaching, but Fullerton, a biographer of Spurgeon, and Scroggie, a vice-president of the League, were exceptions. For people abhorring worldliness the taint of the higher criticism was to be shunned. James Mountain was near the heart of Keswick. In the 1870s he had acted as secretary to Robert Pearsall Smith, the American apostle of holiness teaching. He had conducted the service of song at the first Keswick convention. He was the compiler of the Keswick Hymn Book.[89] Likewise R. B. Jones was probably the chief exponent of Keswick teaching in Wales. He experienced total consecration under the guidance of Meyer at the initial meeting, in 1904, of the first Welsh annual convention, at Llandrindod Wells. He went on to achieve fame at the multiplying lesser conventions throughout Wales, and his magazine existed to propagate the message of holy living. There was a sharp resistance. Critics pointed out, for instance, that the Welsh word used to describe a convention equally meant a herd of swine. R. B. Jones's friend and namesake, W. S. Jones, also

---

[85] BC, July 1924, p. 100.
[86] BC, July–Aug. 1920, p. 1.
[87] Bebbington, 'George Jackson', p. 428.
[88] Bebbington, Evangelicalism, cap. 5.
[89] LF, 29 July 1925, p. 856. R, 21 July 1933, p. 423.

encountered opposition: in 1906 seven of his deacons resigned in protest against Keswick teaching.[90] On the one hand the holiness movement gave these men a fresh dynamic. On the other it accustomed them to withstanding criticism that they saw as unspiritual. It steeled them for the Fundamentalist controversies.

As in America, probably the chief ideological bond between the Fundamentalists was premillennialism, the teaching that Jesus Christ would return to earth in person before the millennium. Far from being an abstruse technicality, this doctrine determined their view of the immediate future and therefore their whole outlook. If the second advent was imminent, there was little point in social reform. The task of the Church was to win as many souls as possible in the short time available. The enterprise would not be easy because convulsions in the world and apostasy in the Church were prophesied for these 'last days'. The expectation of controversy within the Church could often be self-fulfilling.[91] Such premillennialism had become normal among Anglican evangelicals, but in the Free Churches the older postmillennialism still prevailed. According to this teaching, the return of Christ, which might be personal or spiritual, would take place only after the millennium, when the triumph of the Gospel had achieved peace and goodwill throughout the earth. This eschatology generated a far more optimistic world-view. Social reform was worthwhile because it contributed to the purposes of God. The churches had a civilizing mission as well as an evangelistic responsibility, even if the first was usually seen as subordinate to the second. Postmillennialism shaded off imperceptibly into the idea of progress that was still widespread at a popular level. Baptists in general tended to a watered-down version of postmillennialism, but the denomination possessed a larger minority of premillennialists than the other Free Churches. Spurgeon had adopted a premillennial eschatology by 1861,[92] and those such as F. B. Meyer who were associated with Anglican evangelicals in the Keswick movement normally held the same position. Men and women expecting the imminent return of the Lord were likely to perceive those who did not as lukewarm in the faith.

The apocalyptic atmosphere of the First World War gave rise for the

[90] Jones, *King's Champions*, pp. 49, 83, 93, 95, 98.
[91] On America, see T. P. Weber, *Living in the Shadow of the Second Coming: American Premillennialism, 1875–1925* (New York, 1979). On Britain, see D. W. Bebbington, 'The Advent Hope in British Evangelicalism since 1800', *The Scottish Journal of Religious Studies*, 9 (1988), pp. 103–14.
[92] M. T. E. Hopkins, 'Baptists, Congregationalists and Theological Change: Some Late Nineteenth Century Leaders and Controversies' (Oxford D.Phil. thesis, 1988), p. 166.

first time to a popular premillennialist movement. Two Baptist ministers, Alfred Bird and J. S. Harrison, both products of the Pastors' College, suggested to Meyer in the autumn of 1917 that Christians must be urged to prepare themselves to meet the returning Lord. Meyer gathered together like-minded leaders and formed an interdenominational organization that eventually called itself the Advent Testimony and Preparation Movement.[93] In the spring of 1920 the council agreed to add a witness to 'the Fundamentals of Evangelical Christianity' to its purposes. E. L. Langston, an Anglican clergyman at Wimbledon, planned a convention on the theme for later in the year, but mysteriously it failed to take place.[94] Although this scheme for a large-scale British Fundamentalist campaign came to nothing, the potential remained within the Advent Testimony Movement. 'The God-fearing and spiritually-minded amongst the laity are restive', wrote Meyer in its journal in December 1923; 'they will not any longer tolerate the poisoning of their children with the infidelity of the classroom. It means a cleavage.'[95] Advent Testimony mobilized a significant number of Baptists. Six out of the twenty-one members of its council at the start of 1921 were from the denomination.[96] F. E. Marsh wrote one of its handbooks, *The Second Coming of our Lord Jesus Christ in Relation to 'The Millennium'* (1925); another handbook was by Percy Hicks, editor of *The Christian Herald* and formerly Minister of Central Stratford Baptist Church (1913–22).[97] Members included James Mountain of the Baptist Bible Union and Robert Wright Hay of the Bible League, who had gone to India as a missionary with the adventist motto 'Perhaps To-day'.[98] The Welsh circle round R. B. Jones was just as committed to premillennialism. About ten thousand copies of Jones's articles on the second advent were distributed free, and he claimed (probably correctly) to have written the first book in Welsh on the subject.[99] There can be no doubt that common allegiance to the advent hope glued together the Fundamentalist coalition among the Baptists.

A sense of impending crisis reinforced this mentality. *The Christian*,

[93] *The Monthly Bulletin of the Advent Preparation Prayer Union* [hereafter *MBAPPU*], June 1919, p. 1.
[94] *MBAPPU*, June 1920, pp. 97–8; Aug. 1920, p. 120.
[95] *AW*, Dec. 1923, p. 136.
[96] *AW*, Feb. 1921, p. i.
[97] W. P. Hicks, *The Second Coming of our Lord Jesus Christ in Relation to the Present World Crisis* (London, 1925).
[98] *MBAPPU*, June 1920, p. 104; July 1920, p. 112. *AW*, Dec. 1921, p. 282.
[99] Jones, *King's Champions*, p. 101. *C*, 6 Mar. 1919, p. 19.

then edited by an Anglican evangelical, but read by many Baptists, summed up the contemporary feeling that chaos was closing in.

> Every where [ran a commendation of the Advent Testimony Movement in February 1919] there are labour-unrest, the menace of Revolution, the upheaval of Society, the proclamation of war between class and class. Atrocities are being daily committed in Russia and the East, compared with which the tortures of the Inquisition might almost be termed merciful. The professing Christian Church, as a regenerating force, seems bankrupt. After centuries of Christian civilization there are no barriers left against the craft and cruelty of primitive savagery.[100]

Wild rumours circulated. 'Is it not true', asked an article in the BBU journal in 1921, 'that there is a Baptist group of sceptical Critics in London engaged in sceptical propaganda as eager as the Russian Bolsheviks in their anarchical agitation?'[101] The coincidence that Germany, Britain's erstwhile enemy, was the source of higher critical technique and liberal theological trends seemed sinister in the extreme. Meyer declared that Britain had failed to learn the lesson of Germany, where the cause of decadence had been the spirit of criticism of the Bible.[102] Greenwood referred to critical poison manufactured in Germany.[103] And Mountain claimed that the 'rank and file of Biblical Christians are nearing a public revolt against the Germanical Theologians in our midst'.[104] Wars and rumours of wars created an atmosphere in which militancy appeared natural.

Peaceful change also encouraged active Fundamentalism. All change was suspect to the premillennialist, since change meant decay. The emerging cinema, for instance, might possibly have value for education or for innocent recreation, but that was more than balanced by the suggestiveness for the young that led to crime. The Kinema Mission Movement, that aimed to bring the Gospel to the masses through motion pictures, was dismissed in *The Bible Call* as 'just another of the twentieth-century quackeries'.[105] Attempts by the Church to direct social change were more than suspect. Social reform in itself might not be reprehensible, but the

[100] *C*, 20 Feb. 1919, p. 16.
[101] *BC*, Mar.–Apr. 1921, p. 6.
[102] *MBAPPU*, June 1920, p. 97.
[103] *BC*, Jan.–Feb. 1921, p. 2.
[104] J. Mountain, *The Keswick Convention and the Dangers which threaten It* (n.p., 1920), p. 10.
[105] *BC*, July–Aut. 1920, p. 3.

social Gospel certainly was. It was a device of Satan to divert Christians to 'the betterment of this old world system, to the exclusion of the one primary work of getting souls saved and sanctified, and prepared for the next world'.[106] The Church must 'warn men of the approaching judgment of this world, rather than tinker with schemes to save it apart from God'.[107] Premillennialism discouraged political activity in particular, since that was seen as futile.[108] Even organizations as honourable as League of Nations Union branches were rejected by R. B. Jones as unspiritual in motive.[109] The Church was impotent in the midst of change, it was held, because of its abandonment of traditional ways. The service of God was being made subservient to the parading of the choir; a minister was expected to be 'the manager of a sort of social and religious polytechnic'; if he tried to drop amusements in order to reinstate the prayer meeting, he was likely to lose influential families.[110] Only in a few favoured havens were Gospel priorities still observed. Bethesda Hall, Liverpool, for example, raised money only by voluntary giving. 'The people at Bethesda', observed *The Bible Call*, 'believe in the spiritual atmosphere of Pentecost, not in the worldly surroundings of the ball-room.'[111] Even if it did not penetrate very deep, there was a measure of truth in the Fundamentalist critique. The Church was being secularized by attempts to retain the allegiance of a younger generation.[112] The process of secularization was another factor driving the more conservative to shrill calls for a return to the old paths.

The American example was a further stimulus to Fundamentalism. 'Our brethren in America', wrote Meyer in the Advent Testimony magazine in 1923, 'are lifting up a standard against the inrush of a mighty host of deserters from the truth—God bless them! We extend to them the right hand of sympathy, for we are face to face with the same conflict here.'[113] Meyer had several times been to America and so naturally felt a sense of common cause. F. E. Marsh and W. S. Jones had actually held pastorates in the United States; Benjamin Greenwood had been a close

---

[106] *BC*, July 1924, p. 99.
[107] *BC*, Dec. 1924, p. 108.
[108] D. W. Bebbington, 'Baptists and Politics since 1914', in Clements, ed., *Baptists in the Twentieth Century*, pp. 82–3.
[109] Jones, *King's Champions*, p. 147.
[110] *BC*, Nov. 1922, p. 83; Oct. 1925, p. 131; Aug. 1924, p. 115.
[111] *BC*, Jan. 1925, p. 16.
[112] A. D. Gilbert, *The Making of Post-Christian Britain: A History of the Secularization of Modern Society* (London, 1980), cap. 5.
[113] *AW*, Dec. 1923, p. 136.

friend of A. T. Pierson, a proto-Fundamentalist leader of an earlier generation; and James Mountain's D.D. came from an American college supported by W. J. Bryan, the most prominent lay Fundamentalist in the United States.[114] R. B. Jones had been on preaching-tours among the Pennsylvania Welsh, who, in deference to the chief American revivalist of the day, called him 'a Welsh Billy Sunday'. Jones liked American Sunday-school magazines and teaching aids, tried to imitate American techniques, and invited many speakers from the United States to his monthly Bible conferences. They included W. B. Riley, the initiator of the World's Christian Fundamentals Association and a vice-president of the Baptist Bible Union of America, who on one occasion urged total separation from 'impure denominations'.[115] The president of the Southern Baptist Convention, J. S. Gambrell, sent a message of support when Mountain set up the BBU in Britain. 'Distressing word', he wrote, 'has come to us for years concerning the down-grade move in England.' The three million Southern Baptists were 'practically of one mind and one spirit, striving together for the faith of the gospel', and intended to send over a small fund—which seems, however, not to have arrived.[116] Potentially most significant of all was the role of A. C. Dixon, the editor of *The Fundamentals*, an American Baptist who from 1906 to 1911 had been Pastor of Moody Memorial Church, Chicago, and then from 1911 to 1919 occupied Spurgeon's former pulpit at the Metropolitan Tabernacle. Strongly opposed to the notion of Free Church Federation, Dixon suggested the idea of a Baptist Bible Union to Mountain before leaving to put himself at the head of Fundamentalist forces in the United States.[117] In 1923 Mountain publicized Dixon's frustrated effort to move a firm doctrinal resolution at the Baptist World Alliance meetings in Stockholm.[118] In the following year Dixon was back in Britain, denouncing evolution on a Bible League platform, but in 1925 he died.[119] Had Dixon remained at the Metropolitan Tabernacle into the 1920s, he might have provided a rallying-point for Fundamentalists. As it was, he was just one of the American contacts who helped sustain the momentum of the British movement.

[114] *BH*, 1920, p. 189. Jones, *King's Champions*, p. 36. D. L. Pierson, *Arthur T. Pierson: A Biography* (London, 1912), pp. 253, 267. J. Mountain, *Rev. F. C. Spurr and his Bible* (n.p., 1922), p. 2.

[115] Jones, *King's Champions*, pp. 74–8, 101, 138, 202, 246, 279.

[116] J. S. Gambrell to J. Mountain, 5 Nov. 1919, in *BC*, Jan.–Mar. 1920, p. 6.

[117] *BC*, July–Sept. 1919, p. 7; Jan.–Mar. 1920, p. 7. Marsden, *Fundamentalism*, pp. 160–1.

[118] J. Mountain to editor, *LF*, 12 Sept. 1923, p. 1065.

[119] *R*, 23 Oct. 1924, p. 689. *LF*, 17 June 1925, p. 676.

Anti-Catholicism, Keswick teaching, premillennialism, crises in public affairs, secularizing tendencies, the American example—these were the chief factors underlying Fundamentalism among Baptists in Britain. The issues to which they gave rise, though parochial in comparison with the contemporary struggles in America, deserve review. The first was provoked by R. H. Coats, a member of the thread-spinning family of Paisley, who had studied at Glasgow, Oxford, and Leipzig before settling at Handsworth, Birmingham, in 1899.[120] 'The first chapter of the Bible', Coats wrote in *The Baptist Times* Sunday-school notes of 26 December 1919, 'was one of the last to be written, and it gives a priestly lawyer's account of the origin of all things, as believed by the Hebrews four or five centuries before Christ was born.' Principal McCaig of the Pastors' College wrote to protest that 'the guesses of the "higher criticism"' were being presented to young people as 'assured facts'.[121] McCaig was no doubt aware that when, two years before, James Mountain had objected to a *Baptist Times* Sunday-school lesson including similar higher critical theories, the editor, while declining to publish Mountain's letter, had agreed that such lessons should not be repeated.[122] The undertaking had now been broken. For four weeks, correspondents waded in on the two sides until, on 6 February, McCaig exercised the right of reply, and the correspondence was closed.[123] John Thomas, the Welsh minister at Sutton, decided not to let matters drop. For some years he had been lecturing against the higher criticism, and now he published a series of four sermons in *The Baptist Times* defending the Bible against religious scepticism.[124] 'The fundamental cleavage', he wrote in the last of them, '[is] bound to come between those who proclaim the word of God and the gospel of Jesus and those who dishonour both by their speculative rejections.'[125] Leaving his pastorate, Thomas appealed for assistance in a 'holy crusade' to combat error.[126] The 'pernicious teaching' in *The Baptist Times* led to the withdrawal of Toxteth Tabernacle, Liverpool, Philip Street, Bristol, and perhaps other churches from the Baptist Union.[127] Battle had been joined over the attitudes to the Bible.

[120] *BH*, 1920, p. 166.
[121] A. McCaig to editor, *BT*, 9 Jan. 1920, p. 27.
[122] *JWBU*, Dec. 1917, p. 271.
[123] *BT*, 16 Jan. 1920, p. 41; 23 Jan. 1920, p. 57; 30 Jan. 1920, p. 73; 6 Feb. 1920, p. 88.
[124] *JWBU*, Mar. 1915, p. 56. *BT*, 5 Mar. 1920, p. 156; 12 Mar. 1920, p. 173; 19 Mar. 1920, p. 189; 2 Apr. 1920, pp. 222–3.
[125] *BT*, 2 Apr. 1920, p. 223.
[126] J. Thomas to editor, *BT*, 30 Apr. 1920, p. 289.
[127] *BC*, Apr.–June 1920, p. 11; July–Aug. 1920, p. 4.

Charles Brown, approaching the end of a distinguished ministry at Ferme Park Baptist Church, in north London, took up the gage thrown down by John Thomas. On 11 April he preached a sermon, subsequently printed in *The Baptist Times*, on 'How the Bible came to be'. 'There is no need that these men', he declared of the Bible writers, 'be infallible in every particular in order that they may teach us.'[128] Brown, who had in his vestry a portrait of John Clifford, the leader of progressive thought in the denomination, was no premillennialist.[129] He had actively supported Shakespeare's plan for a United Free Church in 1910 and for Free Church Federation in 1918.[130] Perhaps his worst offence in the eyes of Fundamentalists, however, was a commendation of A. S. Peake, the biblical scholar whose commentary had disseminated the conclusions of the milder critics. James Mountain published a reply in which (according to Thomas) Charles Brown was 'crushed'.[131] It so happened that Brown had been invited by his friend Stuart Holden, the Anglican chairman of the council, to speak for the first time at the Keswick Convention that year.[132] Mountain rushed to the defence of what he regarded as the citadel of truth. He despatched a relative and friend from Tunbridge Wells to listen for any critical comment about Keswick made by Brown at his own church; he circulated a pamphlet against Brown at the convention; and shortly afterwards issued a further pamphlet denouncing Brown and two other Keswick speakers.[133] Mountain claimed to receive twenty or thirty letters a day, mostly approving his stand.[134] His case was weakened by the admission that Brown's Keswick address was acceptable.[135] That was an understatement: many hearers thought it the finest address yet given at the convention.[136] Brown, who was never invited to Keswick again, had been hurt: the following month he castigated 'heresy-hunting' in a holiday sermon at Llandudno.[137] Four years later he opened his pulpit to Harry Fosdick, the American minister who was the *bête noire* of Fundamentalists.[138]

[128] *BT*, 16 Apr. 1921, pp. 256–7.
[129] *BW*, 15 Apr. 1920, p. 44. *AW*, March 1922, pp. 39–40.
[130] Jordan, *Free Church Unity*, pp. 127, 134.
[131] *BC*, July–Aug. 1920, pp. 5–10; Sept.–Oct. 1920, p. 3.
[132] H. Cook, *Charles Brown* (London, 1939), p. 62.
[133] C. Brown to editor, *BW*, 14 July 1921, p. 276. Mountain, *Keswick Convention and the Dangers*.
[134] *BC*, Nov.–Dec. 1920, p. 11.
[135] Mountain, *Keswick Convention and the Dangers*, p. 13.
[136] *C*, 29 July 1920, p. 15.
[137] *BW*, 11 Aug. 1921, p. 339.
[138] *BC*, Aug. 1924, p. 128.

Mountain's campaign succeeded only in alienating Brown and the many who respected him from the conservative cause.

Mountain nevertheless redoubled his efforts, now directing his assault against F. C. Spurr, another Baptist minister who had been a first-time Keswick speaker in 1920. Spurr had served as Baptist Union evangelist and as Minister of Collins Street, Melbourne, Australia's leading Baptist church, before taking over at Regent's Park Baptist Church from F. B. Meyer in 1914.[139] He had ventured some incautious remarks in the liberal *Christian World* about the need for Keswick to enter a 'broader path', with praise for the 'historic method of study' and new 'contributions to Theology'.[140] Mountain pursued him relentlessly, particularly when it became known that he was to return to Keswick in 1921. Mountain called for ministers who had disparaged the Bible to be excluded from the convention; he directed an open letter to Spurr expressing the hope that he would disavow his former views; when Spurr replied, Mountain published the results of investigations into Spurr's statements in Australia; when Spurr's friends threatened an action for libel, Meyer intervened with the suggestion that a tribunal of seven should investigate Spurr's views.[141] As the unseemly wrangle dragged on, Spurr withdrew from the convention less than a month before it was due to begin.[142] Eventually the idea of a tribunal was dropped, but Mountain still persevered with his campaign. Professional reporters were sent to record a series of evening lectures on the Bible, from which Mountain concocted another critical pamphlet.[143] In 1922 Spurr moved, perhaps symbolically, to the pulpit in Handsworth of the Coats who had earlier antagonized Principal McCaig.[144] There he could continue to teach that the words of the Bible do not constitute the Word of God, which is 'a living thing inside the words'.[145] The victimizing of Spurr, in excluding him from Keswick, achieved a qualified success. It heartened Mountain and his circle for a fresh assault on Modernism.

The next target was Dr T. R. Glover, a classical scholar, Fellow of St John's College, Cambridge, and a deacon of St Andrew's Street Baptist Church in the town. Glover, a close friend of Charles Brown, was

---

[139] *BH*, 1920, p. 202.
[140] Mountain, *Keswick Convention and the Dangers*, pp. 11–13.
[141] J. Mountain, *What Keswick needs: A Reply to 'What Keswick stands for'* (n.p., 1921), p. 8. *BC*, March–April 1921, pp. 13–14; May–June 1921, p. 7. J. Mountain, *Rev. F. C. Spurr and Keswick* (n.p., 1921), pp. 3–6. *BC*, July–Aug. 1921, pp. 3–4.
[142] *C*, 7 July 1921, p. 11.
[143] Mountain, *Spurr and his Bible*, p. 2.
[144] *BH*, 1926, p. 258.
[145] Mountain, *Spurr and his Bible*, p. 7.

immensely popular as a speaker and writer for the Student Christian Movement.[146] His book *The Jesus of History* (1917) was widely appreciated, even by conservatives such as the devotional writer Oswald Chambers.[147] Later publications attracted less favourable attention. *Jesus in the Experience of Men* (1920), according to John Thomas, was well written but dangerous because built on the higher criticism.[148] *Progress in Religion* (1922), according to the unnamed *Baptist Times* reviewer, said things that would shake the faith of those accepting Scripture as the final court of appeal.[149] Most offence was taken at his weekly religious columns in *The Daily News*, where, for instance, he criticized the Fundamentalist for being weak-headed in spite of having a good heart.[150] In January 1923 Glover was nominated as vice-president of the Baptist Union, with automatic succession to the presidency in the following year. In the month before the election an anonymous article in *The Baptist Times* censured, alongside the ultra-conservative, 'the ultra-radical scholar, who has now left the cloistered charm of the class-room and entered the debating prize-ring'.[151] Glover, recognizing the portrait as himself, was stung into replying, but endorsed the author's plea for Christian reasonableness.[152] It was feared that the election would be a show-down. One of the other candidates, John Bradford, Chairman of Spurgeon's College Committee and a supporter of McCaig in the Sunday-school lesson controversy of 1920, might have made it so, but his backing was small.[153] The most serious opponent was T. S. Penny, Church Secretary at Silver Street, Taunton, whose claims to office rested on his services to the denominational Sustentation Scheme.[154] He was in no sense a candidate of the theological right, and so opinion did not polarize. Furthermore, Glover enjoyed much conservative support, because he had resisted Shakespeare's willingness to accept episcopacy for the sake of church unity.[155] Consequently Glover was elected vice-president by 798 votes to Penny's 544, the announcement being greeted by a 'great cheer'.[156]

---

[146] H. G. Wood, *Terrot Reaveley Glover: A Biography* (Cambridge, 1953), esp. p. 150.
[147] *Oswald Chambers: His Life and Work* (London, 1959 edn.), p. 164.
[148] *BT*, 4 Mar. 1921, p. 132.
[149] *BT*, 6 Oct. 1922, p. 635.
[150] *JWBU*, Mar. 1923, p. 58.
[151] 'The Peril of Extremes', *BT*, 23 Mar. 1923, p. 207.
[152] T. R. Glover to editor, *BT*, 6 Apr. 1923, p. 244.
[153] *BT*, 13 Apr. 1923, p. 259; 20 Apr. 1923, p. 286; 23 Jan. 1920, p. 57.
[154] *BT*, 13 Apr. 1923, p. 259; 2 Mar. 1923, p. 149.
[155] Wood, *Glover*, pp. 152–4.
[156] *BT*, 27 Apr. 1923, pp. 302–3.

On the next day Penny told Glover that he feared his election 'might injure the denomination'.[157] He was right, for the Fundamentalists began to mobilize. The support for Glover, James Mountain noted, showed that it was not just a few Baptists who were tainted with Modernism.[158] Glover's *Daily News* articles, Benjamin Greenwood told the Bible League, discussed the Scriptures with 'flippant humour and half-contemptuous comment'.[159] Greenwood did not improve his case by claiming that Glover supposed Paul to have transformed Jesus into a heathen demigod. Glover was able to point out that he was quoting an outlandish opinion in order to reject it.[160] Yet there was a trickle of churches leaving the Baptist Union: Drummond Road, Bermondsey; Romney Street, Westminster; and Onslow, South Kensington.[161] Mountain himself withdrew and set about creating a counter-Union. In September 1923 the Baptist Bible Union became the Bible Baptist Union, open to affiliation by churches. Onslow Baptist Church became the headquarters, a Workington church joined, and a Thornton Heath correspondent commended the 'New Baptist Union, free from the Modernism which has so long defiled the Old Union'.[162] It was all something of a fiasco. Within a few days of the inaugural meetings in January 1924 the Organizing Secretary resigned, and a few months later the title reverted to Baptist Bible Union.[163] The real alarm in the denomination was caused not by Mountain's antics, but by Fundamentalist activity in south Wales, for Glover was due to preside over the 1924 assembly of the Baptist Union in Cardiff. At the district meeting of the denomination R. B. Jones carried a resolution expressing concern at Glover's election. Copies of Jones's case against Glover were sent to each minister and lay delegate to the assembly.[164] Once more, however, there was an anticlimax. There were no protests at Cardiff, and Glover's impressive presidential address on the continuity of Christian experience down the ages found approval in conservative quarters—even in the journal of the BBU.[165] Baptist Fundamentalism was at its most salient in the Glover case, and yet even here its public impact was small.

Apprehension was all the greater at the time, however, because there

---

[157] Wood, *Glover*, p. 155.
[158] *BC*, June 1923, p. 81.
[159] *R*, 14 June 1923, p. 387.
[160] T. R. Glover to editor, *R*, 21 June 1923, p. 402.
[161] *BC*, July 1923, p. 112; Dec. 1923, p. 186; Feb. 1924, p. 30.
[162] *BC*, Nov. 1923, p. 164; Oct. 1923, pp. 150–3; Dec. 1923, p. 189; Apr. 1924, p. 59.
[163] *BC*, Feb. 1924, pp. 23, 25; June 1924, cover.
[164] Jones, *King's Champions*, p. 204.
[165] *LF*, 14 May 1924, p. 564. *BC*, June 1924, pp. 81–4.

was a parallel assault on the Baptist Missionary Society (BMS). Acting on an appeal from the Bible Union of China, early in 1922, the Bible League called on missionary societies to confirm that they sent out no one who doubted the full inspiration of Scripture.[166] Wright Hay, Secretary of the Bible League, issued a booklet claiming to lay bare the Modernism of the respected missionary Dr George Howells. Glover, who took an active interest in BMS work in India, declared that the booklet showed 'how far folly and venom can carry a man into falsity'.[167] Likewise, Watkin Roberts, a missionary to Assam now resident in Hampstead, published *The Ravages of Higher Criticism in the Indian Mission Field* and prompted fellow Welshmen to insist that the society should investigate the views of its agents. Certain Welshmen around R. B. Jones withdrew from the society's affairs; Henry Oakley, minister of Upper Tooting, left the general committee; and three missionaries resigned.[168] Matters became serious when, following the society's refusal to impose a fresh doctrinal test on candidates, a Missionary Trust Fund was established, with Watkin Roberts as secretary, to divert funds away from the BMS.[169] In the spring of 1923 a special sub-committee examined some twenty accusations made by Wright Hay and Roberts. The general committee endorsed its report vindicating the existing missionaries. At the 1923 assembly—where Glover was elected vice-president—W. Y. Fullerton, an officer of the society, was put up to advertise the loyalty of the denomination and its missionary arm to the evangelical faith.[170] It was doubly reassuring to find at the BMS meetings that the churches had contributed only £20 less than in the previous year and that there was a spontaneous resolution of confidence in the officers and committee.[171] The Missionary Trust, with James Mountain as its Baptist auxiliary leader and D. T. Morgan, one of the BMS men who had resigned, as its sole missionary, raised a total of £831 over the next five years.[172] Once more a Fundamentalist campaign produced scant results except ill feeling.

As a coda to the acrimony of the 1920s there was a further Fundamentalist dispute in the following decade. W. E. Dalling, a student for the ministry under A. C. Underwood, Principal of Rawdon College, resigned

---

[166] D. H. C. Bartlett to editor, *R*, 6 Apr. 1922, p. 224. *BC*, May 1922, pp. 36–8.
[167] T. R. Glover to editor, *R*, 21 June 1923, p. 402.
[168] *BC*, Jan. 1923, p. 10. Jones, *King's Champions*, pp. 192–3.
[169] *BC*, Jan. 1923, p. 8.
[170] *BT*, 27 Apr. 1923, pp. 296, 302.
[171] *BT*, 4 May 1923, p. 323.
[172] *C*, 4 Feb. 1926, p. 11. *BC*, May 1923, p. 75; July–Sept. 1928, p. 33.

in 1930 from the Baptist Union probationers' list in protest against the 'Modernist' teaching in the books he was recommended.[173] In self-vindication he tried to rouse others to witness against the apostasy in high places. He secured the backing of two Spurgeon's-College-trained men, but could not prod Percy Evans, Principal of the College, or Thomas Greenwood, Chairman of the College Council, into action. *The Fundamentalist* magazine, which had incorporated *The Bible Call* in 1928, noisily urged that they should follow Spurgeon in seceding from the Baptist Union.[174] Then a booklet prepared by T. R. Glover for a Baptist Union discipleship campaign fell into the hands of Dalling, who delightedly drew attention to the dismissal of the substitutionary doctrine of the Atonement in this 'subtle piece of modernist propaganda'.[175] To conservatives, the conviction that Christ died as a substitute for sinners rather than merely as their representative was at the heart of the Gospel. Thomas Greenwood felt compelled to request the withdrawal of the booklet. Glover, who had been freshly blooded in another Fundamentalist controversy in Canada in 1928, was disinclined to yield. The matter came to the Baptist Union Council on 7 March 1932. A compromise was worked out whereby Percy Evans would write an alternative booklet including the doctrine of substitution. It was unfortunate that four days later an article prepared some time before by Glover was published in *The Times* containing criticism of Spurgeon.[176] *The Fundamentalist* naturally found it offensive and continued fulminating for several months over 'The Crisis in the Baptist Churches',[177] but the compromise held. Apart from a few hotheads, there was clearly even less inclination to disrupt the denomination in the 1930s than there had been in the 1920s.

It remains to enquire why Fundamentalism, so mighty a force in America, should have made so little impact on British Baptists. The immediate answer lies in its failure to gather extensive support in Britain. Only 130 readers transferred subscriptions from *The Bible Call* to *The Fundamentalist* in 1928, and, although there were no doubt more subscribers in earlier days for which figures are not available, that gives some

---

[173] *The Fundamentalist* [hereafter *F*], Aug. 1930, pp. 176–7.

[174] *F*, Sept. 1931, pp. 206–7; Nov. 1931, pp. 258–60; Jan. 1932, p. 13. Thomas Greenwood was almost certainly Benjamin's brother.

[175] *F*, Dec. 1931, pp. 269–72. This controversy, together with Glover's theology, is reviewed in K. W. Clements, *Lovers of Discord: Twentieth-Century Theological Controversies in England* (London, 1988), pp. 107–29.

[176] Wood, *Glover*, pp. 158–63. The article was republished as 'Nonconformity Old and New' in *Fifty Years: Memories and Contrasts* (London, 1932), pp. 120–6.

[177] *F*, April 1932, p. 83; May 1932, pp. 97–100; July 1932, pp. 161–4; Sept. 1932, pp. 195–8.

indication of the small-scale nature of the operation.[178] Deficiencies in BBU funds were reported several times, and the only two generous donors were Benjamin Greenwood (£75 over 6 years) and J. A. Bolton, a Leicester children's-wear manufacturer, who was a member of Meyer's former church, Melbourne Hall (£163 over 8 years).[179] The substantial giving that sustained American Fundamentalist organizations did not materialize in Britain. That, in turn, is a reflection on the leadership. With Dixon returning to the United States, Wright Hay preoccupied with interdenominational matters, and Tydeman Chilvers disqualified by his Strict Baptist background, leadership devolved on James Mountain. His attention flitted from scheme to scheme—to anti-smoking, to a crusade against Communist Sunday schools, and especially to British Israelism, a fad that consumed his final years.[180] Repeatedly the BBU was restructured, each time on a narrower basis. Other figures—Marsh and Thomas, for example—clearly could not work with him and so moved on to other fields. Mountain was an elderly man with a grasshopper mind. He was not likely to inspire confidence that he could mount a strategy for the defence of western civilization.

Nor were the raw materials of a vigorous movement ready to hand. Both institutionally and ideologically British Fundamentalism was weaker than its American counterpart. Crucially, there was no equivalent to the American network of Bible colleges to encourage alumni to take a stand against denominational trends. In 1920 *The Bible Call* listed the training-colleges where approved teaching was given. Apart from Spurgeon's and Cardiff, there were only four institutions, of which by far the most substantial was the Bible Training Institute, Glasgow.[181] When visiting the United States, R. B. Jones was awed by the great Bible Institutes. Already, in 1919, he had begun a training-school that developed into the South Wales Bible Training Institute, and in 1924 Rees Howells launched the Bible College of Wales, with John Thomas as principal.[182] Both were too late to influence the events of the 1920s. Fundamentalists such as Benjamin Greenwood were still hoping to bring the denominational colleges to heel.[183] R. B. Jones's church, for instance,

---

[178] *F*, Dec. 1928, p. 268.
[179] *BC* donation lists. On Bolton, see E. E. Kendall, *Doing and Daring* (Rushden, n.d.), pp. 124–5.
[180] *BC*, Dec. 1925, p. 174; Oct. 1925, p. 144; Oct.–Dec. 1926, pp. 102–3.
[181] *BC*, Apr.–June 1920, p. 8.
[182] Jones, *King's Champions*, cap. 15. N. P. Grubb, *Rees Howells: Intercessor* (London, 1952), caps 25–37. *JWBU*, July 1924, p. 163.
[183] *BC*, July–Aug. 1921, p. 8.

demanded that Cardiff Baptist College should employ tutors only if they believed in 'the full inspiration of the scriptures'.[184] Spurgeon's, not affiliated to the Baptist Union in the inter-war years and the one institution that had produced a cadre of Fundamentalist activists, was, in fact, steered back by Percy Evans, tutor from 1922 and principal from 1925, towards denominational commitment. The other group of institutional agencies that might conceivably have roused Fundamentalist opinion, the undenominational faith missions, did not normally function in that way. It is true that there were significant personal links—McCaig and Mountain sponsored the Russian Missionary Society, and W. J. Ervine was a director of the Regions Beyond Missionary Union with F. B. Meyer[185]— but such missions served as outlets for separatist feeling that might otherwise have been channelled into domestic controversies. In Britain, Fundamentalism was not grafted on to an existing institutional stock.

The movement was also less ideologically self-assured than in America. The idea of biblical inerrancy, which provided a reference-point in American debates, was less widely canvassed in Britain. F. B. Meyer upheld it, and John Thomas set out the classic form of its *a priori* underpinning when he contended that, since Scripture is the word of God, all forms of human errancy must be excluded.[186] In the United States this axiom had been propagated by B. B. Warfield and other scholars, but in Britain declarations of loyalty to the Bible were less sharply defined and so less divisive.[187] Furthermore, the premillennialists of Britain were less sure of their ground than those across the Atlantic. In America, although there were differences of opinion on various points, the predominant prophetic teaching was dispensationalism, a precise classification of the dispensations, the different eras of human history. It emhasized the expectation that true Christians would have to withdraw from traditional churches in preparation for the Second Coming. In Britain dispensationalism had made less headway. It was often regarded as the distinctive property of the Brethren sect, and therefore suspect. R. B. Jones, for instance, was wary of it and so less inclined to sever his Baptist links.[188] On the other hand, another variety of premillennialism, the historicist school, was much

---

[184] Jones, *King's Champions*, p. 203.
[185] A. McCaig, *Grace Astounding in Bolshevik Russia* (London, n.d.). *R*, 21 July 1933, p. 423. *BC*, Apr. 1924, p. 60.
[186] *MBAPPU*, July 1920, pp. 105–6. *BT*, 5 Mar. 1920, p. 156.
[187] D. F. Wright, 'Soundings in the doctrine of Scripture in British Evangelicalism in the first half of the twentieth century', *Tyndale Bulletin*, 31 (1980), pp. 87–106.
[188] Jones, *King's Champions*, p. 138.

stronger in Britain. Meyer had to stress that controversy over the details of prophetic interpretation must not be introduced into Advent Testimony meetings or into churches.[189] So there was much less dogmatism about the British premillennialists. The ideological cutting-edge of Fundamentalism was less finely honed in Britain.

Moderation was more frequently a mark of the theologically conservative than in America. The early departures from the BBU were a symptom of the British aversion to extremism. So was the attitude of Douglas Brown, Minister of Ramsden Road, Balham, and the main preacher in the East Anglia revival of 1921. In the following year, although he was a keen premillennialist, Brown publicly expressed his abhorrence at the heresy hunters who were 'blackening the characters of good men'.[109] There are good reasons why there should have been more self-restraint than on the other side of the Atlantic. Painful memories of the Downgrade Controversy made certain Spurgeon's men, such as Percy Evans, eager to heal old wounds.[191] The Keswick movement, though encouraging Mountain and some others to take action, also fostered a mildness of manner. F. B. Meyer, who on occasion seems to have been tempted to lead a Fundamentalist coalition, was restrained not only by past services to the denomination, but also by the tone of Keswick. In America in 1926 he declined to discuss Fundamentalism since religion is 'not a matter of argument, but a spiritual force which may and should influence all'.[192] Developments in America also made Britons wish to avoid taking the same path. 'Let us clearly understand', wrote Graham Scroggie from the United States in 1924, 'that the interests of Christ and His Word are not served by raw haste, violent denunciation, presumptuous ignorance, or uncharitableness of spirit.'[193] In that year a desire to witness to basic Christian convictions without controversy led E. A. Carter, a Baptist minister who had led a mission for planting new causes since 1889, to found the Bible Testimony Fellowship.[194] Holding rallies over successive years and drawing in some previous extremists, it represented the conservative evangelical position—orthodox and revivalist, but moderate and charitable. That was far more widely supported among British Baptists than Fundamentalism.

[189] *MBAPPU*, July 1919, p. 203. Bebbington, 'Advent Hope', pp. 108–9.
[190] *BW*, 11 May 1922, p. 124.
[191] Payne, *Baptist Union*, p. 242.
[192] *LF*, 20 Oct. 1926, p. 1189.
[193] *LF*, 30 July 1924, p. 895.
[194] *LF*, 30 Jan. 1924, p. 122.

At bottom, circumstances were unpropitious in Britain for the Fundamentalist movement. In America the sheer size of the country emboldened local spokesmen of limited education, especially in the mid-west, to denounce unknown traitors to biblical truth, especially if they came from the sophisticated big cities of Chicago and the east coast. Britain was altogether different. The small size of the country and of the denomination meant that most Baptists of any standing knew each other personally. The social dynamics of committee meetings made denunciation difficult—for Thomas Greenwood in 1932, for instance. J. H. Shakespeare had done much to centralize denominational affairs.[195] While there were resulting resentments about official interference in individual churches, which led R. B. Jones's church, for example, to withdraw from the Sustentation Fund,[196] centralization permitted tight management. Thus in 1919 Shakespeare was able to use his editorial control over *The Baptist Times* to exclude the BBU's 'Protest and Appeal' against Free Church Federation.[197] Had the document received widespread attention at that point, when restiveness was at its peak, the BBU might have grown much stronger. Shakespeare's successor, M. E. Aubrey, who took up office in 1925, shared many conservative evangelical fears about the direction of denominational life.[198] Even Mountain detected a change for the better in the Baptist Union.[199] And the educational standards encouraged by the Union over the years had their effect. Some 75 per cent of Baptist ministers in the 1920s had been to theological college, and some 15 per cent had been to university as well.[200] Of the ministers on the BBU council in 1919–20, only 4 per cent had a university degree.[201] Higher educational attainments than in America probably explain why evolution was so minor a concern among British Baptists, receiving only occasional adverse comment.[202] They certainly explain why it was so difficult to drum up mass opposition to the higher criticism. Newer critical attitudes had been mediated to the denomination in the last years of the nineteenth

---

[195] Payne, *Baptist Union*, cap. 9.
[196] Jones, *King's Champions*, p. 204.
[197] *BC*, Oct.–Dec. 1919, p. 6.
[198] For example, about recreation eclipsing evangelism. *London City Mission Magazine*, Sept. 1930, p. 142.
[199] *BC*, July–Sept. 1927, p. 34.
[200] The figures are for entrants to the ministry in the period 1890–1919. K. D. Brown, *A Social History of the Nonconformist Ministry in England and Wales, 1800–1930* (Oxford, 1988), p. 60.
[201] That is, one out of twenty-four, excluding Irish representatives: John Thomas. *BC*, July–Sept. 1919, p. 8. *Baptist Bible Union Manifesto*, 3 Nov. 1920.
[202] *BC*, Nov. 1920, p. 3. *C*, 11 Feb. 1926, p. 4 (J. W. Thirtle).

century by John Clifford, Alexander McLaren, and others.[203] Although many Baptists still had their reservations, few were prepared at this late date to reject the higher criticism on principle. The state of the denomination was not receptive to Fundamentalism in the inter-war years.

The disputes of the period nevertheless left a legacy to the future. E. J. Poole-Connor, the chairman of a BBU meeting in 1921, launched in the following year a body to draw together unattached evangelical congregations upholding inerrancy.[204] As the Fellowship of Independent Evangelical Churches, it was to attract a succession of dissident Baptist churches over the years. Several men associated with R. B. Jones were to rise to prominence within it.[205] By 1935, when B. S. Fidler, Senior Tutor of Jones's Bible Training Institute, was the preacher at the thirteenth annual assembly of the F.I.E.C., there were 130 ministers and 22 probationers on its accredited list.[206] Another organization gathering together those troubled by Modernism in the denomination, but in this case remaining loyal to it, was the Baptist Revival Fellowship. It emerged in the 1930s under the leadership of T. M. Bamber, Minister of Rye Lane, Peckham, a speaker at Principal McCaig's farewell from Spurgeon's College in 1926— the so-called 'second R. B. Jones'.[207] In the 1960s the Fellowship was to provide a focus for opposition within the denomination to ecumenical, centralizing, and liberalizing tendencies.[208] In 1944 there was to be a Fundamentalist controversy among the Baptists of Scotland which led for a while to the creation of a separate Bible college.[209] But the greatest effects of Baptist Fundamentalism were in Wales. Under the leadership of R. B. Jones the movement had gathered disproportionate strength in the principality. From the two new Bible colleges flowed a stream of entrants to the ministry whose allegiance to their denomination came second to the beliefs they had imbibed as students. There was potential support for an interdenominational organization emphasizing unity in basic Christian truths. Such a body was to emerge in 1955 as the Evangelical Movement of

[203] W. B. Glover, *Evangelical Nonconformists and Higher Criticism in the Nineteenth Century* (London, 1954), p. 139.

[204] *BC*, Mar.–Apr. 1921, p. 7. D. G. Fountain, *E. J. Poole-Connor (1872–1962): Contender for the Faith* (Worthing, 1966), pp. 121–8. *LF*, 16 Jan. 1924, p. 60.

[205] Jones, *King's Champions*, p. 244 (D. M. Russell-Jones). *AW*, Sept.–Oct. 1928, p. 361 (E. Buckhurst Pinch).

[206] *C*, 7 Mar. 1935, p. 6.

[207] *C*, 22 Apr. 1926, p. 20. *AW*, Jan. 1932, cover. Jones, *King's Champions*, p. 167.

[208] *Liberty in the Lord: Comment on Trends in Baptist Thought Today* (London, 1964).

[209] I. L. S. Balfour, 'The Twentieth Century since 1914', in D. W. Bebbington, ed., *The Baptists in Scotland: A History* (Glasgow, 1988), p. 74.

Wales, under the inspiration of Martyn Lloyd-Jones, the influential Minister of Westminster Chapel, who had been befriended in his early ministry in Wales by R. B. Jones himself.[210] The Fundamentalists did contribute to subsequent developments.

Yet their impact at the time was small. 'In spite of little ripples on the surface', commented *The Baptist Times* on the eve of the 1923 assembly, 'the great deeps of our Denominational life were never stronger nor more peaceful than now . . .'.[211] It was the climax of the BMS controversy, and T. R. Glover's election was imminent, yet, if allowance is made for a little wishful thinking, the assessment is fair. The contrast with strife-ridden America is striking. Only in Wales was there a stir at all comparable with the controversies of the United States. The English leadership failed to mobilize a mass movement; there were few Bible colleges; biblical inerrancy and dispensationalism were weaker; there were conservative evangelicals exercising moderation; the denomination was more tightly knit and better educated. But also, evangelical Christians had less far to fall. In America the long-lasting evangelical cultural hegemony was being displaced by Catholic immigrants and secular-minded entrepreneurs. Fundamentalists saw themselves as the defenders of western civilization. In Wales there had been a comparable evangelical dominance, for the chapels enjoyed the support of about three-quarters of the churchgoers in the early twentieth century. Their place in society was being undermined by English immigrants and secular influences.[212] Certain leaders of Nonconformity, especially Welsh speakers such as R. B. Jones, were naturally inclined to cultural defence. In England, however, Nonconformity had never held sway since the Commonwealth of the mid-seventeenth century. There had been an evangelical social ascendancy in the mid-nineteenth century, but it had been steadily eroded since.[213] Baptists were too marginal to English society for threats to their position to be alarming. In few places, apart from Tunbridge Wells with its continuing evangelical ethos, did Christian civilization seem about to crumble. Fundamentalism could make little headway among English Baptists.

University of Stirling

[210] J. E. Davies, *Striving Together: A Statement of the Principles that have governed the Aims and Policies of the Evangelical Movement of Wales* (Bridgend, 1984), p. 5. I. H. Murray, *David Martyn Lloyd-Jones: The First Forty Years, 1899–1939* (Edinburgh, 1982), p. 193.

[211] *BT*, 20 Apr. 1923, p. 271.

[212] K. O. Morgan, *Rebirth of a Nation: Wales, 1880–1980* (Oxford, 1981), pp. 136, 197–201.

[213] Bebbington, *Evangelicalism*, cap. 4.

THE JUSTIFICATION OF THE GODLESS: HEINRICH VOGEL AND GERMAN GUILT

by HADDON WILLMER

G UILT has proved an irresistible category for making and interpreting the twentieth-century history of which Germany has
been the focus. In that history individuals, organizations, and
nations have become guilty. The history of guilt is not made by the
wrongdoers alone, but also by those who judge them. Doing wrong and
being moralistic often have an evil symbiosis in individuals and communities. Guilt has not always been accurately allocated, and accusations
of guilt have been manipulated for political purposes so producing more
complex evil. There was guilt for the First World War, but it was
untruthfully imposed on Germany alone by Article 231 of the Versailles
Treaty.[1] Within Germany, assigning guilt to political opponents, while
refusing to accept any responsibility for what had happened, intensified
the divisions within the nation and ensured that its policies were inspired
by inward as well as outward enmity and unreality. The theologian H. J.
Iwand argued in 1954 that the Nazis had taken the *Freund-Feind* conception of politics to absurdity, blaming (*versündigt*) the Left for all that
happened after 1918. Consequently, Iwand judged the nationalist front in
the Weimar Republic to have represented *die organisierte Unbussfertigkeit* of
the German people.[2] Too late, after 1945, it had become politically clear
to many, but not to all, that complex historical guilt must be met by a
complex response lest its power escalate yet again beyond the control of
truth, understanding, and humanity.

This history of guilt happened within a nation which could in some
respects still be described as Christian. At least there were many who were
anxious to preserve and work within a Christian interpretation of the
nation. Germany was, moreover, a nation whose evangelical Christianity
had a distinctive understanding of guilt and forgiveness: Luther produced
a tradition which centred attention on the divine suffering of human guilt
in the Cross of Jesus Christ, through which the sinners were forgiven and

---

[1] Klaus Scholder, *Die Kirchen zwischen Republik und Gewaltherrschaft* ed. K. O. von Aretin and
G. Besier (Berlin, 1988), pp. 59–63.
[2] H. J. Iwand, 'Die Verkundigung des Evangeliums und die politische Existenz', *Theologische
Existenz Heute*, NS 41 (1954), pp. 12–16.

justified. Profound sensitivity for, and insight into, the history of political guilt might be expected, if the fear of interpreting politics by Gospel, rather than Law, were overcome. In the twentieth century, the pressure of political guilt helped to break down these inhibitions, but the theme remains confusing and controversial. Christians in Germany did not come without adaptable spiritual resources to the near unimaginable guilts which overtook people in that history, with and without their co-operation. In season, and, it might seem, too often out of season, the Lutheran theologian and hymn-writer, Heinrich Vogel, explored and expounded his theological tradition through various episodes of this history of guilt: his work allows us to see both its resources, obscurities, inhibitions, and possibilities.

Around 1930, when Vogel was a young and lively pastor under General Superintendent Otto Dibelius in Berlin, there was a flurry of anxiety in the Church about the *Gottlosenbewegung*, as it was known.[3] Anticlerical free-thinkers had been active for many years: in 1930, the *Deutsche Freidenkerverband* claimed that in twenty-five years it had recruited 600,000 members, while two million had left the churches.[4] The churches felt any decline in membership as a threat to their power and their credibility as *Volkskirchen*. As the crisis of the Weimar Republic deepened, the Communist minority in this movement, modelling itself on the Russian anti-God movement, became more active: for the Marxist *Gottlosen*, fighting against religion was fighting for Socialism. In these circumstances, the Church found it hard to represent and defend its own cause, however that was understood, without becoming political and yet more anti-socialist. The *Gottlosen* were active in the schools, which churches regarded possessively as their spiritual responsibility and a crucial means of preserving the Christian character of national life. The churches had always resented the socialist determination after 1919 to treat religion as a private matter, taking from it any corporate public status. The *Gottlosen* were seen as the shock-troops and the shocking outcome and warning signal of the secularization. Fear of the *Gottlosen* increased Christians' susceptibility to Hitler's vague and fraudulent avowal of 'positive Christianity'. When the Confessing Church wrote directly to Hitler, in 1936, one of their major complaints about his regime was that the de-

---

[3] Konrad Algermissen, *Die Gottlosenbewegung der Gegenwart und ihre Uberwindung* (Hanover, 1933), pp. 253, 264; Kurt Bohme, 'Die Gottlosen-Bewegung', *Die Christliche Welt*, 12 (1931), pp. 563–5.

[4] H. Waldenmeier, 'Antichristentum und Kirche', *Das Evangelisches Deutschland* (1931), pp. 241–2, 250–1.

Christianizing of public life had speeded up since the end of the Weimar Republic. They had expected Hitler to reverse the trend and were disappointed because his effects on German society were too close to what they had feared from the *Gottlosen*; he was not protecting Germany from the godlessness, which, in the Christian view, was the ultimate danger of Bolshevism.[5]

In 1931, Dibelius rallied his Church to 'make an evangelical Front against the *Gottlosen*', taking banners on to the streets in demonstrations of the Church's popular strength. Vogel brought a *Kirchentag* to a halt by protesting against this plan.[6] His argument was that the Church should not make fronts, because they would always essentially be *against* someone. Even the godless should not find the Church against them, because Christ died not against, but for and in solidarity with, the godless. With the help of Barth's commentary on Romans, but mostly working directly from Paul in a Lutheran way, Vogel thus insisted on reading what was, for the Church, a political issue in strictly theological terms.

Vogel's line of argument could not have been invented by an English Christian. The English Christian is not imbued with Luther's theology or Luther's Bible. The English Authorized Version never used the word godless; Luther used *gottlos* significantly in Romans 5.6 (Christ died for the godless: AV, ungodly). A further deprivation of the English is their not having the German language. For the German *gottlos*, English gives us the cooler 'atheist', which conceals the negation of God behind largely forgotten Greek; the adjective 'ungodly', which has a moral rather than a theological tone and would not be adopted proudly as a self-description by Atheists; 'secularist' makes its positive point without disturbing respectability by the least hint that God is under attack; only for old-fashioned militants, who are prepared to sound cranky, is there 'anti-God'. There is no widely-used word that has the nuance of the German, *gottlos*. The suffix *-los* has an exploitable ambiguity: it means the word can be a shout of liberation, filled with the energy and confidence of humanity in the act of breaking free from the ultimate tyrant, God; it can also pinpoint the essence of sin, as consisting in the rejection of, and sustained opposition to, God, a conception which goes beyond all moralism. In Romans 5. 10, the godless for whom Christ died are identified as the enemies of God.

---

[5] M. Greschat, *Zwischen Widerspruch und Widerstand* (Munich, 1987), pp. 152–3.

[6] Heinrich Vogel, 'Die christliche Solidarität mit dem Gottlosen', *Die Stimme der Gemeinde*, 12 (1960), pp. 679–84; also in *Monatsschrift für Pastoral Theologie*, 27 (1931), pp. 326 ff.; F. W. Marquardt, 'Solidarität mit den Gottlosen', *Vom Herrengeheimnis der Wahrheit*, ed. K. Scharf (Berlin, 1962), pp. 381–405.

In Vogel's work, biblical and dogmatic material became flexible, pointed, and pithy in a poet's hands. The result was an interpretation of Christ's dying for and in solidarity with the godless, which Vogel treated as hard fact. Realistic people simply had to live with it. It was not a mere idea in the theological game. He proclaimed it as though it had fundamental implications for policy-making and action. It was not clear in any detail, however, what would actually happen if the Church were for, rather than against, the *Gottlosen*, except that it would not be mobilized against them as Dibelius wanted. On one hand, Vogel's theology grounded in the Gospel a presumption in favour of action that makes for reconciliation with enemies. On the other, he did not pretend that there were not serious differences between Christians and Marxists. He was passionate in his opposition to what he saw as their *Vergöttlosung* of children. He did not look for a political reconciliation that might allow them to implement their policies. Beyond cultural differences and political conflicts, he saw the *Gottlosen* as people before God, who could not be excluded from those for whom Christ died.

Vogel's main concern was with the Church rather than with secular politics: in this he was typical of what was to become the Confessing Church. Did the Church understand what made it 'Church'? Did it see what it meant that the Church rested on no other basis than that Christ died for the ungodly? If the Church developed itself as though it rested on any other basis, it would be breaking solidarity with the godless and therefore with Christ. When that solidarity was lost, it turned itself into a 'pious party', for whom it would be natural to make fronts against the godless. This concern with the deformed Church recurs throughout Vogel's work. In 1937, he published a book, translated into English in 1941 as *The Iron Ration of a Christian*. There is perhaps too much theological iron in it for the average English stomach. Vogel wrote of the Church's 'most intimate secret': 'those who belong to it are judged and acquitted by none other than by him who came in their place and intercedes for them, by the crucified and risen Lord of the church'. Once more, he attacked the notion that the Church was a limited company for religion or a pious party for good people.

> When I was visiting the house of an intelligent and decent working man, he said to me: 'Herr Pastor, I've told you many a time that I don't go to church. I'm not good—but I'm not godless.' The story pleases me because it illustrates so clearly what they all think, educated and ignorant, men and women from the most varied call-

ings and stations in life: they think that they can see in the church a pious party they would rather not belong to. If the church were really a party of the pious in a godless world, it would be much wiser not to have anything to do with it; for the God of such a pious party would be the very Devil of Pride. Furthermore, it would find a fundamental solidarity with that working man, by accepting the unspoken assumption that we men are capable of knowing and judging whether we are good or wicked. In the church of Jesus Christ, all such self-assessment is impossible. There we are brought under a judgment very different from that of men, and we are acquitted by a forgiveness which no power on earth can affect. He who judges us and acquits us is the Holy Spirit.[7]

A practical churchman like Dibelius might well find Vogel's theological approach to politically charged questions hard to accept both for its apparent impracticability and because it was directed critically to the Church. Would reinterpreting godlessness in the light of the divine justification of sinners overcome the threat to Christianity posed by Marxism, atheism, and secularism? Dibelius wanted observable historical achievement in the preservation and recovery of organized Christianity as a faith with constructive human and cultural consequences. To him, as to the modern secularized person, Vogel's approach offered hardly a foothold, almost no point of contact. The mere assertion of his view was a challenge to people to be converted: to acknowledge their godlessness and to let God be God. Theological practice was to be intellectual obedience to the First Commandment: God was not to be compared or merged with anything other than God, the Source and Judge, Lord and Saviour of all reality. To advocate such a theology was to uncover widespread godlessness, for who revered God in this way as the only Lord of life? It is a way of preaching the Law so that everyone is seen to have no hope if the godless are not justified.

Many observers, then and now, would think that to work with such an intense theological realism as the Weimar Republic staggered into the Third Reich was a failure in immediate human responsibility, resting on a misjudgement of what the situation required. Was this kind of theology merely the effect and the defence of the Church's self-concern in a secularizing context where it was losing status? Were the Marxist

---

[7] Heinrich Vogel, *The Iron Ration of a Christian*, trans. W. A. Whitehouse (London, 1941), pp. 178–98.

Gottlosen not right to argue that such theological concern with God in the purity of his revelation obstructed and displaced relevant action in defence of real human interests?

The question whether Vogel's theological concentration conflicted with the urgent demands of any decent political morality becomes more acute in view of his attempting to respond to the German Christians theologically, just as he had done to the Marxists, on the basis of the divine justification of the godless. Now that we are blessed by hindsight, it is obvious to us that, while it was inappropriate for the Church to be merely anti-Communist, Nazism was an enemy of humanity and of God with which there ought to have been no peace. In that conflict, a theology of reconciliation through God's solidarity with his enemies would be suspected of dangerous unreality. Vogel risked that suspicion when, in 1933, he addressed a set of theses to the German Christians.[8] His theological attack did not imply, he said, an indifference to the new political developments, for he wrote 'in hopeful solidarity with the struggle for our people led by the German National Socialism of Adolf Hitler'. He rather wanted to protest against the way the German Christians were mixing up the godly (*Göttlicher*) and the earthly, the Gospel and politics. He was not protesting against the swastika as a token of 'our German *Volkstum*', but against mixing the swastika with the Cross. His prime aim in making that distinction was to safeguard faith. A genuine *Glaubensbewegung* would come only from the Cross not the swastika, because the movement of faith was from God not from human political work. At a meeting of pastors in Potsdam at this time, Vogel is said to have called out: 'Imagine the Faith Movement of the German Christians without the Party's support, and neither faith nor movement will be there'.[9]

Vogel was concerned to make a theological argument within the Church. Though its occasion was the rise of a blatantly politicized movement within the Church, he looked for a disciplined theological audience: or was his asking that the theses should not be misread as a political statement a sign that he already knew that such a hearing was unlikely? It is hard to believe that Vogel was unaware of the critical political significance of some of the arguments which he developed within the limits, which, because one of his aims was to assert and respect the difference between Church and politics, he accepted for himself. The theses imply a theology of humanity comprised of all human beings. Humanity is perceived at,

---

[8] Heinrich Vogel, 'Kreuz und Hakenkreuz', *Zwischen den Zeiten*, 11. 3 (1933), pp. 201–6.
[9] Vogel, *Iron Ration*, p. 7.

and defined by, the Cross, the point where all human beings were together caught in and overwhelmed by godlessness, so that all sectional pride and judgemental antagonisms were invalidated. Vogel's witness to the unity of humanity is thus coupled with an attack on all self-righteousness. Religion of various kinds might confirm and crown human values, but the Cross, the human failure to recognize and respect God in his coming, cannot be pressed into that service. Rather it reveals that the common human situation was sinful. Vogel resisted any reading of the story of Jesus which saw him as the crown of humanity: Jesus is Lord, but only as the Lamb of God who bears the sin of the world, not as an ethical hero or religious leader. Israel also was to be interpreted in a way which both undercut any confidence in merely human, godless, achievement and upheld human solidarity. Not because of some special inherent virtue was Israel chosen by God, but as the people in whom the Saviour of the world was born and crucified. Where salvation appears, there must be sin to require it. Jesus was crucified amongst the Jews but not by the Jews alone: Vogel immediately said that all peoples, *auch wir Deutschen*, were guilty together (*mitschuldig*) for the Cross of Christ.

In this theological criticism of the German Christians, Vogel can be seen to strike provocatively at some of the central passions of Nazism. He put Germans together with Jews as godless sinners. He made God's reconciliation of all the world through his solidarity with the godless the basis of all judgement about the relations between groups. His fear that the theses might be politically misunderstood and misused was not unreasonable. Some of his later remarks could have stirred the still glowing embers of the *Fall Dehn*, which had run from 1928, when Günther Dehn gave a lecture on *Kirche und Völkerversöhnung*, until 1932, when Nazi opposition forced him to give up the attempt to teach at the University of Halle.[10] In the 1928 lecture, Dehn had argued that war was, at best, a hard necessity in a fallen, disordered world. It should not be romanticized. Theological treatments of war should be honest. It should be acknowledged, for example, that those who were killed in war had themselves been ready to kill, so that it was impossible to liken their death to the sacrificial death of Christ. John 15. 13 (Greater love hath no man than this, that he lay down his life for his friends) should not therefore be inscribed on war memorials, which should be set up in civic places not churches. He was most

---

[10] G. Dehn, *Kirche und Völkerversöhnung* (Berlin, 1931), pp. 6–23, 83–6; E. Bizer, 'Der "Fall Dehn"', in W. Schneemelcher, ed., *Festschrift für Günther Dehn* (Neukirchen, 1957), pp. 238–61.

concerned to draw the line between Church and State clearly, so that Church should be Church. His lecture was neither pacifist nor disrespectful of the war dead but it touched the same raw nationalist and veteran nerves that even Otto Dibelius irritated by his book *Friede auf Erden?*[11]

Vogel was a friend and supporter of Dehn's. In the theses of 1933 he argued, like Dehn, that all life in this world was within the orders of fallen creation. The conditions brought about by the Fall should not be absolutized: they were temporary, lasting only until the Day of Jesus Christ brought the new creation. For the moment, however, this order held; it followed that, if the nations existing within that order were owed loyalty (which Vogel did not doubt) it included war service. Those who gave their lives in war for the nation should therefore be honoured, but without ever suggesting that they had escaped the limits of fallen human achievement. The war dead, however honourable, were not saints. *Kriegsgehorsam* could not be good in itself: it lived only from the forgiveness of sins. War was no part of paradise, but was the hard law over this sinful world, which was preserved only by God in grace.

The word from the Cross could only ever be the seal of the forgiveness of sins. Only in judgement did the word of the Cross promise grace. So the Church was not, as German Christians thought, the expression of the faith-powers of the German people. Those powers were empty: 'we are beggars'.

In 1931, Vogel spoke of the justification of the godless in order to argue for a different attitude on the part of the Church towards those outsiders who were, and who proclaimed themselves, godless. In 1933, the same theological theme was addressed to those who were confident in their contemporary living godliness. If Vogel might be thought to have had a long-term theological strategy, it could be characterized as following Paul in showing how God 'concluded them all in unbelief, that he might have mercy upon all' (Romans 11. 32). Of course, people like the German Christians were too confident for a long time after 1933 to have ears for Vogel's message, but history was not on the side of those who put their trust and hopes in it and believed that they understood and could master it. On the contrary, history took them deep into unlooked-for godlessness.

In 1945, Vogel's theology was more immediately intelligible to many ordinary people than it had been earlier. The confident political religiosity

---

[11] Otto Dibelius, *Friede auf Erden?* (Berlin, 1930); F. Gollert, *Dibelius vor Gericht* (Munich, 1959), pp. 12–31.

of the Third Reich was discredited by its negative achievements. Politics itself had exposed people to, rather than sheltered them against, basic questions about the meaning and worth of humanity. Even in 1945, however, Vogel's theology remained a challenge to faith and humility. And many were too tired and disorientated to grieve or to bother with issues beyond the immediate minimal tasks of ensuring survival.

Vogel told a synod that the question. ' What has the church to say now?' was being put 'with the force of an ultimate question'. 'Because it rises from the cries and the silence of innumerable people who are in the grip of an ultimate question, there is no possibility of softened or evasive answers'. Since an ultimate question was essentially the question of God, it was only before God and from his word that the Church and its responsible synods could find what to say to people. Human tribunals with their own standards properly raised the question of guilt, but more radically it was 'for us to hear it put by God and be silent'.

> The unutterable confusion of conscience in which today countless Christians are worrying about this question . . . can in the last resort be explained only by their ignorance of the only place where this question can be heard and answered in an ultimate sense: that is, before the judgment seat of Him with Whom there is grace . . . those who stand there are in a peculiar way set apart . . . they are taken out of the region of human accusation and human excuse, human assessments of guilt and innocence, relative guilt and relative innocence to a place where, on the one hand, the question of guilt is made immensely more radical, and, on the the other hand, a promise shines of which the world with its thought-forms and judgments knows nothing.[12]

Vogel reckoned seriously though unsystematically with all the dimensions of guilt which Karl Jaspers analysed in *Die Schuldfrage*.[13] There was the political guilt which belonged to a nation in its continuing history, shared by all citizens merely through their historical belonging, regardless of choice or personal actions. Criminal guilt applied to those who could be legally called to account for what they had done. Vogel expected these guilts to be treated in appropriate ways and did nothing to provide a religious escape from them, as though God's forgiveness made legal process

---

[12] Heinrich Vogel, *The Grace of God and German Guilt*, trans. W. A. Whitehouse (London, 1947), pp. 12–13.
[13] Karl Jaspers, *Die Schuldfrage* (Heidelberg, 1946).

redundant. He attacked the widespread 'plague' of self-justification, which arose especially in the face of de-Nazification and the trials of war criminals. Beyond these sorts of guilts which the politicians and lawyers were properly busy with, Vogel spoke with profound sensitivity of guilts which could not be easily treated in these ways, though they were in some way shared public historical realities. At this level, Jaspers distinguished moral and metaphysical guilts. Moral guilt occurred when the conscience was aware of the commission of, or complicity in, evil. Much that lay outside the carefully defined competence of legal process would be caught in this net.

Metaphysical guilt is an especially interesting category for any attempt to understand the relevance to actual human living of what a theologian like Vogel was talking about. Like moral guilt, according to Jaspers, it is known by the conscience, not by public law. Moral guilt is to be felt for actions where there was a failure to do some possible good. Metaphysical guilt may be suffered where people had no power to do good, for failure to do impossible good. It may be useless in a police state to attempt to do anything when one sees people being treated cruelly and unjustly: protest will not save the victims and may merely ensure the protester's death. Almost all who survive such a state will be conscious that they did so by virtue of keeping silent. Because they were powerless, criminal or moral guilt are mostly not appropriate categories. But against metaphysical guilt, powerlessness is no defence, because this guilt arises from a failure of solidarity with the victim. One possible course of action was to die like the victims, not necessarily to protect them or even to protest on their behalf, for both might be impossible to achieve, but to dissociate oneself totally from the society which was cruel and unjust. Jaspers said that thousands had committed suicide rather than continue to live on the terms offered by the regime, which included not acting for those in need but rather systematically distancing oneself in order to protect one's powerless life. On this analysis, survivors were intrinsically guilty, because survival could only have been achieved by a denial of co-humanity with the oppressed. Vogel did not use Jaspers's terms; but Jaspers is useful in any attempt to understand what was happening in Germany immediately after the end of the war. There was a danger that all kinds of guilt would be assimilated to the obvious criminal guilt of some. Most Germans rightly repudiated criminal guilt for themselves, but if that was the only model of guilt available in public awareness, there would be a serious danger of silencing the discussion of guilt altogether and becoming inarticulate about burdensome, albeit 'metaphysical' aspects of experience which ought not to be forgotten. The Germans, in Jaspers' view, faced a vital choice, on which their humanity depended, between accepting guilt truthfully or sinking into merely living without any transcendent meaning, with no more genuine seeking for God (*kein eigentliches Gottsuchen mehr*). For Jaspers, these guilts had to be dealt with by and in the individual conscience; his theory had a privatizing tendency. Vogel was also aware of guilt which went beyond the criminal, but in the Church, he believed, there was a public idiom for the communal sharing of the more than private experience of guilt before God.

He preached sombrely on *Luther's legacy to us today* to mark the four-hundredth anniversary of the Reformer's death. All he could find for this commemoration in 1946 were Luther's words, quoted before in the theses of 1933: ' We are beggars! That's the truth.' [14] This saying summarized 'the message of the justification of the godless in Christ'. He related it to 'our German guilt and our German distress': what had befallen Germany was not incomprehensible tragedy but judgement. The nature of that judgement was recognizable as the mystery of the Cross, 'that Jesus Christ Himself was burnt in the gas-chambers of Auschwitz ... God hangs on the Cross of Jesus Christ, in the midst of our death, of our sin, and of our hell, and hangs there as our brother!' Vogel saw the Cross not only as hope for those who suffer, but as the judgement of the guilty:

> What must it be like for a murderer to hear that Christ has identified himself with the murdered victim, though he be the least of all His brethren, and that the murderer is therefore guilty not only towards men but towards God himself, and deserving therefore of eternal death? And what must it be like for him to go to execution admitting that 'we receive the due reward of our deeds,' and to hear from the lips of the Christ he has murdered the gracious sentence which saves him, not from execution but from eternal judgment? This is a great mystery. To the atheist it is a grotesque fancy, and to the moral religious man it is an outrageous monstrosity. And only from deep humiliation can His grace be experienced and His wisdom adored.

Vogel was not the only theologian to respond to the German situation in such terms. Early in 1945, Barth published a pamphlet, *The Germans and Ourselves*. In a key section, Barth asked what the Swiss owed the Germans, which was not, Barth said, what the Germans deserved, but what they

[14] Vogel, *Grace*, pp. 28, 35.

needed.[15] Above all, they needed friends. 'A man is another man's friend when he is not against him but *for* him.' Being friends meant being unconditionally for them, neither waiting for their conversion nor putting them on probation. Barth distinguished friends from teachers. A teacher was necessarily, in a limited way, against his pupils, judging and examining them. The Germans knew teachers too well to let themselves be helped by them. Barth claimed that the Germans lacked the belief that 'man can be man's friend, that he can be unconditionally for him instead of against him, that such a thing does exist in the world.' Or,

> Put in another way, what the Germans have always lacked and what they must get along without now is a firm grip of what forgiveness is; that men can be for one another in spite of the fact that they have much against one another which they cannot overlook and forget. That this apparently intimate Christian possibility of forgiveness is both strong in itself and the deepest wisdom of a strong policy, has always seemed to the Germans to be a Utopian thought. . . .

A little later, he insists that 'Jesus Christ is unconditionally for them. . . . He is for us in no other way than He is for them.' The parallels with Vogel's language are interesting but not surprising, since Vogel had been closely related to Barth since the 1920s. Barth at the war's end made the argument as concrete and all-embracing as Vogel, when he said that Christ's invitation, 'Come unto me' is addressed to

> you unlikeable ones, you wicked Hitler boys and girls, you brutal S.S. soldiers, you evil Gestapo police, you sad compromisers and collaborationists, all you men of the herd who have moved so long in patient stupidity behind your so-called leader. . . . Come unto me, I know you well, but I do not ask who you are and what you have done, I see only that you have reached the end and must start afresh, for good or ill. I will refresh you, I will start afresh from zero with you. If these Swiss, swollen with democratic and social and Christian ideas which they have always extolled, are not interested in you, I am interested . . . I am for you, I am your friend.

For all the similarities, there is a significant difference between these two addresses. Vogel the German was perhaps more determined to avoid preaching an easy forgiveness through the identification of Christ with the godless, the sinners as well as the victims. Vogel found ways to speak

[15] Karl Barth, *The Germans and Ourselves*, trans. R. Gregor Smith (London, 1945), pp. 34–40.

pastorally to guilty and suffering together, without blurring the distinction between them. He did nothing to undermine the punitive processes dealing with criminal guilt: in his interpretation, the criminal's guilt was deepened by being understood christologically. Such guilt was intensified because of the way forgiveness was possible: it only comes from the hands of the ultimate and representative victim.

Barth the Swiss was primarily addressing his own people, who in his view were in great danger of turning out to be like the Pharisee in the parable of the two men who went to the temple to pray.[16] His target was not the pathetic self-righteousness of the obviously guilty who made excuses, but the plausible self-righteousness of those who had somehow come out on the right side. The Swiss played the role in Barth's argument of the Church as a pious party in Vogel's. To counteract the tendency to self-righteousness, Barth invented 'an instructed German', neither arrogant nor narrow-minded, who questioned whether the political course of Switzerland in relation to Nazi Germany gave the Swiss, including Barth, the moral right to judge or despise the Germans. This long passage amounts to a Swiss *Schulderklärung*.[17]

To expose and eliminate self-righteousness from the politics of victory and the renovation of Europe is an example of a concern that can be found from the earliest stages of Vogel's thought. He and others aimed to avoid a specific corruption of moral criticism in political and social relations which was commonly labelled *Pharisaertum*.

The image of the Pharisee was taken from the Gospels to identify the sort of criticism which stands aloof from and refuses solidarity or friendship with the object of criticism. Even in a genuinely good critic the refusal of solidarity would reduce the moral power of the criticism; but, in many cases, it was probably a device to conceal the badness and self-interest of the critic. In the controversy about how to respond to the *Gottlosenbewegung*, some thought that making fronts against them was almost inevitably pharisaical. Waldenmeier sought to preserve the Church from making pharisaic judgements by asking it to recognize its own responsibility for the development of modern atheism. Penitence on the part of the Church was called for as the only protection against pharisaism.[18] In the same controversy, Benjamin Unruh thought it *pharisaisch* to explain what was happening in the Soviet Union after 1917 by referring only to

---

[16] *Ibid.*, pp. 41, 45–6; Luke 18. 9–14.
[17] *Ibid.*, pp. 49–57.
[18] Waldenmeier, 'Antichristentum', p. 250.

Orthodoxy and tsarist autocracy in pre-revolutionary Rusia. He argued that neither political nor Christian Europe was free from *grossen Mitschuld* for the fearful catastrophe. At the same time, he warned against the discernible tendency for talk of the guilt of Christians to become mere rhetoric: when that occurred, it was easy to behave pharisaically under the guise of the paradoxical righteousness of the tax-collector. The real guilt was not to let God be God: 'Unsere Schuld ist die praktische Gottlosigkeit, die die theoretische dann jederzeit zu ihrer Selbstrechtfertigung hervortreiben kann. Und hier gilt es eine wirkliche Umkehr.'[19]

When the ecumenical representatives went to Stuttgart in October 1945, Pierre Maury said in response to the Declaration made by the Council of the Evangelical Church: 'Wir wollen es annehmen ohne pharisaischen Stolz, sondern auch vor Gott.'[20] Whether the churches outside Germany, any more than the governments and peoples of other nations, generally avoided pharisaism in regard to Germany is open to question, but the sincerity of Maury is as clear as the relevance of the concept for those who wish to work through shared, but rarely equal, guilt towards new hope. Precisely because practical politics in Church as in State often lacks the time and the breadth of spirit to avoid using guilt pharisaically, it is important that its dangers are identified and alternative ways practically explored somewhere in human society.

Pharisaism denies human solidarity. To be pharisaical in any critical judgement upon Nazism would mean that, although it was apparently condemned, its refusal of human solidarity through love and forgiveness was shared by the judges. The political task after 1945 required the re-affirmation of basic and universal human values, the recovery and upholding, or the honest mourning, of the humanity of millions of human beings. There was no way forward in pharisaism. The penitence of the tax-collector was one promising biblical model. Another was the lost sheep, as Barth hinted when he said the Germans were given 'a rare distinction above the ninety-nine righteous', for they had been brought to a situation where they had to start afresh. He looked 'with awe' upon them because historical opportunities for whole peoples to begin again were rare.[21] By suggesting that they needed friends to help them to make this new start, Barth emphasized the central human element in the massive

---

[19] Benjamin Unruh, 'Der Bolschewismus und die Christuskirche', *Die Furche* (1931), pp. 274, 277, 285.

[20] G. Besier and G. Sauter, *Wie Christen ihre Schuld bekennen* (Göttingen, 1985), pp. 32–3.

[21] Barth, *The Germans and Ourselves*, pp. 29, 33.

political problems of the time. Vogel likewise looked for a recovery of humanity together: he called people, hand in hand, to the Cross, where God himself had taken over the defence of those who have not a word to say for themselves. 'It may be that if we do this, we shall not only re-discover God (if one may so put it), God in the divinity of His sovereign grace, but we shall also re-discover man in his true humanity, stained though he is, brutalised and trodden down.' Because Christ died for the godless, he hoped for a rehumanization through solidarity with all people, regardless of superficial features like race, education, possessions, or party loyalty.

> And it may be that we shall thus be set free for human, practical, earthly service, in the realms of culture, economics, and even of politics. For we shall see that education, economics and politics are for the sake of man, and that man is not for the sake of these powers, which again and again he has turned into gods upon whose altars millions have been sacrificed. The Third Reich should be a terrible example and memorial to us of this. For man is never more dangerous than when he is sacrificing to his gods.[22]

So Vogel expounded his favourite theme in a context at least moment-arily different from the partisan and powerfully divisive atmosphere of the early 1930s. Then there had been the glorification of conflict and the sectionalisms of nation, party, and race had blotted out humanity. Argu-ments like Vogel's had been made but not heard: Unruh, for example, reported that in godless Russia people were actually experiencing God, living of necessity out of the hand of God and finding a way from God to human being, the neighbour and the enemy. 'Und dass ein solcher Weg noch da ist, das ist der Sieg der Kirche.'

This way of thinking had little practical value in 1931: could it mean more in 1945 when the only political rhetoric that was allowed respect-ability by the Allies was one of upholding humanity and human rights? Charges at the Nuremberg Tribunal in 1946 included offences against humanity (*Menschlichkeit*). Just over three years later, the Universal Declaration of Human Rights was adopted by the United Nations. In defence of humanity, it was evidently not enough to punish evil-doers and to exclude them from further opportunities of power. It was neces-sary to build the foundations of justice and public responsibility in the State and the life of the people as a whole. Citizenship had to be

---

[22] Vogel, *Grace*, pp. 41, 43–4.

humanized. It was often not easy for Germans to detect the renewal of humanity immediately after the war. The Occupying Powers were not so powerful that they could create human order quickly out of the chaos of Europe; they, too, had been shaped by the war and found it morally and psychologically difficult to affirm the humanity of enemies in genuine solidarity. Many Germans, as Vogel recognized, had the expectations of the self-righteous, who learnt little from experience and repented nothing. But in all the confusion and bitterness of the time, a notable, if limited, recovery of humanity did go on within Germany and its international relationships. Theologians who had kept the Fall in their doctrinal repertoire would not have expected more.

The first synod of the Evangelical Church in Germany, meeting in Bethel, in January 1949, discussed one aspect of the practical reaffirmation of humanity in Germany. What doctrine of rights could be framed on an evangelical rather than a natural law foundation? And how was awareness and respect for rights to be nurtured, built up in society?[23] Delekat gave a lecture on *Kirche, Recht und Rechtsbewusstsein* arguing that the Church could no longer leave the exposition of the Decalogue to the State, while restricting itself to interpreting the commandments of God individualistically in the higher spirit of the Sermon on the Mount. Modern states, not only the Nazi State, were seen to legitimate murder, by gas chambers, hunger, and deportations. Since they could not be trusted to exemplify basic public morality, the Church had to take up the task. He criticized the inflation of talk about rights which bred scepticism when rights did not materialize. The trust of the German people in the newly formed West German State would be greater if, instead of words about human rights in the constitution, promises had been made—and kept—to ensure that each German in '45 would have his own bed and, for 1950, his own dwelling.

It is reported that as soon as the lecture was finished, synod members felt that something decisive had been missed. Did Delekat's emphasis on practical considerations really get at the heart of the problem about rights? Was his optimism about the Germans as a people truly committed to *Recht* consistent with what the Church had declared in Stuttgart in 1945? Vogel was pressed into action: once more he made a dramatic protest, which went beyond the conventions of well-behaved synodical speech. The precise nature of his transgression is unclear; perhaps it was

[23] H. Ehlers, 'Die Frage nach dem Recht vor der Betheler Synode', *Junge Kirche* (1949), pp. 73–9; E. Wolf, *Sozialethik* (Göttingen, 1988), p. 11.

that he spoke, unfortunately, not in the language of the man in the street, but as a theologian with a passionate conviction that central theological themes did get to the root of contemporary human problems. He argued that the key question was how God gets his rights against human self-justification. Ideologies and the partisan politics clustering round the question of human rights would not help: the only help would be that God, who was with everyone, Germans and all peoples, should come to his right. But God's right was trodden under foot and with it human rights. The only way God would get his right was that God should make the concern of the *Rechtsbrecher* his concern; he was in solidarity with the revolutionaries who were caught in the curse (*Fluch*) of their revolt against all divine and human rights. Here Vogel had in view not just the worldly and atheistic revolutionaries, but also the religious and churchly breakers of God's law. In solidarity with such criminals,

> Er ist an die Stelle derer getreten, die das Unmenschliche, das mit dem Recht Gottes Unvereinbare offen tun, und auch an die Stelle derer, die es unter der Maske, wohl gar der frommen Maske tun. Es ist eine unbeschreibliche Solidarität, in der Gott eingegangen ist, als er ein Mensch wurde.

So God's right and human rights were linked in Jesus Christ. Yet once more, Vogel eloquently listed many kinds of the evil-doers and victims with whom Christ was in solidarity. Even the *SS-Leuten* were included, but not to give any *politische Rechtfertigung* to what they had done, for the basis of human rights was not anything a human being was, but what is promised in God's grace.

Post-war hopes for a renewed humanity with an unpartisan fellowship of peoples were soon thwarted or shown to be groundless, most obviously by the development of the Cold War. Vogel's original political application of the justification of the godless to relations with Communists thus regained actuality. The *Darmstädter Wort* (8 August 1947) about the political direction of the German people is an unduly neglected attempt to confess guilt with more political and historical concreteness than the Stuttgart Declaration of 1945.[24] The *Bruderrat* said the Gospel of the

---

[24] G. Heidtmann, ed., *Hat die Kirche geschwiegen?* (Berlin, 1964), pp. 33–5; B. Klappert, 'Die ökumenische Bedeutung des Darmstädter Wortes', *Richte unsere Füssen auf den Weg des Friedens* (Munich, 1979), pp. 632, 640; E. Bethge, 'Geschichtliche Schuld der Kirche', in K. Herbert, ed., *Christliche Freiheit im Dienst am Menschen* (Frankfurt am Main, 1972), pp. 123–4; Marquardt, 'Solidarität . . .', p. 393.

reconciliation with God in Christ could not be heard, done, or communicated unless they allowed themselves to be called back from all the false and evil ways of their previous politics. Amongst the errors from which liberation was needed was that *eine 'christliche Front'* had been made against necessary new social order. They had betrayed Christian freedom when the right to revolution was denied, while at the same time the process leading to dictatorship had been accepted and even approved. They had gone wrong by making a front of good against bad: they had thus confused the offer of the grace of God to all and abandoned the world to self-justification. The echoes of Vogel's thought are noteworthy.

Finding their way in the new Communist German Democratic Republic, some Christians steered their course by the star of the justification of the godless. They wanted to avoid both political indifference and conservative but unavailing opposition to the regime. They also wanted to be active citizens in an atheistic State without surrendering traditional Christian faith. The way between these options was disclosed and grounded in the reconciling action of God in Christ. It was no betrayal of Christian faith to aim beyond co-existence towards 'pro-existence', 'being there for the world, just as Christ was there for the world', even for the godless.[25] In the West, the ideological conjunction of Christianity and anti-Communism became common though not uncontroversial. Dibelius became known in his later years as the NATO Bishop. Gustav Heinemann helped to prepare the way for the *Ostpolitik* by making a political slogan of Christ's dying not against but for the Communists. When Vogel republished his article of 1931 without alteration, he asked the reader to consider why it could have been written just as well for the first time in 1960.[26]

I hope this account does no gross injustice to the interaction of Vogel's theology of the justification of the godless and the recent history of Germany. I am conscious that he could prove a soft target for the kind of criticism W. R. Ward levels against theologians like Barth and Tillich in *Theology, Sociology and Politics: The German Protestant Social Conscience 1890–1933*. That is a book I have been very grateful for, especially since I gave up trying to be a church historian and took to political theology. Theologians who relate to politics cannot afford to be naïve in political calculations or merely wishful in their reading of history. It is foolish for theologians to think they can master history by the power of mere

---

[25] E. Adler, ed., *Pro-Existence* (London, 1964), pp. 11–13; 36.
[26] Vogel, 'Die christliche Solidarität . . .')1960), p. 684.

eloquence or even by faith. It is not acceptable for theology to make political promises and, when they fail, to fall back on an invisible God, deepening the present into 'a sacred void of waiting'.[27] Vogel, like the rest of the theologians, should be put through the mill.

Perhaps, however, there are valuable and viable elements in Vogel's way of thinking which the historian's mill is not designed to refine and collect, but merely throws out as chaff. Ward especially tests theology by its capacity to be realistic and effective in turning the command to love into policy fitting for modern societies. He looks for the movement from theology to policy and is often disappointed. The movement characteristic of Vogel's theology has another direction: in so far as he is political, he begins with the failure of politics, which discloses in painful experience what humanity is before God. His theology is not to be turned into discrete policies which may or may not be realized; rather, it is a search (with a reiterated eureka) for the roots of the possibility of truly human and hopeful politics. Those roots have to include the promise of forgiveness of sin, because there is no hope that through some political change, forgiveness will be made redundant anywhere in human life. Theology is witness to what transcends politics, not as the merely irrelevant but as its source and its hope. Politics operates within relations with the transcendent. Precisely because they are relations with the transcendent, however, these relations never become an obvious fixed part of politics, demonstrably real and operative. Godless interpretations of politics are plausible within limits. Hence the story of politics is likely to be the tale of the repeated disappearance, loss of awareness, and rediscovery of the negligible transcendent, or to put it concretely, of the Pope's divisions.

Vogel did not make theology the basis of specific political programmes. Nor did he promise a particular kind of society to be achieved through godly politics (with God on our side). He developed a theology which kept everyone aware of their own, even more than of others', sin as godlessness. It was a Lutheran theology that did not think the justified are those who have somehow progressed beyond being sinners in moralistic terms. Being justified consisted in God's overcoming the godlessness of human beings by being with them and for them in the history of their godlessness. This generous divine solidarity is with all human beings, uniting them, for all are godless, while only some are

---

[27] W. R. Ward, *Theology, Sociology and Politics: The Protestant Social Conscience 1890–1933* (Bern, 1979), p. 216.

good or pious. A theology which speaks thus might be expected to encourage friendliness and realism in human relations, the will to reconciliation even with enemies, yet without expecting unbroken or cheap peace.

University of Leeds

BIBLIOGRAPHY OF THE WRITINGS OF
W. R. WARD

by ANNE ORDE AND DAVID ROLLASON

1946 'Legal Problems of Planning', *New Epoch* (Spring 1947), pp. 19–21.
–50   'The Rockery School, Headington', *New Epoch* (May 1949),
      pp. 18–22.

1952 'The Administration of the Window and Assessed Taxes, 1696–
      1798', *EHR*, 67, pp. 522–42.
      'The Office for Taxes, 1665–1798', *BIHR*, 25, pp. 205–12.
      REVIEW
      A. Farnsworth, *Addington, Author of the Modern Income Tax*
      (London, 1951), *EHR*, 67, p. 140.

1953 *The English Land Tax in the Eighteenth Century* (London, 1953).
      REVIEW
      F. Shehab, *Progressive Taxation: a Study in the Development of the
      Progressive Principle in the British Income Tax* (London, 1953), *EHR*,
      68, pp. 647–8.

1955 'The Land Tax in Scotland, 1707–98', *BJRL*, 37 (1954–5),
      pp. 288–308.
      'Some Eighteenth-Century Civil Servants: the English Revenue
      Commissioners, 1754–98', *EHR*, 70, pp. 25–54.
      REVIEWS
      Calendar of Treasury Books, 20 (London, 1952), *EHR*, 70, pp. 642–3.
      Calendar of Treasury Books, 21 (London, 1952), *ibid.*, pp. 643–5.
      Calendar of Treasury Books, 22 (London, 1952), *ibid.*, pp. 675–6.

1956 REVIEW
      Calendar of Treasury Books, 26 (London, 1954), *EHR*, 71, pp. 109–
      10.

1957 'County Government c.1660–1835', *A History of Wiltshire*, 5, ed.
      R. B. Pugh and Elizabeth Crittall, *VCH* (London, 1957), pp. 170–
      94.
      REVIEWS
      Calendar of Treasury Books, 27 (London, 1955), *EHR*, 72, pp. 332–3.
      Calendar of Treasury Books, 28 (London, 1955), *ibid.*, pp. 508–10.
      Wiltshire Quarter Sessions and Assizes, 1736, ed. J. P. M. Fowle
      (Devizes, 1955), *History*, 42, pp. 247–8.

1958 *Georgian Oxford. University Politics in the Eighteenth Century* (Oxford, 1958).

REVIEWS

'The New Cambridge Modern History', *Political Studies*, 6, pp. 73–4. [Review of *The New Cambridge Modern History, I: the Renaissance, 1493–1520*, ed. G. R. Potter (Cambridge, 1957) and *The New Cambridge Modern History, VII: the Old Regime, 1713–63*, ed. J. O. Lindsay (Cambridge, 1957)].

I. G. Philip, *William Blackstone and the Reform of the Oxford University Press in the Eighteenth Century* (Oxford, 1957), *EHR*, 73, pp. 359–60.

Stephen B. Baxter, *The Development of the Treasury 1660–1702* (London, 1957), *EHR*, 73, pp. 150–60.

Betty Kemp, *King and Commons, 1660–1832* (London, 1957), *JEH*, 9, pp. 114–15.

1959 REVIEWS

F. W. Bealey and H. M. Pelling, *Labour and Politics, 1900–1906* (London, 1958), *Political Studies*, 7, pp. 93–4.

Calendar of Treasury Books, 29, pt. 1 and 30, pt. 2 (London, 1957), *EHR*, 74, pp. 299–300.

Calendar of Treasury Books, 31 (London, 1957), *ibid.*, pp. 162–3.

1960 REVIEWS

R. R. Palmer, *The Age of Democratic Revolution: a Political History of Europe and America 1760–1800, I: the Challenge* (Princeton and London, 1959), *Parliamentary Affairs*, 13, pp. 263–4.

Calendar of Treasury Books, 30, pt. 1 (London, 1958), *EHR*, 75, p. 170.

Peter Mathias, *The Brewing Industry in England 1700–1830* (Cambridge, 1959), *History*, 45, pp. 60–1.

1961 REVIEWS

D. J. Greene, *The Politics of Samuel Johnson* (New Haven, 1960), *Parliamentary Affairs*, 14 (1960–1), pp. 125–6.

N. C. Hunt, *Two Early Political Associations: the Quakers and the Dissenting Deputies in the Age of Sir Robert Walpole* (Oxford, 1961), *ibid.*, pp. 403–4.

Calendar of Treasury Books, 29, pts 2 and 3 (London, 1959), *EHR*, 76, pp. 159–60.

V. H. H. Green, *The Young Mr. Wesley* (London, 1961), *History*, 46, p. 255.

'The European Idea—Myth and History', *Political Studies*, 9, pp. 298–300 [review of *L'Europe du XIXe et du XXe siècle: problèmes et interpretations historiques*, ed. Max Beloff, Pierre Renouvin, Franz Schnabel, and Franco Valsecchi, 2 vols (Milan, 1959)].

1962 REVIEWS
John Carswell, *The South Sea Bubble* (London, 1960), EHR, 77, pp. 164–5.
Calendar of Treasury Books, 31, pt. 1 (London, 1960), *ibid.*, pp. 779.
M. S. Anderson, *Europe in the Eighteenth Century, 1713–1783* (London, 1961), *History*, 47, pp. 74–5.

1963 *The Administration of the Window and Assessed Taxes* (Bridge Place, 1963) [reprint].
REVIEWS
Dora Mae Clark, *The Rise of the British Treasury: Colonial Administration in the Eighteenth Century* (New Haven, 1961), EHR, 78, pp. 179–80.
Calendar of Treasury Books, 25 (London, 1961), *ibid.*, p. 386.

1964 'Oxford and the origins of Liberal Catholicism in the Church of England', *SCH*, 1, pp. 233–52.
REVIEWS
John G. Sperling, *The South Sea Company: an Historical Essay and Bibliographical Finding List* (Boston, 1962), EHR, 79, p. 420.
Calendar of Treasury Books, 32, pt. 1 (London, 1962), *ibid.*, p. 856.
L. W. Hanson, *Contemporary Printed Sources for British and Irish Economic History, 1701–1750* (Cambridge, 1963), *History*, 49, p. 231.
N. C. Masterman, *John Malcolm Ludlow: the Builder of Christian Socialism* (Cambridge, 1963), *JEH*, 15, pp. 123–4.
G. F. A. Best, *Temporal Pillars: Queen Anne's Bounty, the Ecclesiastical Commissioners and the Church of England* (Cambridge, 1964), *ibid.*, pp. 266–7.

1965 *Victorian Oxford* (London, 1965).
'The Beginnings of Reform in Great Britain, Imperial Problems, Politics and Administration, Economic Growth', *The New Cambridge Modern History, VIII: the American and French Revolutions 1763–93*, ed. A. Goodwin (Cambridge, 1965), pp. 537–64.
'The tithe question in England in the early nineteenth century', *JEH*, 16, pp. 67–81.

REVIEWS

Guide to the Contents of the Public Record Office (London, 1963), *EHR*, 80, p. 883.

V. H. H. Green, *John Wesley* (Edinburgh and London, 1964), *JEH*, 16, p. 270.

1966   'The cost of Establishment: some reflections on church building in Manchester', *SCH*, 3, pp. 277–89.

'Some eighteenth-century civil servants: the English Revenue Commissioners, 1754–98', *Essays in Eighteenth-Century History from the English Historical Review*, ed. R. Mitchison (London, 1966), pp. 201–30 [reprint].

The English Land Tax in the Eighteenth Century [microform edn.].

Georgian Oxford [microform edn.].

REVIEWS

T. J. Williams and A. W. Campbell, *The Park Village Sisterhood* (London, 1965); and Michael Reynolds, *Martyr of Ritualism, Father Mackonochie of St. Alban's, Holborn* (London, 1965), *Theology*, 69, pp. 377–8.

Henry Parris, *Government and the Railways in Nineteenth-Century Britain*, *DUJ*, 58 (1965–6), pp. 101–2.

1967   REVIEWS

A. M. G. Stephenson, *The First Lambeth Conference: 1867* (London, 1967), *Theology*, pp. 517–18.

Bernard Pool, *Navy Board Contracts, 1660–1832* (London, 1966), *History*, 52, pp. 344–5.

Franklin B. Wickwire, *British Subministers and Colonial America 1763–1783* (Princeton, 1966), *History*, 52, p. 346.

John Sparrow, *Mark Pattison and the Idea of a University* (Cambridge, 1967), *JEH*, 18, pp. 271–2.

Robert Blake, *Disraeli* (London, 1966), *DUJ*, 59 (1966–7), pp. 176–8.

'The Last Chronicle of Barset; or the Early Victorian Church Revived', *JEH*, 18, pp. 65–70 [review of Owen Chadwick, *The Victorian Church*, 1 (London, 1966)].

Essays in Modern English Church History in Memory of Norman Sykes, ed. G. V. Bennett and J. D. Walsh (London, 1966); *Religious Controversies of the Nineteenth Century and Selected Documents*, ed. A. O. J. Cockshut (London, 1966); and *Religious Thought in the Nineteenth Century Illustrated from Writers of the Period*, ed. B. M. G.

Reardon (London and New York, 1966), *Victorian Studies*, 10, pp. 312–14.

Articles for *Encyclopaedia Britannica* (Chicago, 1967) on 'Bolingbroke, Henry St. John'; 'Cadogan, William Cadogan'; 'Craggs, James'; 'Godolphin, Sidney Godolphin'; 'Marlborough, John Churchill'; 'Marlborough, Sarah Jennings'; 'Masham, Lady Abigail'; 'Ormonde, James Butler'; 'Oxford, Robert Harley'; 'Sacheverell, Henry'; 'Stanhope, James Stanhope'; 'Sunderland, Charles Spencer'; 'Townshend, Charles'; and 'Wyndham, Sir William'.

1968 REVIEWS

P. G. M. Dickson, *The Financial Revolution in England: a Study of the Development of Public Credit, 1688–1756* (London, 1967), *History*, 53, pp. 124–6.

Desmond Bowen, *The Idea of the Victorian Church: a Study of the Church of England 1833–1889* (Montreal, 1968), *ibid.*, pp. 453–4.

Romilly's Cambridge Diary, 1832–42, ed. J. P. T. Bury (Cambridge, 1967), *DUJ*, 60 (1967–8), pp. 53–5.

Maurice Cowling, *Disraeli, Gladstone and Revolution: the Passing of the Second Reform Bill* (Cambridge, 1967), *ibid.*, pp. 126–9.

1969 REVIEWS

I. K. Steele, *Politics of Colonial Policy: the Board of Trade in Colonial Administration, 1696–1720* (Oxford, 1968), *History*, 54, p. 284.

G. S. R. Kitson Clark, *An Expanding Society: Britain 1830–1900* (Cambridge, 1967), *DUJ*, 61 (1968–9), pp. 44–5.

Hedva Ben Israel, *English Historians on the French Revolution* (Cambridge, 1968), *ibid.*, pp. 99–100.

1970 'James II and the Universities', Winston S. Churchill, *History of the English-Speaking Peoples* (London, 1970), pp. 1820–1.

REVIEWS

E. R. Norman, *Anticatholicism in Victorian England* (London, 1968), *EHR*, 85, p. 196.

Robert Currie, *Methodism Divided: a Study in the Sociology of Ecumenism* (London, 1968), *ibid.*, pp. 369–74.

J. M. Sherwig, *Guineas and Gunpowder: British Foreign Aid in the Wars with France 1793–1815* (Harvard, 1969), *History*, 55, p. 281.

J. H. Grainger, *Character and Style in English Politics* (Cambridge, 1969), *DUJ*, 62 (1969–70), pp. 185–6.

1971 'The Religion of the People and the Problem of Control', *SCH*, 8, pp. 237–57.
REVIEWS
P. T. Marsh, *The Victorian Church in Decline* (London, 1969), *EHR*, 86, pp. 433–4.
R. A. Soloway, *Prelates and People: Ecclesiastical Social Thought in England 1783–1852* (London, 1969), *ibid.*, pp. 632–3.
Owen Chadwick, *The Victorian Church*, 2 (London, 1970), *JEH*, 22, pp. 158–60.
E. G. W. Bill and J. F. A. Mason, *Christ Church and Reform, 1850–1867* (Oxford, 1970), *ibid.*, p. 272.
M. A. Crowther, *Church Embattled: Religious Controversy in Mid-Victorian England* (Newton Abbot and Hamden, Conn., 1970), *ibid.*, pp. 380–1.
John Cannon, *The Fox–North Coalition: Crisis of the Constitution, 1782–4* (Cambridge, 1969), *DUJ*, 63 (1970–1), pp. 66–7.
Higher Education: Demand and Response, ed. W. R. Niblett (London and Tavistock, 1969); and E. P. Thompson, *Warwick University Ltd: Industry, Management and the Universities* (Harmondsworth, 1970), *ibid.*, pp. 230–2.
The Correspondence of Edmund Burke, VII: January 1792–August 1794, ed. P. J. Marshall and J. A. Woods (Chicago, 1968), *AHR*, 76, p. 503.

1972 *Religion and Society in England, 1790–1850* (London, 1972).
The Early Correspondence of Jabez Bunting 1820–1829, *CSer*, ser. 4, 11 (1972) [edition].
'The French Revolution and the English Churches: a case study in the impact of revolution upon the Church', *Miscellanea historiae ecclesiasticae*, 4 = *Bibliothèque de la revue d'histoire ecclésiastique*, fasc. 56, pp. 55–84.
'Swedenborgianism: Heresy, Schism or Religious Protest?', *SCH*, 9, pp. 303–9.
REVIEWS
Kenneth A. Thompson, *Bureaucracy and Church Reform: the Organizational Response of the Church of England to Social Change, 1800–1965* (Oxford, 1970), *EHR*, 87, pp. 206–7.
Dorothy M. Owen, *The Records of the Established Church in England, excluding Parochial Records* (Cambridge, 1970), *ibid.*, 663.
Brian Harrison, *Drink and the Victorians: the Temperance Question in England, 1815–1872* (London, 1971), *JEH*, 23, pp. 92–3.

Literature and Politics in the Nineteenth Century, ed. John Lucas (London, 1971), *DUJ*, 64 (1971–2), pp. 167–9.

S. G. Checkland, *The Gladstones: a Family Biography 1764–1851* (Cambridge, 1971), *ibid.*, pp. 251–3.

1973   'Will Herberg: an American hypothesis seen from Europe', *DUJ*, 65 (1972–3), pp. 260–70.

'The Legacy of John Wesley: the Pastoral Office in Britain and America', *Statesmen, Scholars and Merchants: Essays in Eighteenth-Century History presented to Dame Lucy Sutherland*, ed. Anne Whiteman, J. S. Bromley, and P. G. M. Dickson (Oxford, 1973), pp. 323–50.

'The Baptists and the transformation of the Church, 1780–1830', *BQ*, 25, pp. 167–84.

REVIEWS

The Autobiography of Francis Place 1771–1854, ed. Mary Thrale (Cambridge, 1972), *DUJ*, 65 (1972–3), pp. 109–11.

Herbert Tingsten, *Victoria and the Victorians* (London, 1972), *ibid.*, pp. 111–12.

Alan Bell, *Sydney Smith, Rector of Foston 1806–1829* (York, 1972), *NH*, 8, p. 176.

1974   REVIEWS

Sydney E. Ahlstrom, *A Religious History of the American People* (New Haven, 1972), *EHR*, 89, pp. 122–5.

Bruce E. Steiner, *Samuel Seabury 1729–1796: a Study in the High Church Tradition* (Athens, Ohio, 1972), *ibid.*, pp. 670–1.

Wiltshire Returns to Bishop's Visitation Queries, 1783, ed. Mary Ransome (Devizes, 1972), *ibid.*, p. 672.

Cynthia Griffin Wolff, *Samuel Richardson and the Eighteenth-Century Puritan Character* (Hamden, Conn., 1972), *ibid.*, pp. 906–7.

Anthony Armstrong, *The Church of England, the Methodists and Society 1700–1850* (London, 1973), *History*, 59, p. 476.

Clyde Binfield, *George Williams and the YMCA: a Study in Victorian Social Attitudes* (London, 1973), *DUJ*, 66 (1973–4), pp. 327–9.

Robert Moats Miller, *How Shall They Hear without a Preacher? The Life of Ernest Fremont Tittle* (Chapel Hill, North Carolina, 1971), *JEH*, 25, pp. 107–9.

Kenneth Young, *Chapel: the Joyous Days and Prayerful Nights of the Non-Conformists in their Hey-day, circa 1850–1950* (London, 1972), *NH*, 9, pp. 183–4.

1975 REVIEWS
Carol V. R. George, *Segregated Sabbaths: Richard Allan and the Rise of Independent Black Churches, 1760–1880* (New York, 1973), *EHR*, 90, p. 907.
M. L. Clarke, *Paley, Evidences for the Man* (London, 1974), *ibid.*, p. 909.
Michael Brock, *The Great Reform Act* (London, 1973), *JEH*, 26, pp. 99–100.
Bernard Semmel, *The Methodist Revolution* (London, 1974); and John Foster, *Class Struggle and the Industrial Revolution: Early Industrial Capitalism in Three English Towns* (London, 1974), *History*, 60, pp. 310–11.
W. P. Morrell, *The Anglican Church in New Zealand* (Dunedin, 1973), *EHR*, 90, p. 456.
E. R. Sandeen, *The Roots of Fundamentalism: British and American Millenarianism 1800–1930* (Chicago, 1974), *DUJ*, 67 (1974–5), pp. 109–11.
Politics and Literature in the Eighteenth Century, ed. H. T. Dickinson (London, 1974), *ibid.*, pp. 245–6.
Thorvald Köllstad, *John Wesley and the Bible: a Psychological Study* (Uppsala, 1974), *Kyrkhistorisk årsskrift* (1975), pp. 296–7.
Hugh McLeod, *Class and Religion in the Late Victorian City* (London, 1974), *JEH*, 26, pp. 424–5.

1976 *Early Victorian Methodism: the Correspondence of Jabez Bunting 1830–1858* (London, 1976) [edition].
REVIEWS
S.P.G. Papers in Lambeth Palace Library: Calendar and Indexes, ed. W. W. Manross (Oxford, 1974), *EHR*, 91, pp. 432–3.
Walter Goddijn, *The Deferred Revolution: a Social Experiment in Church Innovation in Holland, 1960–70* (Amsterdam, 1975), *JEH*, 27, pp. 95–6.
A. R. Winnett, *Peter Browne: Provost, Bishop, Metaphysician* (London, 1974), *EHR*, 91, p. 206.
Harry Carter, *A History of the Oxford University Press, to the Year 1780* (Oxford, 1975), *ibid.*, pp. 912–13.
Geoffrey Rowell, *Hell and the Victorians: a Study of the Nineteenth-Century Theological Controversies concerning Eternal Punishment and the Future Life* (Oxford, 1974), *DUJ*, 68 (1975–6), pp. 94–5.
J. R. C. Wright, *'Above Parties': the Political Attitudes of the German*

Protestant Church Leadership 1918–1933 (Oxford, 1974), *ibid.*, pp. 211–13.
The University in Society, ed. Lawrence Stone (Princeton, 1975), *EHR*, 91, pp. 378–81.
Harold P. Simonson, *Jonathan Edwards: Theologian of the Heart* (Grand Rapids, 1974), *ibid.*, p. 650.
Frank Baker, *From Wesley to Asbury: Studies in Early American Methodism* (Durham, North Carolina, 1976), *Times Literary Supplement*, no. 3888 (17 Sept. 1976), p. 1146.
Robert Moore, *Pitmen, Preachers and Politics: the Effects of Methodism in a Durham Mining Community* (Cambridge, 1974), *NH*, 12, pp. 273–4.

1977   REVIEWS
Sheldon Rothblatt, *Tradition and Change in English Liberal Education: an Essay in History and Culture* (London, 1976), *EHR*, 92, p. 666.
Eric J. Evans, *The Contentious Tithe: the Tithe Problem and English Agriculture 1750–1850* (London, 1976), *ibid.*, p. 911.
John Roberts, *Revolution and Improvement: the Western World, 1775–1847* (London, 1976), *History*, 62, pp. 495–6.
The Works of John Wesley, II: the Appeals to Men of Reason and Religion and Certain Related Open Letters, ed. Gerald R. Cragg (Oxford 1975); and John C. Bowmer, *Pastor and People: a Study of Church and Ministry in Wesleyan Methodism from the Death of John Wesley (1791) to the Death of Jabez Bunting (1858)* (London, 1975), *JEH*, 28, pp. 92–3.
Elisabeth Kovacs, *Ultramontanismus und Staatskirchentum im Theresianisch-Josephinischen Staat: der Kampf der Kardinale Migazzi und Franckenberg gegen den Wiener Professor der Kirchengeschichte Ferdinand Stoger* (Vienna, 1975), *ibid.*, pp. 93–4.
Stephen Yeo, *Religion and Voluntary Organisations in Crisis* (London, 1976), *ibid.*, pp. 326–7.
Owen Chadwick, *The Secularization of the European Mind in the Nineteenth Century: the Gifford Lectures in the University of Edinburgh for 1973–4* (Cambridge, 1975), *DUJ*, 69 (1976–7), pp. 293–5.
Hugh McLeod, *Class and Religion in the late Victorian City* (London, 1974), *Catholic Historical Review*, 63, pp. 608–9.
A. J. Hayes, *Edinburgh Methodism 1761–1975* (Edinburgh, 1976), *ScHR*, 56, pp. 223–4.

1978 'Church and Society in the First Half of the Nineteenth Century', *A History of the Methodist Church in Great Britain*, 2, ed. Rupert Davies, A. Raymond George, and Gordon Rupp (London, 1978), pp. 11–96.

'The Protestant Churches, especially in Britain, and the Social Problems of the Industrial Revolution', *Religion und Kirchen im industriellen Zeitalter*, Schriftenreihe des Georg-Eckert-Instituts für internationale Schulbuchforschung, 23 (Brunswick, 1978), pp. 63–77.

REVIEWS

D. L. Le Mahieu, *The Mind of William Paley: a Philosopher and his Age* (Lincoln, Neb., 1976), *EHR*, 93, pp. 206–7.

T. W. Laqueur, *Religion and Respectability: Sunday Schools and Working Class Culture, 1780–1850* (New Haven and London, 1976), *PWHS*, 41 (1977–8), pp. 33–4.

G. I. T. Machin, *Politics and the Churches in Great Britain, 1832–1868* (Oxford, 1977), *ibid.*, p. 160.

G. I. T. Machin, *Politics and the Churches in Great Britain, 1832–1868* (Oxford, 1977), *JTS*, ns 29, pp. 607–8.

Reinhard Rurup, *Emanzipation und Antisemitismus: Studien zur 'Judenfrage' der bürgerlichen Gesellschaft* (Göttingen, 1975), *Religion*, 8, pp. 245–7.

John Pollock, *Wilberforce* (London, 1977), *History*, 63, p. 314.

W. O. Henderson, *The Life of Friedrich Engels* (London, 1976), *DUJ*, 70 (1977–8), pp. 87–8.

Steven Lukes, *Émile Durkheim: his Life and Work. A Historical and Critical Study* (London, 1975), *ibid.*, pp. 227–9.

Clyde Binfield, *So Down to Prayers: Studies in English Nonconformity 1780–1920* (London, 1977), *NH*, 14, p. 277.

1979 'Scottish Methodism in the Age of Jabez Bunting', *Records of the Scottish Church History Society*, 20, pt. 1, pp. 47–63.

'The relations of Enlightenment and religious revival in Central Europe and in the English-speaking world', in *Reform and Reformation: England and the Continent c 1500–c 1750*, ed. Derek Baker, *SCH.S*, 2 (Oxford, 1979), pp. 281–305.

Theology, Sociology and Politics: the German Protestant Social Conscience, 1890–1933 (Bern, 1979).

REVIEWS

R. C. Pritchard, *The Story of Woodhouse Grove School* (Bradford, 1978), *British Journal of Educational Studies*, 27, pp. 89–90.

Roland Marx, *Religion et Société en Angleterre de la Réforme à nos jours* (Paris, 1978), *History*, 64, p. 77.

John Kent, *Holding the Fort: Studies in Victorian Revivalism* (London, 1978), *ibid.*, p. 314.

Frederick V. Mills Sr, *Bishops by Ballot: an Eighteenth-Century Ecclesiastical Revolution* (Oxford, 1979), *ibid.*, p. 405.

Émile Poulat, *Catholicisme, démocratie et socialisme: le mouvement catholique et Mgr. Benigni de la naissance du socialisme à la victoire du fascisme*, *DUJ*, 71 (1978–8), pp. 113–14.

Michael R. Watts, *The Dissenters, I: from the Reformation to the French Revolution* (Oxford, 1978), *EHR*, 94, pp. 389–90.

Walter Grossman, *Johann Christian Edelmann: from Orthodoxy to Enlightenment* (The Hague and Paris, 1976), *JEH*, 30, pp. 298–9.

The Letters and Diaries of John Henry Newman, I: Ealing, Trinity, Oriel, February 1801 to December 1826, ed. I. T. Ker and T. Gornall (Oxford, 1978), *JTS*, ns 30, pp. 378–9.

R. L. Moore, *In Search of White Crows: Spiritualism, Parapsychology and American Culture* (New York, 1976), *The Christian Parapsychologist*, 3 (1978–9), pp. 19–20.

Sidney E. Mead, *The Old Religion in the Brave New World: Reflections on the Relation between Christendom and the Republic* (Berkeley, Los Angeles, and London, 1977); and Theodore Dwight Bozeman, *Protestants in an Age of Science: the Baconian Ideal and Antebellum American Religious Thought* (Chapel Hill, North Carolina, 1977), *Journal of American Studies*, 13, pp. 136–7.

Nicolas Barker, *The Oxford University Press and the Spread of Learning: an Illustrated History* (Oxford, 1978), *EHR*, 94, pp. 903–4.

Ian Bradley, *The Call to Seriousness: the Evangelical Impact on the Victorians* (London, 1976), *Journal of the Historical Society of the Church in Wales*, 26 (1979) (no. 31 for 1978–9), pp. 86–8.

1980   REVIEWS

Herbert Hovenkamp, *Science and Religion in America, 1800–1860* (Philadelphia, 1978); and James R. Moore, *The Post-Darwinian Controversies* (Cambridge, 1979), *Heythrop Journal*, 21, pp. 73–5.

Clyde Binfield, *So Down to Prayers: Studies in English Nonconformity 1780–1920* (London, 1977), *DUJ*, 72 (1979–80), pp. 103–5.

Victorian America, ed. Daniel Walker Howe (Philadelphia, 1976); and R. D. Thomas, *The Man who would be Perfect: John Humphrey Noyes and the Utopian Impulse* (Philadelphia, 1977), *ibid.*, 105–6.

Heinz Brunotte, *Bekenntnis und Kirchenverfassung: Aufsätze zur kirchlichen Zeitgeschichte* (Göttingen, 1977), *JEH*, 31, p. 128.

Christopher Weber, *Kardinäle und Prälaten in den letzten Jahrzehnten des Kirchenstaates, 1846–1878* (Stuttgart, 1978), *ibid.*, pp. 242–4.

Johanna Vogel, *Kirche und Wiederbewaffnung: die Haltung der Evangelischen Kirche in Deutschland in den Auseinandersetzungen um die Wiederbewaffnung der Bundesrepublik, 1949–1956* (Göttingen, 1978), *ibid.*, pp. 248–9.

Joseph Hubert Reinkens: Briefe an seinen Bruder Wilhelm (1840–1873), ed. H. J. Sieben (Cologne and Vienna, 1979), *ibid.*, pp. 511–12.

Stephen Yeo, *Religion and Voluntary Organisations in Crisis* (London, 1976), *Catholic Historical Review*, 66, pp. 62–3.

Ben Knights, *The Idea of the Clerisy in the Nineteenth Century* (Cambridge, 1978), *DUJ*, 72 (1979–80), pp. 235–6.

Todd M. Endelman, *The Jews of Georgian England, 1714–1830: Tradition and Change in a Liberal Society* (Philadelphia, 1979), *AHR*, 85, pp. 883–4.

Calendar of the Correspondence of Philip Doddridge DD (1702–1751), ed. G. F. Nuttall (London, 1979), *JTS* ns 31, pp. 654–5.

The Letters and Diaries of John Henry Newman, II: Tutor of Oriel, January 1827 to December 1831, ed. I. T. Ker and T. Gornall (Oxford, 1979), *ibid.*, pp. 666–7.

Church and Society in Catholic Europe of the Eighteenth Century, ed. W. J. Callaghan and D. Higgs (Cambridge, 1979), *Religious Studies*, 16, pp. 127–8.

Leonard J. Arrington and Davis Bilton, *The Mormon Experience: a History of Latterday Saints* (London, 1979), *Religion*, 10, pp. 238–9.

D. A. Gowland, *Methodist Secessions. The Origins of Free Methodism in Three Lancashire Towns: Manchester, Rochdale, Liverpool*, Chetham Society, ser. 3, 26 (Manchester, 1979), *Urban History Yearbook 1980*, pp. 162–3.

1981 'Power and Piety: the Origins of Religious Revival in the Early Eighteenth Century', *BJRL*, 63, pp. 231–52.
REVIEWS
Herbert Hovenkamp, *Science and Religion in America, 1800–1860* (Pennsylvania, 1978), *DUJ*, 73 (1980–1), pp. 96–7.

Klaus Scholder, *Die Kirchen und das Dritte Reich: Band 1. Vorgeschichte und Zeit der Illusionen 1918–1934* (Frankfurt, Berlin, and Vienna, 1977), *ibid.*, pp. 104–5.

The Letters and Diaries of John Henry Cardinal Newman, IV: the Oxford Movement, July 1833 to December 1834, ed. I. T. Ker and T. Gornall (Oxford, 1980), *JTS*, ns 32, pp. 298–300.

Owen Chadwick, *The Popes and European Revolution* (Oxford, 1981), *THES*, no. 443 (1 May 1981), p. 14.

Robert Currie, Alan Gilbert, and Lee Horsley, *Churches and Churchgoers: Patterns of Church Growth in the British Isles since 1700* (Oxford, 1977), *Catholic Historical Review*, 67, pp. 299–300.

Hillel Schwartz, *The French Prophets: the History of a Millenarian Group in Eighteenth-century England* (London, 1980), *History*, 66, p. 306.

Frank Booth, *Robert Raikes of Gloucester* (Redhill, 1980), *ibid.*, pp. 326–7.

J. F. C. Harrison, *The Second Coming: Popular Millenarianism, 1780–1850* (London and Henley, 1979), *Southern History*, 3, pp. 268–9.

Barclay Fox's Journal, ed. R. L. Brett (London, 1979), *EHR*, 96, pp. 663–4.

'The Watch on the Rhine', *JEH*, 32, pp. 509–12 [review of J. Van den Berg and J. P. Van Dooren, *Pietismus und Réveil: Referate der internationalen Tagung: Der Pietismus in den Niederlanden und seine internationalen Beziehungen: Zeit 18–22 Juni, 1974* (Leiden, 1978); William G. Willoughby, *Counting the Cost: the Life of Alexander Mack 1679–1735* (Elgin, Illinois, 1979); A. Loschhorn and W. Zeller, *Gerhard Tersteegen: Geistliche Reden* (Göttingen and Zürich, 1980); Sigrid Grossmann, *Friedrich Christoph Oetingers Gottesvorstellung: Versuch einer Analyse seiner Theologie* (Göttingen, 1979)].

Bernard Frank, *Actualité nouvelle des synodes: le synode commun des diocèses allemands (1971–75)* (Paris, 1980), *ibid.*, pp. 561–2.

1982 'Orthodoxy, Enlightenment and Religious Revival', *SCH*, 17, pp. 275–96.

REVIEWS

Annemarie Smith-von Osten, *Von Treysa 1945 bis Eisenach 1948: zur Geschichte der Grundordnung der Evangelischen Kirche in Deutschland* (Göttingen, 1980), *JEH*, 33, pp. 154–5.

Richard Carwardine, *Transatlantic Revivalism: Popular Evangelicalism in Britain and America, 1790–1865* (Westport, Conn., 1978), *EHR*, 97, pp. 437–8.

David Blackbourn, *Class, Religion and Local Politics in Wilhelmine*

Germany: the Centre Party in Württemberg before 1914 (New Haven, 1980), *Heythrop Journal*, 23, pp. 223–5.

Martin Scharfe, *Die Relgion des Volkes. Kleine Kultur- und Sozialgeschichte des Pietismus* (Gütersloh, 1980), *JEH*, 33, pp. 338–9.

L. Binder and J. Scheerer, *Die Bischöfe des Evangelischen Kirche A. B. in Siebenbürgen, Teil 2: die bischöfe des Jahres 1867–1969* (Cologne, 1980), *ibid.*, pp. 481–2.

J. Beckmann, *Hoffnung für die Kirche in dieser Zeit: Beiträge zur kirchlichen Zeitgeschichte 1964–1974*, Arbeiten zur kirchlichen Zeitgeschichte, Reihe B 10 (Göttingen, 1981), *ibid.*, pp. 484–5.

Friedrich von Hügel-Nathan Söderblom – Friedrich Heiler Briefwechsel 1909–31, ed. Paul Misner (Paderborn, 1981), *ibid.*, pp. 510–11.

Hilary Evans, *Intrusions: Society and the Paranormal* (London, 1982), *The Christian Parapsychologist*, 4, pp. 200–2.

The Letters and Diaries of John Henry Newman, V: Liberalism in Oxford, January 1835 to December 1836, ed. I. T. Ker and T. Gornall (Oxford, 1981), *JTS*, ns 33, pp. 324–5.

Ruth K. McClure, *Coram's Children: the London Foundling Hospital in the Eighteenth Century* (London, 1981), *History*, 67, p. 377.

W. J. Baker, *Beyond Port and Prejudice: Charles Lloyd of Oxford, 1784–1829* (Orono, Maine, 1981), *ibid.*, p. 495.

T. W. Heyck, *The Transformation of Intellectual Life in Victorian England* (London, 1982), *THES*, no. 516 (24 Sept. 1982), p. 14.

Hugh McLeod, *Religion and the People of Western Europe 1789–1970* (Oxford, 1980), *JTS*, ns 33, p. 622.

Katholische Aufklärung und Josephinismus, ed. E. Kovacs (Vienna, 1979), *DUJ*, 74 (1981–2), pp. 286–7.

Michael Dion, *État, église et luttes populaires* (Paris, 1980), *ibid.*, pp. 290–1.

1983   REVIEWS

Gary D. Stark, *Entrepreneurs of Ideology: Neoconservative Publishers in Germany, 1890–1933* (Chapel Hill, North Carolina, 1981), *DUJ*, 75 (1982–3), pp. 120–1.

Émile Poulat, *Une église ébranlée. Changement, conflit et continuité de Pie XII à Jean-Paul II* (Paris, 1980), *ibid.*, pp. 125–6.

Mack Walker, *Johann Jakob Moser and the Holy Romam Empire of the German Nation* (Chapel Hill, North Carolina, 1981), *ibid.*, p. 147.

James Bentley, *Between Marx and Christ: the Dialogue in German-speaking Europe 1870–1970* (London, 1982), *JEH*, 34, p. 158.

Andrew Louth, *Discerning the Mystery: an Essay on the Nature of Theology* (Oxford, 1983), *ibid.*, pp. 639–40.

Margaret Lavinia Anderson, *Windthorst: a Political Biography* (Oxford, 1981), *Heythrop Journal*, 24, pp. 347–8.

J. W. Boyer, *Political Radicalism in late Imperial Vienna: Origins of the Christian Social Movement* (Chicago, 1981), *ibid.*, pp. 348–50.

C. T. McIntire, *England against the Papacy 1858–1861: Tories, Liberals, and the Overthrow of Papal Temporal Power during the Italian Risorgimento* (Cambridge, 1983), *THES*, no. 568 (23 Sept. 1983), p. 16.

Grete Klingenstein, *Der Aufstieg des Hauses Kaunitz* (Göttingen, 1975), *British Journal for Eighteenth-Century Studies*, 6, pp. 234–6.

A Social History of the Diocese of Newcastle, ed. W. S. F. Pickering (Stocksfield, 1981), *NH*, 19, pp. 274–5.

David Clark, *Between Pulpit and Pew: Folk Religion in a North Yorkshire Fishing Village* (Cambridge, 1982), *ibid.*, pp. 279–81.

1984 'Aufklärung und religiöser Aufbruch im europäischen Protestantismus des 18.Jahrhunderts', *Österreich in Geschichte und Literatur*, 28, pp. 1–14.

'Class, Denomination and the Development of the Connexional Frame of Mind in the Age of Bunting', *Canadian Methodist Historical Society Papers*, 4, pp. 1–12.

REVIEWS

F. J. McLynn, *The Jacobite Army in England, 1745: the Final Campaign* (Edinburgh, 1983), *NH*, 20, pp. 254–5.

D. W. Bebbington, *The Nonconformist Conscience: Chapel and Politics, 1870–1914* (London, 1982), *Heythrop Journal*, 25, pp. 242–3.

Marilyn Chapin Massey, *Christ Unmasked: the Meaning of 'The Life of Jesus' in German Politics* (Chapel Hill, North Carolina, 1983), *JEH*, 35, pp. 325–6.

Robert J. Rubenowice, *Crisis in Consciousness: the Thought of Ernst Troeltsch* (Gainsville, 1983), *ibid.*, pp. 328–9.

K. H. Voigt, *Friedrich Wunderlich, ein Brückenbauer Gottes* (Stuttgart, 1982), *PWHS*, 44 (1983–4), pp. 40–1.

Roger H. Martin, *Evangelicals United: Ecumenical Stirrings in Pre-Victorian Britain 1795–1830* (Metuchen, New Jersey, 1983), *ibid.*, pp. 111–12.

Konrad H. Jarausch, *Students, Society and Politics in Imperial Germany: the Rise of Academic Illiberalism* (Princeton, 1982), *DUJ*, 76 (1983–4), pp. 289–90.

H. F. May, *Ideas, Faiths and Feelings: Essays on American Intellectual and Religious History 1952–1982* (Oxford, 1983), *British Journal for Eighteenth-Century Studies*, 7, pp. 107–8.

A History of the Methodist Church in Great Britain, 3, ed. Rupert Davies, A. Raymond George, and Gordon Rupp; and *Geschichte der Evangelisch-methodistischen Kirche*, ed. K. Steckel and C. E. Sommers (Stuttgart, 1982), *EHR*, 99, pp. 577–8.

Robert C. Fuller, *Mesmerism and the American Cure of Souls* (Philadelphia, 1982), *Journal of American Studies*, 18, pp. 117–18.

1985 'John Wesley', *Gestalten der Kirchengeschichte*, ed. M. Greschat, 9, pt. 1 (Stuttgart, 1985), pp. 43–58.
'William Booth', *Gestalten der Kirchengeschichte*, ed. M. Greschat, 9, pt. 2 (Stuttgart, 1985), pp. 233–43.
'Dwight L. Moody', *ibid.*, pp. 308–18.
'John Raleigh Mott', *Gestalten der Kirchengeschichte*, ed. M. Greschat, 10, pt. 1 (Stuttgart, 1985), pp. 204–13.
REVIEWS
John Rogerson, *Old Testament Criticism in the Nineteenth Century: England and Germany* (London, 1984), *JEH*, 36, pp. 329–30.
History, Society and the Churches: Essays in Honour of Owen Chadwick, ed. D. Beales and Geoffrey Best (Cambridge, 1985), *The Tablet* (15 June 1985), pp. 630–1.
Troeltsch — Studien Bd 3. Protestantismus und Neuzeit, ed. H. Renz and F. W. Graf (Gütersloh, 1984), *DUJ*, 77 (1984–5), pp. 294–5.
Edward Norman, *The English Catholic Church in the Nineteenth Century* (Oxford, 1985), *History*, 70, pp. 325–7.
Geoffrey E. Milburn, *Piety, Profit and Paternalism: Methodists in Business in the North East of England, c 1760–1920* (Banbury, 1983), *Durham County Local History Society Bulletin*, 34, pp. 45–6.
Kirche, Staat und Gesellschaft im 19. Jahrhundert = Prinz-Albert-Studien, 2, ed. A. M. Birke and K. Kluxon (Munich, 1984), *JEH*, 36, p. 681.
P. P. Streiff, *Jean Guillaume de la Flechere. John William Fletcher, 1729–1785. Ein Beiträg zur Geschichte des Methodismus* (Frankfurt, 1984), *PWHS*, 45 (1985–6), pp. 91–2.
Hugh McLeod, *Religion and the Working Class in Nineteenth-Century Britain* (London, 1984), *PWHS*, 45 (1985–6), pp. 92–3.

1986 'Revival and Class Conflict in Early Nineteenth-Century Britain', *Erweckung am Beginn des 19. Jahrhunderts: Referate einer Tagung an der*

Bibliography of the Writings of W. R. Ward

freien Universität Amsterdam 26.–29. März 1985, ed. Ulrich Gabler and Peter Schram (Amsterdam, 1986), pp. 87–104.

'Dissenters', *Evangelisches Kirchenlexikon* (Göttingen, 1986), 1, pp. 882–4.

REVIEWS

Julia Stewart Werner, *The Primitive Methodist Connexion: Its Background and Early History* (Madison, 1985), *History*, 71, p. 175–6.

Philipp Jakob Spener, *Die Klagen über das verdorbene Christentum: Misbrauch und rechter Gebrauch (1685)*, and *Natur und Gnade (1687)*, ed. Dietrich Blaufuss and Erich Beyreuther (Hildesheim, 1984), *JEH*, 37, pp. 179–80.

Janet Oppenheim, *The Other World: Spiritualism and Psychical Research in England 1850–1914* (Cambridge, 1985), *The Christian Parapsychologist*, 6, pp. 188–90.

The Papers of Benjamin Franklin, 24, *May 1 through September 30, 1777*, ed. William B. Willcox (New Haven and London, 1984), *British Journal for Eighteenth-Century Studies*, 9, pp. 209–10.

Die Habsburgermonarchie 1848–1918, Bd 4, *Die Konfessionen*, ed. Adam Wandruszka and Peter Urbanitsch (Vienna, 1985), *History*, 71, pp. 292–3.

Bibliographie der Buch- und Bibliothekgeschichte, Bd 3, ed. Horst Meyer (Bad Iburg, 1983), *Journal of Newspaper and Periodical History*, 2, p. 44.

Bernard M. G. Reardon, *Religion in the Age of Romanticism* (Cambridge, 1985), *JEH*, 37, pp. 477–8.

Allan Horstmann, *Victorian Divorce* (London, 1985), *DUJ*, 78 (1986), p. 371.

The Works of Jonathan Edwards, 7, *The Life of David Brainerd*, ed. Norman Pettit (New Haven and London, 1985), *British Journal for Eighteenth-Century Studies*, 9, pp. 275–6.

Nineteenth-Century Religious Thought in the West, ed. Ninian Smart, John Clayton, Patrick Sherry, and Steven Katz, 2 and 3 (Cambridge, 1985), *JEH*, 37, pp. 640–1.

Alfred Plummer. Conversations with Dr Döllinger 1870–1890, ed. Robredt Boudens (Louvain, 1985), *JEH*, pp. 662–3.

1987 'Max Weber and the Lutherans', *Max Weber and His Contemporaries*, ed. Wolfgang Mommsen and Jürgen Osterhammel (London, 1987), pp. 203–14.

'Zinzendorf and Money', *SCH*, 24, pp. 283–305.

ANNE ORDE AND DAVID ROLLASON

REVIEWS

The Correspondence and Miscellaneous Papers of Benjamin Harry Latrobe, 1, 1784–1804, ed. John C. Van Horne and Lee W. Turneelt (New Haven, 1984), British Journal for Eighteenth-Century Studies, 10, pp. 65–6.

Mary Fulbrook, Piety and Politics. Religion and the Rise of Absolutism in England, Württemberg and Prussia (Cambridge, 1983), Pietismus und Neuzeit, 12, pp. 199–202.

Alistair E. McGrath, The Making of Modern German Christology: From the Enlightenment to Pannenberg (Oxford, 1986), JEH, 38, p. 158.

Erich Naab, Die eine grosse Sakrament des Lebens. Studie zum Kirchentraktat des Joseph Ernst (1804–1869), mit Berucksichtigung der Lehrentwicklung in der von ihn begrundeten Schule (Regensburg, 1985), JEH, 38, pp. 161–2.

Kurt Rudolph, Historical Fundamentals and the Study of Religions (London, 1986), History, 72, p. 95.

Mary Fulbrook, Piety and Politics. Religion and the Rise of Absolutism in England, Württemberg and Prussia (Cambridge, 1983), Heythrop Journal, 28, pp. 233–5.

Internationaler Schleiermacher-Kongress Berlin 1984, ed. Kurt-Viktor Selge (Berlin and New York, 1985), and Schleiermacher. Ein Verzeichnis westeuropäischer und nordamerikanischer Hochschulschriften 1880–1980, ed. G. V. Gabel (Cologne, 1986), JEH, 38, pp. 319–20.

Pietismus-forschungen. Zu Philipp Jakob Spener und zum spiritualistisch-radikalpietistischer Umfeld, ed. Dietrich Blaufuss (Frankfurt, Bern, and New York, 1986), JEH, 38, p. 503.

Jorg Olemacher, Das Reich Gottes in Deutschland Bauen. Ein Beitrag zur vorgeschichte und Theologie der deutschen Gemeinschaftsbewegung (Göttingen, 1986), JEH, 38, pp. 508–9.

Walter H. Conser, Church and Confession. Conservative Theologians in Germany, England and America, 1815–1866 (Macon, Ga., 1984), EHR, 102, p. 1060.

Karl Stestell, Die Bibel in deutschsprachigen Methodismus mit Thesen zum heutigen Schriftverständnis aus evangelischer-methodistischer Sicht (Stuttgart, 1987), PWHS, 46 (1986–7), pp. 82–3.

Religion and Society in Early Modern Europe 1500–1800, ed. Kaspar von Greyerz (London, 1984), Heythrop Journal, 28, pp. 483–4.

Pietismus und Neuzeit. Ein Jahrbuch zur Geschichte des neuren Protestantismus, 8–11 (Göttingen, 1982–5), JEH, 38, pp. 649–50.

1988   *The Works of John Wesley*, 18, *Journals and Diaries. I* (*1735–1738*), ed. W. Reginald Ward and Richard P. Heitzenrater (Nashville, 1988). 'Enlightenment in Early Moravianism', *Kerkhistorische Opstellen aangeboden aan Prof. Dr. J. van der Berg*, ed. C. Augustijn, P. N. Haltrop, G. H. M. Posthumus Meyjes, and E. G. E. van der Wall (Kampen, 1987), pp. 114–27.

'Episcopacy in Early Methodism', *Miscellanea Historiae Ecclesiasticae*, 8, pp. 398–406.

'The Way of the World. The Rise and Decline of Protestant Social Christianity in Britain', *Kirchliche Zeitgeschichte*, 1, pp. 293–305.

'Asa Briggs', *The Blackwell Dictionary of Historians*, ed. John Cannon, R. H. C. Davis, William Doyle, and Jack P. Greene (Oxford, 1988), pp. 51–2.

'Thomas Carlyle', *ibid.*, pp. 69–70.

'William Owen Chadwick', *ibid.*, p. 73.

'Harry Hallam', *ibid.*, pp. 175–6.

'Max Weber und die Schule Albrecht Ritschls', *Max Weber und seine Zeitgenossen*, ed. Wolfgang J. Mommsen and Wolfgang Schwentker (Göttingen, 1988), pp. 296–312.

REVIEWS

Gordon Rupp, *Religion in England, 1688–1791* (Oxford, 1986), *Epworth Review*, 15, pp. 105–6.

Geoffrey Milburn, *The Travelling Preacher. John Wesley in the North-East 1742–90* (Sunderland, 1987), *Durham County Local History Society Bulletin*, 37, p. 44.

Disciplines of Faith. Studies in Religion, Politics and Patriarchy, ed. James Obelkevich and others (London, 1987), *PWHS*, 16, pp. 113–14.

Diary of an Oxford Methodist, Benjamin Ingham, 1733–1734, ed. Richard P. Heitzenrater (Durham, N.C., 1985), *EHR*, 103, pp. 508–9.

Karl Heinz Voigt, *Die Predigt durch Laien in der Evangelisch-Methodistischen Kirche damals und heute* (Stuttgart, 1987), *PWHS*, 46 (1987–8), p. 158.

Lief Gran, *Die Kirche in 19. Jahrhundert. Europäische Perspektiven* (Göttingen, 1987), *JEH*, 39, p. 318.

The Great Chronicle of the Hutterian Brethren, trans. and ed. the Hutterian Brethren (Rifton, N.Y., 1987), *JEH*, 39, pp. 313–14.

J. van den Berg and G. F. Nuttall, *Philip Doddridge (1702–51) and the Netherlands* (Leiden, 1987), *JTS*, 39, pp. 314–15.

Gordon Rupp, *Religion in England, 1688–1791* (Oxford, 1986), *British Journal for Eighteenth-Century Studies*, 11, pp. 119–20.

Jonathan Sperber, *Popular Catholicism in Nineteenth-Century Germany* (Princeton, 1984), *Heythrop Journal*, 29, pp. 373–5.

The Journal of John Wesley. A Selection, ed. Elisabeth Jay (Oxford, 1987), *JEH*, 39, p. 487.

Michael Eckert, *Gott-Glauben und Wissen. Friedrich Schleiermachers Philosophische Theologie* (Berlin and New York, 1987), *JEH*, 39, pp. 640–1.

1989   'The Renewed Unity of the Brethren: Ancient Church, New Sect, or Interconfessional Movement', *BJRL*, 73, pp. 77–92.

'"An Awakened Christianity". The Austrian Protestants and their Neighbours in the Eighteenth Century', *JEH*, 40, pp. 53–73.

'University Friends and Colleagues II', *A Memorial. William Henry Chaloner MA, PhD, 1914–1987*, ed. J. H. G. Archer and G. B. Hindle, *TLCAS*, 85 (1988), pp. 72–3.

REVIEWS

The Papers of Benjamin Franklin, 25, *October 1, 1777 through February 28, 1778*, ed. William B. Willcox (New Haven and London, 1986), *British Journal for Eighteenth-Century Studies*, 11, pp. 205–6.

Joachim Whaley, *Religious Toleration and Social Change in Hamburg, 1512–1819* (Cambridge, 1985), *Heythrop Journal*, 30, pp. 103–4.

William L. Patch, *Christian Trade Unions in the Weimar Republic, 1918–33. The Failure of Corporate Pluralism* (New Haven, 1985), *Heythrop Journal*, 30, pp. 110–11.

Deborah M. Valenze, *Prophetic Sons and Daughters. Female Preaching and Popular Religion in Industrial England* (Princeton, 1985), *EHR*, 104, pp. 224–5.

Norman W. Taggart, *The Irish in World Methodism, 1760–1900* (London, 1986), *EHR*, 104, pp. 518–19.

Deryck W. Lovegrove, *Established Church, Sectarian People. Itinerancy and the Transformation of English Dissent, 1780–1830* (Cambridge, 1988), *PWHS*, 47 (1989–90), p. 25.

Derec Llwyd Morgan, *The Great Awakening in Wales* (London, 1988), *PWHS*, 17, pp. 54–5.

Deryck W. Lovegrove, *Established Church, Sectarian People. Itinerancy and the Transformation of English Dissent, 1780–1830* (Cambridge, 1988), *Journal of the United Reformed Church History Society*, 4, pp. 280–1.

Truth, Liberty, Religion. Essays Celebrating Two Hundred Years of Manchester College, ed. Barbara Smith (Oxford, 1986), *British Journal for Eighteenth-Century Studies*, 12, pp. 88–9.

Betty M. Jarboe, *John and Charles Wesley. A Bibliography* (Metuchen, N.J. and London, 1987), *JEH*, 40, p. 468.

Friedrich Schleiermacher. Theologische Enziklopädie (1831/32). Nachschrift David Friedrich Strauss, ed. Walter Sachs (Berlin and New York, 1987), *JEH*, 40, p. 472.

ABBREVIATIONS

Abbreviated titles are adopted within each paper after first full citation. In addition, the following abbreviations are used throughout the volume.

AHR	*American Historical Review* (New York, 1895 ff.)
AV	Authorized Version
BIHR	*Bulletin of the Institute of Historical Research* (London, 1923–86) [superseded by HR]
BJRL	*Bulletin of the John Rylands Library* (Manchester, 1903 ff.)
BQ	*Baptist Quarterly* (London, 1922 ff.)
ChH	*Church History* (New York/Chicago, 1932 ff.)
CSer	*Camden Series of the Royal Historical Society*, ser. 3 (London, 1900–63); ser. 4 (London, 1964 ff.)
DNB	*Dictionary of National Biography* (London, 1885 ff.)
DUJ	*Durham University Journal* (Durham, 1876–32), ns (1940 ff.)
EHR	*English Historical Review* (London, 1886 ff.)
HJ	*Historical Journal* (Cambridge, 1958 ff.)
HMC	*Historical Manuscripts Commission*
HThR	*Harvard Theological Review* (New York/Cambridge, Mass., 1908 ff.)
HZ	*Historische Zeitschrift* (Munich, 1859 ff.)
IHS	*Irish Historical Studies* (Dublin, 1938 ff.)
JEH	*Journal of Ecclesiastical History* (Cambridge, 1950 ff.)
JTS	*Journal of Theological Studies* (London, 1899 ff.)
JURCHS	*Journal of the United Reformed Church History Society* (London, 1973 ff.)
NH	*Northern History* (Leeds, 1966 ff.)
ns	new series
PWHS	*Proceedings of the Wesley Historical Society* (Burnley, 1896/7 ff.)
RE	*Realencyklopädie für protestantische Theologie*, ed. A. Hauck, 24 vols, 3rd edn. (Leipzig, 1896–1913)
SCH	*Studies in Church History* (London/Oxford, 1964 ff.)
ScHR	*Scottish Historical Review* (Edinburgh/Glasgow, 1904 ff.)
SCH.S	*Studies in Church History. Subsidia* (Oxford, 1978 ff.)
TCHS	*Transactions of the Congregational Historical Society* (London, 1901 ff.)
THSLC	*Transactions of the Historic Society of Lancashire and Cheshire* (Liverpool, 1848 ff.)
TLCAS	*Transactions of the Lancashire and Cheshire Antiquarian Society* (Manchester, 1883 ff.)
TRHS	*Transactions of the Royal Historical Society* (London, 1871 ff.)
VCH	*Victoria County History* (London, 1900 ff.)